Local Democracy under Siege

Local Democracy under Siege

Activism, Public Interests, and Private Politics

DOROTHY HOLLAND, DONALD M. NONINI,
CATHERINE LUTZ, LESLEY BARTLETT,
MARLA FREDERICK-McGLATHERY,
THADDEUS C. GULDBRANDSEN,
AND ENRIQUE G. MURILLO, JR.

NEW YORK UNIVERSITY PRESS
New York and London

NEW YORK UNIVERSITY PRESS
New York and London
www.nyupress.org

Library of Congress Cataloging-in-Publication Data

Local democracy under siege : activism, public interests, and private
politics / Dorothy Holland ... [et al.].
  p. cm.
Includes bibliographical references and index.
ISBN-13: 978-0-8147-3677-7 (cloth : alk. paper)
ISBN-10: 0-8147-3677-7 (cloth : alk. paper)
ISBN-13: 978-0-8147-3678-4 (pbk. : alk. paper)
ISBN-10: 0-8147-3678-5 (pbk. : alk. paper)
1. Political participation—North Carolina. 2. Political anthropology—North
Carolina. 3. Political culture—North Carolina. 4. Democracy—North Carolina.
5. North Carolina—Politics and government. I. Holland, Dorothy C.
JK4189.L63   2006
320.809756—dc22   2006030098

New York University Press books are printed on acid-free paper,
and their binding materials are chosen for strength and durability.

Manufactured in the United States of America
c 10 9 8 7 6 5 4 3 2 1
p 10 9 8 7 6 5 4 3 2 1

Democratic nations care but little for what has been, but they are haunted by visions of what will be; in this direction their unbounded imagination grows and dilates beyond all measure.

—Alexis de Tocqueville, *Democracy in America*

Democracy is still upon its trial.
The civic genius of our people is its only bulwark.

—William James, *Oration upon the Unveiling of the Monument to Robert Gould Shaw*

Contents

Acknowledgments

The fact that this book has seven authors means that the debts and gratitude that any writer develops over the course of a project have been unusually multiple.

We need to begin, though, by acknowledging one another. Our gratitude to each other as collaborators begins with the recognition of the way we were able to develop a team atmosphere of great resilience, productivity, and mutual support. Meeting intensely for hundreds of hours over a number of years, we developed a group ethos that was remarkably harmonious and intellectually demanding. The meeting of many minds that occurred from the beginning of this project helped us create something that is much more than the sum of our abilities and time devoted to it. Collective work has its challenges, especially in academic cultures that continue to reward individualism and antagonistic display. None of us has come away unchanged or unimproved from the process of working together.

The group that we put together initially consisted of professors and graduate students, and it developed, to our pride and mutual admiration, into a cohort of seven colleagues. We especially thank the then graduate students who did the very hardest work of living in the field and took on the challenges of learning about a new place and its people.

We would particularly like to thank Kim Allen, whose administrative and intellectual contributions to the project were consistently of the highest order and integrity. We especially appreciate the model she provided for clear and compassionate communication. Gretchen Fox, Marsha Michie, Josh Boyer, and Marc David also provided superb research assistance.

We would like to thank Stuart Plattner of the Cultural Anthropology Program at the National Science Foundation for his good advice and his shepherding of a generous grant (SBR-9514912) that allowed us to carry out this ambitious project of multisited fieldwork. Funding also came from the University of North Carolina at Chapel Hill's College of Arts and Sciences and its University Research Council. Some of us received support from UNC's University Center for International Studies (UCIS), the Mellon Dissertation Writing Grant, UNC's Weiss Urban Livability Program, the Center for the Study of the American South, and the Latané Human Science Program.

Numerous colleagues gave feedback on the ideas presented here, commenting on early drafts of various chapters. We would like to thank John Clarke, Gretchen Fox, Jeff Boyer, William Lachicotte, Louise Lamphere, Brett Williams, Jim Peacock, Peter Redfield, and Raymond Parker, as well as audiences at UNC,

Duke University, and the meetings of the American Anthropological Association and the Society for the Anthropology of North America. The book was greatly improved from the inception of our relationship with Eric Zinner, a very patient and enthusiastic editor at New York University Press, and, more recently, by the press's addition of Ilene Kalish as their executive editor for sociology, politics, and anthropology. We also benefited immensely from Karen Brodkin, who read the entire manuscript, and from three other terrific anonymous reviewers for the press, whose thoughts prompted us to undertake major rewriting of sections of the book. Karina Lutz's expert copyediting made the final result a much more readable document. Laura Oakes and Rebecca Schaffer also contributed valued editing work.

Most importantly, we would like to thank all of the hundreds of people who participated in the study. Some contributed by providing long, vibrant, and fascinating interviews, others by befriending us and helping us to learn our way around the towns and cities in which we worked. We hope this book honors their life stories and their commitments to democracy. Together they produced the wisdom and the productive dialogues and conflicts that are the core of any contribution this book will make to the reader's understanding of local democracy and the challenges it faces today. As perhaps some kind of repayment to them, the authors' royalties from this book are going to the organization Democracy North Carolina.

Finally, we would like to thank our families and friends for their support and love during the process of research and writing that took us away from them for so many hours.

Preface

Turn-of-the-century America was supposedly a place of widespread skepticism, cynicism, and disillusionment about government and about the possibilities for democratic input. We went out to live for a year in several communities spread across one state of the United States to see if *local* democracy was in fact in trouble and if so, why. The specific questions we asked are still at the center of debates across the United States: Who is being excluded from a putatively imperfect democracy? Which issues are being settled behind closed doors? How can we account for the current limitations of U.S. democracy, and how do we create remedies that ensure more meaningful participation by a greater range of people? What are the ethical imperatives and sources of democratic hope that continue to spur some residents to undertake political action in the new millennium?

Local democracy has contended with distinctive and sometimes formidable new social, political, and economic conditions over the last three decades. Various changes, often called "globalization," have shaped people's jobs and affected where they work and live. These "post-Fordist" changes in corporate flexibility and reorganization include downsizing, outsourcing, deindustrialization, the emergence of the service economy, the rise of factory farming and decline of the independent family farm, and increased domestic and transnational migration in response to changing U.S. labor markets.[1]

When we began the project in the late 1990s, we suspected that these economic changes were relevant to claims by pollsters and media pundits about "apathetic" and "angry" voters, though we saw such claims as superficial at best, uninformative or misleading at worst. It seemed plausible that reactions by people to these vast social and economic transformations could include as well the scapegoating of minorities and immigrants by the victims of downsizing; new forms of apolitical consumerism; middle-class withdrawal from participation arising from preoccupations with work and time; the functional disenfranchisement of large numbers of workers due to economic duress; and anxieties generated by the presence of new migrants, including mobile professionals, transnational labor migrants, retirees, and tourists.

Rapid political change has also altered the conditions for local democratic participation. Privatization and devolution of social services to state and local municipalities—initially associated with the Reagan/Bush/Gingrich "revolution of government" of the 1980s and early 1990s—have affected the way government itself works and prompted fairly dramatic changes in the way public monies have been allocated. For example, relatively less is spent on schools and more on speculative economic development projects, less on pollution control and more on prisons. The role of government has been radically questioned, as has the definition of public resources and, indeed, whether a public sector should exist at all.

The institutional changes wrought by this "revolution" and the economic transformations just mentioned have been joined by the rise of neoliberalism—briefly, the idea that the market offers the best solutions to social problems and that governments' attempted solutions, in contrast, are inefficient and antithetical to the value of freedom. Together these processes—privatization, devolution, and neoliberalism—have constituted what we call "market rule." Market rule is an experiment of grand proportions that has fundamentally shifted the meaning of American democracy in the late twentieth century, as we observed it being played out in the five communities we studied in North Carolina.

As all this begins to suggest, there is not one simple story about the changing shape of democracy. Thirty-five years of dramatic economic change have affected communities across the country in very different ways. Some have experienced an influx of new capital; others have undergone deindustrialization or the reorientation of production, as with new forms of agribusiness. Some have experienced in-migration of retirees, labor from Central America, or high-tech workers from other regions. Others have experienced depopulation. In virtually all areas, there is a widening gap between the rich and poor. This gap not only threatens the principles of equality and fairness in life chances but also creates a democracy gap as well as an ethical challenge to those who profit from a diminished government.

This study illustrates the value of a comparative anthropological approach to U.S. politics, the study of which has been dominated by a narrow definition of democratic political participation as voting, political party membership, and financial contributions to candidates. By following up with participants to the disputes, we learned about local activism, and we eventually came to agree with theorists of democracy who argue that, under current conditions, such activist associations are the best hope for revitalizing democracy in America.

Collaboration

We should say a bit about the more unusual aspects of researching and writing this book. It results from a unique collaborative, comparative, ethnographic research project.[2] Ethnography is a research method that involves living with and listening to people as they make their daily lives. We observed public meetings of all sorts, listening as people spoke about local issues with each other at bus shelters and barber shops, at soccer games and workplaces, at government meetings and in their homes. We had informal conversations and formal interviews with people who participated in the publicly aired disagreements that we studied. We attended school board, city council, and other meetings. We watched the way people were welcomed or not welcomed into debates on issues to be decided. And we listened to people tell their political autobiographies and reflect on their relationship to democracy and the powerful challenges history has presented to them and their communities. All told, the book, which was written through a collaborative process among all the authors, reports on almost five years of ethnographic field research.

Survey research based on a priori questions and categories and media pronouncements have often been constrained sources of orthodoxy on democracy's problems. Ethnography's value is that it allows us to understand how diverse members of a community—not just the elites and better-off residents whom journalists and other social scientists mainly interview—think and live; it allows the extensive ideas and modes of living of the people we met to challenge prevailing understandings. Further, an ethnography of local politics redefines the meaning of the political, discovering how people seek to achieve the public good not only in one way—such as in voting—but in many ways.[3]

We met the challenge of doing ethnography across many sites by meeting extensively before, during, and after conducting a year's fieldwork in each of the five communities. Finally, over several months of intense discussions, we came to agree that the book reporting our findings should be organized by a number of themes, which extend like braided strands across and through different chapters to weave, as it were, our larger argument. Each multisited and comparative chapter therefore treats a theme on local democracy and its variations. In organizing our book this way, we have resisted a common temptation among anthropologists to structure the book sequentially by site, as would a cultural gazetteer touring from one community to another.[4]

The outcome, we hope, is not simply to defamiliarize the familiar but to focus on the intimate processes of local democracy as experienced by the people we met, and to discover the implications for American democracy as a whole.

Our research opens wider the debate about democracy, asking questions scholars have not adequately explored regarding how contemporary political, economic, and cultural processes have changed the conditions for political participation. The new conditions are arguably more open, providing some space for vitally expanding democracy through what Fung and Wright call "empowered participatory governance," but input and inclusivity are not guaranteed.[5] Instead, effort is necessary to nurture the development of more participatory forms, identify and address the needs of underserved populations, and ensure inclusion in decision-making processes.

It seems crucial, as our government putatively works to bring democracy overseas, to examine our democracy and ask whether it has been downsized or diminished at home and, if so, how we might cultivate its renewal. What difference would it make in people's lives were local democracy to become a reality here? The people we spoke with across one state told us very clearly.

1   Experimenting with Democracy

Duany and the Water Bill: A Puzzle of Contemporary U.S. Democracy

A hot Sunbelt day in 1997 presented us with a puzzle about contemporary U.S. democracy. It was the kind of July North Carolina afternoon that makes a person break into a sweat walking from the air-conditioned car to the air-conditioned building.

Inside the City Hall complex, members and associates of Durham Inner Village, a nonprofit group of nonelected citizens, were brainstorming about how to create a better future for Durham. Seated around the conference table, in a room they had requested, were a real estate developer, two medical doctors, an IBM developer, the city planner, a leader of a nonprofit real estate development partnership, a computer engineer, and an anthropology graduate student.

They had recently invited the famed architect and New Urbanist guru, Andres Duany, to town as a consultant and they were planning his visit. In the midst of delegating key tasks—event planning, public relations, advertisement, news media involvement, and invitations for "key players"—Timothy, one of the medical doctors in the group, interrupted the discussion to ask everyone to take stock of specific goals.[1]

> Timothy: Andres Duany and Elizabeth Plater-Zyberk are the leaders of the New Urbanist . . . movement in architecture and community planning. . . . Duany is coming to Durham to offer his assessment of the future of Durham and to offer insights into how that future might be more "livable." What do we want out of this visit?[2]

Barry, the real estate developer: To affect the way the typical citizen thinks about the future of development. I want them to see New Urbanism as an alternative to [suburban] sprawl.

Calvin, a physician: I see a more concrete focus. I want to affect the key decision makers. [The ones] that generally buy into this stuff [New Urbanism or Smart Growth] but only give lip service. . . . I want to move up the scale of enthusiasm. We should address the key political players, like the city manager, the key bankers, and the key developers.

Stephanie, the computer engineer who neither lives nor works in Durham but was nonetheless interested in urban planning in the city: We should help people [understand how to participate] when things need to be done [for the city]. . . . We could have a slogan like "Reinventing Durham."

Outside, two Durham residents gazed at the city office complex with what appeared to be apprehension. There were no parked cars around, so it was clear that the couple had walked some distance. With modest clothing, uncertain expressions, and papers in hand, the man and woman approached Thad Guldbrandsen, the anthropology graduate student and member of our research team who had just come from the meeting to the sidewalk outside City Hall.

"Can I help you find something?" Thad asked.

"Do you know where we go to deal with our water bill?"

"Sure, the cashier is right inside City Hall in the building right here."

The couple seemed to stagger backward expressing anxiety, saying something to the effect of, "Oh no, City Hall is not for us."

"Oh, it's very easy," Thad told them. "I just walked through the room where several people were standing in line waiting to pay their own bills. It's no big deal."

Without much more communication, the couple abruptly changed direction and walked away.

These events provide starkly contrasting images of two relationships to government. Inside the air-conditioned building eight private citizens were at home in City Hall, taking ownership of a process intended to shape the city and engaging in high-level civic engagement and participatory governance. Outside on the searing sidewalk, two people lacked the confidence to even enter the building to pay a routine bill. This couple is not alone. We know from our research that many people neither identify with their own government nor otherwise see themselves as meaningfully involved in their own governance.

So here is the puzzle: How are these contradictory images—one of empowerment, the other of estrangement—reflections of the changing shape of democracy in the United States? The reaction of the couple calls to mind widespread debates about the health of American democracy. Fall-offs in voting since the 1960s and in memberships in older, hierarchically organized federations of civic associations suggest the weakening of long-standing links between government and the people, and thus estrangement. At the same time, those bringing Andres Duany to Durham were directly engaged in participatory governance. What are the underlying conditions that make both estrangement and empowerment possible? How are they interacting? The subsequent pages of this book introduce a discussion about people with everyday problems, in everyday American towns, as they all struggle to make lives. We will show the many ways in which the American political terrain has changed during the past three decades in relation to globalization, widespread economic changes, and bold new policy initiatives. In the process, we will show how these changes matter in the lives of regular people and constitute as yet unanswered challenges to contemporary democracy.

Market Rule and the Three-Legged Stool of Democracy

In the United States, democracy is popularly associated with voting. Voting booths have clear symbolic importance. Less clearly defined, but equally important, is the expectation that U.S. society enjoys certain entitlements and guarantees, such as life, liberty, the pursuit of happiness, promotion of the common good, and justice. Likewise, related values lay out the conditions necessary for democracy to flourish. Societies that claim to be democratic are expected to promote three interrelated core values: liberty—freedom from government tyranny and from unwanted government intrusion into private spheres; equality— equality of input into decision-making about public resources regardless of birth, gender, race, religion, or wealth; and community— voluntary, communal bonds and common concerns that transcend individual self-interest.

Yet, the exact content of these values is never permanently defined once and for all. People contest the interpretation of liberty, equality, and community with different versions becoming dominant at different times.[3] Today, those in power define freedom and liberty in a neoliberal fashion, as freedom of the market from government interference. Other versions of liberty continue to be intensely debated, for example, freedom from the polluting effects of industry or women's freedom of choice over their bodies, but "freedom of the market" carries the day.

The meaning of equality is disputed as well. Does it simply mean that there shall be no laws or other barriers that directly bar the participation of anyone in governmental decision-making? Or, is it necessary to take the broader view that equality of input necessitates broad economic and social equality?

Nor do people across historical periods or even in any one historical period necessarily assign the same priority to each of the core democratic values. Since the 1980s, the rhetorical focus in political discussion has been dominated by elite and other voices calling for freedom of markets from government. "Freedom" is read as freedom for corporations from government regulation and interference, and freedom for consumers/citizens to choose among providers of public services. Now in the driver's seat are market-based interpretations of what it means to be free.

Emergence of Neoliberalism as Received Wisdom

Neoliberalism, or market fundamentalism, currently represents the dominant governing ethos and discourse in American political life.[4] Widely promulgated and accepted by elites in American politics, it has two basic premises:

1. the unfettered market, not government, is the optimal mechanism for allocating social resources;
2. governments must allow the market to function freely, without regulation, providing only the law and order that the market and its participants need to function efficiently.[5]

American governments from the New Deal 1930s onward mistakenly, in the eyes of the neoliberals, expanded government to provide economic support to the poor, the unemployed, and other inadequate market performers. This has led to waste, inefficiency, corruption, and parasitism, instead of the salutary discipline of market forces. To bring about the revitalization of the country, this legacy must be purged. Public policy must

- reduce, if not eliminate, Social Security and other government programs that provide assistance to the aged, the poor, and other low market performers, and stress instead individual personal responsibility;
- deregulate corporate practices, give relief from onerous environmental and labor standards set by government, and in general get government "off the backs" of business people;
- privatize government schooling, incarceration, welfare administration, and other such functions by outsourcing them to the business or philanthropic sectors whenever they cannot be eliminated outright;
- reduce taxes on income, wealth, and property, especially the estate tax, on the grounds that individuals, not government, know best how to spend their wealth.[6]

Given the encounter of American communities with globalization over the last thirty years, there are three additional claims within this discourse and worldview that have had uptake among local economic and political elites:

- major sources of investment, especially in capital, come from outside the unit in question (locale, region, state, country);
- thus, each person, each local community, each state, and each national government must view itself as a competitor with every other and promote its distinctive comparative advantage to outside market players to attract global capital;
- competition requires that the costs of investment to outsiders be reduced to a minimum, no matter what the broader expense to the individual, local community, or government.[7]

These premises of neoliberalism are widely if not universally shared among American political elites.[8] We heard them, adapted to local conditions, articulated by many of the local economic and political leaders in the five communities we studied.

What about Equality and Community?

In neoliberal doctrine, equality, to the degree that it is considered at all, is supposed to come from the marketplace, where each citizen is empowered to choose among programs, much as each consumer (one with the necessary monetary means) is able to choose among consumer products. Instead of determining the public's service needs and methods of provision through democratic means—e.g., debate about the merit of one set of needs against others—the public's needs are set by corporations, business people, and politicians, who interpret, with an eye toward profit making, the choices of individual citizen/consumers. This is a radical redefinition of the common good and how to achieve it.

The third value of a democratic society, that of nurturing community and its well-being, is understood under market rule to mean ensuring the well-being of the business community. Most policymakers now see private corporations and businesses as crucial to the conduct of government and to the provision of government-like goods and services. Market rule sees special expertise in the businessperson and places special value on corporations and the wealth they produce. Their rights and well-being are therefore presumed to be above those of ordinary people. They have in effect become supercitizens. Market rule, in short, is a striking reformulation of the roles and responsibilities of government, business, and the public. Proponents of market rule direct their policies and rhetoric toward ensuring liberty and strengthening the family. They ignore the solidarity of the larger unit, the community, and are virtually silent about equality. Using the metaphor of democracy as a three-legged stool, we might say that the leg of liberty is enlarged and strengthened while those of equality and community suffer neglect and are allowed to splinter.

For those who consider all three legs to be structurally necessary for democracy to survive, market rule challenges democratic governance. The challenges have been articulated most clearly with respect to equality. Market rule generates fears of capitalism's tendency, when left unchecked, to produce large and growing wealth gaps. In fact, wealth disparities among Americans have grown since the late 1970s. The wealth gap in the United States is now the largest of all advanced industrialized countries, and it continues to increase. When it comes to homes, other real estate, ownership of small businesses, savings accounts, CDs and money market funds, bonds, stocks, and such, middle-class and lower-income Americans own relatively little compared to the wealthy.[9] These differences translate into stark differences between the lives of the rich and the poor and create the risk of further decline even for those who think of themselves as middle class. Reduced income through retirement, severe illness, and other not so uncommon financial downturns put the nonrich at continuing risk.

Wealth inequalities matter in a democracy, even, or perhaps especially, in a representative democracy like that of the United States. Marked wealth differences very easily translate into disparities in political influence. As spelled out in a later chapter, we concur, in fact, with scholars who hold that the United States tends strongly toward plutocracy, not democracy, wherein wealth determines who has significant input into energy, environmental, health, education, race, and other policies.

Even assuming that efforts to erase race and gender privilege have allowed the input of African Americans and women to count as much as that of whites and men (which they have not), greater wealth can be, and often is, transformed into greater political capital or influence. Elections are relatively infrequent and, especially in national elections, restricted de facto to a handful of candidates, most of whom are wealthy. Consequently, the bulk of the population must rely on representatives who tend to look out above all for the well-being of business donors, and fail to recognize the problems of the 80 percent of the population who have relatively limited resources and/or face discrimination on the basis of race or ethnicity.

Many people are now worried about the effects of inequality on politics. A person in one of our research areas summed up the point when he said, "Our water quality standards are so low because those kinds of decisions have been left up to people who . . . don't have to drink the water." Commentators make similar connections in the popular media. In an article in *Esquire*, Ron Reagan, son of the late president, Ronald Reagan, wrote, "Wealthy politicians and government officials, of which there are many including the current president, have little idea of what life is like for the average American who makes a little less than $32,000 per year. The two live in different worlds."[10] Senator John McCain in his 2000 campaign for president said elections today are nothing less than an "influence peddling scheme in which both parties compete to stay in office by selling the country to the highest bidder."[11] And *Time* magazine investigative journalists Donald Bartlett and James Steele declared that America now has "government for the few at the expense of the many."[12]

Another issue associated with inequality is whether alternative views are aired in the public sphere, especially when their circulation depends on the news media.[13] The conventional view is that the role of the media in a democracy is to allow its citizens to be better informed when they participate in decision making as voters and in other capacities. However, as Robert McChesney, Ben Bagdikian, and others have observed, the concentrated corporate ownership of the electronic and print media means that the media plays a major role in furthering corporate agendas and keeping many concerns of citizens from becoming public issues for democratic deliberation and decision making.[14]

Market rule's version of liberty is central to the challenges faced by locales such as the ones we studied. It promotes policies that enhance global flows of goods and labor, but destabilizes local places. The "creative destruction" of textile, furniture, and, now, many white-collar jobs in the United States enabled by neoliberal free trade and, in some cases, underwritten by the government, undermines and challenges many local communities, even while providing a privileged few with new economic resources.[15]

Not only do relatively few enjoy the fruits of market rule's peculiar definition of liberty, but the stool itself, democracy, threatens to topple over. Is representative democracy, skewed as it is by wealth disparities, still effective and inclusive? Many of the people we interviewed and got to know answered negatively. To them, even voting, a symbol of one of the core rights of a citizen in representative democracy, seemed a hollow act. Should the current practices of representative democracy, so swayed as they are by wealth, even be called democracy? This book argues that neoliberal doctrines and the market rule they advocate are virtually blind to structural inequalities, allowing race and other structures of privilege to operate at will. Moreover, market rule has so inflamed the wealth gap and so exacerbated the plutocratic tendencies of American democracy that the very possibility of preserving, not to mention expanding, the democratic potential of the United States is in peril.

At the same time, we argue from our research that important counter experiments to market rule are underway. Community and activist organizations in local towns and cities are developing and acting on alternatives to the neoliberal vision. Moreover, their efforts are often interlinked through environmental and other translocal movements. They are also, as we argue in detail, conceivably part of a potential democracy movement aimed at greater empowerment and participation of all residents of the country. At this historical juncture, nurturing these counter experiments, contributing to the development of the translocal movements that link them, and building a U.S.A. democracy movement are crucial tasks for those who care about U.S. democracy.

Part I of the Research Story: Questions about Estrangement

In the mid-1990s, when we were initially planning our research, measures of voter turnout in national, state, and local elections showed a downward trend. For federal elections, voting had dropped from a high of 63 percent in 1960 to a low in the 1996 election of 49 percent.[16] Political analysts, social scientists, and civic-oriented people were alarmed by these numbers. Why were people turning away from the voting booth? Why were they neglecting one of the key rights of American democracy: the right to choose politicians who would then represent them when it came time to make decisions? At the time, popular and academic interpretations of the dwindling participation in and satisfaction with U.S. representative democracy ranged from the "apathetic electorate" to "angry voters."[17]

Around the same time, Robert Putnam highlighted an apparently related trend in his article, "Bowling Alone," and in a subsequent book of the same title.[18] He described what he took to be a general decline in civic participation in voluntary associations such as the PTA (Parent-Teacher Association) and Lion's Club—types of organizations judged crucial to America's democracy. Scholars have since challenged Putnam's data and his interpretation of them. Nonetheless, his work created alarm about the state of democracy in the United States. Participation in the PTA and other such groups, he argued, created cross-cutting ties important for building trust and encouraging moral behavior. Declining memberships in those groups meant the splintering of the third leg of democracy, community, in the sense of solidarity described above, and thus the erosion of the human bonds that make possible the relations of democratic governance.[19]

Thus, when we began the research, we focused on estrangement from democratic institutions and on what, if anything, this estrangement had to do with market rule and its challenges to democracy. Were people acting out the estrangement from representative democracy that the disinterest in voting seemed to suggest? If people were not taking political action to influence elected officials, then how were they responding locally to the massive economic shifts brought on by the expansion and mobility of global corporations?

We were also familiar with research charting the emergence of multiple social movements beginning in the 1950s and 1960s and continuing to the present, e.g., the Civil Rights movement, the anti-war movement, the women's movement, the environmental movement, the human rights movement, and the Christian Right movement. Local activism, including that associated with regional and national social movements in the towns and areas we studied, was at odds with the picture of civic engagement that Putnam's work seemed to signal. While many residents might indeed have been retreating into the relative isolation of their households and engaging in virtual connections through television and other media, we knew there was a proactive minority whose efforts deserved a look.

One of us (Holland) was simultaneously engaged in an ethnographic and survey study of local grassroots environmental groups in North Carolina. That research was finding a relatively high level of participation in activist groups.[20] We wanted to learn more about the people who were participating in movement groups and networks, what those groups were trying to accomplish, and how they related to market rule and the associated reorganization of government.

What we learned through our research has convinced us that the lack of engagement with voting—and so, one might conclude, with representative democracy—on the part of roughly half the population is only one part of the story of ongoing changes in the way the United States is being governed. Current changes in governance cannot be fully grasped by thinking only of representative democracy with its emphasis on elections and communicating with representatives through visiting their offices, writing letters, and staging protests. Instead, the view must be more comprehensive and include a focus on how the experiment with market rule is reshaping local, and thus potentially state and national, politics.

What struck us most, even more than many people's relative disinterest and disenchantment with representative democracy, was a variety of new and alternative forms of participatory governance. An important development in the modern democratic story is the ascendancy of a confusing array of hybrid forms of government referred to by terms such as "public-private partnerships" and "nonprofit organizations" ("nonprofits"). We became interested in these organizations and the way people related to them and, in some cases, as with the group excitedly gathered in the Durham City Hall complex, participated in them.

Part II: Experiment and Counter Experiment: Possibilities for Empowerment

The public-private partnerships so common to the experiment in market rule pose deep challenges to democracy, but, at the same time, the arrangement, ironically, creates an opening, albeit a small one, for democratic empowerment. These points require some explanation. Market rule's favored institution for conducting government policy is not government agencies but businesses, or, in cases where the market or private sector cannot take over the function altogether, the public-private partnership. It relies on these businesses and hybrid governmental entities, including nonprofits with which it partners, to provide educational services, for example, or to run prisons or to house and feed soldiers.

Public-private partnerships are not new, but they are now depended upon to deliver heretofore politically adjudicated educational, health, and other such programs to a much greater extent than at any time in the past. Moreover, in the present era, they are resonant with the ascendant ideology and with the decreased government revenues market rule produces. Governments, whose budgets have diminished, turn to outsourcing government services as a means to cut costs.

This transformation of the provision of government services is a fundamental one. Government sets general policy guidelines and program specifications, but realizes the provision of public goods not through funding government agencies that design programs by political decisions but, ideally, through funding businesses that contract services according to economic decisions geared to making profits for owners of the business.

Market rule is primarily an experiment with public services and the degree to which the motivation to profit affects the quality of for-profit efforts and sets their limits. The experiment gives cause for concern. Surely, some needs, perhaps basic ones, cannot be transformed into profit-making schemes. Likewise some clients, especially those with more than an average number of needs, may be conveniently ignored because they interfere with profit making. We also note that private organizations—especially businesses with their proprietary interests—are not required to be transparent and have open meetings. Later chapters provide insight into these concerns.

At the same time that this transformative experiment raises red flags about its compatibility with democracy, it also, paradoxically, creates possibilities for people favoring nonprofit visions of the public good. As noted above, in cases where the neoliberal priority of profit making is difficult to achieve, outsourcing to nonprofit organizations is acceptable. As a result, governments also partner with nonprofit organizations that are community oriented rather than market oriented. Organizations agree to meet government goals, specifications, and reporting functions and maintain an acceptable tax status with the Internal Revenue Service (in the case of nonprofits, for example, a 501(c)(3) designation). Otherwise, they enjoy the freedom, however constrained, to pursue their own missions.

We were struck by the variety of arrangements between government and public-private partnerships that we saw in the locales that we studied. They ran the gamut from government outsourcing arrangements with businesses to market-oriented nonprofit organizations designed to improve conditions for the business community to not-for-profit groups that had originally formed as grassroots, voluntary organizations with ties to environmentalist, feminist, or some other social movement.

These organizations ranged from ones purposively developed to provide public services for a profit to preexisting organizations that were willing to forego overt political activities, necessary for 501(c)(3) status, and accepting of the need to adapt their agendas to match government mandates. They also spanned the spectrum from nonprofits that were heavily dependent on government monies to others that were much less so. Some of these partnerships served elite interests, while others were steered more toward goals of social and material equality and the achievement of communal bonds across a broader spectrum.

We were especially intrigued by nonprofits run by community, activist, and social movement–related associations. Leaders of voluntary associations, we noted, sometimes enlisted their organizations as government partners not to make a profit, but to promote their vision of community well-being and social justice. It is this latter set of community-based, non–market-oriented nonprofits that provides for the possible constitution of a counter experiment to market rule.

In short, the partnership arrangement allows public monies to flow to a variety of organizations, including activist and community organizations, with a variety of interpretations of the common good. The current public-private partnering arrangements make more resources available to these sorts of community-oriented groups than in the past. Market rule has inadvertently created the possibility for an intensified role for voluntary associations and networks such as neighborhood associations, mutual aid societies, women's groups, religious organizations, and the type of group we met from Durham in the opening vignette.

Here, we come to another striking point: Although market rule is indifferent to this special feature, many of these not-for-profit organizations are outgrowths of the sort of secondary associations much discussed in democratic theory. While analysts dispute their overall significance and their specific effects in bringing about a democratic society, voluntary associations are usually thought to be important to the health of American democracy. Observers, from de Tocqueville in the first half of the nineteenth century up through the present, have considered voluntary associations to be a hallmark of American democracy.[21] Unlike market-oriented public-private partnerships and nonprofits, they nurture, so it is claimed, the integral structure of democracy. They offer possibilities for participatory democracy where residents, as members of these voluntary associations-turned-community-oriented nonprofits, have hands-on input into the design of government programs and, potentially more importantly, have become active in relinking local concerns to state and national politics.

Recent commentators, such as Skocpol, Evans, and Boyte, resonate with earlier theorists when they argue that voluntary associations can serve as schools for democracy, providing a crucial training ground for developing democratic sensibilities and skills among the population.[22] These organizations often serve as sources of empowerment and bases for translocal mobilization. Holland and her research associates, for example, followed people involved in grassroots environmental organizations and found many cases where members reformulated their ideas about how local, state, and national governments work, and became resolved to insist on more participatory input.[23] The present research describes some spectacular examples of such organizations.

Such organizations are relevant to the other core democratic values of equality and community as well. Some provide services, distribute food and other material resources, or give awards and other symbolic resources by criteria other than those of the market. They can help to cushion the roller coaster cycles of capital accumulation and the loss of livelihood that may accompany them. They constitute a brake against the sacrifice of equality to unrestrained capitalism. With celebrations and awards they recognize the importance of common resources and good stewardship of them. They also advocate for the interests of particular segments of the population, including those who, especially as lone individuals, lack political clout.[24]

In fact, some of the scholars of what we will call "associational democracy," with its focus on these voluntary associations and their capacity for solving community problems, favor schemes to develop voluntary associations for an even more integral role in U.S. democracy. Noting the current openings in market rule, advocates of associational democracy argue that these voluntary associations should be provided with more resources and recognized as providing crucial government-like services.

Our research led us to appreciate such organizations, and we concentrate on five such groups in part 3 of the book. It is in such organizations that we see the development and impetus for counter experiments to market rule. Along with others who are excited by the potential of current conditions to support the expansion of such associations, we focus on the importance of participatory democracy, particularly empowered participatory government, as the most promising counter experiment to the neoliberal projects of the past thirty years.[25]

If This Is Going to Be Democracy

Clearly, our ethnographic study took place during an experimental moment in the development of American democracy—an experimental moment that continues today. Market rule, with its centerpiece of public-private partnerships, has created what Dagnino calls, describing similar trends in Brazil, a "perverse confluence" between the otherwise oppositional projects of expanded participatory governance on the one hand, and neoliberal governance on the other.[26] Market rule's encouragement of an active, proactive civil society suits the counter experiments envisioned by champions of associational democracy. Ironically, it opens the door for more participatory forms of governance and thus the empowerment of citizens and residents who become accustomed to having more say in decision making than is afforded them in a representative government through which wealth rules.

If market rule continues to dominate what currently passes for democracy in the United States—and it appears that it will for some time to come—serious questions, both empirical and normative, need to be answered and serious shortcomings addressed. Does this new arrangement for meeting public needs sufficiently provide for core democratic values? Does it promote greater economic equality? Does it otherwise promote equality by engaging new groups in democratic action? Does it strengthen community?

If market rule is going to be what passes for democracy, then those alarmed by the neglect of equality and community are advised to treat seriously the counter experiments taking place in some of the voluntary organizations described later in the book. Activism has changed in response to the new political terrain and these local efforts have become even more important. Likewise, they should look closely at the theoretical proposals of scholars such as Fung and Wright, Cohen and Rogers, Hirst, and Amin, whose writings propose (competing) visions of associational democracy as an alternative to market rule and to the shortcomings of representative democracy geared to the wealthy.

Our research presents a picture of local democracy as profoundly changed and curtailed by the powerful emergence of market rule. At the same time, it reveals the possibility of other democratic outcomes through innovative, participatory avenues that community-oriented organizations are exploring and that are, in some cases, already linked through translocal social movements. The counter experiments they offer are key to the struggle for democracy in this country. They are part of a vision that democratic theory offers for building a more participatory democracy and for challenging the plutocratic structures that are increasingly being rigidified in the name of neoliberal values. Taking up this possibility is all the more urgent since such openings are highly exceptional given the plutocratic tendencies of the American political system as a whole. We are at a moment of danger and opportunity. It is imperative not only to understand this moment and the counter experiments of activist groups it has engendered but also to support, work with, and participate in such groups.

Studying Local Democracy in Everyday Life

For close to a year, we lived in five areas of North Carolina (two urban and three smaller towns). We listened to the radio stations that people in the community did, read the same newspapers, went to the same meetings, and attended the same churches. We visited people in their homes and had both informal conversations and formal interviews with them. The systematic notes we took at meetings and other events, the interviews we recorded, and the documents we studied from each place aimed to capture a holistic picture of the way U.S. democracy is changing in the present historical period.

Our research focused on *local* democracy, meaning the experience and making of democratic governance and democratic values as they are conceptualized, idealized, lived out, and struggled over in the places where people live. Politics and democracy, as we studied them and report their condition in this book, were local in the sense that they were closely connected to the everyday experiences and practices of a heterogeneous body of citizens and residents. These are the politics surrounding the passing of city budgets, the evaluating by PTAs of school staffing plans, or the complaining to county commissioners about the location nearby of "intensive livestock operations," a.k.a. "hog farms."

We explored the way people personally related to the public institutions and to the goods and services that flowed from them. We wanted to know, for example, which issues came before town councils and other governing bodies and which did not, how such issues were framed, and how they were debated. We noted practices of inclusion and exclusion from "the public" and from public debates, and analyzed the construction of social categories of citizenship that suggest who should participate. By examining the cultural work required to create and sustain public political dramas, we observed various mechanisms used to diffuse or discredit certain debates and to prevent others from even forming as discussions. In addition, we were interested in how everyday people developed a sense of themselves as participants in a democracy and in how they felt about their involvement in civic affairs.

Among our primary methods, we pursued dramas of contention—conflicts and differences of opinion that captured public attention. In order to have some comparability across the areas, each researcher pursued at least two dramas of contention in depth, one related to an educational issue, another, to a land use/environmental issue.[27]

Mindful of media processes that artificially limit coverage to a restricted set of issues and resolutely produce narratives alien to participants, we studied these dramas in depth by attending meetings where they were debated, interviewing as many participants as we could. We also pursued people who, though they stood to be affected by the outcomes, were ignored by the media or did not show up at the events where the issues were discussed. It is not difficult to imagine people like the couple described above who hurried away from the Durham courthouse, for example, as people who might not have tried to have input into a conflict, even one directly affecting them. Chapters in all three sections of the book analyze material from these dramas.

Tracing these dramas led us to grassroots and movement groups and networks where we learned about the organizations and about their political actions, whether targeted at the local level, at state or national governments, or at cultural issues. People and associations working to protect—and sometimes to reshape and expand—the possibilities and opportunities for everyday life where they lived undertook much of this action. We also interviewed some hundred people selected according to their activity in local politics—roughly half had long-term experience and half did not. In these political autobiography interviews, people told us about their dreams and disappointments with the state of democracy writ large.

Focusing on Similarities

Each region of the country has a different economic, political, and social history that shapes its democratic structures and influences the way it changes. As the differences among our five sites so clearly show, areas within states also present very different profiles and possibilities for democratic expansion. We took account of some of the range in conditions affecting democratic opportunities by examining three different cultural and economic landscapes common to the whole of North Carolina and every other state: *landscapes of consumption,* dominated by values and experiences organized around consuming goods and services; *landscapes of production,* organized around agricultural or industrial production; and *landscapes of the state,* dominated by government installations and facilities.[28]

These landscapes combined with local, state, and regional histories and conditions to form the stage on which North Carolinians confront, as do the other residents of the United States, the effects of globalization and government restructuring. Despite local differences, today's global economic institutions, e.g., NAFTA (North American Free Trade Agreement) and WTO (World Trade Organization), operate on such a grand scale that their effects challenge equality and community in these landscapes in similar ways across the country. This is a book about these large-scale economic and social changes as they intersect with the visions, hopes, and actualities of democracy in everyday life. North Carolina is like the other forty-nine U.S. states in that it is participating in and affected by major transformations—by economic restructuring and by government reorganization—that have affected every part of the United States over the last thirty to thirty-five years.

As with other places in the country, North Carolina has produced key leaders of core institutions such as the Bank of America, now headquartered in Charlotte, that have been directly involved in economic restructuring. It has produced the Research Triangle Park, a major technology center like Silicon Valley and others across the country, and has generated Boone and other resort and retirement communities primarily oriented to consumption, just as Colorado, Hawaii, Nevada, and California have with Vail, Maui, Las Vegas, and Disneyland.

The state, too, as with many other places in the country, has suffered wrenching dislocations wrought by globalization. The devastating effects of the loss of manufacturing jobs in the textile- and furniture-producing towns in North Carolina over the past fifteen years rival those of steel and automotive jobs lost in the other parts of the country in the 1980s and early 1990s.

Likewise, as with the rest of the country, social movements have, over the past four decades, strongly affected the development of civil society in North Carolina by encouraging and supporting voluntary associations that undertake political action. Some of the activists we got to know, for example, drew on their experience in the Civil Rights movement, and some of the local environmental groups we studied were aided by regional environmental organizations. North Carolina, by the same token, has contributed to these movements. Protests in the late 1970s and early 1980s in Warren County are often heralded as the birthplace of the environmental justice movement, for example, a movement now with national as well as global influence. North Carolina residents, too, are participating in the remarkable emergence of evangelical Christians as a powerful force in national politics, described in Liebman and in Wuthnow and Smith.[29]

Certainly, the book is about North Carolina, but it is primarily about local democracy in the United States as people carry it out under conditions of great economic transformations and particular, neoliberal interpretations of those changes. As suggested in the opening descriptions of the excited group planning for Duany's visit and that of the couple who fled the courtroom vicinity, it is likely that people across the country have differing opportunities for democracy. In some communities, estrangement may be more prevalent than in Durham; in others, empowerment may be. Nonetheless, the conditions producing estrangement versus empowerment are likely to be similar and the struggle between market rule and the counter experiment of empowered participatory governance, equally significant. The narratives of different areas are not exactly the same; the details differ, but there are striking similarities across the country and they call for attention just as the discrepancies do. Moreover, one of the major challenges to those organizing to transform the current structures of U.S. plutocratic rule is to mobilize across locales as well as within them, and we hope that this book will call attention to the similarities and solidarities that local groups share with one another across the United States that could serve as bases for their broader geographic mobilization.

Organization of the Book

Following the next chapter, which briefly introduces the landscapes and places of the book (chapter 2), *Local Democracy under Siege* is divided into three parts. Part 1, "Limiting Democracy," focuses on personal reactions and experiences with local government both from the point of view of individuals (chapter 3) and from that of racial and ethnic communities (chapter 4). Through these chapters, we see forces that, for the most part, constrain people's political lives. Education is considered as well (chapter 5). The potential of schooling for social mobility and for cultivating the democratic imagination has been dimmed in its neoliberal reformulation.

Part 2, "Governing under Neoliberalism," begins with an account of the remarkable changes in governance that have, along with economic restructuring, transformed local government and its challenges over the last thirty years (chapter 6). Two ethnographic chapters follow. They describe issues of governance: the way plans for the future of cities and locales are developed (chapter 7), and the practices of inclusion and exclusion that determine who has input and who does not (chapter 8).

The last section, part 3, conveys stories of empowerment and activism and places them in the larger drama of American democracy. Its first chapter (chapter 9) stands back from our ethnographic examination of local politics to examine U.S. politics more broadly. It considers conditions required for empowered participatory governance to be brought about locally and to play a role in broader systemic transformation. Here we point out that although the U.S. political system is structurally plutocratic and racially unequal, theoretical preconditions exist for local groups to broaden the political participation and inclusion of citizens, enhance their democratic internal organization, and seek out transnational coalitions with like-minded groups elsewhere. The second chapter in part 3 (chapter 10) demonstrates that such groups actually exist now, and not just in theory, and provides ethnographic accounts of community-oriented organizations and their ties to regional and national social movements as they struggled for democratic visions of the public good. This chapter demonstrates that the opportunity to begin this broader transformation exists now—and points to the imperative that citizens seize it while it exists. The concluding chapter (chapter 11) lays out the major findings of the book, and proposes steps that citizens might take on the path from local participatory democracy toward the democratization of the American political system as a whole.

2 Landscapes in Transition

If we could go back through time, we would watch places like Houston, Texas; Lee, Massachusetts; or Boone, North Carolina, change with each new historical era and its emerging economy. New buildings of the latest architectural design might go up; services dedicated to agriculture dwindle; residences in one area multiply rapidly while major highways shoot through; and newcomers move into particular sections of town.

We might get the impression that such changes simply happen to places as inevitable spin-offs of broad-scale regional, national, and international forces. But a closer look reveals efforts to jump start and to steer these changes. Every place has people whose projects and plans are ambitious, large scale, and future oriented. Responding to conditions such as the appearance of high-tech industries nearby or the deterioration of their neighborhood, these people create development strategies for their communities. They understand these conditions in relation to competing on the global market, or fighting environmental racism, or some other idea espoused by people they admire or circulated in the electronic media. To the extent that some persons and groups have power and their development strategies coalesce, their decisions can affect the directions in which places grow. These different development strategies and local histories and ecologies come together in what we referred to earlier as landscapes of power.

We have chosen to introduce the five places of the book through a brief glance at the landscape of power dominant in them at the time of our study: Chatham and Halifax Counties were characterized by a landscape of production; Durham and Watauga Counties, of consumption; and Fayetteville and Cumberland County, of the state.[1] (See figure 2.1.) These landscapes had been shaped by economic and political decisions and by cultural values, and they showed both national and regional patterns and as well as local individuality.

Stories from Landscapes of Production:
Chatham and Halifax Counties

> At times now, it almost feels like I have to apologize for being a farmer. It's been my life's work, and my father's life's work before me, his father's before him. It's hard. You try; you can't make a living at it, no matter what anybody says.
>
> —Lynn Mann, dairy farmer, Chatham County, 1996

> There were over three hundred farms in Thornton [in Halifax County]. There are no black farmers there today. They [the U.S. Dept. of Agriculture officials] treat us like fourth-class citizens who have no right to participate in democracy.
>
> —Ashby Odoms, Halifax County, 1997

> After being away several years I moved back to the Triangle. I found not the home I had left, but another congested rat race. The people had changed, the farms were gone, and strip malls had replaced the country stores. . . . And people are losing what is important, the sense of community, identity, and values.
>
> —Letter to the editor from Chatham County resident, 1996

Each of these people had different stories to tell about the condition of North Carolina's rural landscapes of production at century's end. They told of the passing of the family farm in North Carolina and the gross differences between large corporate operations and small farms, and reminded us that even the phrase "family farmer" is contested terrain. The writer of the letter to the editor displayed a commonly invoked nostalgia for a past bucolic period in the Carolina Piedmont. Lynn Mann appeared at a public hearing to oppose new proposed regulations on intensive livestock operations (ILOs), which were aimed at huge hog farms whose excrement floods the land in lyrically named "lagoons," while their ammonia-laden fumes assault the senses of rural neighbors.[2]

Small farmers across North Carolina are in economic crisis, their numbers in decline and incomes static or even declining.[3] Small farmers in North Carolina, like those elsewhere in the South, suffer from low farm-commodity prices, fixed pricing of fertilizer and other farm inputs by agribusiness corporations, decreases in tobacco and other farm subsidies for small farmers, and increases in land prices, assessments, and taxes due to competing uses of farmland. Meanwhile, those farms that remain viable have grown larger.

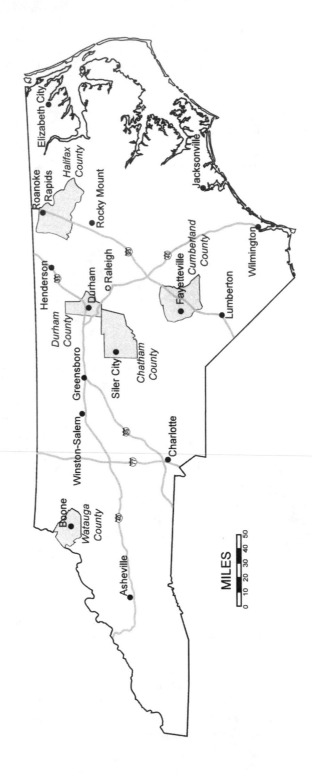

Figure 2.1 Five Research Sites

In Clinton, North Carolina, Greg Stephens is the 1995 version of the North Carolina hog farmer: He owns no hogs.

Stephens carries a mortgage on four new confinement barns that cost him $300,000 to build. The 3,000 hogs inside belong to a company called Prestage Farms Inc. Prestage simply pays Stephens a fee to raise them. For the next 10 years, most of Stephens' earnings will go toward paying off his debt. Then, if all goes well, he can start making money—enough, he hopes, to put his kids through college. The arrangement is called contract farming.[4]

Ashby Odoms's testimony above points to a related story—but one in which race exacerbates the already difficult, and at times desperate, situation of Tarheel small farmers. The decline in the number of small farms owned and worked by Odoms and other African-Americans has been even more precipitous than that of farms owned by whites.

Although the causes of the decline are similar in many respects for both minority and white farmers, African-Americans suffered additionally from discrimination by USDA extension officials. For decades these officials were selected by committees of local white farmers, and for decades they withheld loans and technical assistance from African-American farmers in favor of whites.[5] In Halifax County, poor rural African-Americans, like the rural residents of southern Chatham County, have been encroached on by ILOs—hog grow-out pens and processors—but have developed a distinctive critique of hog farms as a supposed index of progress and a better way of life.

The writer of the letter to the editor quoted above witnessed such changes. As the population in the Research Triangle Park region grew over the last two decades with the area's ascent to high-tech "new economy" status, growth coalitions of private developers and local governments eager for jobs and tax revenues built roads and constructed middle- and upper-middle-class housing projects in urban fringe areas such as northern Chatham County. This has put pressure on rural land prices, and has led to local property tax increases, making it even more difficult for small farmers to sustain operations.

We have found it most helpful to think of this change as the displacement and succession of a landscape of production by a rising landscape of consumption. For Chatham County, we could almost mark out a spatial boundary of contestation between these two landscapes and their ethos: one of production in the county's southern areas and one of consumption in its northeast. One of the principal disputes we followed during our fieldwork concerned whether the county government should allow the upscale Astoria housing construction project to proceed in the northern part of the county. While the project advocates pointed to its advantages in increasing local property taxes and providing construction jobs, environmentalist opponents and local new home owners, including many newcomer residents, argued that it would jeopardize the rural character of the county and threaten nearby Lake Jordan with sewage run-off.

The Shell Building

> Eighty percent [of all businesses seeking to locate in North Carolina] are looking for a good Class A structure in which to house their industry. . . . You can't build out of an empty wagon. The project is significant . . . because it will create three things: one, traffic, which will create two, a sale, which will create three, jobs, which will enhance the tax base.
> —State government official, speaking at the opening of the "shell building"
> of the Halifax County Industrial Center, 1997

Over the last several years, rural county governments with North Carolina State assistance have been constructing industrial parks centered around "shell buildings" containing the future space and utilities facilities for factories, which each government hopes to attract to its county. For many such counties like Halifax, the "shell building" is the material centerpiece of a set of incentives that rural counties put together to lure mobile capital, including tax credits and outright grants. In some rural counties, however, these shell buildings lie largely unoccupied years after their construction.

North Carolina has long been one of the most industrialized states in the country. From the mid-1800s, production of textiles, apparel, and furniture became North Carolina's "big three" until the 1970s, when "deindustrialization" began to take its toll.[6] Its relatively large rural population is explained by the location of many small factories in areas where family livelihoods combine farming with factory work. Characteristic of North Carolina labor markets has been the use of nonunionized laborers who receive low wages and few fringe benefits, and who work long but at times erratic hours. Across the country, this is the pattern industrial employers have converged on.

North Carolina has been a pioneer in such practices of industrial restructuring, and its rural factory workers have borne the brunt of the resulting deindustrialization in the state's landscapes of production, as corporations—many of which fled decades previously to North Carolina from high-wage, unionized, industrial states elsewhere—have closed down operations altogether, moved to Mexico, Central America, and the Caribbean, or subcontracted their operations to these locations. The state has experienced a major net loss of such jobs relative to its increased population and the size of the available labor pool. The shift to service work is dramatically depicted in Figure 2.2.

Despite the loss of family farms in North Carolina, there is a remarkable growth in the rise of restructured agroindustrial concerns relocating to rural

Figure 2.2
From Landscapes of Production to Landscapes of Consumption:
Employment Patterns in North Carolina over Four Decades

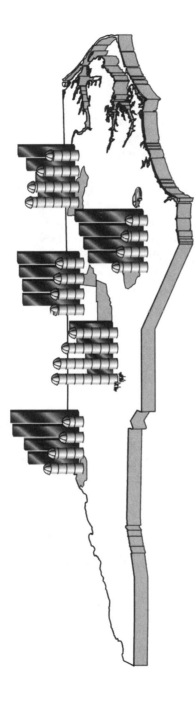

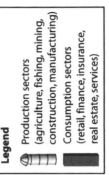

Legend

Production sectors
(agriculture, fishing, mining, construction, manufacturing)

Consumption sectors
(retail, finance, insurance, real estate, services)

Silos and skyscrapers represent the relative percentage of employment in the production and consumption sectors in 1970, 1980, 1990, and 1999 in five counties in North Carolina (left to right: Watauga, Chatham, Durham, Cumberland, and Halifax). For each year represented, the "production" and "consumption" figures for each county add to a total of 100% of employment in these two sectors.

All data are from the U.S. Dept of Commerce, Bureau of Economic Analysis. Employment in government, military, and in two other BEA categories ("Transportation, communication, and public utilities" and "Wholesale trade," neither of which is easily categorized as either production or consumption) is not included in this chart.

North Carolina, as with the following case of the Perdue/Goldkist poultry plant in Chatham County.

Processing Poultry, People, Communities:
Political Externalities of Industrial Restructuring

> If Perdue Farms doesn't find a buyer for its local poultry operation . . . the
> fallout will affect more than the 800 persons losing jobs. The town of Siler
> City, Chatham County, a large number of farmers, and a host of other busi-
> nesses all stand to be big losers in the fallout of the announcement Friday
> that the poultry giant is closing its facilities.
> —*Chapel Hill News,* May 23, 1996

Fortunately for those who would have faced immediate hardship, Golden Poultry Co. of Atlanta agreed to purchase these facilities, and after a brief interlude, production in its Goldkist facility went on as before.[7] All the same, times of uncertainty like this produce the anxieties about the future evinced in many locales that have faced globalization's effects over the last two decades.

The advent of poultry and pork processors in rural North Carolina is recent. Poultry and hogs are no longer raised by farmers, killed in slaughterhouses, and then butchered for sale by retail butchers. They are instead processed in production chains of technologically sophisticated, computerized steps that control the life course of the animal product from birth to maturity to death to meat.[8] It was this new industrial system that brought eight hundred immigrants from Mexico and Central America to work in the Perdue plant in Siler City, and helped make immigrants from these places 40 percent of the town's population by 1997.

Private transactions in the market have public consequences that are treated by the corporations as externalities, that is, as costs that those other than employers and laborers have to bear. This corporate stance results in anxiety, confusion, and often anger. One externality consisted of poultry waste from the two large processing plants. Even after passing through the town's sewage treatment plant, fats, feathers, and foam detergents flushed out of the plants through their use of an average 830,000 gallons of water each day then went into local rivers.[9] Moreover, Latino laborers in Siler City placed demands on the small rural community's public schools and social services, as well as social system.

Landscapes of Consumption: Durham and Watauga Counties

Roads Are Good, Roads Are Bad

Over the past thirty years, the local economy of Watauga County in the north-western part of the state has shifted almost completely from manufacturing and farming to service and retail. With the growth of tourism, the local univer-sity, and the general population, snarled traffic has increasingly plagued the area. The possibility of widened roads pleases most residents and tourists. How-ever, plans for one highway project have occasioned intense debate. The road in question passes through Blowing Rock, a tourist and retiree destination with a large seasonal population. (About 45 percent of housing is seasonal and 60 percent of owners reside outside the county.) "Transplants"—"newcomers" coming in from outside—feared a four-lane road would destroy the town's charm.

The debate sparked a series of letters to the editor of the local paper. Trans-plants argued that "development can ruin a once quiet, picturesque town," and the road widening would "destroy our beautiful, quaint mountain village." Others complained of the huge "visual impact" of a road. Natives resented the efforts of a small but powerful group of transplants to impede road improve-ment. They complained that "seasonals" don't pay North Carolina income taxes and retirees don't travel the road each day to work. Others complained of the loss of community and retail institutions geared toward the local commu-nity that resulted from the growth of tourism and the second-home industry.

Converting land once dedicated to food production or to services for leisure and recreation areas requires that food and goods be brought in. Natives view the wider road as a physical link to the outside made necessary by the restric-tions on economic activities imposed by newcomers. Letters to the editor implicitly contrast the natives' enduring Protestant work ethic to the lack of productiveness of temporary residents, and harshly judge the selfishness of those unconcerned with the safety of others.

Concentrating on Consumption

People living in mountainous Watauga County have made money from tourists for a long time. Roadside stands have welcomed visitors with local sourwood honey, apples in season, quilts, and other crafts for sale. Neither are luxury mountain resorts new to the area. Textile magnates such as the Cone family and other wealthy Americans summered regularly in the famous Blow-ing Rock area. Today's rough-hewn stands similarly line the roads, although they sell more goods from further away. But now, instead of hard-to-reach resorts, the roads travel to concentrated tourist areas crowded with motels, inns, malls, and restaurants. Hiking trails, ski slopes with manufactured snow, and canoes entertain the tourists.

Prior to the 1970s, commercial tourist interests and the local college explicitly discouraged the expansion of a manufacturing base in Watauga. As a result, working people were limited to two primary economic strategies. If they inherited land, they could farm; if not, they could work in the small number of local factories or go "off the mountain" to the furniture factories thirty miles to the south. Nevertheless, through the postwar period Watauga could be characterized as having a mixed economy of small distribution centers, food processing plants, small-scale factories, family farms, some tourist resorts, and a state teachers college turned public university in 1979.[10]

Over the past thirty years, manufacturing employment fell by two-thirds while the percentage of the workforce employed in retail and the number of people employed in the service sector doubled. The burgeoning interest in Watauga's stunning landscapes and mild summers has pushed up land prices and taxes, the latter by an estimated 500 percent from 1980 to 1997, forcing many farmers to sell. Between 1970 and 1990, Watauga's farming population fell by more than two-thirds, and new and seasonal homeowners flooded the area. Further, the local university expanded significantly and is now the area's largest employer. Watauga County, in short, has become a landscape of consumption, a place that makes its living by selling services and experiences, from education to leisure to beautiful views from one's retirement porch.

Locals of working age are caught in the middle. Except for an affluent few who have made good, they are squeezed out of farming and manufacturing jobs in the area and now face one of two choices. Either they must continue to drive "off the mountain" to find higher-paying jobs in industry, or they must settle for lower-paying, less steady local service and retail work, with few benefits, which services the affluent and culturally different newcomers.

County economic planners have placed some focus on nurturing small businesses, but tourism and the retail and construction boom from second-home construction dominated economic development schemes. Watauga's status as a landscape of consumption is evident in the rhetoric about its future that packages its unique attractiveness as a site for consumable services, including scenery, within a national or even global competition between similar places— in contrast to a landscape of production like Halifax that would lure in outside capital with a shell building and cheap local labor. This self-assigned town identity guides discussions of public spending and the future.

Similarly over the last several decades, elites in Durham County have reoriented their locale away from a landscape of production toward one of consumption. Government planners and entrepreneurs have worked to transform Durham from a city oriented to the tobacco industry with high-paying manufacturing jobs, especially for African-Americans, to one oriented to consumers of high-quality university and medical services. They have also sought successfully to transform Durham into a site of FIRE industries (financial, insurance, and real estate).

Durham now promotes itself as the "City of Medicine." Local elites have sought to cater to the highly paid doctors, researchers, and support staff who constitute its high-profile workers, and to the area's well-remunerated knowledge workers. Upscale shops and high-end housing developments beckon those with wealth and boutique tastes.

In doing this work of urban transformation, Durham planners see the city as complementary to the nearby Research Triangle Park, and strive to compete with Chapel Hill, Raleigh, and Cary to attract the knowledge workers employed in those towns. They also promote the construction of new shopping malls that provide large profits and minimum-wage jobs, respectively, to commercial developers who build them, and to hundreds of less well-off whites and African-Americans who work in them servicing both upscale and middle-brow clienteles.

Housekeepers, Knowledge Workers, Retirees: Those Who Serve and Those Who Are Served

In both Watauga and Durham Counties, the markets for high-priced homes, merchandise, education, and other services are strong given the influx of the people whom landscapes of consumption are known to attract: well-paid knowledge workers employed in the finance houses and high-tech firms, upper-level managers in the insurance business, doctors and researchers in the medical centers, professors and administrators in the universities. These are the people whose lives are highlighted in the public relations efforts of the two counties.

In fact, landscapes of consumption depend on an abundance of cheap but socially invisible laborers. Hotel rooms need to be cleaned, fast-food restaurants need low-paid workers, universities need food-service workers, and medical complexes need orderlies. Then there are the people who make their living in lower-paid service work, the retail clerks in Dillard's, Wal-Mart, and other department stores, the wait staff at restaurants, the administrative assistants at IBM in the Research Triangle Park, the housekeepers at Duke University and local hotels, the orderlies working at Duke or Durham Regional Hospitals, the people who drive the vans at Raleigh/Durham International Airport, the child care workers, and the private gardeners. Thus, low-wage work and poverty exist side by side with high-tech development and conspicuous wealth.

In successful landscapes of consumption, the people who hold the lower-paid jobs of the service economy represent a separate market, one not catered to with as much enthusiasm. While affordable housing stock deteriorates and is not replenished, one new high-end subdivision after another springs up. New schools and water and sewer lines are required, and so property taxes and land prices go up. Long-time residents often sell their property, and they (and their relatives with little or no land to sell) end up in housing further away from their jobs, or rent lower-quality housing or trailers.

And then there are the people who are unable to make ends meet at all. While the lower-end service jobs are not that hard to get, those who hold them without additional income or the possibility of farming for their families' own consumption struggle mightily to make ends meet. Betty Haw was a registered nurse who hit hard times when she became addicted to drugs and lost her job. She then moved to Watauga County, using the money her mother had left her to buy a modest home. On her way to a job interview, she slipped on the ice and fell, breaking her leg. Betty lost her house because she couldn't work, and spent the next four months moving in and out of the homeless shelter. Betty accepted a job cleaning hotel rooms for $6.50 an hour with no benefits. Over the past eight years, she has continued to work at various Blowing Rock hotels. She now lives in a rented trailer.

Low-end service jobs are seldom celebrated or attributed moral value. The high value placed on one's manual labor in farming or blue-collar work is absent when one waits tables or washes dishes in a restaurant, in part because the latter is often seen as more feminine or less "white" and thus of lower status than the work done by previous generations. Many people now holding lower-end service jobs grew up on farms or come from families that combined factory work with farming, where a stigma was attached to such service work, which they still feel keenly.

In Durham, low-income African-Americans carry the burden of North Carolina's legacy of racism—in underfunded schools leading to a lack of marketable skills and the bitter memories left by a desegregation process that closed down black-run schools. Like many whites, they come from backgrounds where kin relations organize daily life, where churches are major institutions of community organization, where small farms and small independent businesses shape work lives, and where the accountants' definition of their net worth is relatively low. The newcomers and those who return with education and skills not only secure the majority of the higher-paying jobs but also have different lifestyles and, in some cases, conflicting styles of activism and political culture.

Landscapes of the State: Fayetteville

John Sokowski, like many residents of Fayetteville, North Carolina, was passionately interested in local issues. Like some tens of thousands of his neighbors, he was a retired soldier, brought to the city by the government and kept there by the incentives of hospital and PX services and long-term local relationships. More than most, he became deeply engaged in local politics. Although he was not particularly interested in political parties or elections, he tried to promote a certain set of ideas about how the city he lived in should plan its future and develop. He was not always so involved, however, and told the story of his political awakening and of the city where he lived in a way that provides a feel for the city and its qualities as a landscape of the state.

He came to Fayetteville in 1970 and for the twenty years he was on active duty, like many others in the military, was very uninterested in the fate of the city. It was, he said, just a place the government had sent him. "The attitude is hands-off, and tolerate almost anything because there's no sense of permanence, there's no sense of kinship with the community."

If anything, he was more likely to see the fate of Vietnam as his concern and doing than that of Fayetteville. But while he served in the military, local political life in his city was under challenge. The way things went for the city seemed determined by decisions in the Pentagon or by the base commander rather than in the chambers of City Hall. When Washington set wage rates and housing allowances for the enlisted ranks of soldiers, the local economy could be radically altered. When the Pentagon or local commanders decided that uniforms did or did not require dry cleaning, local businesses closed down or opened up. Perhaps as important, the long Cold War years created a sense of permanence to the army base's economic effects and cultural climate. Efforts to imagine a new or expanded vision of Fayetteville's future seemed to be more chimerical here than in places organized around smaller, less powerful, or more local economic and cultural institutions.

Throughout the United States, there are places like this that show a large, enduring influence of state institutions such as military bases, state universities, parks, and the expanding prison system.[11] The large payrolls of these institutions provide major contributions to local economies. There are about ten such counties in North Carolina (out of one hundred) where federal, North Carolina, or local government employees make up more than one-fourth of the labor force.

Economically, a landscape of the state consists not only of this workforce's earnings, spending, and taxes but also of the transfer payments through contracts made by these institutions to residents and local businesses and through government retirees' pensions. Fayetteville, like some other landscapes of the state, has either a higher tax rate or lower levels of local government services, or both, since the area's government properties pay no taxes. This both puts a burden on residents and makes the area less attractive to business. Legally, a landscape of the state is expressed not only in the state's rights of eminent domain to claim private land for forest and park preserves, military bases, and roadways[12] but also in the complex jurisdictional divisions of legal rights among federal, state, and local governments related to taxes, the prosecution of crime, the environment, and contractual disputes.

The migrations to Fayetteville by soldiers that the federal government underwrites has created enclaves of outsiders who appeal to universal standards of administrative rationality to make a place for themselves within a preexisting political community where, in contrast, participation is based on personal ties and the privileges accumulated through years of cultivating such ties in situ. The experience within military bureaucracies that such migrants bring or acquire in the course of government service often leads them to argue for the values of regulatory transparency, efficiency, and rationality, values that conflict with other political modes of operating that natives use.

Landscapes of the state may develop hand in glove with landscapes of consumption as they supersede landscapes of production. This is widely recognized where federal and state governments have invested in higher education, research, and development—that is, the high-end services provided in a few select areas such as the Research Triangle Park and Durham County, which benefit from government subsidies to the region's public universities. In these few instances, government institutions have been crucial to "jump starting" the transition from a landscape of production to one of consumption—with the latter showing the characteristics we have discussed elsewhere in this chapter. Transfer payments also subsidize the lower-end markets for the service workers of landscapes of consumption. Moreover, that money may flow right back out to franchise headquarters in New York or Chicago. It leaves behind some of the lowest wages (those paid to retail workers) and a relatively small economic elite, intensifying the growing economic gap, which is also intrinsically a political one.

Landscapes, Transitions, and Local Issues

As this brief survey reveals, the different places to be visited in subsequent chapters mirror places around the country. Landscapes of production like those of Halifax and Chatham Counties are also found in places like Ames, Iowa (with its beef processing), for example, and Flint, Michigan (with its auto workers). Durham County and the Research Triangle Park, the high-tech center, and Watauga County and its scenic attractions have commonalities with places like Orlando, Las Vegas, Manhattan, the 128 corridor in Boston, and other landscapes of consumption. Landscapes of the state, besides Fayetteville, include obvious places like Washington, DC, and places with state universities and/or the state capital like Austin, Texas.

It is necessary to complicate the term "landscapes." First, each of these landscapes does not simply house people who produce things or people who consume things or people who work for the state. Virtually every locale in America has people engaged in all three activities. Second, although we can characterize each place as having a single dominant landscape and a history of being developed as such, some of the most interesting and important aspects of the politics of a place have to do with the overlap or border conflict points created when development strategies shift. At times two different landscapes—and the people who have made their lives in them—coexist uneasily, and even collide, as when one—a rising landscape of consumption—supersedes the other—a declining landscape of production. Many of the dramas of contention we studied could be situated in reactions to these shifts or intensifications of the dominant landscape.

PART I

Limiting Democracy

3 Hope, Fear, and Political Autobiography

From the outset, we were interested in how people have responded to the last decades' momentous changes in their economic, political, and social environment. Knowing that the possibilities for democratic action have grown in some ways, but mostly shrunk, we went on to question people about how they see the relationship between their own lives and local democracy. How, we asked nearly one hundred people from all walks of life, have you been involved in local politics? What *is* politics to you? What are your sources of hope, anger, or fear when you think about getting involved or have gotten involved? We were listening to hear how they described, in the stories of their lives, the many transformations occurring around them: changing neighborhood demographics and affluence, crime, environmental quality, cultural diversity, and sometime racial tensions. How had these changed their willingness to engage in local politics? We learned whether they had had stable employment with a living wage or not—how they had fared as the rich had gotten richer and the poor poorer—and how their economic circumstances might have remade their sense of what democracy is or could be and reshaped their engagement with the idea of "the common good." Had such an idea even survived the corruptions, inequalities, and unfairness in politics described in the media?

How had their religious engagements and beliefs, sometimes in flux as well over this time, structured or restructured their attempts to change things in their community? Did they see themselves and their life chances as being liberated or diminished by the moves to shrink government institutions and programs? Given all the changes that have occurred in local democratic practice, we asked, in effect, how do you think about your place and potential in this democracy? What has prompted you to act politically through your life, and what has discouraged you from doing so?

We asked people across North Carolina to talk about what can be called their political autobiographies. Their lives could hardly be more varied: a deeply religious woman committed to home schooling her daughter, a migrant from Mexico working in a chicken processing factory, a wealthy retired man new to his county, a homeless man focused on maintaining his sobriety, an illiterate woman living with her illiterate son, and a libertarian very involved in efforts to change his urban neighborhood. We asked each of them to talk about their life experiences in relating to the problems facing them and their community. In listening to them, we found that their views were structured by passions that have moved them toward and repelled them from collective action to change their communities. And we discovered what some of the barriers to full citizenship are, and what has allowed some people to make change, at times in spite of those barriers and not infrequently because of them, and what has acted to exclude them.

We divided our conversations about equally between people who were or had been active in public matters and those who had not, relatively speaking. We discovered much commitment, and sometimes enthusiasm, among the former group for their public work. Others had not been encouraged in their attempts to understand and act on their vision of what needs to change, or in their desire to make history move in a particular direction. With either group of people, we can see how their experiences have changed as their communities changed.

First, we should note that Americans relate to politics in ways that are cross-culturally distinctive. Democracy has been enacted very differently in other countries, with the differences depending not only on formal legal variation but also on historical and cultural dynamics and differences.[1] In contrast to some other nations, most people in the United States mobilize themselves to go beyond their private lives only under special circumstances, such as a threat to their values or household economy. To do so, however, they first have to connect their private worlds with public ones.[2] The size of a credit card bill has to be connected to state regulation of banks, or to a decline in one's economic security and purchasing power. A neighbor's violent attacks on his wife have to be seen as preventable, perhaps by the creation of a shelter for battered women or a change in popular culture views of what it means to be a man. Comparing Americans with people from other nations, however, researchers have found that people in the United States are less likely to make those connections. For example, they are more likely to see their personal well-being as changing independently from societal well-being, that is, they can argue that the country is sliding rapidly downhill while still seeing their own life as on the upswing.[3] Or they see their personal problems as idiosyncratic or simply signs of personal or moral failing. As a result, these moments of connecting private and public, individual and collective woes are relatively rare. Habitual activists, at least, are a small percentage of the American population. But when people do see their problems as having public solutions, they may start or join an activist group, speak their mind at a public meeting, or join a church or temple social action committee. Or they may simply complain to neighbors, hoping that their concerns will resonate with others' problems and move others to act.

Whether or not people *can* actually change the world once they make that connection is another matter. There are, of course, more and less powerful people—people who decide interest rates, move armies in the night, or even allocate local school funds versus those whose jobs mainly entail being told what to do. A Citibank vice-president can remake the wider world in a way that a person working the steam table at a cafeteria cannot, and it is people like that who readily acquire the sense of importance, status, and leverage that moves them forward. On the other hand, organized groups of the less powerful have voted scoundrels out, boycotted segregated movie theaters, or come together to speak out on issues.

The people we spoke to across North Carolina vary in degrees of power, primarily by virtue of their wealth, education, race, gender, and charisma. On account of this variation, they have very different stories to tell. Some people see the personal and the historical as intimately connected. Others see their personal problems as quite unrelated to politics. Some see themselves as personally incapable of entering the public domain and making a difference. Others feel a sense of duty or obligation to civic life, a trait that has been called "republican virtue."

Each of these various perspectives provides some support to the theorists of democracy who have written in the past on what motivates political participation. The most well-known thinkers in the tradition that sees political participation in terms of the republican virtue just mentioned are the authors of *Habits of the Heart: Individualism and Commitment in American Life.*[4] They argued that Americans are sorely lacking in civic orientation, primarily because of their tradition of individualism. But they argue from the premise that democracy requires altruism and effort from the citizenry. Critics of this perspective on civic virtue say it asks impossible levels of goodwill and exertion on the part of people whom it would count as good citizens. In order for this classic model to work, critics say, there must be homogeneity of public interest or at least homogeneity in the way people view the public interest; feminists launched an especially important critique of this assumption in relationship to the lives of women and men as citizens.[5] Critics of the classic model include the *realists,* who see the citizenry as fleeting sources of input, too ill informed, too intolerant, and too involved with their own private lives to be effective, and the *participatory theorists,* who have a more positive view.[6] The participatory theorists see citizens as no more enlightened or less self-serving, but instead argue two things. The first is that citizens are the products and blamed victims of a political system that thwarts them at every turn. The second is that people's day-to-day work and family activities should not be sharply separated from their public or political activities. Many theorists, especially those who have turned away from survey methods to give more in-depth attention to citizen talk, have argued that "citizens' political capabilities have been underestimated significantly."[7]

It is with these last, more positive outlooks in mind that we asked ninety-three people across the state to talk to us about what orients them to the public good.[8] The interviews revealed a rich galaxy of understanding and action. These narratives provide diverse insights derived from what is, collectively, thousands of years of experience. Juxtaposed to each other, the narratives can tell us *why* local democracy operates as it does. This is both because people's understandings are cultural—that is, widely shared—and so exert broad cross-societal influence and because they are individually distinctive. In a huge and diverse country, the different ways that life is lived can get lost to each other. While constraints of space and time are one obvious reason why this is so, more important are our class- and race-based segregation from each other, even within small communities, and the often homogenized images of American life that television suggests. People's political autobiographies tell us about the cultural assumptions—shared and diverse—that shape our understandings of democracy and society. They should *not* suggest that people's ideas are at the root of local democracy's fate. They should tell us how people make sense of a world they have inherited, a world overwhelmingly not of their own making.

Cultures of Political Action and Their Basis in Everyday Social Conditions

Sources of Action: Cultures of Family, Media, Church, and School

The people who felt very confident that they could make a public contribution often spoke of a family history of participation. For most, as one man said, it was "through a process of osmosis that it became ingrained in me to be involved." Not everyone felt this family legacy meant that their change efforts would be successful. Their admiration for their parents' democratic involvement meant that they persevered nonetheless.

> My parents were involved, and were the kinds of people and still are the kinds of people who believe that you make an effort. You know, if you have a concern you try to do something about it. And one of my father's heroes is

Don Quixote, you know, sometimes you don't win the battles, but you know, there's some kind of glory about the trying. And that really is, that's a model that I did grow up with.

Some of those families were mobilized by the Civil Rights or other social movements. These were not families, then, that *invented* the ideas they worked with or the methods they used to pursue their idea of the public good. Broader social and historical forces resonated through families, who took them up and configured them in their own ways and built a family culture of activism. In places where the conditions that prompted those movements have changed relatively little—as for example in Halifax, where exclusion from economic opportunities continues to plague black people of the county—the continuing experience of discrimination reinforces that family culture.

While these people act publicly with the confidence that the *we* with whom they most identify—the family—speaks out or works for change, they are not necessarily the most powerful of people we interviewed. They do include, however, many people with long-standing roots in their county. This geographical continuity allows them to inherit and accumulate valuable knowledge about how things work in the particular place where they live. Knowledge of local history and political networks and resources is a priceless commodity that can be parlayed into political action and efficacy. While some more recent migrants have made contacts that give them access to local knowledge, the people with broad-based connections and information are clearly at an advantage when it comes to working for change. And while this is true whether they come from wealthy, politically connected families or not, some kinds of knowledge, of course, can take one farther than others.

The family is an important source of political action in another sense. Family has often determined one's political affiliation, and especially in the rural areas of North Carolina, it frequently defined one's reputation as well. Some people feel that peace and acceptance within their own families depend on their joining the same political party and taking the same stands on issues as other members of the family. More consequentially, shared political memberships and attitudes can affect one's economic opportunities; jobs and other resources are regularly doled out on a political basis.

This has clearly been true of elite families in several of the areas we studied. In Fayetteville, the woman put in charge of a downtown revitalization group came from an at least century-long lineage of powerful civic figures, including a major historic preservationist, a mayor, and men who lobbied the state legislature for transportation resources for the city. She had both the symbolic capital and the personal sense of leadership to take on this task. And like those who came before, her efforts both were civic minded and maintained or enhanced the value of the family's properties. So, too, one of the founders of the Laurel Valley Preservation and Development group in Watauga County was a member of prominent, long-resident family. For the less wealthy, as well, kinship provides more limited but still important connections to people who work, for example, in the schools or know people in local government offices.

Having family in the community where one lives has additional benefits and prompts to action. As one woman said, being married and "rooted in the community"—being able to claim her town as "home"—has made her more visible and legitimate as a political actor. A retiree who moved into Watauga County felt not being a native or permanent resident left him open to attack for his political activity. The motive works in reverse ways as well: a Mexican immigrant who came alone—without family or English skills—remembers the pain this caused him and a number of years later this memory led him to feel he ought to help other immigrants. Overall, though, the new waves of migration into and within the United States on account of economic restructuring have meant that more and more citizens are less strategically and emotionally connected to the communities they live in.

In the classic view, religious organizations, media, and schools are prime cultivators of democratic involvement. Of the people we spoke with, however, only the church or temple emerged as a central place of political engagement, and then only in certain of the communities. What people did in their churches was sometimes called political action but often seen as religious or social action, as noted by one person from the city of Durham: "People go to church for socializing, and they almost automatically reject what they call politics in the church, at least in the white community churches. They don't do that in the black community churches. They very much talk about politics there." This racial difference has obvious roots in the long mobilization or politicization of the black community for social justice ends. Using a broader definition of politics, however—as discussion and action oriented toward the public good—we can say that church action and activists are more often political than not.

Regardless of how they classified the work they did at church, people drew knowledge about political issues from church friends and acquaintances. The importance of the church to political thought and activity derived at least partly from the fact that churchgoers often form most of their social relationships with other church members. People who want to become active find easy access and social comfort in first working in the church organizations that are to become the vehicle for their activism. Said one woman who moved to Watauga County in retirement and became active, "I would have had difficulty knowing where to tap in [to the community without the church, and] until I got actively involved in the church, [I had no] awareness of the dimensions of problems" that needed solving. A woman in Halifax County heard about the pollution caused by large-scale hog operations from another church member;

and she subsequently put a notice in her church bulletin to recruit others to join her in doing something about it. And most obviously, social action committees have been long-term sources of mobilization for a number of people in this group. By the figuring of many people, "church people" are more likely to put themselves out: said one man, "I feel like they care more about it than somebody else would who don't go to church." On the other hand, there were numerous people who described their church experiences as very apolitical, their ministers arguing that politics and religion shouldn't mix, and there were others who saw religious realities as being in conflict with religious principles: "if the churches in the world would do what they're supposed to, we wouldn't have all these problems either. [But] a lot of people . . . use Him to get ahead and that shouldn't be done."

In classic theory, the media create an informed citizenry who can act with, or even *only because of,* the knowledge they acquire from it. A few people do mention becoming aware of problems through the media, and talk with their friends and family about public issues that they hear about in the newspaper or on television. Several politically active people looked back gratefully on help the local newspaper gave their efforts, such as advertising Farm Heritage events in Watauga County and thus educating people to have more pride in their sometimes maligned community.

The people we spoke with, though, were more likely to criticize the media than see it as a helpful tool. Many feel it is not just indifferent to their needs but actually anti-democratic in its practices or effects. Some say the media's role in scandal mongering has discouraged political participation in people who fear falling victim to unfounded criticism or charges. Others see their local news outlets as selling products rather than solving problems, or even as contributing to those problems. They do this, in common view, by trafficking in sensationalism and stereotypes—whether of Latinos in Chatham County or native people in Watauga's mountains.

Some complained about the values promulgated via the media, especially television and the Internet, characterizing them as anti-Christian, coarse, or scary. Critical media reading/watching skills, though, are not as available as they should be, one person noted: "I'm afraid [people] might say, 'oh, it's in print, so that must be true.'" Rather than seeing the media itself as an object for political scrutiny, though, he said, it's the parent's responsibility to steer their children's use of it: "If they are grounded in Christianity, maybe they can stop and say, 'well, that's not what we believe, or what I believe.'"

The activists, who are most likely to want to collaborate with the media in educating the public for democratic action, had in several instances became so wary of the media that they had at least temporarily refused to grant interviews to the local paper or television news. The attention that they or their issues received in the media was often negative, or in a newspaper's attempt to "present both sides," for example, gave further airing and advantage to official or more powerful positions on an issue. In one case, an activist watched the local media turn a story about official racism against Latinos in Siler City into a story about the good intentions and suffering caused to those officials. Another activist who raised questions about law enforcement in the media found himself the recipient of physical threats from the police themselves.

The fundamental changes in the way media are organized that have taken place over the last decades—the mergers and concentration in media ownership especially as a result of federal deregulation—have remade local politics. As one highly educated activist from Durham observed, he is more likely to watch CNN than to read editorials in his own city's paper. The broader impact was identified by a black activist in Halifax County who said, "people don't understand that they have a right to [call into or write media outlets]. That the airwaves are actually *theirs.*"

Contrary to the expectation that the schools impart civic education, we found that virtually no one mentioned them as important in their development as citizens. This does not mean that schools are not actively engaged everyday in defining democracy and citizenship. They train children in particular principles of democracy and in political culture—like the idea of freedom as a pinnacle value or the favoring of representative over direct participatory democracy. The learning of these ideas, however, may fade into the background of other cultural experiences of these ubiquitous notions. This civics training in schools presents abstracted and ideal knowledge that is nonetheless at odds with some popular or informal knowledge acquired later. Many only learn in adulthood about the race- or class-based social conflicts and other political economic realities that structure local political life—for example, that a town's "first families" may have tacit political power or that developers meet over golf with government officials to get things done. This may be what people count as their political education. Such experiences violate the normative accounts they learned in school and thereby get called "politics."

Ideas about democracy are clearly first encountered in an articulated form in primary and secondary school, however. Civics textbooks often tell us that we should vote, or volunteer for civic activity, because democratic values require our participation. A textbook used by North Carolina high school students in the 1990s, for example, says that voting is "one of the major responsibilities of citizenship." Almost everyone grew up being exposed to similar ideas in their school years. Many of the people we spoke with believe it, and those who feel they have not lived up to the ideal express much guilt over not participating. American individualism contributes to this pressure, because it suggests that each person must take responsibility for his or her fate and that of his or her community. It also makes difficult the kind of collective organizing that is key to political action.

For the significant number of people who have been overseas (either because they are immigrants or because they traveled for work, volunteer missions, or pleasure), that experience was a source of political awareness and action. One man identified as a crucial motivator the time he spent in the Peace Corps, when he not only saw poverty and injustice but also experienced how much impact his actions could have. Another first developed curiosity about how our political system works after having lived overseas and seen how another kind of political life was practiced. And a woman who emigrated from Latin America was surprised to see how American individualism prevented many here from becoming political. Focused on their work and family, they did not inquire into how others live and where injustice might be occurring, imperatives she took for granted from her more communally oriented upbringing.

The relatively thin role of the schools and media in people's accounts of their political lives may also reflect historical change in the idea of citizenship. In his book *The Good Citizen*, Michael Schudson has identified a shift in American post–World War II history from the ideal of the "well-informed citizen"— who would rely on the expertise of objective journalists, teachers, or political scientists in making political decisions—to that of the "rights-bearing citizen"—whose citizenship and decisions emerge from a sense of the authority of the notion of universal human rights to which individuals can lay claim.[9] These ideals, of course, sit in some conflict with the disempowerment people feel in relationship to their citizenship, but they represent the changing terms within which people can make arguments for their political points of view.

The shift to a rights-based view of citizenship does not mean that the knowledge involved in the informed citizen type is no longer important in the political arena. Contemporary civic intervention very much continues to require factual, impassive presentations. In addition, an important source of knowledge about political life comes from the grassroots organizations that people join. The groups we observed—like Concerned Citizens of Thornton— spend an intensive amount of time training people how to understand issues like environmental racism and the health effects of industrial hog farming. And they provide education on how government works and how to have an effect on one's community.

The Textbook Ideal and Motives for Action

Despite not mentioning their school experience, many people describe their motives for doing what they have done in the public arena during their lifetimes in the terms of the textbook ideals.

> I just wanted to be civic. Overall I wanted to do something and I almost picked that [issue] out of a hat. I thought about getting involved with

schools, or something. Part of it was that I was getting to a point in my life where I was going to do something useful in the community. Sort of a Jeffersonian concept of a civic life and I thought it was a duty.

Similarly, one person said, "There is sort of an obligation to yourself, to your family, [and] to the social good to try and do something to impact things." Another woman, a highly educated black female activist, described her sense of this duty through the lens of the inequality she sees in her community, and the duty to love and help others.

> I am really thinking that the first strongest force would be the love for mankind, and wanting to help. The next thing is feeling that it becomes our obligation after we, if you want to say, quote, "arrive," and unquote. It behooves us to give back, to give something back to the community in which we live. . . . And the next thing that I would say is I do have an American dream. But, that American dream can never be complete until everybody has the right to a street light. And *everybody* should have the right to a paved road. And *everybody* should have the right to sewage.

Sometimes it is not so much virtue or duty or an American dream of equality that people identify as the source of their involvement, but rather a kind of common sense. Something is needed and therefore someone must fill the need. The language of choice—so rife elsewhere in the culture of consumerism and in spreading neoliberal rhetoric—sometimes disappears. And these may be two sides of the same coin: internalized political values so compel some people that they seem beyond choice. And so a woman who teaches in Durham and works in her spare time to organize children's sports programs said, "if somebody isn't there to run the games and make sure everything is OK, then they don't happen. So, it's got to be done, somebody's got to do it." The people who speak of themselves in the language of the textbook ideal are often relatively highly educated. This gives them the formidable power of a legitimated language dialect when they enter the public arena. So, too, their formal schooling often gives them civic skills, such as knowledge of how to organize a meeting or make public speeches.[10]

Active people sometimes described their work as motivated by the fact that they get to work with other people, who are or become friends, allies, and inspirational figures. By one Durham woman's account, the people she became involved with in politics were a "great group of people, smart and witty and feisty and sassy." Explaining his participation, another man said,

> You meet a lot of good people that way. . . . I'm pretty much a social animal. So I derive encouragement from the fact that there are other people out there

that think like me. [They] don't [necessarily] take a perspective like me, but they are good people that are unselfish with their time.

These other active people model leadership and inspire perseverance, reenergizing those around them with the attitude that they can get things done. They also inspire some by their insistence on the value of having a vision of what change is needed, a vision that can reveal a path out of the problematic present. Some of the people mentioned as models are political figures, local and national; others are activists or volunteers with some charisma.

Passions, Values, and the Motive for Action

More frequently than an abstract sense of duty or the imperatives of common sense or sociability, an attachment to certain values moves people to act. Passions, religious and secular, have an honorable tradition of motivating democratic participation. Righteous indignation at injustice, inequality, or unfairness, hatred of incompetence, fear of loss of a way of life, compassion for others in need, and love for a supreme being or religious principle are all political motives. During an early 1960s march against segregated lunch counters in her city, one woman remembered that

> someone in one of those downtown buildings threw ammonia out of a window that fell on a girl and burned her face. That really got my attention. Prior to that I was one of those people who wasn't going to get involved. I understood the point but I didn't feel like walking up and down the street. But after that, it was time for me to walk too.

Another man began to contest downtown redevelopment plans in Fayetteville out of anger:

> [I]t offends me to no end that they want to put $28 million of public money into the Marvin Plan, as they have described it so far, when our schools need more money, public safety needs more money, and we need overpasses downtown.

And an African-American woman's emotional identification with the injustice done to new immigrant Latinos in her community moved her to act:

> There is a new generation or new ethnic group of people that has been picked on and enslaved and kicked down and pushed down as we were. And I think it gives me a sense of encouragement that we can struggle and come from these struggles, not that we have overcome all of them. It gives me that sense that we must fight for these changes.

For some, the motive for participating is their passionate belief in the value of liberty. It orients them towards political issues but does not dictate which issues they work on. So one man described his political encounter with anti–Vietnam War activists years before. They tried to close down classes at his university in protest, and he took exception.

> I guess it was a civil libertarian point of view. My brand of conservatism is a libertarian kind of a thing. I thought it [the boycott of classes] was an encroachment on a personal liberty, if you want to look at it that way. . . . [My objection] wasn't about the war. I was never involved in any Republican or political groups.

Very often the passion seems to be about failures of the democratic process itself. People get enflamed and then involved because a politician runs unopposed, because tax dollars are used to enrich the few while politicians pretend they benefit the many, because the police routinely swoop down on carloads of black teenagers at a corner, leaving white teens undisturbed at the next, or because they discover that the deal on a zoning variance is already done before they come to a public meeting. A poor white man in Fayetteville summarized the problem as one of corruption, which levels all political difference and debate.

> It all boils down to money. The people that have money have influenced our political system. . . . If you listen to their platforms, Democrats and Republicans, nowadays they got good qualities about themselves and they both have bad qualities. Twenty years ago they were different. Now they are a little indifferent. They are agreeing on things that they shouldn't agree on.

Whether this last thought on party "indifferences" was a malapropism or not, the simple dishonesty of calling a virtual one-party system a two-party system makes people mad.

Nonetheless, emotion has a bad reputation and is used to discredit some people politically. Some see it as mere turbulence, interfering with problem solving rather than motivating it. Thus, some people talk about common sense rather than feeling as the force that moves them to act. Politicians are often portrayed as at the mercy of their emotions, fearful to act, or arrogant, filled with self-important pride, while the citizen who steps forward to act in public ways does so with quiet, rational common sense. Political insiders, on the other hand, paint activists as overly emotional and out-of-touch with the cold, hard facts.

Many people we interviewed seem to share the democratic theorist and activist Michael Parenti's view that democracy is ideally "a system of governance that represents both in form and content the interests of the ruled . . . [but that] too often we are free to say what we want, while those of wealth and power are free to do what they want regardless of what we say."[11] And for some, freedom seems not to extend even that far. As one man said of the media,

> I think it has no interest in uncovering facts. . . . It's like the last letter I wrote to the [local newspaper] that never got published. They never gave me any kind of a reason except, well, we have the right to refuse. . . . It's like we have freedom of speech as long as we say the right thing.

Unlike many democracy theorists, some North Carolinians might argue that democracy is, again in Parenti's words, "not a seminar," or a polite debate between equals whose outcome hinges on the pure merit of the argument, "but a system of power, like any other form of governance."[12] In the lifetimes of both those who have been active and those who have been less so, a power experienced as external to them has prevented them from making government respond to the urgent social problems that beset them.

Barriers to Democratic Action: Dirty Politics, Subcitizens Silenced, and the Psychological Ethic

The Forms of Repulsion: Dirty Politics and Shaming to Silence

Whether politically active or not, everyone spoke of the barriers to living the ideals of democratic life. Not enough time. Not enough money. The boredom of meetings. The lack of involvement by other people: the sense of having to pull too much weight by oneself without others' support. The fear of offending others or simply being the object of others' gaze. And the feeling, as one black man in Halifax County said, that "it ain't going to be no good and they'll go to one or two meetings and they [get] shut right out, you see."

Another reason people gave for avoidance is the "dirty" or even repulsive nature of politics, which includes their sense that the fix is already in by the time "the public" is called in. Many people express skepticism about things labeled politics. If only through their knowledge of the corruption, narrowly defined interests, bureaucratic rigidities or overreach, and corporate purchasing power in Washington, such skepticism would be explicable. In addition, however, their local political institutions often have similar, if smaller-scale, tendencies. While politics has long had a sometimes unsavory reputation, it has become stronger and more generalized (to include the presidency as well as city hall politicians) more recently. In part, this is the result of a concerted attack by some business and political interests on the very notion of government or the public interest.

The repellent cultural image of politics often centers on the character or personality of those who do it: they are often believed to be self-serving, manipulative, corrupt people who hide their actual motives.[13] Politics, in this view, is virtually the opposite of principled, reasonable action, or of impartial decision making; it is the self-interested pursuit of power. One man in Fayetteville who had dipped his foot into the overtly political arena by serving on a government board said that

> it drew some people too that I thought were real low-lives. And I said if what I got to do to be in this kind of arena [is] to deal with this kind of [expletive deleted], well then I just got better things to do. Maybe I don't have the stomach for it. I saw people who were clearly lying and manipulating the situation for their own benefit.

While this latter barrier clearly dissuades many, people take fascinating linguistic routes around this problem in order to go ahead and participate. So someone noted, "politics is a dirty word for some people now. If you call it volunteerism, by the way, it's all right." Nonetheless, "civic work" or "volunteering to help in the community" feed directly into larger public concerns or democratic processes, as when people go out to lobby their neighbors for money to support a rape crisis center or local fire rescue services. There is much in a name—by calling the political something else, people assert an identity and a set of motives quite different from the self-interestedness and ugly contentiousness of stereotyped politics. Being active in the community is seen as a valid and valuable thing only if it is done for others or the group as a whole, not in pursuit of self-interest, self-display, and antagonistic desire.

Secrecy is another forbidding practice of government in some people's eyes. So one woman, who for years tenaciously worked to keep a landfill out of her neighborhood, described the government practices that most dispirited her at times:

> The City Council itself is discouraging. Particularly when they lie to you. They keep you at meetings until 2 to 3 in the morning and then don't make decisions. Then they make one decision, and you come back in two weeks and they have been in a closed session, took a secret vote that you or nobody else knows about, and they turned around what they had spoken two weeks ago.

For some people, the antidote to such secrecy is the use of a business model for government. This was not just a view expressed by businesspeople, because it was a homeless man in Watauga County who told us, "I believe Perot was the right man for the job: he was going to run the government like a business, you know, to where all the records would be made known, their budget, everything." In seeing the market as a preferable model, this man follows many

Americans who view economic exchange as less morally ambiguous or compromised than politics, because economic pursuits are necessary to make a life for oneself and one's family.[14] Moreover, the very idea of "the economy" is, as the political theorist Timothy Mitchell has argued, a set of ideas and practices that began to take the shape they have today starting from the mid-twentieth century.[15] The economy is assumed to be both a thing and a set of underlying logics or rules by which exchange takes place, a natural or universal logic with no master and no politics. Politicians may attempt to manipulate the economy, in this framework, but its operation, left untouched, should produce outcomes that are both natural, and, since the rise of neoliberalism and its reinterpretation of economic matters, good.

While this belief in the market has long-standing roots in American political culture, it has been strengthened and amplified by the ascendance of neoliberal rhetoric over the last two decades. Despite the fact that business is usually private and closed to nonmembers, and the government public and at least partially open, that rhetoric, expounded at the highest levels, encourages many to see what is called the "open market" as a transparent place where unfairness or corruption could not go on. It is a place supposedly structured objectively to produce the greatest good for the greatest number: there are therefore no selfish or corrupt motives or activities to hide. Government, neoliberalism suggests, has its own counter public interests—for example, to expand and pay its employees and units or to control the populace—and it is here then that secrecy has an (illegitimate) role. While many people have learned from fifty years of Cold War and national security rhetoric that federal secrecy can be patriotic when applied to this one government function that neoliberalism legitimates, many seem to feel that the rules elsewhere, especially on the local level, should be different.

Another dissuading factor beyond politics' reputation and secrecy is the silencing that often happens in the public arena. The muting comes from the perceived attitudes of those who sit at the front table or in the audience at public meetings. So of town meetings, one woman said, "you get in there, and whenever you say something, they look at you like 'What are you doing? You ain't supposed to say nothing. Don't say nothing,'" she said, laughing at the uncomfortable memory.

Most people who complain of the time barrier to participation see it as something developmental, which falls away as their children grow up. Others see the press of time as related to economic restructuring. As one woman from Durham said, in an impassioned tone,

> The past twenty years of income stagnation . . . really led to a situation where both my spouse and myself have to work full-time in order to have a reasonable standard of living. I think that that very fact has seriously served to

squelch the kind of level of community involvement that's possible for people. And in paranoid moments, I wonder if that was intentional, that that was the plan all along, to make sure that we're all working like dogs so that nobody has the time or the energy to translate their vision into reality, except the people with a lot more money than most of us have.

Sociologist Juliet Schor, in *The Overworked American,* summarizes studies that show that people on average have less time than in the past for anything beyond paid work and maintaining their household,[16] a trend that has accelerated with the economic reorganizations of the end of the twentieth century.[17] So, too, have the hours of commuting to work increased and the hours of television viewing.

Democracy's Barrier of Fear and the Prison of the Self

But what most struck us about the barriers that people talk about were two stumbling blocks that have not often been addressed in the many volumes on democracy. First, fear is an important factor in people's political autobiographies, and it has an anti-political effect. Second, what we can call "psychologism" pushes people to flee from public work.

The fear that people talked to us about includes the anxiety about being different or alienating neighbors by disagreeing with them. Some fear street crime so much that they would not go out for evening meetings or to canvass their neighbors. More importantly, and in some places around the state much more than others, the fear is of retaliation, either economic or physical violence, should one try to change the status quo through political activity.

Trust is commonly seen as a foundation stone of democratic life, in fact of any successful social life. Yet America's social divisions—especially of race and gender—have often been reinforced through violence. Women walking out at night to meetings have rape to fear, subconsciously if not overtly. Blacks have police attention to worry about. Everyone of middle age or older remembers the assassinations of Martin Luther King, Jr., other black leaders, and Civil Rights workers—and many people brought these incidents up to us. These experiences were fundamentally formative of people's political autobiographies. Some people's accounts of the most important changes of the last decades center on the rise of fear of others. Without specifying events, they point to the rise of the perception of a more criminal or lawless environment and also a heightened individualism. As one person said, "And that's what I see has changed most of all. It's a fear. It is a looking-out-for-only-oneself type of attitude."

Imagining herself going to people's homes to do service work or a canvass of some kind, a Durham woman who had done some volunteering to raise money for Toys for Tots in the past and had thought about helping out with a local literacy campaign said, "I'm so afraid that if I go and knock on this door somebody's probably going to fuss me out, cuss me out, knock me in the head or something, just because." No particular experience prompted her fear; for her and many others the prompt must be mainly the media's constant crime coverage—despite the fact that U.S. crime rates have dropped or remained constant over a long period.[18] But too many others have personal tales to tell.

One Watauga woman described the violence woven through her relationship to the immediate public space of her neighborhood. She described calling the police to break up a late and loud drinking party in her condominium complex, which spilled into her yard and flowerbed, only to have the policeman warn her that her complaint would only get the revelers angry at her. The fine he levied in fact did just that. Afterward, the peace-disturbing neighbor took his dog to defecate on her lawn and cut her Christmas lights.

And for an even more distressing number, their past political activity has brought violence or the threat of violence.[19] While this sometimes prompted resistance and a public call for apology, reform, or exposure of wrongdoing, it could also bring on more aggressive attention. An activist assisting workers in the meat processing industry worried about retaliation; rumor told her a group of police met and discussed taking revenge after it was announced (incorrectly, she felt) that she would criticize their misconduct at a meeting in another town. One man in Durham who spoke out similarly told of the police stopping him, and "telling me that I was going to be beat up. It was going to be a couple of police officers—nonuniform—that were going to kick my [behind]."

And the harassment or violence does not have to happen to each person him- or herself to chill the atmosphere for those who identify with the attacked or threatened. This is what has been called violence's "demonstration effect." So one man—currently unemployed and struggling with a drug addiction—said that the assassinations of Martin Luther King, Jr., and John Kennedy made him feel that he was not going to get into politics because he would end up "at the bottom of a river or blown up." The violence may occasionally, though, be a prompt to action, as with the woman who saw Civil Rights protestors attacked with ammonia.

There is also the fear of economic retaliation. Immigrants worried about being deported if they stuck out in any way. Even life-long residents worried aloud about losing a job if they spoke out or got involved and so alienated their employer. One man who was politically active in Halifax County was frustrated with such fear, however, when the people who hold back for fear of reprisal would lose a minimum-wage service job he felt was hardly worth having.

Finally, some people felt that the basic processes of collective or individual democratic action had been delegitimated. Others did not just disagree with them on matters of substance when they had been active in citizen movements; the powerful saw their organizing as an antisocial threat. The activists absorbed that sense of danger themselves, fearing the labels, from "troublemaker" to "socialist," that could be put on them, and sometime speaking to the ethnographer in lowered voices about their concerns.

We can return for a minute to the question of power raised early in this chapter. The people who have experienced this fear have not been the elite of these five communities. To the extent that neoliberalism suggests the market is an impartial, invisible, and helping hand to all, it disguises the nonrandomness of such experiences of violence, retaliation, or fear. And it suggests that anyone not acting as a full citizen—that is, making contributions in the public arena and speaking out—is making a choice rather than responding to constraints and forces beyond choice.

We can ask how people experience their lack of power—whether it is to make a decent living or to make other kinds of social change happen—and whether they experience it via "the sociological imagination." That is the phrase the thinker C. Wright Mills coined in the 1950s for that which "enables us to grasp history and biography and the relations between the two within society." It is the route, he said, by which "the personal uneasiness of individuals is focused upon explicit troubles and the indifference of publics is transformed into involvement with public issues."[20]

The sociological imagination flowers in many places through the interviews. It is absent, however, in intriguing or discouraging places, for example, in the man whose home had no sewer and water services but who answered the ethnographer's question about the relationship of local government to his life by saying that there was no relationship, either actual or hypothetical. At the other end of the social spectrum, several elite or wealthy individuals characterized themselves as politically inactive, and yet mentioned their personal relationships with powerful political figures and their ability to speak frequently to these figures (and presumably influence them) about the direction they thought things should go in their communities.

Where the sociological imagination is absent—where private troubles cannot be made into the stuff of broader public debate or historical frame—what theorists call "the psychological imagination" takes its place.[21] Psychological explanations were commonly used to account for political engagement or efficacy. One woman, whose paid job involved developing alternative education for homeless children, explained why she didn't pursue this goal more vigorously, especially outside work.

My own work situation . . . has kind of led to such a level of self-doubt about my own efficacy in articulating what I want to do and making it happen. That I've honestly been very fearful of stepping out of the safety of the environment where I'm working and trying it out on somebody else, because I'm really afraid of finding out that it's not the people around me, it's me.

Although she was concerned about moral decline in the nation and also saw racism and the good ol' boy network at work in excluding some from local politics, one Republican woman saw her political reticence as the product of her personality:

> I have a temper. I really do have a temper and I know it. And I know my limitations and my limitations are when somebody looks at me in a condescending manner or when somebody says to me anything that is going to make me think that they think that I don't belong somewhere, I know that I would not be effective, because I know that I would lose it.

Yet another woman expressed a view of herself as inadequate to the task of democracy because she was more a listener than a vocal leader. And on this she shares an assumption with many political theorists who associate democracy with talking, debate, or deliberation (although an alternative account of democracy, feminist in orientation, argues that listening is just as central a capacity for democratic life but is undervalued [Bickford 1996]): "I can't imagine with my personality getting involved in speaking out or things like that. I pretty much will listen. I vote, if there's an issue that you vote on. But I'm usually not very vocal that way." The psychological imagination is closely related to the culture of individualism. This culture centers analysis of the world on the person and what she does, the choices she makes, the virtues or vices she displays. Such individualism favors a view of political solutions that an autonomous person might engage in, such as voting or expressing opinions, rather than group activities, like forming organizations to pressure the government.

Finally, there is the discouragement of seeing how little things change despite a lifetime of one's own or others' political work. Even more disheartening for some is the sense that the basic things people once took for granted as the contribution of normal government to their communities require struggle to attain in the new neoliberal era. A long-time activist and businessman in Fayetteville said, of a local controversy over funding of the county library system, pushing for "this is something that twenty years ago you didn't have to do. You were going to have libraries." Now, he said, the people working to prevent loss of these basic public resources are so tied up in such rear-guard actions that they are unable to attend to "the bigger picture kind of things," like longer-term environmental problems. Moreover, he said,

> years ago there was a leadership of the community who were merchants who did what needed to be done. The industry people like Kelly Springfield [a

large nationally owned tire factory] frankly are just taking care of their own thing. . . . They go to the Chamber of Commerce meeting and that's it. And the [managers] at Wal-Mart wouldn't know where to *find* the Chamber of Commerce meeting. And they certainly wouldn't go to a Sierra Club meeting or work at the local library.

What this man is referencing is the following striking change that Fayetteville has undergone, along with the rest of the country: 95 percent of the nonanchor stores in the city's largest mall were locally owned businesses when the mall first opened in the mid-1970s; today, just 5 percent are owned by people who live nearby. This man, who had a brilliant sociological imagination and a long enough history of residence and activism in one town, could see the changes over his lifetime in what politics focuses on and in *how* people have to work for the common good: the neoliberal faith that the market will provide means politics is now a struggle for basic public needs once taken for granted, and the consolidation of capital into larger and larger organizations (such as Wal-Mart, Lowe's, and McDonald's) means that local business is no longer truly local and has much less investment in community health.

Economic Restructuring, the Meaning of History, and Political Autobiography

As people told us their political autobiographies, we saw how important the everyday conditions of their lives were to their relationship to public life. It is far too simple to say, then, as many assume, that people participate out of a simple will to make a difference or with the knowledge that advancing levels of education build. However important these may be, more fundamental are histories of highly variable school funding, or local cultures of racism, or privileged hope. While the people speaking here have made history, history has in turn made them and American places in different ways. And the economic restructuring of the last thirty years—the changing material basis of people's lives—has shaped the way the possibilities for making history are perceived, understood, and physically and socially enabled. In ending, we can summarize how these five North Carolina communities have presented the political possibilities to the people who live there, and what people make of that history.

In Fayetteville, the local government has had to take a passive role in relationship to its main economic counterpart, the military base. Directives from the Department of Defense are not negotiable at the local level, and so a habit of waiting has generally descended on the community. The city, for example, has no recycling program. Moreover, active-duty soldiers have rarely gotten involved in local politics, a reality due both to their retaining their residence in other, non–income-tax states, and to (an eroding) tradition that says the army should be apolitical. A restructuring army, however, has meant longer stays in town for more soldiers, up to and including retirement, when their political lives often begin, sometimes with vigor. And the even higher status as citizens that has been allocated to soldiers as a class—the sense that this is the proper exchange for their service to the country—has meant that when retirees do participate, they are sometimes seen as more rational, capable, and selfless contributors to public debate than others. They are, on the other hand, subject to the exclusionary practices of that part of the community who are native or see themselves as the only true and permanent citizens of the locality.

Halifax County's residents can in some ways see the least difference in their political and economic lives over the last decades. Economic opportunities remain restricted, and a racial regime of segregation and coercion remains present, if somewhat muted. People's autobiographies reflect this sense of limited possibility for shifting history off its course. Another form of waiting oppresses Halifax, and that is the dominant leadership's anticipation that economic development will come to the county from the outside, once they provide tax incentives and building shells. On the other hand, Halifax is the place that has generated the most remarkable, wide-ranging, and vigorous citizen movement in the form of the Concerned Citizens of Thornton. In one sense, one could say that as the decades have stretched into centuries of democratic exclusion in this county, there has been a kind of alternative government or public arena that has arisen for black citizens of the county, through their own leadership and efforts.

Durham County has an increasingly large segment of people who are empowered by their class and education to see themselves as the makers of Durham, as we will see with the activists of Durham Inner Village. There political optimism is at its highest in some segments, including both the white and black middle class. But racial polarization remains strong and has potentially been sharpened as manufacturing—which included both black and white workers in its relatively high-wage opportunities—was replaced with service work and corporate headquarters, and the usual racial suspects disproportionately filled the varied new job slots. But racial inequality is not new; historical memory easily recalls the devastation of the Hayti neighborhood by urban renewal and the city has always had comfortable and poor halves as sharply marked as any other across the state.

Change has come to Watauga County in a way that pits two very different styles of political engagement with each other. The confidence—overweening at times—of the county's many in-migrants confronts the muted, nonconfrontational, and kinship-based style of natives. Political culture—the medium in which and by which political participation takes place—has undergone seismic shifts in the last several decades. And if the rules are changing like this, it will not be surprising if fewer feel they can play. More palpably, the new economy of tourism, retail business, and service work that has replaced farming and industry present the horns of a dilemma for native families because retirees and tourists are both an economic opportunity and a political threat to longer-term residents. They come down on different sides of the issues on which natives today can still politically prevail as a majority of the population. But migrations, fueled by national economies and changes, may soon end the regularity of that political outcome.

Siler City residents tell moral tales that obviously relate to the impact of migration on their local economies and values. The influx of Latinos appears as a kind of "return of the repressed" for black-white relations, and in ways both productive and destructive, people reenact the earlier Civil Rights era. Memories of previous mobilization are generally empowering. But the onslaught of public officials and media stereotyping of Latinos as inferior and as interlopers sets political culture on a course it has already run with African-Americans. Participation is dogged by these racial exclusions.

But the situation is new in ways that parallel the difference between the economic basis of wealth in the Siler City area in the 1950s and today. The changes have made citizenship then and now quite different. In her book, *Flexible Citizenship,* anthropologist Aihwa Ong has argued that neoliberal economic change has not so much overwhelmed nation-state boundaries as resulted in the state's strategic allocation of differing degrees of citizenship to residents within its boundaries. Mexican migrants with limited citizenship rights who work the poultry processing plants are that much less likely than a native black or white workforce to challenge local political practice, much less the business practice of their employers. The sheer pace of capital flow into the county, moreover, poses challenges for activists concerned about how it shapes their community.

Each one of the people who spoke about their experience with politics speaks to the possibilities of remaking society as they see it. When we broaden the horizon beyond individual lives to the political and economic frameworks of those lives, as well as the cultural frames these interviews reveal, we can see that the remaking of democratic process and outcome requires the reshaping, not so much of people's attitudes, as of the material and social conditions of possibility for action and inclusiveness. And it requires that we see the cultural frameworks that people use to understand participation and that thereby make democracy more or less likely to wither or take root.

4   Racial Framing

[T]he silence of white people on issues of race continues to be the critical problem of race relations in this country—that people who are not minority won't raise their voice to talk about how structures of racial inequality are being perpetuated in this country.

—North Carolina resident, 1997

The last thing the Senate should do is engage in clearly an inflammatory action. As far as I know, race relations in North Carolina are excellent. They may not be in Illinois or Ohio. I do not know about that, but in North Carolina they are fine.

—U.S. Senator Jesse Helms, North Carolina,
in a 1993 Senate floor speech about Confederate symbols

The Story of One Ethnographer

I was scheduled to meet with Tom Moses one Thursday afternoon in September at his home in the country. Prior to leaving I gave a quick precautionary call to a couple of friends to let them know where I would be that afternoon, the time of the interview, and when to expect me back . . . just in case. Stories about the long-term public official painted him as malicious and conniving, short of feeling and bent on hatred. According to county lore, he loathes African-Americans. Despite my attempts at dismissing my anxieties, I saw little reason to be less than cautious about a private meeting. When I arrived at his extensive farm, his dogs barked ceaselessly as my car came up the long driveway. Tom Moses greeted me from the porch, waved away the dogs, and signaled for me to come inside. I went in, masking my anxiety with an air of scholarly confidence and professionalism.

He offered iced tea and a seat on the couch beside his reclining chair, and our conversation soon flowed smoothly. When I asked about his support of the segregated school system, he explained that he did not believe blacks and whites should intermarry and share social worlds. Moreover, he thought that industrial development in the area suffered from the fact that affirmative action had brought in a wave of incompetent people who received their positions based on quotas. In response to a query about his presence on the school board of the predominantly black school system, he said that the taxpayers elected him and that he has worked to improve the quality of education. He did not mention that he had voted against every nomination of a black superintendent for the district.

As the interview came to an end, he thanked me for coming and mentioned that when some people write up interviews with him all they see is racism. He, however, does not see himself as a racist and seemed a bit baffled by the characterization.

Mention of the concepts of racism and racial inequality often brings to mind the dehumanizing mistreatment and overtly malicious discourses of the pre–Civil Rights days: "white" and "colored" restroom signs, water hoses, police dogs, and angry white protestors. Contemporary day-to-day confrontations with racism and racial inequality, however, are frequently removed from this type of open hostility. Present struggles with race have much more to do with worldviews and institutionalized processes of privilege and exclusion. Much less accessible to the eye, these processes are often naturalized into everyday patterns that reinforce stereotypical norms and exaggerate foundational inequalities. The purpose of this chapter is to present issues of race in North Carolina in such a way as to open up an understanding of racializing processes, and to relate these to the state of local democracy today.

By bringing to light processes of racialized exclusion, we do not mean to suggest that overt and malicious racism does not still exist in North Carolina and throughout the country. Despite the fact that incidents of overt racism have declined since their heyday in earlier decades, North Carolinians Against Racist and Religious Violence (NCARRV) reported 138 incidents of hate crimes in North Carolina in 1992, the highest number in nearly a decade.[1] This report did not include the resurgence of black church burnings between 1994 and 1996, which left several North Carolina churches and scores of other black churches across the South in ashes. Neither did it report reflect the significance of hate crimes that capture widespread public attention. In 1995, the murders in Fayetteville of an African-American man and woman by white Fort Bragg soldiers, members of a neo-Nazi hate group, caught state and national attention. Crimes such as these, coupled with ongoing reports of police harassment, racial leafleting, and other activity, create among people of color a continued climate of fear and distrust.

While it is important to acknowledge the presence of overt and dehumanizing racism, it is clear that many today condemn such acts of terror. Durham residents were infuriated in 2005 when three crosses were burned in separate locations around the city. Ironically for some, vigils and protests in opposition to the symbolic gesture were attended largely by white residents. When questioned about why few African-Americans turned out for vigils, historian and resident John Hope Franklin pointed out that African-Americans in Durham are exposed to structural and symbolic violence on a daily basis and did not find the cross burnings as remarkable as whites did. Nevertheless, acknowledging the heinousness of certain crimes does not preclude intentional or unintentional participation in other forms of exclusion. Within the sites we studied, the more subtle practices of racial inequality are illustrated in decisions about economic development, quality of life, and democracy. Regardless of site, race and class privilege tend to sway the outcome of public policy, affecting access to funds and to votes.

If North Carolina is a progressive state, as many elected officials claim, how then do its "progressive" people allow and maintain racist and racialized polarity in present-day North Carolina? How do the process of white privilege and the mystique of progress operate to allow these inequalities to continue? Finally, how different are the sites in our study from one another given the differences in local economic and political histories?

Answers to these questions are evident in the vastly different ways whites versus people of color describe issues that inform their lives. For example, what does "economic development" mean to a community of African-American seniors who live in Halifax County? What might this same idea represent for local development officials? Likewise, how do Latino residents of Chatham County understand "quality of life" and what might other residents see as challenges to their quality of life? And, given the presence of a sizeable African-American middle class in Durham, how do residents of Durham evaluate their access to the democratic process?

Again, it is important to remember that our characterizations of the different sites are meant to describe the general milieu and dominant forms. We do not claim that *all* residents embrace these forms. Indeed, some fight against them. Neither are the situations peculiar to the counties mentioned. A range of similar situations occurs throughout the state and nation. In these pages we aim to capture dominant themes in public discourse—themes that in many instances reinforce political polarity and hinder the growth of racial equality.

What Is Economic Development?

If you travel Interstate 95 between Enfield and Roanoke Rapids, you are sure to see signs of development. The industrial park in Weldon constantly spews steam, the paper mill in Roanoke Rapids emits the "smell of money," and the retail signs leading you to lodge, dine, or fill up give travelers the distinct impression that things are happening in Halifax County. An empty industrial shell building, completed in 1998, seems to promise imminent growth. Extolling the county as the place where "the spirit of independence was born," business and civic leaders proclaim economic progress, describing Halifax as a "progressive county" with "progressive leadership." Industries such as textiles, lumber, and rubber keep this former agricultural center alive, while the number of small farmers continues to dwindle. Compared to the local school systems and government offices, these industries or similar ones across the border in Virginia or in surrounding counties employ an equally significant proportion of Halifax residents.

Electoral politics seem to have progressed as well. Since 1985, the county has seen the election of African-American school superintendents, African-American county council members, and African-American heads of two county departments, the Department of Social Services and the Health Department. These elections and appointments alone signal progress for many in a county where black political leadership has been historically opposed by more power-ful political forces, despite the population majority that blacks hold. According to the 2000 census, of the 57,370 residents in Halifax County, 53 percent iden-tified themselves as Black/African-American, 42.6 percent as white.

County statistics serve as indicators of the imbalance of power and access in the county. In this small county, there are three school systems, one 80 percent white, the other two 90 percent and 95 percent African-American. In addition, segregated residential conditions perpetuate patterns of inequality. As with many other towns in the state, several townships in Halifax County have what are referred to as "extraterritorial districts" stretching in a one-mile radius around the town. These districts, which house a disproportionate number of African-Americans, lack adequate water or sewer service. Residents are not forced to live in extraterritorial jurisdictions; however, the circumstances of their lives sometimes provide little choice. Citizens who can afford to pay town taxes and choose to live in town gain the benefits of running water, sewer, and adequately paved roads. One of the conclusions reached by the 1993 Confer-ence on Poverty in North Carolina is that in what are called "black belt" coun-ties like Halifax, although poverty plagues all groups, blacks are the poorest.[2] Poor conditions reflect both a general lack of suitably paying jobs and poor graduation rates among high school students.[3] It is no coincidence that cou-

pled with these statistics on poverty rates and education is the disproportionately high number of toxic waste and hog industries in these areas of North
Carolina.

North Carolina has advanced rapidly in swine production since the 1990s
and has been a national leader in vertically integrated, industrially structured
hog farming.[4] Well over 90 percent of the industry today is found in former
black belt counties with histories rooted in cotton and tobacco farming.[5] The
disproportionate presence of these farms in African-American communities has
excited concern among environmental justice groups. Likewise, the presence of
toxic-waste dumping sites also raises the question of race and the privilege of
whites who are less likely to be exposed to such sites.

One of the ways the process of racialized privilege manifests itself is in relation to the question of the *quality* of economic development. Developers,
entrepreneurs, and council members often see development projects simply as
the influx of industry into the area, bringing an increase in jobs, profits, and
tax base. While these changes suggest quantitative growth, they do not necessarily imply quality economic development. These changes bring threats to air
and water quality, health, and safety, forcing a broader understanding of economic development. This broader understanding often illuminates the importance of making a race-conscious analysis of development plans because the
negative impacts of certain types of development are most often felt in predominantly black and rural communities.

During one interview, Nancy Rowles, a middle-aged white woman, spoke of
the need for more industry to come to Halifax. She, like several other informants, is a native of the county and is deeply concerned about her children's
possible futures. She has remained in the area and established a local business
with her husband and in-laws. Rowles appears to genuinely desire improvement in the life of people in Halifax County, both white and black. At the
same time, she "does not understand" why some residents do not welcome
opportunities for "economic development." For her, businesses that promise to
bring more jobs into the area should be celebrated as advancing the industrial
base of the county. Of hog farming in the area, she acknowledged, "I'm sorry it
stinks, but you know, you got to have it. People need jobs. . . . Get a grip, you
know? [laughs] Circle off the land around them and let them be there and provide work opportunities. Somebody's going to do it." She went on to note the
objections to a human feces–recycling plant proposed for Enfield:

> Enfield has nothing as far as industry, major industry. And this was going to
> be something like a recycling plant. They were going to do something with
> tires or something and a committee went to check out a similar plant and
> they came back and reported that neighbors didn't complain around this
> other plant and that everything was . . . I mean they were, they blended into

the community fine. [But, still,] people didn't want the idea of having the possibility of odor or pollution or whatever around the town. And so the town's going to die. You know? It just makes absolutely no sense to me.

Because she was not directly affected by either the hog industry or the human feces–recycling plant, she had not studied information on the health and environmental hazards that these industries could bring. Plans for the plant, we learned through a county economic development officer, were scuttled by an African-American congregation whose homes and church were located across from the proposed site. Rowles's physical, social, and economic distance from the affected communities, however, allowed her to ignore the pollution problems. She also overlooked the relationship between race and quality of life and instead presented a color-blind assessment of development. Her disconnection from such issues symbolizes the type of white middle-class privilege that allows for ongoing racial inequality. Her color-blind view of economic development allows her to support local leaders who campaign for these industries to come without strict environmental regulations.

African-American critics of the proposed industries did not disapprove because they lacked concern for economic development. Rather, they discriminated among economic development projects out of a deep concern for their community. For these residents good economic development brings jobs that do not endanger, but rather support, the health and well-being of the community.

In 1992 a community group, the Concerned Citizens of Thornton, lobbied the county commissioners to impose a moratorium on the hog industry in Halifax. As a part of their campaign, they leafleted local African-American churches, including several that had been active in past civil rights struggles. In the end, they were successful in establishing strict water quality regulations for these industries. Since then, no new hog industries have located to the area.

When asked what local issues concerned him, one African-American community leader, George Givens, replied, "Environmental degradation, environmental racism, black land loss, voter registration education, triple school districts in the county, administration of the social services programs, hogs, hogs, and more hogs." He saw *true* economic development as something that takes into consideration obscured costs that may be levied upon disenfranchised groups:

Well I actually got involved with the environmental degradation and racism when we discovered that the corporate hog world was planning to enter Halifax County as economic development. . . . And it was at that point that I began to fully understand that [environmental] degradation really is not just the air, water, and land, but what is actually happening to communities and especially communities of color.

This community leader's understanding of the problems associated with certain types of economic development allowed him to see that blindness to race is not a neutral act. The areas impacted by low-quality development projects are most often poor African-American communities, not white middle-class ones. The history of limited development in Halifax, as in other northeastern North Carolina counties, leaves blacks in rural areas vulnerable to any type of development project that presents the possibility of jobs, even if these projects mean "the town dies" literally. White privilege in this case accounts for one of the processes at work allowing racial inequality to continue in the face of otherwise progressive leadership.

Fred Smyth, one of Halifax County's chief economic development specialists, defined progress as being open to industrial growth. Speaking of areas and people as a "product" (presumably to be marketed to itinerant capital), he emphasized the complexity of achieving economic development:

> Economic development encompasses a lot of different areas. Product development is one of them. Not only does it involve going out and finding somebody to come in and build or establish a company and provide jobs and tax base for the county, but it also means that, you know, you've got to develop your product.

For Smyth, Halifax as a product includes the shell building, the already operating industrial park, and a trainable workforce able to compete with global production rates. Production rates, he insisted, are key in "selling" Halifax County to interested corporations, workers in other areas must not out-produce workers in Halifax:

> Unfortunately, in today's climate, every company is in a global economy and a global market. They've got to compete with companies that have very, very low labor costs, so productivity becomes an issue. Each employee has to be as productive as possible to compete with those low-wage countries, like the Caribbean basin and Mexico and areas like that.

Smyth's neoliberal discourse of progress, combined with white privilege that does not recognize itself, here casts "employees" as individuals who must be pressed to be more productive, but whose safety or health takes a back seat. In eastern North Carolina a large portion of such low- and semi-skilled workers are African-American. These workers, often descendants of sharecroppers, are the ones most negatively affected by the narrow, market-driven notions of progress employed by local officials. Steady production rates can create unrealistic job responsibilities that turn into health problems. Likewise, competition with "low-wage countries" requires the suppression of wage demands.

Smyth's vision of progress stands in contrast to the vision of progressive economic development presented by African-American workers and leaders in the area. David Cummings, an African-American official who sees himself as constantly working against the dominant political structure in Halifax, explained the transition from farming the land to industrial work in these terms:

> The only difference between working in the sewing factory and slavery is that they've taken us out of the fields and put us in the mills—so we're picking corporate cotton. . . . We're still in cotton. . . . When you're poor and unemployed, you don't have a lot to say about what happens in your community. Unless you get someone elected to represent your issues.

Cummings believes he was elected to represent poor and disenfranchised African-Americans who live and work in Halifax. Having observed the trends in his community, Cummings notes that there is a gender distinction in the experience of laborers. Women and men often pay different prices for certain types of development. According to Cummings, African-American women overwhelmingly supply the labor for sewing factories as well as poultry industries. These high-risk, high-production jobs requiring repetitive motion and hard physical labor go to semi- to low-skilled workers.

Lisa Jackson, who lives and works in an adjoining county, works on behalf of women industrial workers in northeastern North Carolina. The women that Jackson supports are most often women who work in the sewing or poultry industries who have been injured on the job and are seeking disability payments. She noted,

> The [poultry] plant has been in the area for twenty-one years . . . and what I've seen in the last seven years [since working here] is that it's totally destroying the community, the African-American communities, because you have women [with job-related disabilities] who can no longer sustain their households—can't do anything but take medicine.

As a former employee in the sewing factory and an advocate for women factory workers, Jackson is familiar with the high rates of carpal tunnel syndrome caused by the high-paced repetition of work tasks coupled with the risks of operating heavy equipment.[6] When asked who generally works in these types of floor positions, Jackson responded that in the poultry plant "they have three shifts and it's 98 percent African-American women." Women in the rubber industry indicated the same type of disproportionate representation of African-American men and women in their plants. One woman explained, "All the white people was in the office," while African-Americans worked the floor.

"When I left there on third shift, no white people. On second shift, I think about two." Factories competing for an edge in the global market are most likely to require rigid production rates in these types of assembly-line jobs.

The plight of African-American workers in high-risk, low-pay industries raises questions about the meaning of the term "progress" in North Carolina. During eleven months of ethnographic research, we heard "progress" used as the buzzword by local officials and school board members to express a particular amount of distance from the past, one recalled as racist, poor, and isolated. Their remembering suggests, "We are not where we used to be, nor are we where we want to be, but we are moving forward." School board members express this idea in relationship to school desegregation. Economic development officers express it in relationship to industrial development. City officials express it in relationship to citizens' access to public goods and the recent ascent of African-Americans to the county commission. Yet, this notion of progress is misleading.

From their long history of struggle for equal rights and fair pay, African-Americans and those sensitive to the plight of industrial workers in eastern North Carolina do not necessarily subscribe to the vision of Halifax County as progressive. Progress for them is defined by the success of citizens who have organized *against* unwanted industry. The women's activist organization is presently lobbying for state regulation of processing lines in poultry plants. Progress for them does not simply mean more industry; it means safer industry and living wages. Using *these* notions of progress, Halifax County may be progressing.

What Is Quality of Life?

In the western section of Chatham County, in the small town of Siler City, there has been significant change in the area's racial composition over the last ten years. The expanding poultry plants, with their need for unskilled labor, have recruited Latino immigrant laborers. Where once only male Latinos were recruited to work in seasonal and contracted farm labor, Latino immigrants now bring families and settle permanently in year-round employment. An unofficial conservative estimate of the Latino population is 38 percent, but is more likely close to 50 percent.[7] Many of the new laborers come from rural backgrounds in Mexico, El Salvador, and other Central American countries. Others move to Siler City from states like California, Florida, or Texas.

Unlike these states, North Carolina has little history and experience in absorbing new immigrants. Latino immigrant laborers are directly linked to the market forces of the county's economic restructuring, and not since the colonial period in Chatham County have the "locals" had to deal with such increased diversity due to workforce reconfiguration. Spanish-speaking immigrants on average have less formal schooling and a lower socioeconomic position than the local population. For the most part, they have settled in dilapidated rental housing in the segregated African-American neighborhoods. They have taken on some of the most difficult, tiring, and hazardous jobs, although many with gratitude and even enthusiasm.

Many North Carolinians have no clear idea who Latinos are, and in Siler City there is a tremendous tendency to racialize this group. Most often, the local immigrant population is labeled under the umbrella term of "Hispanic," commonly referred to as though it were a single ethnic group. But in Siler City, the immigrants come from Mexico, Central and South America, and the Caribbean—the majority being Mexicans.

Local industries, particularly poultry, lumber, and textiles, maintain their globally competitive edge by relying upon immigrant labor. In the state as a whole, the increased numbers of immigrant laborers permit North Carolina to continue as a haven for low-wage industries. Employers welcome the new arrivals because they represent a pool of unskilled and low-wage labor, are not union organized, and are enthusiastic about the opportunity despite harsh working conditions.

Many economic studies have found that low-skilled immigrants take jobs that others shun, often creating tension between them and poor blacks and whites. In poultry processing, one of the most hazardous jobs in commercial agriculture, occupational injuries like carpal tunnel syndrome are commonplace, especially where as many as ninety-five chickens are processed per minute. Interviews with Latino workers revealed that when injured, many could not receive any compensation or care from medical doctors, many of whom they suspect of working in cahoots with the poultry companies. Others reported having to work extra hours for free or face losing their jobs, and several described being fired for complaining about hazardous work conditions, particularly if they made an issue of any injuries. Immigrants are the most contingent of all contingent workers. What these companies call "job flexibility" most commonly means little to no health insurance, no paid vacation, and no pension or job security. Together with constant fear of INS raids and threat of deportation to get rid of surplus workers, working conditions are ugly evidence of economic exploitation bordering on overt violence. With the companies focusing strictly on the product, these labor practices degenerate into commodification and dehumanization that recalls slavery.

Under these conditions, only the labor is welcomed—not the immigrant. Many racial tensions arise when the immigrant refuses to be strictly labor, and instead becomes a person with a family, human necessities, and diverse cultural practices and beliefs. The settlement of entire families in this locale has placed particular stresses on the county infrastructure, with serious consequences for quality of life. Lack of appropriate housing is a prime example. Interviews with workers and advocates revealed that the poultry companies initially advertised their jobs at the U.S./Mexican border. They faulted the companies for recruiting workers and issuing promises but failing to provide or even facilitate housing for them. Serious overcrowding is the result, to the point where some people actually sleep in shifts: sleeping for eight hours and then going to work, a person leaves the bed for the next worker who is just getting off work. These shifts coincide with the three eight-hour shifts of factory work. Latino renters report discriminatory practices and unsafe, sometimes condemned housing units with no water or heat. In addition, egregious rent price gouging by some of the local landlords stands as a major barrier in securing adequate housing.

The presence of the Spanish-speaking laborers in Siler City raises serious quality-of-life issues. The issues are racialized because of the drastic difference in the way Latinos are marginalized from public goods and services, despite contributing to public coffers. Latinos face major challenges in gaining access to adequate health care and housing; yet these very real quality-of-life issues have only been marginally addressed. The plight of the Latino workers often becomes secondary to citizens' speculative concerns *about* the new arrivals. In one example, nonwhite anxieties about the possibilities of Latino gang activity became an immediate issue to be addressed by the citizens' council and local officials. In this case white privilege determined whose quality-of-life issues were voiced and prioritized.

White locals exhibited increased anxiety over the use of public resources, despite the fact that immigrants supply the needed labor and their presence stimulates the economy and creates new jobs. In interviews, long-time residents described Siler City as a "ghost-town" before the immigrant workers arrived. Yet ethnographer Enrique Murillo's fieldwork revealed a popular myth that Latinos are getting a free ride—that they don't pay taxes, live off welfare, and overutilize county social services. One letter to the editor in the local newspaper read,

> I am an American citizen, I know for a fact, the government pays the first six months salary for a Hispanic. . . . They do not pay federal tax or social security for three years, just state tax. . . . The American people made this country, but we have been pushed aside.

Such comments demonstrate that Latinos are often thought of and portrayed as problems for the community. Such attitudes also reflect the logic of privilege. One is entitled to certain public goods because "the American people" built the country. Who, though, we can ask, are the American people? What entitles someone to be considered part of the American people?

One petition to the town board by the local residents of a particular neighborhood read,

> There is trash all over the yards. We thought littering was against the law. Clothes all over bushes, trees, and walls, wherever they can throw them. Ducks, roosters, and chickens running wild. We deserve more respect than we are given, we were here trying to make our community a better place to live, long before the new arrivals. . . . They infringe on our rights. Although the new arrivals work in our city, they . . . are basically doing as they please with no restrictions [and] do not pay city and county taxes.

Local media also propagates these myths of Latinos as chaotic and dirty. One radio personality, commenting on an effort to clean the town, reported,

> It's going to take effort from everyone who lives or works in Siler City, even those who don't pay taxes here. They need to clean up their own backyards. In fact, that's where a lot of the litter is coming from. Folks are moving to the area and don't appreciate our way of life, or understand our culture, you know, where we use trashcans. You know, it's folks coming from other places who are not accustomed to our culture—the same people who throw their baby diapers out on the side of the street, and the beer bottles and all that.

Nativist backlash in Siler City, Chatham County, be it from local white residents, local government officials, radio commentators, or newspaper writers, clearly indicates the connection of racism with nationalism.[8] That is, Latinos are accused of receiving unfair tax breaks and otherwise failing to fit understandings of what it means to be a good citizen. Yet undocumented laborers, like legal residents, pay taxes, but use falsified Social Security numbers or a special code for undocumented workers on their tax returns. Some reports estimate that Latinos pay five to ten times as much in taxes as the cost of the services they actually use.[9]

In absolute numbers, Latinos and African-Americans in Siler City now make up the demographic majority, yet local decision-making power is retained in the hands of the white minority. New racial pressures have become marked in this manufacturing-based town as the presence of entire Spanish-speaking immigrant families adds to the already ongoing black-white racial tensions. One orange bumper sticker on a Chatham County state road sign read, "Earth's Most Endangered Species: THE WHITE RACE. Help Preserve It." Though this sticker is certainly not indicative of every white American in Chatham County, our ethnographic data clearly suggests that Latinos experience economic exploitation, multiple incidents of overt racial insults, and widespread cultural indifference.

In this small town, Latinos have boosted the economy with their labor, taxes, and local spending on goods and services. Yet, with respect to the government and local debates over the distribution of public resources, Latinos have no decision-making standing, no voice, and no political representation. Most cannot vote because of their status as undocumented laborers, and so far no political leaders have taken on their issues. Whites rule despite minority numbers and racial subordination predominates. The situation is one of "taxation without representation."

The social processes of white privilege and civility in race relations facilitates the disregard of immigrants' poor quality of life. The progressive mystique and its emphasis on rituals of civility disguises negative feelings about both Latinos and African-Americans, who are often portrayed as lacking civility. In Siler City, for example, many locals believe that Spanish-speaking immigrants were "by nature" chaotic and violent. A local newspaper article appeared with the prominent headline "Statistics Show Latinos More Prone to Violence," and its opening read, "Living to a ripe old age may not be a reality for Siler City Latinos (Hispanics). The North Carolina State Center for Health and Environmental Statistics reports the top five causes of mortality for Latinos in N.C. are cardiovascular disease, motor vehicle accidents, homicide, nonvehicular accidents, and cancer." It is noteworthy that three of the five were attributed to Latino behavior. The article suggested that the Latino population in the state is quite young, prone to injury and violence, and engaged in more dangerous habits and practices than the population as a whole. The article goes on to cite "problems" that Latinos face. However, it generates a negative social and cultural portrayal of Spanish-speaking immigrants, distancing the reader from the Latinos' situation by offering purportedly neutral statistics to support its claims. Although the article was not about violence primarily, but about health and social issues, it helped construct images of Latinos as chaotic and violent.

These negative images of Spanish-speaking immigrants feed and are fed by exaggerated responses of local commentators and officials. One early morning, the local Siler City radio station broadcast its local news report. The main subject was the rumor of a drive-by threat on the last day of school. Purportedly the shooters were gang members. Even though the rumor proved false, the radio station announcer (and owner) reported the incident as an example that Latinos (conflated with gangs and drugs) now marked the end of their "very friendly city," which he laughingly called "Mayberry." He also spoke of the incident as a lost opportunity to call the Immigration and Naturalization Service and "find out who's here illegally."

The announcer warned the town folks that with the presence of Spanish-speaking immigrants came all the "bad" from the big cities. Problems were "coming like a freight train," and locals, he said, had to decide whether to "get out of the way" or "get in the way" and "do something about it." The news broadcast, which contributed to a rising tide of concern, went on:

> We had some rather tense moments, I guess you might say, here in Siler City yesterday. As rumors were going around, that there was going to be some kind of trouble on the last day of school. . . . And we want to salute our Siler City Police Department, Chatham County's Sheriff's Department, a lot of officers volunteered to hang around . . . stick around all throughout the day, even though they may not have been on duty officially. It was the last day of school. There were rumors that there was going to be some trouble at the middle school. Now, I'm not even going to say what the rumor was in effect, but that there was to be some trouble at the school. A disturbance. And security was high at both the high school and the middle school, by the Siler City Police Department, the Chatham County Sheriff's Department. And officers from both departments, some of them weren't even on duty, volunteered to stick around and be on hand to protect the public safety of our community—whether or not anything was actually going on. You know, better safe than sorry! And you can't be too sure. . . . Rumors of violence have been going on. Law enforcement and school officials believed that this is the beginning of gang activities here in Siler City. Now they've spotted several clues that there might be gang activity brewing in Siler City . . . they found symbols painted on the walls that they traced to gang symbols—gang activity.

Months later, when the new school year began, the front-page headlines of the local paper read, "Police Set Meeting on Gang Activity." The article that followed spoke to the local Siler City police's efforts to stop the spread of gang activity and "save Smalltown U.S.A." from all the serious problems of city life that they bring:

> One of the downsides of living in a large city, north or south, is the presence of street gangs and their activity. From random acts of violence or vandalism to more serious offenses, they're a problem for police to deal with in those cities. It's enough to make you want to live in a small town like Siler City where none of that stuff goes on, isn't it? Guess what. It's not just the big cities. It's here, Smalltown, U.S.A., right here. And local police say they want to stop its spread before it grows any larger. To that end, says detective Dan Stewart, the police need the community and have organized a public forum to talk about the issue. "Street gangs are here," Stewart says, "and more and more signs of them are popping up. Remember the last day of school at the middle and high schools last year?"

Enrique attended the public forum on gangs, sponsored by the local police department and a community-interest group. Officer Stewart lectured the audience of approximately 130 people that most of what the police had seen of gang culture had been at places where youth approximately twelve to fourteen years old concentrate, like ball fields, schools, and so forth. He anecdotally described the adversarial relationship between Crips and Bloods. This information followed a display of slides wherein the officer explained names, symbols, and colors. Examples of what he showed were graffiti from the Folk Nation and People Nation, the 4-corner Hustlers, Vatos Locos, and others.

The officer was adamant that people were wrong to make this incipient gang activity out to be "a racial thing," meaning biologically or genetically based. Instead, he argued that "for Hispanics it [gangs] is very much a cultural thing! . . . Just like Martin Luther King is part of our culture, so are gangs part of theirs."

Officer Stewart said that public concern really escalated when those rumors of a drive-by shooting circulated on graduation day. A man stood up and said that gang activity was not just at the middle and high schools, but that it was also present in the elementary schools. Mayor Ditts proclaimed that "it all starts at home," suggesting that children are not getting proper guidance.

White privilege means that white concerns are taken in the public sphere not as *white* concerns, but as everyone's concerns. Racially unmarked, they are simply "concerns." Likewise, whites are not liable to have their behavior, disapproved or otherwise, interpreted as *white* behavior. Thus, whites are not as susceptible to being interpreted as lacking in civility simply because they are white.

Enrique tried to make this point in the meeting. He raised his hand to speak, and stated, "I am from Los Angeles and grew up around gangs and peripherally was in one myself as a youth . . . and there is a tremendous difference between youth culture and hard-core gangs." He went on to ask,

What are the police doing to differentiate between the two? . . . I've been harassed my whole life by police, and being young and Latino, or being young and black, were not crimes. If police work from a criminal profile, or racial profiling, then the question remains, How are you differentiating the run-of-the-mill youth wearing football attire, and the like, from those of serious hard-core gang activity?

The police representatives said that that was a good point, and that someone "needed to educate us Southerners on the difference."

The vulnerability of nonwhites to being treated as though they were chaotic, violent, and uncivil deeply concerned youth in all of our sites. Popular imagery associates minority youth with violence so strongly that even trained police officers have without hesitation shot young men—as in one notorious California example, mistaking playing with a broom for threatening with a firearm. That night in the auditorium, people said such things as "these kids come from bad environments" and "these children are victims and the product of bad parenting," their comments suggesting that only the good parents in town showed up to the meeting.

These racist stereotypes and the fear they evoke seem credible to white locals shielded from the quality-of-life issues faced by Latino immigrants. From their point of privilege, the startling inadequacy of their town's infrastructure appears to be the fault of the newly arrived immigrants, and they can easily imagine that rumors of a drive-by are true and gangs, likely. The image making, perceptions, and actions of whites trying to defend themselves from the possibility of harm are strangely compatible with the local rituals of civility and race etiquette that purport to value racial egalitarianism and color-blind behavior. These processes encourage blindness to quality-of-life issues for nonwhites and treat as benign the social distance that allows for racial profiling. What makes racist interpretations possible is that racial identity or nationalism seems to explain in common-sense terms broader cultural processes at work in everyday life. The rumor of a drive-by on the last day of school encouraged and was encouraged by the idea that "Hispanics are violent and chaotic, it's part of their culture," "our [white] children are not violent as they are," "they are harmful and less-deserving," "they are taking over the town," and, moreover, "they are taking over the country." In plain words, one African-American woman interviewed afterwards stated, "The white people there last night didn't care about the youth, but just about themselves. They just wanted information on how they themselves could further segregate themselves more away from us blacks and Latinos."

What Is Democracy?

The processes of stereotyping, privilege, and civility further relate to questions of democracy and its attainability across all of our sites. Again, perspectives on and appreciation of the possibilities for democracy vary according to whether one is white or nonwhite in North Carolina. For residents in North Carolina, this question of democracy comes up in discussions about how local and state governments should operate. More often than not these discussions of democracy and pleas for the "democratic process" are complicated because of the racial past and present of the counties.

Under these circumstances white privilege allows whites to exclude minorities from the political process and access to public goods in both formal and informal ways. Informal exclusion is manifested in the patterns of consultation used by developers and officials, which often leave minorities out of decisions affecting their lives. Formal exclusion occurs in the electoral process when whites gain a voting majority on a board or council simply because of numbers. In two of the five sites covered in 1997, major conflicts surrounded board or council votes split (4–3 and 5–4) along racial lines. Taking up James Madison's concerns about majority rule in the founding of the republic, legal scholar Lani Guinear questions what often emerges as tyranny of the majority, where the majority rules without the checks and balances of minority input because of their sheer numerical advantage. In other words, tyranny of the majority means that minority representation exists but that there is never sufficient numerical representation to ensure that the issues and concerns of the minority are brought before the council, heard, and finally acted upon.

In Halifax and Durham Counties in 1997, there arose two major incidents of this power differential. Enfield, one of the six major townships in Halifax County, ceased operating for nearly twelve months in 1997–1998 because of internal racialized strife. Three African-American elected officials began a boycott of the regular town council meeting because they felt that the concerns of African-American residents were not being addressed by the majority white board. In this scenario the progress implied by their election was short-circuited by the reality that they were merely treated as a token presence on the board. Their input was not taken seriously. Unable to form a majority voting bloc, these elected officials complained of not being able to secure paved roads in majority black communities, fair electricity prices, or a host of other amenities for their constituents. Journalists in one news magazine have called these types of majority/minority votes that end in an actual boycott of a meeting "quorum busters."[10] Likening the boycotts to legislative filibustering, the author states that "in all these places, race is the defining factor. The boycotting members share similar grievances related to the inadequate provision of services to minority communities."

In Durham, a conflict on the school board came on the heels of the merger of the city and county school systems. The predominantly African-American city school system and the predominantly white county school system were merged in 1992 in order to adjust the racial and economic imbalance created by the two separate school systems. The 1997 discussion surrounding the hiring of the new school district's superintendent erupted into heated debates about the qualifications of the white female candidate versus the African-American male candidate. In the end, the school board hired the white female candidate, with a 4–3 vote split along racial lines. One white businessman, Jeff Davis, gave his interpretation of the event:

> They came up with this convoluted way of electing the school board, which is why we had the sparks that we did in this superintendent's election. You've

got three [of the seven people on the school board] that are . . . elected almost exclusively by the black community, and three by the white community, and they don't really have any need to be loyal. Now they're supposed to represent the whole city, but if you live in the white section of town, you know that's who elected you, [so] you're going to tend to be an advocate for them. Now, I don't think the white school board members have done that, but the black school board members have. You know, see it's a polarizing sort of thing. You've got these two sides that are locked in conflict with each other because they want different things, and there's no clear mandate, one way or the other, from the whole city or county about what we want our school board to do.

Davis illustrates the point clearly. Under the terms of majoritarian tyranny, despite the presence of free elections and open debate, the final outcome of debate ends in majority/minority splits. In North Carolina these splits are all too often along racial lines. To understand the persistence of this logic on the everyday level, it is important to further note the dynamics of this businessman's analysis. While speaking of the problematics of the white/black divide on the school board, Davis did not recognize his own bias. In his summation, the white school board members voted according to the objective facts of the matter before the board. Black school board members on the other hand, voted purely along racial lines. The concerns of the black members are treated as *black* concerns; those of the white members, simply as concerns. The consequence is that whites are seen as thinking and acting according to an objective and nonracialized standard, while African-Americans are perceived as acting according to a subjective and racialized standard.

These instances of majority/minority divisions occur in formal processes within institutions of the state. Yet, how do these issues of white privilege maintain themselves in informal ways on the everyday level, where people confront them regularly? How does or how can the majority not hear the minority? In Durham, this issue of white privilege is seen through what some residents suggest is their invisibility. Durham has a large African-American middle class, yet the concerns of poorer African-Americans in Durham are left out of most public consideration. Whether the issue relates to funding for schools in poorer areas of the county, the location of an alternative school, or provision of adequate housing, the ability to make invisible those different from the taken-for-granted middle class stands as a sharp marker of privilege. Yet, the presence of a sizeable African-American middle class allows marginal access. This access speaks to another kind of privilege, one less powerful and less overbearing, but one that, left unchecked, could reinforce similar patterns of exclusion that poorer residents of the city endure.

In several interviews, developers and elected officials spoke of the need to further plans they have conceived by consulting the black community. One developer, Clyde Barksdale, identified powerful groups who need to be consulted before actions begin.

> My past experience in Durham is that there are a lot of power centers, and you can't get anything done at all unless you get each one engaged. And the two main ones are, I guess sort of generally, the black community and the white community, although there is no such thing as either. . . . The power groups [are] the government group, the university groups [one of which is the historically black NCCU], the developer group, and the do-gooder group [people who want to see good things happen]. So we put together a bit of a steering committee, which represented Duke and NCCU and some of the political leaders of the black community, people in the planning movement, and started talking about how we do this.

This developer's belief that an African-American voice is crucial for the success of any project is rooted in Durham's long history of an organized and active African-American community. African-American churches, the NAACP, and the Durham Committee on the Affairs of Black People have made significant strides in attaining access for marginalized groups. Black churches in particular have continued what is seen as their Civil Rights legacy by serving as black public spheres, central locations for the dispersal of information and the rallying of support for local concerns. E. Franklin Frazier's idea of the black church as a "nation within a nation" captures the historic meaning of the black church for countless African-Americans who were excluded from the workings of local, state, and national government.[11] Yet, the questions of how this African-American voice is included in larger democratic contexts and how much power this presumed monolithic voice has are related to the issues of privilege and civility. Several African-American respondents were reluctant to talk about the extent to which their input is fully considered against the broader goals of planning and development. A developer in Durham argued in a conversation with us that the diverse racial makeup of Durham "gets in the way" of progress:

> If I can talk to any of these people one on one [African-American leaders in Durham], I feel I can convince them, as long as I feel confident about it. But if I go in the audience and try to convince people, there's always the other process, and that's a political process, and that can be combined from a racial point of view, on some issues, not all issues obviously.

The developer identified talking publicly as a political process, where, by definition, race would inevitably come up. Yet, he did not associate talking "one on one" with African-American leaders about development plans as part of a "political process." Civility, or the rules of polite society, requires that the African-American community be consulted. In fact, however, only a few members of the community are being contacted out of fear that in a group setting issues will become racialized and a compromise more difficult to reach. One on one, however, compromises are easier because race is less likely to become a leveraging point.

For developers and officials to single out certain African-Americans as consultants for the community is problematic for some African-American leaders. It creates division and can allow African-American individual interest to take precedence over community interests. At the same time, it marginalizes those who refuse to play by these same rules of civility. One activist, Sylvia Boyd, frustrated with the process and some of the outcomes of such meetings, expressed her concern when she talked about how the former Hayti Community was developed:

> I see Rick Hendrick's [white car dealer] and he's got a nice landscape and the bricks and the lights and all of that. It's like two different worlds. So I wonder what the African-Americans—and I'm African-American myself—I wonder what these African-Americans that supposed to be power brokers, what are they doing in these meetings? What are they doing when it comes to planning, and zoning, and monies? What are you getting for your community? They are not doing it. They are not doing what they're supposed to be doing, because I think everybody is so glad to be socially accepted.

In Durham, the presence of an organized and sizable African-American middle class could lead one to believe that privilege lies on two levels—that the economic privilege of being counted among the middle class, for African-Americans, offsets the realities of racial inequality. However, the realities of privilege are far broader than simple economic gains. To be black *and* poor virtually guarantees exclusion marked by the invisibility of your needs. One reporter recalled an incident that set off emotions in a Durham City Council meeting:

> Once the Chamber was bringing a group of people to the Angus Barn for dinner and they decided to take Holloway Street. While they were driving, someone threw a typewriter in the middle of the road to stop the car. Everybody in the car was pretty upset when they saw that the car was surrounded by black men. Nothing really happened. But in city council, Mayor Hanks said that if she was taking people to the Angus Barn, she would not have taken Holloway Street. Eric Jones jumped in and said, "that is the problem, you just want to ignore the problems over there and pretend they don't exist." There is a lot of public denial about east Durham.

The "denial" suggested by the reporter that renders east Durham invisible is a type of process that comes with both race and class privilege. As in Halifax, with its extraterritorial districts, people are often ignored by geographic location and geographic location often coincides with socioeconomic differences. Because of these correlations, the legitimate concerns of the poor are often overlooked or, worse still, trivialized.

Residents of east Durham recently challenged the placement of an alternative school in their community. The school, seen by some as the "dumping ground" for "disruptive kids," was placed in the community without its consent. When several residents heard about the district's plans, they organized to prevent the school board from expanding the facility. Residents were concerned that the students were being placed in their neighborhood, a neighborhood without adequate resources, simply in order to distance them from other students, not necessarily to work on their academic development. One resident explained her concerns in these terms:

> Well, basically, what concerns me the most is the fact that Durham Public School System has a lack of interest in Afro-American youth   . The advancement center, it seemed to me, was more of a dumping ground for kids that the school system just refused to deal with. Basically all of the kids were Afro-American, and they were not addressing the real issues and the problems that were going on with the kids. . . . [I]t was kind of just a dumping area, [a] dumpsite.

Similar issues are raised in regard to the placement of businesses. While the "black community" is not overlooked per se, middle-class African-Americans, who have no immediate stake in the placement of certain projects, have been consulted but the residents themselves have not. And though African-American power brokers may be consulted, ultimate privilege lies not in being consulted but in being the one who does the consulting. In Durham and throughout the country, this position is reserved for a privileged few—often upper middle class, often white.

Invisibility and the Plight of Poor Whites

These questions of race- and class-based exclusion from political and economic processes raise legitimate questions about the plight of yet another group of people—those who experience the pain of poverty, yet have not been racialized. In other words, what about poor whites? Are they not also ignored and disenfranchised? Is not their plight as important as that of those who have been explicitly racialized into exclusion?

According to some scholars, poor whites *are* the nonracialized race of people who make up the invisible masses. Though the vast majority of people on welfare in this country are white, "poverty has a black face—not in reality, but in the public imagination."[12] According to anthropologist Kirby Moss, "Narratives and prevailing images of poor Whites are conveniently missing from the middle-class ideological portrait of itself because to acknowledge poverty and banality within its own ranks erodes the eminent, constructed image of Whiteness."[13]

In Watauga, where whites make up over 95 percent of the population, race would seem to be irrelevant. Yet, the issues in this small county raise further questions about the complexity of race and class, and their collective power in American society. In Watauga, two separate experiences speak to the realities of exclusion: the experience of the homeless and the experience of native residents. As noted in chapter 3, long-time residents of the county, or those native to Watauga, struggle to maintain political control in the face of increasing numbers of newcomers with more spare time and money to affect decisions. The presence of a solidly middle-class-to-wealthy group of newcomers creates a social hierarchy where natives, often with fewer resources and less access to leisure time, are being marginalized as citizens. The struggle to have their voices heard in the midst of economic restructuring decisions is a growing challenge. Often pejoratively referred to as "hillbillies" and "rednecks," this group of citizens represents the working poor, as in Halifax and Chatham.

The struggle over how best to develop Watauga magnifies ongoing social divisions, with individuals marginalized, and community concerns of the poor ignored. Although the county has experienced economic growth due to tourism, poor natives rarely benefit. Both direct political marginalization and poverty are means of exclusion, and the numbers of poor and even homeless whites are increasing. One resident of the local homeless shelter expressed the need to build yet another one. "I would try to build at least one more shelter like this because certain times in the year we get completely overrun." For him, as for other residents of the shelter, experiences with "bad luck," as they would call it, lead them to the shelter. "You don't have any idea what can happen to you," says one resident. "One day you can be just perfectly fine sitting right up there, and tomorrow you could have nothing. I know because I've been there and it's happened to me."

While the process of immiserization remains a mystery for this man and others, the reality for many Watauga residents is that the economic boom in the economy has positively affected some while leaving many poorer natives, people not immediately vested in the economic boom, to suffer the consequences. Unable to compete with rising costs of living, many natives find their ways of life vanishing and their sense of stability completely disrupted. The idea that their concerns are invisible to the public eye resonates with feelings of invisibility found among other poor African-American and Latino residents of North Carolina. Though seemingly less overt and racist, the processes of exclusion leave similar results.

Interpreting Processes and Progress

According to political theorist Howard Winant, there has been a movement away from domination to hegemony in the post–Civil Rights era. That is, overt forms of racism have been on the decline, replaced by more subtle processes that work to reinforce the status quo in race relations. People now hold to a value system—in many cases a neoconservative, purportedly color-blind approach—that precludes overt racial labeling, yet at the same time reinforces stereotypes and patterns of exclusion. As we describe, such acts are often veiled, not only from those whom they might negatively affect but also in some instances from those who actually perpetuate them. In other words, people tend not to see their practices as racist. Instead they see themselves as maintaining a system of meritocratic values.

In this present period of racial hegemony, the claim is made that racial inequality is no longer the result of built-in biases against nonwhites in schools, jobs, and other institutions because all legal and institutional barriers have been eliminated. To bring up race in this context is to "play the race card," even when legitimate instances of racialized inequality are witnessed. In their study of race and religion Hinojosa and Park inform us that "scholars have noted an apparent paradox surrounding racial inequality: while white Americans believe inequality is a bad thing, they consistently oppose government programs to solve it." Several reasons underlie this attitude, most importantly the belief that racial inequality is a result of individual failures as opposed to structural inequality. According to Hinojosa and Park,

> White Americans do not believe that inequality is a structural problem, thus negating the need for a structural (or government policy) solution. Instead, the explanation for inequality lies within the individual—whites appear to believe that individual blacks have made and continue to make bad choices, leading to unequal outcomes.[14]

According to these analysts, religious conservatism contributes significantly to these beliefs. Beyond the political and economic influences on racialized inequality, it is important to consider the significance of religion in shaping social opinions, especially in a state like North Carolina where the majority of the population identifies with Protestant Christianity. In their pivotal work, *Divided by Faith: Evangelical Religion and the Problem of Race in America*, sociologists Christian Smith and Michael Emerson argue that because religious conservatism hinges almost exclusively on the transformation and/or salvation of the individual, power for change is seen by most evangelicals at least as an act of individual will. Thus, "white conservative Protestants are more individualistic and less structural in their explanations of black-white inequality than other whites."[15] In order to explain racial economic inequality, most conservative Protestant Christians rely heavily on their understandings of God and the equality of individuals. According to Smith and Emerson,

> Much of conservative Protestant theological thought views humans as free actors who are personally responsible for and in control of their own destinies. It takes but a limited extension of this freewill individualist perspective to arrive at equal opportunity. . . . [F]reewill individualism requires a belief in equal opportunity, or the world would be grossly unfair and God unjust.[16]

The rise of conservative Protestantism over the last three decades, along with its access to and domination of religious broadcasting, has created a means of organizing and disseminating such views to a broader public. The formation of the Moral Majority, the Christian Coalition, and other conservative institutions of Protestantism have effectively bolstered arguments for a color-blind, race-neutral society. While the tendency toward conventional views of social inequality cannot be reduced to a discussion of religious conservatism, the tendency to eschew structural problems as a reason for racial inequality runs parallel with the rise of religious conservatism throughout the country.

Our ethnographic research, however, challenges the view that U.S. institutions no longer promote racial inequality. A genealogy of racism in North Carolina points to the historic governance of the majority over the minority coupled with practices that marginalize minority interests. Especially excluded from the mainstream political process are those who are socially and economically disadvantaged.

In today's political climate, white privilege, along with continuing patterns of civility, subtly maintain a social and economic order of inequality set in motion in centuries past. Privilege operates by allowing whites to "benefit from a host of apparently neutral social arrangements and institutional operations, all of which seem to whites at least to have no racial bias."[17] Historic privilege-granting processes include such things as inheritance of wealth, alumni advantages in college admissions, and acceptance of white culture as the standard for proper behavior and language in schools. These racialized advantages go unchecked because they are treated as natural patterns of everyday practice. There are no legal forces or abrasive crowds demanding privilege. The operations of daily living already guarantee it.

Similarly, an etiquette of civility, scholars argue, largely governs day-to-day interracial interactions. Pleasantries are exchanged and opposing positions may get a polite hearing, but there is not significant uptake of minority views. Civility suggests definite progress has been made in the treatment of African-Americans; however, ongoing and deliberate blindness to structures that continue economic and social inequality make this progress hollow or at best paradoxical.[18]

The progressive mystique, as historian William Chafe argues,

> involves a set of ground rules that support the notion of North Carolina as a more civilized, enlightened and tolerant place than the rest of the Old Confederacy. . . . What all this amounts to is a culture of civility, a world characterized by politeness, respect, and an acknowledgment of civic obligation—but firmly based in everyone's accepting his or her "place" and not rocking the boat.[19]

Together, naturalized white privilege and the mystique of progress promote a social contract that resists profound change to the status quo of racial inequality and associated income disparities.

Conclusion

As North Carolina has grown, so has its image as a place of cultural diversity and racial progress. As with the rest of the South, the desegregation of public school systems along with the advancement of African-Americans, Latinos, and other minorities to key positions of leadership in state and local government contribute to this view of progress. True to this image is the steady growth of a black middle class, particularly around metropolitan centers such as Research Triangle Park, Charlotte, and Fayetteville. Furthermore, the decline of public outcry over discrimination and racial violence since the sixties supports assumptions of improved racial conditions. These changes over the last thirty years coincide with North Carolina's progressive image.

Missing from this view, however, is discussion of the divides increasingly separating North Carolinians. Disparities in school funding and increasing disparities in income are only some of the factors that dispute this notion of progress. As evidenced, race often organizes local labor and local politics, and figures into a process of uneven development in our sites. As compared to the majority of North Carolinians, the major issues of economic development, democracy, and quality of life often look quite different to African-American and Latino North Carolinians, especially those whose social and economic capital does not place them among the middle class. In many cases neoliberal goals of economic development and democracy are in competition with local views that champion social issues ahead of market issues. In our five fieldwork sites, questions and dramas of contention have developed that consistently challenge neoliberal images of progress.

These same conditions prevail on the national stage. While an average of 11 percent of all Americans fell below the poverty line in 1995, 9 percent of all whites, 26 percent of all African-Americans, and 27 percent of Latinos were in poverty.[20] With massive reconfigurations in the structure of the economy, the devolution and disintegration of social programs, and a fading of the national will to ensure civil rights, racialized inequalities have shifted in character, if not worsened in degree. Economic restructuring has been accompanied by cultural and demographic shifts. Improvement in race relations is especially in question in North Carolina towns such as Siler City, where nonwhites have rapidly become majority populations.

The ongoing struggle to realize the possibilities for American democracy with growing diversity are what most citizens, however, strive to realize. Despite the declaration of a new world order and neoconservative claims to the moral victory of color blindness, race is neither a social illusion nor a vestige of the past. On the contrary, as Winant writes, "In a range of manifestations wider and wilder than the most fertile imaginations could have dreamed up, race continues to operate as a fundamental factor in political and cultural life."[21]

Since its inception, the United States has long embodied this fundamental contradiction between the promise of equality and the reality of inequality.[22] Encouraging ongoing struggle for the realization of America's promise, Thurgood Marshall noted the reality of the United States's contradiction. "I do not believe," stated Marshall,

> that the meaning of the Constitution was forever "fixed" at the Philadelphia Convention. Nor do I find the wisdom, foresight and sense of justice exhibited by the framers particularly profound. To the contrary, the government they devised was defective from the start, requiring several amendments, a civil war and momentous social transformation to attain the system of constitutional government, and its respect for the individual freedoms and human rights we hold as fundamental today.

Such a struggle requires an understanding of the complexity of race and racialized exclusion in the United States. Nevertheless, in light of the situation of poor residents of Watauga, the question looms: *Does race no longer matter?* If poor white residents as well as African-American and Latino residents each experience invisibility and exclusion within a larger political and economic system, can we still speak in terms of racialized exclusion? The answer is, *Certainly*. Race matters. Race is built into the fabric of American life. The United States is, as literary scholar Wahneema Lubiano suggests, "the house that race built." In fact, Lubiano maintains that "if race and its strategic social and ideological deployment as racism didn't exist, the United States' severe inequalities and betrayal of its formal commitments to social equality and social justice would be readily apparent to anyone existing on this ground." Yet, because race (albeit a cultural construction) exists, white privilege and middle-class privilege can be unrecognized as such. White middle-class perspectives on economic development, quality-of-life issues, and democracy are not marked as white or middle-class and instead are put forward as a universalist view. Thus, the perspectives of people of color and poor people are either rendered invisible or, at best, labeled as perspectives peculiar to a so-called special-interest group.

The challenge facing residents is to ensure that their issues are heard and addressed, regardless of race and class, with the same degree of influence and urgency as those who predominate in public discourse. While neoliberal rhetoric ensures that the market remains at the center, residents throughout the state have consistently engaged the public to bring to light issues related to marginalized communities. Their success in bringing these perspectives to bear in shaping and informing political and economic policy speaks to the level of the state's true progress in reconciling race and class tensions and the promise of equality as a guarantor of democracy.

5 Public Goods for Private Ends

The Redirection of Schooling

The common school represents something basic about who we are as a people and what kind of society we can become.
—David Labaree, "No Exit: Public Education as an Inescapably Public Good"

Haw Creek, a rural community in Watauga County, lost its high school in the 1960s national trend toward consolidation. Several residents have pressed unsuccessfully since then for its reinstatement, complaining that rural students are discriminated against at the consolidated high school and that the school board does not grasp the value of community schools. Then, in the early 1990s, over much protest, the school board removed its elementary school from the heart of the community. One woman explained the resulting sense of loss and political impotence:

> People need to feel like they're cared about and their opinions mean something. If you put somebody down for so many years, how are they going to feel? If you give them hand-me-downs through the system for forty years, how are they going to feel? . . . If somebody gets you down and says to you, "you don't know anything, you'll never be nothing," and they tell you that for twenty years, how is your mind going to work? You take stuff away from them. You take their schools away, you bus their kids for two hours a day, you won't give them a chance to participate, how are they going to feel?

In the town schools, the children of poor rural whites were ethnicized as hillbilly, second class, and stupid. This small group's desire to re-create community schools in order to revalue their own input to school decisions represents a resistance to exclusionary practices as well as an alternative vision of schooling's purpose—one of schools as a community institution, not as a commodity, and one in symbiotic relationship with civic participation.

This is only one of the many goals that Americans have historically attached to our public schools. Others include individual intellectual and character development, the formation of an informed and/or patriotic citizenry, the expansion of social and economic mobility, and the creation of a more socially just society. Over the course of America's history, the balance between these goals has shifted continuously.[1] However, as part of the neoliberal revolution described in this book, economic justifications for schooling have gradually edged out political rationales, and individualist goals have replaced collectivist ones. Since the 1970s public education has become marketized, or subject to the intensified application of market principles such as deregulation, competition, and stratification.[2] And economic ways of talking about and justifying the purpose of schooling have become dominant.

In this chapter, we discuss the impact of neoliberalism on educational policy and practice. We argue that neoliberalism has influenced education in two primary ways. First, it has resulted in a series of educational experiments—privatization, vouchers, charters, and accountability programs—that have on the whole had negative effects for equity. In terms of the "three-legged stool" of democracy discussed in chapter 1, neoliberal educational reforms privilege liberty to the detriment of equality. Second, our ethnographic research revealed that, by normalizing the assumption that schools should provide primarily for economic growth, neoliberal rhetoric has privileged the perspectives of wealthier, whiter stakeholders (e.g., business leaders) in local policy debates, while inhibiting democratic debate and marginalizing other claims on the public resource of education.[3] As we show in the second section of this chapter, this market discourse has negatively affected the goal of social equity and reduced opportunities for democratic participation.

Neoliberal Educational Policies

As previously noted, equity concerns and collectivist goals for schooling have not always been relegated to a secondary role. Common schools were initiated in the nineteenth century by reformers such as Horace Mann in the hopes that publicly funded, locally controlled schools open to all children would teach basic literacy, strengthen moral character, instill common democratic values, ensure social stability, and enable citizens to fulfill their civic duties. Schools were mainly regarded for their important contribution to political socialization. In the early 1900s, during the intensification of the industrial economy, schools began to be valued more for their potential economic contribution. Vocational education flourished; the factory model of schooling was consolidated. At the same time, schools were relied upon to Americanize immigrant children and incorporate them into subordinate positions in the political economic structure. The invention of human capital theory in the 1960s, which posited that investments in the education of the labor force resulted in greater productivity and therefore increased profits, furthered the association in the public's mind between schooling and economic development. When Sputnik shocked Americans into realizing their comparative disadvantage in the fields of math and science, they turned to the schools to recoup their standing. Around the same time, the country was gradually acknowledging the shame and inequity of racial segregation, and the courts relied on public schooling, that singular public institution, to implement integration measures. Concern with international competitiveness and internal equity greatly influenced the passage of the landmark Elementary and Secondary Education Act of 1965. Though the primary purposes of schooling shifted over this period, faith in the utility of public education for national development and stability remained constant. Over the last quarter of the twentieth century, this collectivist orientation and commitment to using schools to promote equity was gradually eclipsed by approaches to schooling that emphasized competition, consumption, and prioritizing the use of schools for economic development. This shift was facilitated by the application of neoliberal principles to schooling.

Marketization applies principles taken from the realm of free market economics to other institutions, like schools. These principles entail the following assumptions, which have been extensively challenged:

1. The state is an inefficient provider of goods and services (such as education) compared to the market.
2. Competition between public and private schools and among public institutions will force all schools to become more efficacious providers of service.
3. Deregulation of schools will improve their performance.
4. Citizen-consumers, who make rational choices, will select the best educational service, forcing schools to compete and bringing about the extinction of inefficient schools.
5. Standardized tests measure student learning and provide an optimal basis upon which stakeholders (including parents, the business community, and the state) can evaluate the performance of schools, and therefore make informed choices and hold schools accountable.

In the United States, these market principles have become concrete in a variety of educational reforms. Several local and state governments, most notably those of Cleveland, Milwaukee, and Florida, have offered vouchers to allow students in low-performing schools to take their per-pupil expenditure to another (public or private) school. New York City, Washington, DC, and Dayton, Ohio, have privately financed voucher experiments underway. Charter schools, or schools supported by public monies but autonomous of much of the regulation imposed by local school districts, are now firmly in place in thirty-nine states; more than six hundred thousand students nationwide now study in charter schools. All states have instituted widespread accountability, or standardized testing programs, the results of which are meant to enable parents and the state to hold schools responsible for individual student learning. Further, in many schools across the nation, school functions have been outsourced; the administration of schools has been privatized, as when schools are run by for-profit organizations. School-business partnerships have proliferated, as has a more general pro-business climate in and around schools.[4]

Educational scholars have conducted and continue to carry out comprehensive studies of vouchers, charters, and accountability programs. No clear evidence shows that vouchers have provided significant educational benefits to those who elected them, and there are reasons to worry that vouchers will be detrimental to equity goals. There is mixed evidence that private (mostly Catholic) schools provide modest gains for students.[5] Studies of the private voucher programs in New York, Dayton, and Washington, DC, suggest quite modest gains for African-American voucher students and no gains for other minority students.[6] However, competition with private schools does not seem to have improved public school efficiency or the educational experience of those left behind in the sending schools.[7] The rhetoric of choice implies that all parents are equally informed, politically connected, and capable of securing for their own children the best education. Yet parents' school selections are thoroughly constrained by availability of information, familiarity, sense of "fit," transportation, access to after-school care, and other factors such as attitudes about race and class. Parents with higher educational levels are more likely to take advantage of vouchers. Since vouchers do not guarantee the full tuition, families with lower incomes are limited to private schools that charge less. Obviously, private schools can deny admission to any student; they are not obligated to provide services to all children, as are public schools. Such choice mechanisms tend to leave the most disadvantaged students behind. Since studies have demonstrated that student achievement correlates with the average socioeconomic status of peers, we might expect that, when more advantaged students exit the public school, the achievement of the students left behind would decline; however, there is not yet reliable evidence on such effects.

Charter schools also suggest problematic effects for equity.[8] Charter schools are not outperforming public schools, and therefore are not forcing their regulated counterparts to improve.[9] The low and often unequal levels of public funding for charter schools have led them to rely upon private resources; this trend favors charter schools in or serving wealthier communities. The immense institutional demands placed on charters, which among other tasks must provide their own financial management, have two negative consequences. First, charters in poor neighborhoods tend to rely upon educational management organizations (EMOs) for assistance. These organizations too frequently preclude community control; many of the for-profit EMOs have been found to divert critical funds from students' needs to the management company.[10] Second, the demands caused many charter schools to fold, creating instability in the lives of poor students (which is correlated with educational failure). Further, charter schools are facilitating the segregation of students by ethnicity, income level, and special needs.[11] National evidence suggests that charter schools are even more racially segregated than public schools, which themselves have become more segregated than at any point since the landmark 1954 *Brown vs. Board of Education* decision.[12] The same holds true for social-class segregation. Charters in general do not provide for and may not welcome special needs students.[13]

Accountability movements and high-stakes standardized testing, the third major and most widespread reform influenced by neoliberal principles of choice and competition, have proven highly controversial. Standardized tests are now implemented in every state of the nation; a majority of states either already use or plan to use such tests as the sole or a significant criterion for retention and graduation decisions.[14] Critics argue that standardized testing reduces education to rote memorization of basic facts and standardized outcomes, rather than creative exploration of ideas and construction of knowledge.[15] Creditable studies have demonstrated that testing has negative effects for minority students, disabled students, and especially English language learners.[16] The high stakes attached to these tests are disproportionately affecting African-American, Latino, and Native American students, leading to an overall increase in the dropout rate among these students.[17]

Overall, the evidence to date suggests that these neoliberal educational experiments offer few benefits but might hinder efforts to use schools to promote greater equity. As educational scholar Henry Levin has suggested, the goals of free choice, efficiency, equity, and social cohesion are at odds in these reforms.[18]

The gradual marketization of education was evident during our fieldwork. In fact, North Carolina governor James B. Hunt built a national reputation as a classic Democratic modernizer who promoted economic growth through educational investments.[19] In his early terms, he increased educational appropriations significantly, funding teacher salary increases, training grants, the employment of aides in early elementary classrooms, huge investments in early childhood education, and the institution of a state-wide science-and-math magnet school. During his hiatus from the governor's office in the 1980s, Hunt promulgated the "growth through education" approach nationally by cochairing the National Task Force on Education and Economic Growth, a public-private advisory council, with Carnegie Corporation president David Hamburg. Reelected as governor, Hunt continued to support education within a narrowly meritocratic frame. While he avoided the more neoliberal reforms, such as outright privatization and vouchers, under Hunt the state adopted charter schools and implemented widespread, mandated competition among individual schools through standardized testing (the accountability program).

Legislation authorizing charter schools in North Carolina was passed in 1996, and the first charter schools opened in fall 1997. By 2000–2001 there were ninety such schools with fifteen thousand students. "As of 2002, only 5 [states] had a greater concentration of charter schools."[20] North Carolina charter schools receive operating funding at the same level as the traditional public schools, and the students in charter schools are subject to the same state testing requirements as other students.

Charters in North Carolina have not provided the benefits that proponents of neoliberal educational reform promised. A recent analysis by educational policy experts painted an unflattering portrait of North Carolina charters. The authors found that (1) "students make considerably smaller achievement gains in charter schools than they would have in public schools"; (2) "about 30 percent of the negative effect of charter schools is attributable to high rates of student turnover"; and (3) "charter schools appear to have no statistically significant effects on the achievement of the traditional public school students in North Carolina."[21] Charters have proven fairly unstable:

> Between 1997 and 2002 the State Board of Education revoked seven charters, and seven more relinquished their charter voluntarily or closed due to low enrollment or financial problems. Overall, about 12 percent of the charter schools that have been opened are now closed. However, in no case was the decision to revoke a charter or to close due primarily to low student performance.[22]

Further, charters in North Carolina have been remarkably segregated.[23]

Likewise, standardized testing has proven to be a problematic educational reform. North Carolina originally adopted widespread standardized testing in 1996 as a tool that parents and community members could utilize to hold the schools accountable. End-of-grade tests were used to determine the overall performance of schools and award bonuses for teachers whose students did well; persistently low-performing schools were subject to state assistance or takeover. However, in a few short years the tests came to be used to measure each individual student's progress as well. By 2001, the North Carolina Student Accountability Standards directed that third, fifth, and eighth graders who failed end-of-grade exams in math, reading, or writing should repeat their current grade in most instances; the policy will be phased in for high school graduation in 2005. Though parents have the right to appeal such a decision, the appeal process varies by district and parents may not know they have such a right or how to execute it.

The decision to base promotion largely or fully on a student's performance on the end-of-grade test has had a major impact on the education of poor minority students. In North Carolina, as in other states, poor minority students tend not to score well on these standardized tests. For example, in 1998–1999, only 49 percent of African-American students and only 56 percent of Hispanic students in grades three through eight scored at or above grade level on math and reading tests.[24] In 2001, while 87 percent of white and 85 percent of Asian fifth-grade students passed the exam on the first try, only 62 percent of African-American and 67 percent of Hispanic students did.[25] There is a marked racial gap of approximately 30 points between white and black students; the gap has proven relatively constant since 1993, when end-of-grade tests were instituted.[26] That means that, by and large, it is poor minority students—African-American, Hispanic, and Native American—who are being retained on the basis of test scores.[27] In 2001 across North Carolina, even after retests, appeals, and other safeguards, blacks and Latinos were still retained at four times the rate as whites and Asians.[28] Yet studies suggest that retention has an incredibly negative impact on a student's chances of completing school: retention predicts who drops out even more strongly than race, income, or parental education.[29] Therefore, the current promotion policy promises to exacerbate the minority student dropout rate. Advocates for minority children object to this policy, arguing that the tests are punitive rather than diagnostic, that the state should invest in remedial services for underperforming students, and that students spend too much time preparing for and taking tests rather than learning valuable information.[30]

Neoliberal Educational Discourse: The Social Consequences of Education's Marketization

During the time of our fieldwork, these neoliberal reforms were slowly taking shape. Charter schools were forming; in PTA meetings across the state, principals were introducing the notion of accountability to mute and often bewildered parents who privately expressed perplexity over what these new measures had to do with their core concerns. Charters and standardized testing were not hot topics in the educational arena during our year of fieldwork in five sites; those broad reforms were quietly implemented while most parents and other citizens were busy looking the other way, worrying about topics such as unwieldy school population growth, educational finance, school bonds, and new school construction, the education of so-labeled disruptive students, or the maintenance of community schools.

However, we did find evidence of the impact of neoliberalism at the very local level of educational politics. Our ethnographic research revealed that local elites used a growth discourse to justify their preferred plans for the public schools—schemes that often ran directly contrary to policies that would promote equity. Local growth elites, people such as professional economic developers, realtors, large landowners, bankers, owners of retail and service-based businesses, and chamber of commerce representatives who stood to gain from the kind of economic development underway in North Carolina, argued that "good schools" were necessary to attract businesses and/or maintain a healthy economy—even if erecting or maintaining good schools meant denying quality education to local poor and/or minority students.[31]

This growth discourse undoubtedly predated neoliberal political reforms; indeed, it is evident in many of the discussions of schooling's purpose that have emerged since the early twentieth century. It was balanced by a concern for equity in the 1960s and 1970s. However, neoliberal economic and political shifts seem to have rejuvenated it. The rhetoric of strong educational systems as the lure for business has radically expanded during the last thirty years, when capital's new mobility has forced rival prospective sites into competitive bidding. Accordingly, this discourse was most pronounced in the sites (Halifax, Durham, and Cumberland) that aggressively recruit new industry and/or (young) residents, offering education as "the new amenity." It was less pronounced in Watauga, where local economic developers have abandoned the attempt to recruit industry in favor of promoting the county as a tourist and retirement destination. But reliance on education to promote economic expansion posed a serious dilemma: the growth elite wanted to offer exclusive, reputable schools to attract relocating businesses and professionals, yet they needed to avoid contentious charges of racism or classism. By arguing that school systems that attracted the right kind of development would ultimately benefit everyone (i.e. "lift all boats"), they were able to resolve this quandary. Below, we describe how local elites used the rhetoric that schools should serve economic development to further their private agendas.

"White by Design": Halifax County

Halifax County is part of the poorer, traditionally agricultural eastern third of the state. Its de facto segregated school districts resulted from a hyperdependence on a textile industry that resolutely manipulated racial differences to depress labor costs, creating racialized and segregated classes. In the early twentieth century, textile magnates donated land and money for the construction of a town school; in exchange, they secured business education and industrial arts classes and a future white labor pool.[32] One-room schoolhouses, with significantly fewer resources at their disposal, spread haphazardly throughout the county. Segregationists took advantage of arbitrary historical boundaries to declare racialized school districts. In fact, Roanoke Rapids essentially expelled its remaining minority school population. The city had one black school: the Chaloner School. The school board argued that of the school's one thousand one hundred students, only three hundred lived within town limits. So they ceded the school to the county for four years, while the county built new schools to house the eight hundred county black students. Then the city reappropriated it, and by 1971 it was a predominantly white middle school. Segregated districts, and internal segregation by schools, proved a feasible solution until federally mandated integration prompted many white county students to flee to the private schools that seemingly sprouted overnight.

Segregation continues undisturbed in the county's three school districts. In 1995–1996, Halifax County schools were 86 percent black, Weldon City schools were 92 percent black, and Roanoke Rapids City schools were 77 percent white. Given the differing economic bases as well as social class and racial composition of the cities and county, it is not surprising to find a considerable difference in per pupil expenditures and performance on standardized tests among the school systems. According to a Halifax County–sponsored survey in 1994, two-thirds of Halifax students were reading below grade level.[33] In 1996, on the SAT scores of 121 school systems, Weldon placed last and Halifax 117th, while Roanoke Rapids ranked 43rd. In fact, two of the four schools in Weldon were among the fifteen lowest-performing in the state that received "assistance teams."

The intermittent debate over the merger of Halifax's segregated systems illustrates the predominance of economic interests and discourse over concerns for racial equity. The different concerns and justifications used by black and white parents were striking. Black parents, without hesitation, denounced the current arrangement as unfair and detrimental to black students. Many favored merger but coldly accepted that white power interests would never allow it to transpire. The demonstrated hostility of whites to the topic checked black aspirations for more equitable schooling arrangements. Parents specifically feared "submitting" their children to such hostility from white teachers or peers in a merged system. One parent commented,

> We wouldn't want to subject our children to a lot of hostility just to say that they're in a better [school], or, they're getting a better opportunity. For instance, last year was the first time that we've had black students to go to private schools. . . . Would I send my kids there? No. It might be better. They might get better educated. I don't have the slightest idea. But I would not send my children there. And the reason I say that is because it has always

been a white-only school. Just because you have a minority there, it might change the outlook, but not necessarily the *inlook*. See what I'm saying?

Other black parents calculated the destruction of black political control that a merger would bring. Communities suffered heavy losses during integration, when black schools were shut down and black teachers and administrators lost their professional positions.[34] Many parents remembered the absolute dearth, until recently, of black educational representation. The first black representative was appointed to the Roanoke Rapids school board only in 1970; the county's third district, Weldon (predominantly black), achieved a majority black board only when granted the right to elect members in 1984. Parents recognized that merger would eliminate black administrators, black teachers, and black culture from the schools:

> [Whites are] controlling. I see the white power structure in Roanoke Rapids. If you look at their central office, you might find two blacks, the rest are whites. See this stuff is outdated. It shouldn't be that way. If you look at your principals, what do you have in leadership over there? *All* white. If you look into the schools, you might find one black teacher among all the teachers. . . . Because see, the way they're set up, our kids wouldn't see a black teacher. They could go through the whole day and never experience being taught by a black teacher. It would be white oriented. We lose a lot of values that way. We lose a lot of culture that way, because whites, they do not understand.

Those more cognizant of black political and cultural losses in integrated systems argued for the maintenance of separate systems but under more equitable funding arrangements. As one county policymaker said,

> We got to go the same distance that Roanoke Rapids goes. We get enough gas to get halfway there and we got to push and pull to try to get there, but we get there. Give us the same amount of money and we'll get there when you get there. And that's the way I feel about it. We don't need merger. What we need is equity in funding.

Yet, while Roanoke Rapids and Weldon schools voted their own supplemental taxes, race and class politics in the county have precluded increased county taxes for school funding. The same school board member continued,

> We had [a supplemental tax proposal] about eight or ten years ago, which the county commissioners, the politics in the county, didn't support. . . . The black board members supported it [but others didn't]. Most of the resources in this county are in the white community. The black community should

have supported the bond issue, it wouldn't have cost them that much because they didn't own anything that much. . . . And when you talk about tax increase in Halifax County, you know, you're hitting the people that own the resources in the county. . . . When we ran we got a 2 percent increase. When the other commissioners ran two years prior to that they got a 2 percent reduction. So it's a nip and tuck kind of thing.

Wealthy white county landowners, who themselves placed their children and grandchildren in private schools, continuously mobilized the opposition of the county's poor whites with anti-tax rhetoric, supplemented by charges of "school mediocrity" and implications of biological intellectual inferiority. These race and class politics simultaneously obstructed tax increases for county schools and system merger, perpetually fueling the reproduction of inequality.

White parents enjoying the benefits of the city school system justified the continued segregation in two ways: as tradition and as economically feasible. Proponents of the segregated system use words like "community," "tradition," "identity," and "loyalty" to defend their opposition to merger. For example, a Roanoke Rapids politician claimed publicly that a merger would damage "community spirit." A city school board member said, "we want to keep our identity." This rhetoric accorded with the neoconservative call for restoring community values and tradition in schools. In the Halifax case, "community" and "identity" euphemistically camouflaged acts of institutional racism. Likewise, a city administrator argued,

> Well it's been said that there is a move on at the state level to have one hundred school districts just like one hundred counties, and the saying in Roanoke Rapids is, when we're down to 101, Roanoke Rapids will be number 101, because there's a loyalty, and the fact that the school district is small, we have like three thousand two hundred or three thousand three hundred students. . . . And it has nothing to do with trying to set ourselves apart and say, "We're better than you," or anything like that, it has more to do with a certain, a loyalty and a feeling of more like family and not wanting to be swallowed up in a larger entity so that we would lose our own identity.

This discussion of tradition ignored the historical struggles over the institution and maintenance of school district borders.

Further, people took for granted the economic advantages enjoyed within those arbitrary borders, ignoring the fact that the borders resulted from specific practices and policies that concentrate development in the white area of the county. One white city educator posited,

> One reason Roanoke Rapids has had a better school system is because we have our own tax base here. People who go to this school system, they live

inside the school district and have to pay a little bit higher tax, which goes directly to the school system. So we can offer higher supplements for teachers to come in. And so we can pick out better teachers to come in. But now if there's merger, then I don't have to pay this higher property tax because then I can move out to the country and my children can go wherever. And the real estate values will go down. Because some of these houses, these big fancy houses you know, who's going to buy them if there's no special school system to keep people together?

Her comments implied the universal desirability of separate systems that maintain housing stock (above equitable education). The supplemental school tax allows the white middle class to be selectively and locally communitarian.

White parents and teachers in the city system naturalized the advantages of their students, attributing them to "higher standards" and better "quality," as evident in the comments of one teacher:

Well, really, it's sort of like Roanoke Rapids has always had higher standards and the kids have excelled more here. In the other systems the standards have been lower, the attendance has been bad. It hasn't been equal education. It hasn't been quality education out there. And I really think if we merge, instead of having one system out of three that is achieving some learning, I think we'll just have three that don't do anything.

Notably, in the midst of her comments she admitted that the education provided is unequal, and then immediately covered by using the word "quality" (rather than "equality") to explain the difference. Similarly, while a white city administrator attributed the success of systems like Chapel Hill to an advantaged population, he credited "expectations" for his own system's success:

Traditionally, our students score pretty well on standardized tests and the SAT, certainly nothing like Chapel Hill, but we don't have the highly educated population to draw on that the Research Triangle area does. But our students for our area do well on tests because we have high expectations and high standards.

Whites frequently talked about the need to bring the other systems "up" before merger is conceivable. "Why tear a good thing down?" one informant queried. He feared a merger "would lower the standards in the Roanoke Rapids school." Yet they never proposed improving the two predominantly black systems.

Issues of taxation and school funding point to the firmest base for the maintenance of these segregated systems: the current arrangement encourages economic development, because the town offers "at least one good school system." As one former city school board member explained,

> When you're talking about economic development, attracting industry, you know this is one of the first things that they look at when an industry is getting ready to come into an area. "What type of educational system do you have?" Roanoke Rapids graded school district has been a drawing card for what business and for what industry that has come to the area, hasn't been a lot, but it's been some, and I think that's been a part of it by Roanoke Rapids being in the top ten percent school systems in the whole state.

People in positions of power, who stood to benefit from development, worked to ensure the continued separation of the systems. A large landowner who shaped education policy in the county for more than a decade reasoned this way:

> Merging would no doubt help the Halifax system, but it would damage Roanoke Rapids city system, and then I think the doctors and lawyers would leave the city to pay for education elsewhere. . . . We know [Halifax] schools are in trouble, but I would hate to see the only school that is halfway right be taken over by the county. . . . I'm not sure what to do. I don't know if it would bring to ruin the manufacturing out in Roanoke Rapids, or what it would do. That's our biggest tax base in Roanoke Rapids. That's where all the jobs and manufacturing is in Roanoke Rapids. And those folks won't come into Halifax County and put their kids in the county schools. So what would it do economically for the county?

The school board member implied that everyone in the county should support whatever policies promote the economic development of the town, because such development would eventually "trickle down" and would benefit a great number of residents. But this is inaccurate in many ways. The economic development experienced in Halifax County has benefited a remarkably small number of people, while the remainder of the populace continues working full-time while experiencing near-poverty incomes. Further, such a rhetoric of economic utility obfuscates a key question: Who bears the cost?

The predominantly black student bodies of these two underfunded school districts bear the costs in two ways. First, they must continue to attend poorer quality schools in order to keep one system attractive for prospective industries. Second, the location of development in Roanoke Rapids at the expense of other areas of the county further marginalizes those areas, because a system with an industrial base can levy higher taxes without unduly burdening property owners and therefore can dedicate even more money to educational facilities and teacher supplements. Hence, the economic development of Roanoke Rapids, thanks largely to the maintenance of race- and class-segregated school systems, generates a downward spiral from which the other systems are unlikely to ever recover. Thus, an alliance of white county land owners, private school owners (at least one of whom served over a decade on the county's school board), city school parents, black city politicians (whose silence on merger was the price of election), and a few black separatists continually deprived the large majority of Halifax's poor and/or black students an equal education.

From Private Interests to Public Good:
The Redefinition of Business Involvement in Durham Public Schools

The economic use of schools to attract business and relocating professionals proved a major concern in Durham County as well. Durham's experience with desegregation and, later, merger echoes themes presented in the Halifax case. The Durham case also makes clear the ways in which business leaders are currently privileged as political actors in the realm of educational policy. In the 1980s, conservatives argued that schools were not serving economic growth and proposed business leaders as the appropriate educational policy makers. This approach released the growth elite from the appearance of self-interest in their educational activism, despite the fact that business leaders (especially those with real estate, retail, or service interests) obviously stood to gain economically from the relocation of industry or professionals to the area. Thus, private, corporate interests were redefined as "public" or "civic," and their decisions, made without reference to the welfare of the extended community, nevertheless assumed the appearance of "democratic deliberation." The popularity of economic uses of schools granted corporations an undue authority that minimized competing interests. Further, because we think of schools as meritocratic institutions, business involvement with school issues is interpreted as socially progressive, when in fact steering of issues frequently results in *less* social mobility for subordinate race and class groups. This process is well illustrated by the chamber of commerce's involvement in Durham educational politics, culminating in their push to establish an alternative school.

In the wake of integration, white flight from the city to county and/or private schools left two separate, almost totally segregated systems, with vast disparities in resources and quality of education. When occasionally broached, the topic of merger was squelched by white middle-class animosity and black middle-class concern that merger would deny them professional positions as well as influence over the education of black students.[35] Old-school local elites had little reason to support the merger, since the maintenance of separate systems encouraged the relocation of mobile industry and knowledge workers to Research Triangle Park (RTP) and the suburbs of Durham. However, by the late 1980s the chasm of disparity between city and county schools prompted the state legislature to threaten a takeover.

The merger plan developed under duress over several years, amidst foot-dragging by many county teachers, parents, and students and charges of racism from middle-class black activists. The historical animosity between some black and white political leaders, the vehement opposition of many county teachers to merger, and the racialization of poverty in Durham set the stage for height-ened race and class tension within and surrounding the schools. The tacit issue behind merger negotiations was class privilege, although race featured most prominently in discussions. One informant said, "The question became, 'How do you establish a school system that meets the needs of middle-class black and white students when there is a 50 to 60 percent disadvantaged minority population?'"

Magnet schools with racial quotas were set up to integrate several of the tra-ditionally African-American city schools. Middle-class parents anxiously secured advantages for their own children by advocating elaborate tracking sys-tems within the schools that essentially kept their children in socioeconomi-cally homogeneous classrooms. With tracking to satisfy vocal white parents, few advocates remained for the education of the students remaining in "regu-lar" classes, whose parents lacked the necessary connections and social capital to have them transferred. These students were, as educator Lisa Delpit aptly phrases it, "other people's children," children whose welfare was beyond the concern of those with power in the system.[36]

In the wake of merger, Durham schools developed a negative reputation that sent some builders out of the county and into neighboring Wake, Orange, and Chatham Counties. This diversion of residential dollars prompted real estate interests to get involved with educational issues. As one seller's agent explained,

> I was fighting to try to get this [student code of conduct] changed, and of course, get these stats [on violation of conduct] down, because Durham was getting a bad name. Ever since I sell real estate, that's part of that image prob-lem, and I'm just trying to get my nose in there to help solve it.

The attempt by business interests to "clean up the schools" in order to fos-ter economic growth, paired with the entree provided for business interests in the 1980s and 1990s, prompted Durham's chamber of commerce to become more formally involved in educational issues through a variety of means. A participant described the chamber's School-to-Work (a.k.a. Job Ready) program as an attempt to join a "community focus" and a "capitalist focus," since "there is no split between the two."

The chamber was drawn into policy decisions when, in the first year of merger, members began complaining about "disruptive" students in their children's classrooms. John, a white parent of a school-aged child, developer, and chamber leader, explained,

> My son would be in some AG [academically gifted] classes and some regular classes. And when he was in the regular classes, there were disruptive students which prevented him from learning. And this bothered him and it bothered me . . . I didn't want those classes disrupted so that's why I became involved on a personal level, which happened to translate to a more system-wide level being in the position I was at that time with the chamber.

John was satisfied with the new merger arrangement as long as his son remained in tracked classes for so-labeled academically gifted children (classes with a remarkable class and race homogeneity). Yet he and his son were "bothered" by the populations in his "regular" classes. Following the merger, "disruptive" became the dominant code word for poor minority students, and chamber members proposed an alternative school to make these disruptive students into more "productive citizens." Much like the at-risk educational discourse, "disruptive" prejudicially references a host of stereotypes about race, class, and family. As John stated, his personal interests quickly translated into institutional policy, by virtue of his position with the chamber and the chamber's exalted role in education policy. John continued,

> There were lots of fights and lots of truancy. And really, whether you mix kids of different socioeconomic backgrounds and what chips on the shoulders people may have brought to school manifest themselves in a lot of bad behavior and a lot of fights at school. And that was sort of a lightning rod, if you will, for the Chamber's Public Education Committee and me to get involved with it.

The chamber quickly and easily translated the interests of its parents into new policy, with very little public input. As John explained it,

> Our question was, What was the school system doing about this? And what we found out was, not much. So, we at the chamber said, "There needs to be alternative classroom settings for these kids who disrupt so these kids who want to learn can learn. And the disruptive kids need to be in this setting until they are ready to play by the rules." So that is how we got involved with it.

John invoked the ubiquitous sports metaphor to present schools as meritocratic, where success is equally available to all children and fitting into school structures is a mere matter of "playing by the rules." Such metaphors ignore the complicated social history that, as educational anthropologists have shown, has created race and class stereotypes such as "the good student," "the disruptive student," and "the problem child."[37] Talk of "fair play" allows people to mistake white privilege for a greater willingness to work hard and "disruption" for an individual's free choice within a meritocratic institution.

The chamber faced the difficult situation of needing both to develop a solution that would satisfy chamber members and to prevent further damage to Durham's image among relocating companies and employees.[38] The chamber sought a mechanism to further stratify the schools and hence appease the relocated business community, but in a way that would avoid charges of racism and scandal. Durham chamber members led fund-raising efforts to make an alternative school possible. State grants and the popularity of alternative programs among professional educators also helped.

The resulting school, however, lacked such basics as textbooks and pupil desks, and overwhelmingly schooled poor, black, male youth. Locked doors, windowless rooms, strictly controlled entrance and exit, a dilapidated physical plant, and police officers on site gave the institution a decidedly penal feeling. "Dumped" as we have described already, with no consultation, in a poor, black neighborhood, the school usurped part of the building that the community development volunteer coalition was using for community programs. Thus, the personal, parental interests of middle-class, predominantly white chamber members were translated into new policy and institutions affecting black youth with minimal public involvement. Several years later, school conditions prompted a local judge to summon education policy makers and demand a reexamination of the abysmal institution. To defuse the controversy, the local school system established the "task force" we describe in chapter 8.

Such is the danger of according narrow interests the status of common good, of reducing the public sphere to the interventions of a few privileged actors. Without continual, critical discussions about educational processes that acknowledge the history of inequality built into the system, we cannot hope for more democratic schools or a public culture that treats all children as equally valuable and teachable.

Marketing Schools: Cumberland's School Bond

The school bond campaign in Cumberland County also illustrates the use of public schools for business ends, the way the interests of local populations are ignored, and the privileged position of business interests in educational policy debates. In 1997, after securing the cooperation of the county commissioners, the Cumberland school board and the chamber of commerce assembled a coalition to promote the passage of a $98 million school bond for capital improvements. That alliance, consisting almost exclusively of middle- and upper-middle-class people, was recruited from the chamber, the Kiwanis and Civitan groups, the African-American professional and business organization, school faculty, the parent-teacher associations (PTAs), and the Junior League. Anxious to present themselves as a citizen-led, grassroots effort, they carefully selected a prominent member of the business community to lead the group, reflecting the extent to which private, corporate interests had already been redefined as public. Task force members raised one hundred thousand dollars, using the funds to hire an opinion-polling firm and purchase advertising. They trained members of the community to attend meetings of local groups and stump for the bond.

Task force members justified the bond by arguing, as one member did, that

> whether this community is going to progress or not economically is totally, not totally, but critically dependent on the quality of schools. Both from a work-force education point of view and from the point of view of improving the quality of life in the community, so that high-tech and professional employers want to bring their families here. They aren't going to do that if the schools aren't available for them, for their children.

Essentially, the group wanted schools to produce a disciplined, punctual, blue-collar labor force with basic skills to attract industry. They also wanted high-quality education for the children of relocating professionals that would provide those students with critical thinking skills, preparing them for college and professional careers. The economic future of the city hinged upon the schools' ability to fulfill both functions. Another task force member remarked, "The first thing an industry asks for, other than, 'Is the property going to be fairly inexpensive?' is 'Am I going to have a labor force? What kind of schools are my employees going to find for their children?' So this is very, very important." The shared rhetoric of task force members suggests how deeply socialized they are in this extraordinary view of schools. Both define education as a *quality of life* (whose life? what qualities?) indicator for relocating business. Both identify dual populations and dual purposes for the public schools.

While the growth the task force called for might increase the tax base, it would also multiply demands on infrastructure and services. If incentives packages trade a lower tax rate for jobs, if the jobs do not provide a living wage, and/or if the industry entails hidden environmental or other costs, then communities lose through growth. Yet the sense of urgency in the competition between sites for the recruitment of industry overshadows such concerns. The link between schools and growth that economic developers repeatedly pro-

moted was readily accepted by the middle-class participants whose own professional positions relied on their educational credentials.

The curious and rather anti-democratic effect of such planning is that powerful development interests make educational decisions on behalf of people
who are not yet and probably never will be citizens of the county, rather than
referring to the requirements of those who are. In the case of Cumberland, the
needs of relocating industry and migrant military families were overwhelmingly represented in the public discussions. One informant stated,

> We have so many people that pass through Fayetteville on a yearly basis,
> coming here in the military, visiting other people in the military, visiting
> family here; if it's a good place to stay we may capture some of those people.
> But I think one of the keys in attracting people who pass through, or have
> any acquaintance with the area, is a sound and attractive public education
> system.

She proposes that improved schools will "capture" "quality," i.e., middle-class,
people. And it is the exchange value rather than the use value of schools that
gets the most attention.

The authority granted to these assertions marginalizes other possible justifications for educational investment, impoverishing politics by diminishing
debate. In such a climate, a school bond campaign that acknowledged the
unequal physical plants of schools within the system or criticized the investment in programs benefiting middle- and upper-income students at the
expense of low-income students would not warrant much attention. What
other ways might emerge to talk about the school's responsibilities if the dominant, economic model did not overemphasize the needs of relocating industry
or middle-class managerial families?

The Myth of Schooling for Uniform Economic Development:
The Pressures of Success in Chatham County

Chatham provides a counter factual case to the notion that growth and educational quality depend on each other. Indeed, Chatham demonstrates the consequences of uncontrolled growth for public schools. Chatham has experienced
exponential residential growth of out-commuting professionals, drawn by
Chatham's reputation for good schools (predominantly white and middle class,
in contrast to Durham) and inexpensive land. Western Chatham has witnessed
a rapid expansion of the low-wage hog and poultry industries and Latino immigrant workers. As a consequence, Chatham schools have grown at a rate of
roughly two hundred new students per year since 1993; Latino enrollment has

increased by 72 percent since 1990.[39] Bonds passed in 1989, 1993, and 1995 have proven inadequate to accompany capital needs and new demands for English as a Second Language (ESL) curriculum and instruction.

Recently, Chatham studied the idea of an impact fee, by which purchasers of newly constructed homes would pay an extra fee dedicated to school construction; the purpose is to transfer some of the cost of growth from existing to new taxpayers. Opposition to the fee was vociferous, especially among those with real estate interests. As a result of the impact fee's failure, all Chatham citizens are subsidizing handsome profits for the farmer who sells his or her family's tract for development, lavish returns for the real estate and construction industries, and lower-cost housing for the hundreds of professional people moving into the northeastern end of the county.

Likewise, Chatham County and Siler City are financing the profits of the poultry industry that has located in the western part of the county by attempting to provide services for the hundreds of immigrant poultry workers recruited to the area.[40] The plants pay very little in commercial taxes to help meet the needs of the workforce (especially health, housing, and education).[41] They rely on extremely low-wage Latino labor. Siler City poultry workers begin at a wage of $6.00/hour, increasing to $6.75/hour after ninety days of perfect attendance. These wages are significantly lower than the average U.S. food manufacturing wage.[42] Plants routinely deduct the cost of safety equipment from workers' pay. Further, prominent Siler City poultry companies have been found guilty of requiring employees to work off the clock in order to maintain their jobs.[43] The low-wage jobs that the industry brings by definition contribute little to the local tax base, yet the industry relies upon corporate subsidies of water treatment and tax forgiveness.

These economic uses of the school run counter to the goal of providing socially just schooling and instead reproduce race and class structures. The overwhelmingly white, professional, middle-class families of northeastern Chatham, who themselves secured their careers through their educational credentials, invest the equivalent of an impact fee in their children's schools. The more racially diverse working-class families in the western county schools must settle for the meager county funding remaining at the close of an overly strained county budget. Poor facilities and instruction contribute to a dropout rate double that of students in the northern high school.

Conclusion

These ethnographic case studies demonstrate that the marketization of education has privileged a growth discourse and elite interests in the local policy arena, to the detriment of efforts to use schools to promote greater equity. At this historical juncture, the argument that schools should be cultivated to attract mobile capital and professionals overwhelms other possible rationales for schools; it has achieved hegemony. We found that upper- and middle-class parents use this discourse to promote their own race and class interests, to the detriment of social equity and democratic participation. The data, however, shows the false logic of growth. In Chatham County, the influx of newcomers has stressed limited educational resources, caused the quality of public schooling to decline in poor areas of the county, and generated a sharp, unequal race and class division within the public school system as wealthier parents in the northern end of the county pay to supplement the schools of their children.

The marketization of education, made possible by a larger political and economic project, has validated nonegalitarian uses of schools. By couching their justifications in terms of economic benefits (whether for attracting new businesses or residents, benefiting real estate, or serving local business and economic interests), local elites have managed to present their private interests as a public good.

For those desiring to use schools to promote social equity and democratic participation, we recommend assiduous attention to the naturalization of economic justifications and business activism in local education policy. We can still recover a vision of schooling that would promote a more inclusive vision of "who we are as a people and what kind of society we can become." This historically contingent moment will undoubtedly shape public education for generations to come.

PART II

Governing under Neoliberalism

6   Local Politics and the Contemporary American Scene

In this chapter, we ask two related questions. First, what new conditions have local politics faced over the last three decades due to national governmental reform, economic restructuring, globalization, suburban sprawl, and the delinkage of local from national politics? Second, how have local political systems responded to these conditions through the invention of new hybrid practices and institutions of governance—privatization and public-private partnerships, which partner local governments with for-profit corporations on one hand, and with nonprofit organizations on the other? What brave new world have Americans entered?

What Has Happened to Local Democratic Politics over the Last Three Decades?

American society has changed greatly over the last thirty years, in ways that have increasingly threatened the viability of democracy, although in a few vital respects these changes have provided new opportunities and openings for democratic practices. From the middle to late 1970s to the present, those changes have included the reduction of federal funding for locales combined with the paradoxical centralization of policies concomitant with devolution; the emergence of new private financial constraints over local government budgets associated with an entrepreneurial reinventing of government; the effects of economic restructuring, globalization, and suburban sprawl on local communities and their governance structures; and the delinkage of local politics from state and national political processes.

Federal Funding: Less Support for Locales,
More Support for Individuals and Corporations

Since the 1970s, local governments have had to deal with shrinking U.S. government funding for their programs. During certain periods, and for specific programs, these declines have been severe. The conservative trend in national politics since 1980 has led to the elimination or substantial defunding of Lyndon Johnson's 1960s Great Society programs for job training, schooling, the building of physical infrastructure and transport facilities, and, above all, welfare for the poor and disabled. Peaks of defunding occurred during the early years of Reagan's first term (1980–1981), then during the 104th Congress and Newt Gingrich's "Contract with America" (and Clinton's "welfare reform") in 1994–1996. Large cities and highly urbanized states, whose residents are grossly underrepresented in Congress and a large proportion of whom are poor, have been particularly hard hit by these declines.[1]

For instance, federal aid to state and local governments, exclusive of Medicaid and military-related expenditures, remained more or less steady at $100 billion (in real 1980 dollars) from 1980 to 1995, while federal aid as a percentage of total state and local government outlays declined from 28 percent to 23 percent over the same period.[2] Over the period 1957 to 1990, federal grants to local governments for development (transportation, natural resources, safety, education, etc.) rose steadily from 1957 to peaks in 1977 in both absolute amounts ($26.4 billion in real 1990 dollars) and as percentages of GNP (0.68 percent) but then declined from 1977 to 1990.[3] Combined federal aid to *both* state and local governments for development from 1957 to 1990 showed the same pattern, rising from 1957 to peaks in 1977 (at $74.5 billion in real 1990 dollars and 1.8 percent of GNP), but declining from 1977 to 1990.[4] As Kincaid puts it, for city and local governments, there has been "a defunding revolution that began during the Carter years after federal aid to states and localities reached its historic peak in 1978."[5]

These changes involved a move *away* from funding places and their local and state governments, and *toward* funding individuals and corporations— who/which are not necessarily tied to place. Over the same postwar period, federal costs for entitlement or social insurance programs (Social Security and Medicare) to individuals and for redistributive programs (especially Medicaid) have increased steeply, especially since the 1970s. From 1978 to 1998, federal aid for state and local governments that was in the form of payments for individuals jumped from 32 to 63 percent.[6]

What is far less acknowledged is that the federal government since the 1970s has engaged in a massive shift in the way it imposes relative costs and benefits on different segments of the citizenry. The federal government has put in place new subsidies and passed new tax credits, deductions, and exemptions—which represent revenues foregone and remaining in the hands of wealthy individuals and corporations—estimated at $815 billion per year.[7] Excepting Medicaid and the Earned Income Tax Credit, most of these programs are aimed at benefiting not poor individuals or families but the American middle class (conventionally defined as all those who are not poor), the super-wealthy, and, disproportionately, corporations.[8]

As a result, local governments and their communities have fallen into situations of chronic underfunding and financial decline vis-à-vis the federal government—not because national public wealth in the form of actual or potential federal revenues is insufficient but because the vast majority of money spent by the federal government now goes toward supporting the entitled middle class and making richer those increasingly mobile wealthy individuals and corporations with few overriding place-specific loyalties.

"Devolution Revolution" or Increased Centralization?

Even if federal funding to local governments has decreased significantly since the 1970s, some policy analysts and pundits have argued that "devolution," or passing down of policy making and of funds to implement it from the federal to state and local levels, has given local leaders more discretion to do what they want with the funding they do get. As a result, the argument goes, government policy making is now "closer to the people," and government is more "efficient" and "responsive" to their needs, norms, and values, and so less costly. In fact, it has been asserted that American politics has since the 1980s experienced a "devolution revolution."[9]

If these claims could be accepted, this would indeed be good news, even if somewhat dampened by the actual reduction from prior funding amounts. However, a close examination suggests that a better case can be made that presidents and Congress have engaged in increased centralization of both regulatory policy making and fiscal control at the federal level since the 1970s, and that only in a few policy areas—but notably in so-called welfare reform and the provision of other social services—has there been devolution. There is at most a "tepid trend" in devolution, one of "great expectations [but] modest results."[10]

If so, the situation facing local governments has been made much worse by *partial* devolutionary efforts. What we may be seeing in important policy areas is a tendency for *responsibilities* to be devolved to lower-level governments, while policy-making *capacities* are centralized to the federal level and the *funding* essential to implement policy are not devolved, but instead are cut drastically or even disappear. The United States appears to be entering an intensified period of unfunded mandates, conditions to aid, and preemptions—signs of centralization where the federal government increases its policy demands on state and local governments without providing either funding support or the means to raise new revenues to meet the new requirements imposed.

The term "devolution," with its associations within political rhetoric of local empowerment and rejuvenation, has more often than not served as a beautification effort for budget cuts as such. This has been evident in the use of the congressional "block grant" favored by conservatives. A block grant is one in which many programs, previously defined by funding regulations specifying their expenditures in "categorical grants," are consolidated into a single package with vague or general guidelines for its use. As an aide on a 1990s Senate Budget Committee put it, "Block grants are one of the best ways to cut the budget. The cuts are so ethereal. You just give the states less money and let them decide."[11]

Although there are many scattered examples of administrative devolution, when it comes to substantive devolution,[12] the prime exhibit for the devolution revolution is the welfare reform law, the "Personal Responsibility and Work Opportunity Reconciliation Act" (PRWORA) of 1996. PRWORA shifted the administration and enforcement of welfare-based Aid to Dependent Families and Children (AFDC) from the federal level to the workfare-based Temporary Aid to Needy Families (TANF) at state levels of government. In most states, TANF administration remains the responsibility of state governments.

What such discretion and flexibility mean for the wider case for devolution is unclear. We have evidence suggesting that state and local officials perceive that the influence of the national government in areas belonging to the states has diminished in the late 1990s,[13] since the campaign against unfunded mandates of the 104th Congress and the Clinton second term. We know that local officials perceive that devolution has lessened welfare workers' caseloads, lowered the poverty rate, and increased workforce participation—but we also know that there is no clear correlation between such perceptions and these outcomes.[14] While TANF has reduced welfare caseworker case loads and moved people off TANF support into the workforce,[15] it has not succeeded in its greater goal of reducing poverty.[16]

However, not as well publicized as the flexibility that PRORWA has provided for lower-level officials are the centralized regulatory features of the law and related subsequent legislation. The federal government has required state governments to remove families who have received TANF aid for more than five years from their rolls; to comply with federal paternity-establishment and child-support rules or lose TANF funds; to suspend the drivers' and professional licenses of TANF recipients if their child-support payments were in arrears; and to operate abstinence-only sex education programs.[17] In short, PRWORA has been hedged with federal dictates that required state and local governments to abdicate their rights to set fundamental policies in areas as intimate as child support and drivers license use.[18] Moreover, the federal dictates align with racist and paternalistic stereotypes about poor African-Americans and other minorities, which portray them as lazy, sexually promiscuous, unreliable, and deservedly indigent.

Readers may be surprised to read of these signs of centralization in a period supposedly marked by increased state and local flexibility. They illustrate a profound point about the American political system: despite its origins in postwar conservatism and the Republican Party, devolution has been accompanied or even neutralized by centralizing policies enacted by opportunistic presidents and Congresses—Republicans as well as Democrats. While one might assume that it would be primarily Democrats who have centralized controls when the interests of their powerful constituencies have been challenged, conservative congressional Republicans and presidents have maintained or further centralized decision making whenever their pro-business policies have come under serious threat. This was especially the case whenever states and locales have become active and vigilant in regulating product liability issues, food and drug labeling, Internet taxation, truck transport and road use, and affirmative action programs.[19]

In fact, centralization of policy making by the U.S. government appears to be the dominant trend of the postwar period. According to Bowman and Krause, regarding federal laws and executive orders that set out the division of powers between federal and state or local levels of government, "the 1947–1998 period can be accurately characterized by a significant shift in policymaking authority away from subnational governments toward the federal level."[20]

To sum up, the balance of forces favoring centralization versus those favoring devolution has inclined toward centralization during most of the postwar period, and if anything the balance has shifted more toward centralization in the last two decades. Much of what has passed for devolution has been purely administrative, not substantive, and hides deep budget cuts in services.

Most crucially, federal funding for local governments has declined as part of the broader shift in the most powerful constituencies of the federal government away from places—states and locales—toward groups and categories of rights-bearing individuals and corporations.[21] Since the 1980s, federal programs to protect the constitutional rights and entitlements of individuals have greatly expanded. State reapportionment during this period, following on the Supreme Court's 1964 "one person one vote" decision, weakened local- and state-based political parties in favor of an electorate of individuals. There has been a proliferation of advocacy groups working against what they perceive as state- and locally imposed restrictions on group rights.[22] As Kincaid concludes,

> the greatest federal encroachments upon state and local powers occurred not during the New Deal . . . but during and after the Great Society. Since then,

Congress and presidents . . . have acquired powerful incentives to legislate directly for persons regardless of the effects of such legislation on places (i.e., states and local governments).[23]

Financial Dire Straits and the Emergence of "Entrepreneurial" Local Governments

As we have seen, federal government funding directed specifically to the development of economic and social infrastructures of cities and of local governments has steeply declined in this period—even as the federal government has increased its social benefits to rights-bearing individuals in the form of Social Security, Medicare, and related entitlement programs, and to wealthy individuals and corporations through the subsidies it pays them and the tax revenues from them it foregoes. This has forced local governments to turn to new, nongovernmental sources of funding in order to pay for many of the basic services citizens expect them to provide. There have been two consequences. First, bond-rating agencies have become the new financial governors of local governments. Second, and partly as a result, entrepreneurial local governments have emerged that seek new forms of revenue by issuing bonds that subsidize the creation of new private enterprises that would increase the tax base of locales, and thus tax revenues.[24] The new financial exigencies have also been integral to the field of force constraining local governments to seek to "reinvent government" through a new entrepreneurialism, one we found much in evidence in our field sites in North Carolina.

Over the past two decades, alternative sources for revenues to offset reduced federal funding for local economic and social infrastructure have been few. Since their founding, because they are legal creatures of state governments within the federal system, city and local governments have been quite limited in their powers to increase taxes and find new sources of taxation. In the case of property taxes—their major local source of revenues—local governments have been severely constrained from raising such taxes by new laws brought about by taxpayer revolts, beginning with Proposition 13 in California in 1978, but spreading nationally after that.[25]

Prior to the 1970s, local governments had been able to secure loans from commercial banks. In many instances the lending banks were actually located in the locales for which borrowing was being sought, which gave local banks an economic stake in actual communities. However, as a result of the urban financial crises of the 1960s and 1970s (e.g., New York's 1975 fiscal crisis) and the beginning of withdrawal of federal funding support and financial backstopping to cities and locales, by the 1970s commercial banks refused to lend to local governments. The latter had to turn directly to private capital markets to find buyers—wealthy private individuals and institutional lenders—for the municipal bonds they issued.[26]

THE NEW FISCAL OVERLORDS OF LOCAL GOVERNMENTS

This shift has come at a price: city and local governments have become subject to a new kind of governance—by bond ratings and the three bond-rating agencies (Standard and Poors, Moody's, and Fitch IBCA) that set them. Bond ratings indicate to potential lenders the degree of risk of loan default associated with the bond issued by a specific borrower. The major ranking distinction is whether a borrower has an "investment grade" rating (one not liable to default) or "speculative grade" rating (liable to default).

This matters because lenders use these bond ratings to determine whether they will buy the bonds issued by the borrower, and, if so, at what rate of interest. Simply put, the more speculative the rating of a government borrower is, the higher the rate of interest it will have to pay—if it can find lenders, i.e., successfully issue a bond. Investors—both wealthy individuals and institutional lenders—rely on these bond ratings in their decisions as to whether to buy bonds, and which ones. Large institutional investors, such as mutual funds, pension funds, and insurance companies, which now buy the majority (in terms of dollar value) of municipal bonds, pay close attention to bond ratings because they are limited by federal law from carrying more than a small proportion of speculative-grade bond holdings in their portfolios.[27]

Under the circumstances, bond ratings are cultural artifacts of great power because they discipline local governments to manage their budgets in ways that bond-rating analysts perceive reduce the risk of default. Borrowing governments are expected to operate at surpluses, which implies that both staff and services are to be cut during tax shortfalls. This financial expectation is not politically innocent, for it makes impossible even minor deficit spending by local governments to "prime the pump" of their economies during times of recession. Moreover, borrowers are expected to engage in the work of government in increasingly "business-like" ways—to operate with "efficiency" and "transparency"—with these worthy financial qualities being defined by the bond-rating analysts.

Discipline takes the form of bond-rating analysts threatening to "downgrade" the bond ratings of local and city governments whose leaders—in the analysts' opinions—have shown insufficient commitment to operating in a business-like manner. Past downgrades have led institutional investors and wealthy individuals to suddenly unload large volumes of the offending government's bonds on the municipal bond market. This has led to catastrophe—the closedown of municipal services, flight of businesses and wealthy families, massive layoffs of public employees, and widespread citizen dissatisfaction. Elected officials seen as responsible for such imbroglios rarely retain office in the next elections. Demonstration cases include large cities like New York, Philadelphia, and Detroit, whose municipalities have undergone multiple rating downgrades over many years—leading to protracted financial and political instability and the flight of investors.[28] Thus, banks, mutual funds, and bond-rating agencies hold tightly the new fiscal reins on public life.

In addition to being influenced by the doctrine of neoliberalism, therefore, local governing elites have become entrepreneurial in their efforts to raise new revenues by using loans to underwrite private business ventures, such as the construction of malls and sports stadia, and by participating in the new hybrid public-private partnerships first discussed in chapter 1. Again, the bond-rating agencies are implicated, for being entrepreneurial "has become nothing less than an axiom of 'good governance.' The increasingly heavy-handed analyses of bond-rating agencies are thus not only uncontested, they are often enthusiastically *supported* as the roadmap toward economic sustainability."[29]

Local government officials, constrained by local business boosters, thus come to discipline themselves, as in this statement of one of "Ten Reasons to Locate Your Business in Durham," found on the web site of the Durham, North Carolina, Chamber of Commerce: *"A Government that Works for Business—Durham's City and County Governments enforce sound fiscal policies that enable these governmental bodies to hold AAA bond ratings by both Standard and Poors and Moody's. Durham has professionally managed governments that are skilled and experienced in responding to the needs of the high technology business community."*[30]

At the same time, the cultural revolution of the new entrepreneurialism arising from neoliberal influences should not be underestimated. Margit Mayer summarizes the redefined relationship between the federal government and local actors by observing that the role of the municipality "has changed from being the local arm of the welfare state to acting as the catalyst of processes of innovation and cooperation, which it seeks to steer in the direction of improving the city's (or community's) economic and social situation."[31]

Challenges to Local Communities: Economic Restructuring, Globalization, Suburban Sprawl

In the last thirty years, local communities and governments have also experienced the realities of economic restructuring, globalization, and suburban sprawl.

ECONOMIC RESTRUCTURING

By now, the effects of economic restructuring have been experienced by all Americans. Changes from the 1970s onward from an industrial to a service-based economy have transformed the lives of most. Shifts from Fordist mass production to flexible industrialism, emergence of "lean and mean" management, workforce rationalizations, mass layoffs and outsourcing, successive waves of mergers and acquisitions, and cycles of speculative booms and busts have been widely noted.[32] In the last fifteen years the effects of economic restructuring have moved up the value chain from blue-collar factory workers of the 1980s to white-collar middle-level managers and professionals, many of whom have seen their jobs disappear or outsourced to subcontractors.[33] The search for new employment and job opportunities has led large numbers of white-collar workers to seek work in more economically flourishing areas of the country. In combination with affirmative action policies, static or declining real family incomes have led increasing numbers of women from middle-class families to enter the formal labor force to maintain the affluent lifestyles that their parents' generation attained in the 1950s and 1960s.[34] Over this period, consumer debt has mounted and an increasing proportion of families' discretionary income has gone toward debt servicing.[35]

CORPORATE GLOBALIZATION

During the last three decades, the process of globalization has greatly affected the American economy.[36] Since its principal effects on local communities have been plant closings and large-scale job loss associated with corporate relocation and offshoring, we speak of "corporate globalization": while firms can move overseas, workers—not to speak of the communities they live in—cannot. So-called free trade treaties and agreements entered into by the United States, from the North American Free Trade Agreement (NAFTA) in 1994 to others negotiated since, have allowed the import of goods at prices that have undercut those of domestic producers, which have either closed down their factories or moved them offshore.[37] The outcomes have been large-scale layoffs in many areas, but particularly in the southern United States, where a new Rust Belt is rapidly emerging.[38] U.S.-initiated globalization in neighboring countries has redounded in blowback consequences for the United States. Regions such as the Southeast and Southwest have experienced an influx of impoverished immigrants from Mexico and Central America who have arrived to work at the lowest-paid, least legally protected, and most dangerous work available in the United States.[39]

To summarize, economic restructuring and globalization have led to a situation where most people are experiencing increased economic and social insecurity associated with various kinds of risk, where new opportunities must be seized by geographic mobility, and where new residents are often newcomers from elsewhere in the United States or from foreign countries.

SUBURBAN SPRAWL

Over the last three decades, the American landscape has been increasingly characterized by suburban sprawl. Sprawl is not a fact of nature but rather the result of policy decisions brought about by the influence of the national "corporate community" and allied "local growth coalitions" discussed in a later chapter. These processes have intensified, not abated, since the 1970s, and have generated enormous pressures on local governments to construct the new infrastructures that suburbs require—roads, sewage and water services, schools, hospitals, police departments, electricity grids, etc. Suburban sprawl invariably imposes high costs on local governments due to the externalities it generates from traffic congestion, accidents, air pollution abatement, and loss of open land that could otherwise be used for parks and farms.[40] Sprawl creates "throwaway cities" that suffer devaluation when their better-off residents flee for the suburbs, property values deteriorate, buildings are not repaired, tax revenues fall, and city infrastructures decay from lack of municipal funds to fix them. The construction of new suburbs both promotes and results from "white flight" from the cities that leads to extreme racial and class segregation.[41]

CHALLENGES TO LOCAL COMMUNITIES

While the economic, social, and personal effects of economic restructuring and globalization and suburban sprawl have been widely analyzed, their effects on local politics are far less often discussed. These processes have created new problems as well as opportunities for local communities and governments. In many locales, large job layoffs with the attendant downstream losses to local businesses have jeopardized local governments' revenues from property and sales taxes. Uncertain employment and high consumer debt make many people reluctant to support tax increases even if these are needed for vital government services. Consumerism and increased working hours for many people mean that precious free time is taken away, not only from family and recreation but also from civic involvement, and invested in personal consumption instead.[42] Even the *possibility* of plant closings casts into doubt the fiscal stability of local governments and gives large-scale employers and real estate entrepreneurs disproportionate power to influence local government policies relative to ordinary citizens. When large-scale layoffs do occur, those residents most able to leave for better economic opportunities elsewhere—professionals and the well educated—are those most active in local politics, and when they depart they leave vacant local activist roles vital to a democracy.[43] In the face of extensive and protracted lay-offs, cities, towns, and rural areas may even experience widespread depopulation and their government infrastructures may collapse, as in the worst-hit cities and towns in the midwestern Rust Bowl.

The influx of migrants has also posed new challenges to local governments. In-migration of relatively uneducated Latin Americans has required that they be provided local government services, even though many residents view them as culturally alien and do not understand their needs. In contrast, in-migrants from elsewhere in the United States who are professionals, managers, and skilled white-collar workers are newcomers eagerly sought by local officials for the enhanced tax base they provide. Still, they quickly begin to make political demands on local governments and to challenge the dominance of "natives" or "old-timers" in local politics, as well as their ways of conducting it.

Suburban sprawl exacerbates the new demands that economic restructuring and globalization make on locales. The new public costs of suburban expansion must be paid for, needs of residents of throw-away cities met, and environmental effects of sprawl remediated. Williamson, Imbroscio, Alperovitz, and others point out that sprawl's low-density development lessens informal interactions among residents and discourages civic involvement.[44] We also wonder whether the search by many citizens to satisfy their individual dreams of suburban consumption places in jeopardy their capacity to imagine shared public goods and the imperative to find common solutions to collective problems. The white flight that sprawl both promotes and makes possible makes it more difficult for people of different races to find common ground on local issues and to deal with shared place-based concerns that cross races and classes. Sprawl also generates conflicts when urban areas seek to increase their revenue base by annexing surrounding unincorporated areas, whose residents often resist because it will increase their property taxes, as we found in Fayetteville.

The Delinkage of Local Politics from State and National Politics

The trend of governments to support individuals and corporations and drain resources away from places has had important consequences for the organization of translocal relationships. There has been an advanced but still incomplete delinkage of local politics from other levels of American politics due to the demobilization of citizens. This change is of decisive importance to our analysis of local democracy because it has shifted the scale of much effective citizen mobilization away from national and state levels toward local politics. Up to the 1960s, the argument goes, Americans organized themselves in federations of voluntary organizations—labor unions, the American Automobile Association, and many more—through hierarchical ties that closely connected active leaders to mobilized followers in local chapters, state federations, and national federations—each of which had effective clout at their respective levels of federal politics. Political elites needed the energies, ideas, and support of followers in order to advance their own agendas.[45]

Today, in stark contrast, much of what passes for citizen activism at national and state levels is instead the work of activist-professionals who manage and articulate the interests and dissent of rights-bearing individuals, but who almost never mobilize citizens through organizing—because they have no need to. Instead, professional advocates working for nonprofit and political NGOs are concentrated in a few locations (especially Washington, DC) where they conduct survey polls, raise funds from foundations, hold press conferences, write op-ed pieces, directly lobby Congress, and litigate—all *on behalf of* individual citizens living in different locales, but not *with* citizens in any collective social way.[46]

Local politics in contrast is now, as a consequence, the most vital arena in which ordinary citizen activism, engagement, and mobilization occur—which makes local politics both an extremely crucial diagnostic site in which to study the ills of American democracy and a site of hope in which to seek the sources for its revitalization.

Local Politics Up Close:
The Rise of Market Rule or Neoliberal Governance

The various shifts we outline above have brought on a broader cultural and political transformation we refer to as the rise of market rule or neoliberal governance and has created a wide set of institutional changes throughout the American political system. While market rule and neoliberal views have now completely displaced the previously prevailing institutions of "big government" associated with the social liberalism that justified the American welfare state of the 1950s–1960s, market rule is characterized by its own tensions and gaps between its reach and its grasp that must be explored.

The New Local Institutions of Market Rule

Market rule since the 1980s has been associated with the appearance of new processes of governance in America's communities: the privatization (outsourcing) of government services, the emergence of new institutions called "public-private partnerships," and the increasing tendency of the nonprofit and philanthropic sectors to play essential governance roles. Although since the beginning of the republic there has been private-sector participation in some functions of governance (e.g., contracting out for construction and road building), the last two decades are exceptional in that local government by itself has come to perform far fewer of these governance functions than at any time since the 1930s. Moreover, the internal operation of local government has also been transformed by the application of market logics (such as competitive cost-accounting and surplus-imperative budgeting) to supersede what had been (from the late 1940s to the 1970s) civil service norms of public service bound by hierarchical rules and technocratic measurements of performance, and budgets determined as much by technical requirements for program success as by legislative or executive cutbacks.

Privatization as Part of "Reinventing Government"

During the 1980s, the movement to "reinvent government" by seeking out business and nonprofit organizations' participation in governance came to play a larger role in public life under the impetus of the new neoliberal wisdom and, more specifically, the first Reagan administration's goal to "shrink the size of government."[47] This movement, of course, presupposed that then-current public-service practices favored inefficiency, rule-bound rigidity, wastefulness, a structured incapacity to empathize with citizens' demands, and a "bloated" civil service. Both for-profit enterprises that "radiate a capitalist halo of competitive spirit, efficiency, flexibility, and discipline" and nonprofit or philanthropic organizations that are "supposed to bring a sense of mission to their missions" were to be a cure for this government disease.[48]

Central to this movement has been privatization, something that in recent American history has meant not the sale of government assets to for-profit purchasers but the putting out of what had previously been a function provided by a (monopolistic) public agency to a for-profit enterprise through competitive bidding, or to a "voluntary" nonprofit organization in areas where the for-profit sector showed little interest.[49] From the early 1980s onward, privatization initiatives have led to the increased role of for-profit enterprises in areas of governance as widely varied as Medicaid, highway maintenance, child care, waste collection and recycling, prison and jail administration, the operation of youth counseling and custodial services, and the supply of ambulance services.[50] And in some locales, school vouchers have allowed for both for-profit and nonprofit (e.g., religious-based) schools to be cross-subsidized by public school systems.[51]

Governance functions now contracted out to for-profit enterprises raise questions about efficiency, equity, and democracy. First, despite claims by privatization advocates that services cost less and are provided more efficiently by private rather than public providers,[52] the evidence is far more mixed. According to the economist Sclar in his aptly named book, *You Don't Always Get What You Pay For,* "comparative cost studies [show that] . . . although there are clearly situations in which [private] contracting works well, there are at least as many, if not more, in which the existence of direct public service is a rational economic strategy."[53] Sclar's data show that privatization appears to be less costly and more efficient where the services provided require relatively low levels of skills and have results that are readily transparent (e.g., turf is either mowed or not), where the services are discrete tasks that are not part of more complex long-term suites of services, and where the number of people served and the geographical scope of such services are relatively small. In contrast, public agencies appear to be less costly and more efficient in providing services that require highly educated personnel, consist of a complex series of tasks that must be coordinated over a long period of time (e.g., highway maintenance or police or fire-fighting services), and serve a relatively large number of people with a wide geographic scope that make the use of fixed public assets (e.g., road-paving equipment) efficient. Publicly operated transit systems may "work best," in this sense, for large cities, while privately operated systems make sense for some suburban areas and small towns. But what would be less expensive and more efficient in the case of a highly dispersed rural population, say, a historically underserved, impoverished one? Or is this even the (only) right question to ask?

These reflections lead us to ask several related questions. *First, in a democracy, how are ordinary citizens going to be able to participate in such difficult and complex decisions about whether a local governance function should be public or contracted out to a private firm?* Because it is claimed that most citizens lack the accounting and technical expertise that such decisions appear to require, how are they to avoid being disempowered from participation in decision making, even though they have their own common sense and "local knowledge"—for instance, how well a service operates in their neighborhood—which arguably should play a role in such consequential decisions? Moreover, how are ordinary citizens—who are neither certified experts nor members of the local economic and political elites who employ experts—to play a role equal to those of the latter groups in making decisions that directly affect citizens? After all, such decisions require attention not only to efficiency but also to equity of treatment in the receipt of services to which all citizens are entitled. How in particular can those marginalized groups, treated as subcitizens because of their poverty, racial identities, or national origins, participate on an equal footing with the supercitizens made up of members of the business community and other local elites?

Second, how can citizens and local governments be sure that a newly contracted-out function has actually been adequately performed by a for-profit contractor? Sclar points out how complex public services are, and how often, therefore, their total costs are not known or even well understood. He analyzes the case study of highway maintenance in Massachusetts, where the public agency MassHighway, under pressure from Governor William Weld, an ardent privatizer, contracted out highway maintenance to a private contractor in the early 1990s. However, Sclar argues that this was done almost certainly at greater cost than if highway maintenance had continued to be done in-house. Sclar concludes that this difference was due to the failure by MassHighway to undertake a complete accounting of the actual long-term costs of highway maintenance.[54] By underestimating the costs, MassHighway made its operation appear more wasteful and inefficient in comparison to that of the private contractor than it actually was. How are citizens going to be more informed about such complex services so that—local power structures permitting—they can play a larger role in deci-sion making about the adequacy of their performance?

How, short of accepting on faith the cost-efficiency claims of privatizers, can citi-zens assess the performance of a private contractor, if not through the monitoring by a public agency of that performance? There is every reason to believe that the knowledge, objectives, tactics, and perspectives of for-profit private contractors will be significantly different from those of government officials and the public they are elected to represent. For-profit contractors rarely have a comprehen-sive sense of the total set of services required to meet a major public need, while public agencies that have long performed this set of services generally have an inherited knowledge of how to carry out these services at lowest cost—even if they may be unable to comprehensively specify their costs. As Sclar puts it, "history matters."[55] Private contractors not only lack such local knowl-edge, but their profit objectives often lead them to "cut corners" in order to save costs, and to secretly "cherry-pick" the situations in which they will ren-der services, thus leading to cost-shifting at public expense.[56] Another tempta-tion is for contractors (either out of greed or a failure to adequately predict their costs in a contract) to intentionally misrepresent their actual service per-formance,[57] in other words, to defraud the government.

Under the circumstances, the monitoring by public agencies of private con-tractor performance is imperative. Such monitoring, however, has its own costs. Before it can be determined which option is less costly, these monitoring costs must be fully accounted for and added to the direct costs of the private service contractor, and the total compared to the direct costs of providing a service through a public agency. It is possible that in the case of complex serv-ices contracted out, the costs of monitoring performance, when added to the cost of the private service itself, will make privatization more costly. Clearly, there are temptations to cut corners: where privatization is being contemplated or is already in effect, are citizens willing to trade off their rights to preexisting levels of service, e.g., to highways made safe through proper maintenance, or to demand that local governments figure in the full costs of monitoring the performance of private contractors when figuring their true costs?

Since privatization advocates assume that the virtues of efficiency and flexibility of privatization arise from market competition, can competition in the bidding process actually be ensured? What happens where instead a monopoly situation pre-vails? Sclar provides evidence that there are serious barriers to entry by private competitors. Where the services privatized are complex and require multiyear commitments, only a very limited number of firms, perhaps only one, have the technical expertise and resources to manage a service. Sclar gives the example of a waste-treatment contract that demands a high initial capital investment and technological expertise by any prospective bidder—thus severely filtering the field of competitors down to an oligopoly or even monopoly situation.[58]

Finally, are there dangers to citizens' exercise of rights arising from private contractors treating them more as customers with preferences than as citizens with rights? Citizens are treated primarily as customers with whom service providers have a limited relationship as vendors of a commodity, and critics charge that this has an individualizing effect on citizens that can lead to their collective demobilization.[59] If citizens see themselves first as individuals whose buying preferences are not satisfied by private contractors, are they going to be less inclined to mobilize themselves with like-minded others through local politics to solve their common problems?

Given all these questions, claims about the achievements and potential of the privatization movement since the 1980s appear to be seriously exaggerated.

Market-Oriented Public-Private Partnerships: New Forms of Governance

What we discovered in our research on five North Carolina communities was the widespread experimentation with new hybrid institutions of governance— public-private partnerships—that frequently operate at the fuzzy, ambiguous boundaries between local governments, on one side, and either for-profit enterprises or nonprofit organizations, on the other. The new public-private partnerships are hybrid legal entities that combine the traits of local governments with either private enterprise or nonprofit, nongovernment organizations. Our research provides an illuminating window on an increasingly prevalent form of governance that has emerged since the 1970s throughout the United States.[60] These partnerships have functioned in such areas as urban revitalization, welfare administration, community financing, and health-care provision.

Peters provides a very useful definition of a public-private partnership as having the following characteristics: (a) they are composed of "two or more actors," at least one of which is a public entity; (b) each of the participating actors can bargain on its own behalf; (c) the partnership involves a long-term or "enduring" relationship; (d) each actor must be able to bring some goods, whether material or symbolic, to the relationship; (e) all parties have a "shared responsibility" for the outcomes.[61] If we accept this definition, we can make three helpful conceptual distinctions to start with. First, public-private partnerships are quite distinct from the privatization arrangements such as procurement contracts discussed above. Partnership governance functions are—at least in theory—comanaged and coordinated over a long period through ongoing negotiation between both sides of the partnership, not subcontracted out from government to the for-profit sector.

Second, these characteristics of a public-private partnership (it is an enduring relationship, with each side bringing resources to the table and sharing responsibility for outcomes) imply that we are referring to a private partner with some degree of formal institutionalization. This would reflect parity in the partnership with the government in question. That is, the private partner has a high degree of permanence, has a defined organization and set of objectives stated (usually in a legal charter), has the capacity to enter into contracts, possesses resources, and employs personnel in an internal division of labor.   Third, as long as one side is a public entity, then the other side may be either a for-profit enterprise or a nonprofit, e.g., philanthropic or political organization. However, it is essential to distinguish public-private partnerships between governments and for-profit partners from those between governments and nonprofit organizations, since the dynamics of the two kinds of partnerships are very different. Some of the major problems of democratic accountability in the case of public-private partnerships lie in the blurred boundaries within them between practices appropriate to public agencies, those suited to private enterprise, and those geared to nonprofit organizations. In this section, we deal first *only* with partnerships where the private partner is a for-profit enterprise.[62]

The local experimentation with public-private partnerships of the last two decades continues throughout the United States, and examples of the public-private partnership experiments and their outcomes are discussed in the chapters that follow. Indeed, public-private partnerships have been widely acclaimed successes by some, while others have pointed to demonstrable failures.[63] Whether these partnerships can be deemed successes or not depends on how one measures success—and whose success, after all, we are talking about. Presumably, at the very least, a successful public-private partnership is one that advances the public good, and protects local democratic institutions.

In this book, we are most concerned with whether public-private partnerships do or do not enhance the possibilities for local democracy. What questions then arise about the direction of local politics when these partnerships come to play a prominent role in governance, as they do in so many communities today?

Can public-private partnerships be more efficient in their use of public resources than government alone when government officials do not have access to the same market knowledge as their for-profit corporate partner, given their own territorial fixity compared to the mobility of corporations? How will a local government know whether other for-profit corporations than the one it is seeking to partner with could compete with it and possibly be less expensive and provide better service? Absent market knowledge, how can local governments avoid entering into unnecessary or even virtual bidding wars against competing locales or making more generous concessions than necessary to a potential partner or investor? When officials lack such market information and agree to a partnership, should it not be assumed that the for-profit partner is gaining excess profits at public expense? And what of the funds required for building the infrastructure (roads, industrial estates, sewage and water treatment plants) needed to entice private partners *and* for maintaining it into the future—how is their efficient allocation to be determined under these conditions?[64]

How can the attractiveness for government officials of public-private partnerships with for-profit partners be reconciled with democratic needs of accountability? Elected officials have many incentives for working on projects with private partners— to create physical symbols of progress or prosperity to show to voters, to create new jobs (the one almost always given), to attract other businesses, or to provide vitally needed services for residents, among others. But officials also require campaign financing, and this is most readily available from prospective for-profit partners, rather than poor community residents or their associations. As a consequence, officials often are in a conflict-of-interest position vis-à-vis their private partners. Under the circumstances, how can citizens be assured that the public good, rather than the personal interests of officials, is being attended to? It has been argued that "many public-private partnerships are not accountable directly to the public for their activities."[65] Moreover, the twilight status of the new quasi-public, quasi-private development organizations that are often set up in partnerships—where it is unclear whether public standards of disclosure or private standards favoring secrecy about market decisions should apply—make the problem of accountability for public funds spent and official decisions made even more difficult to solve.[66] Can democracy flourish under these conditions?

How can the "structural mismatch" in knowledge, timing, project stakes, and ethical commitments between government officials and for-profit partners be dealt with in order to make partnership negotiations fair to government and thus further the public good? According to Stephenson, public and private partners bring entirely different endowments to the table in these areas.[67] Prospective private partners have knowledge about possible competitors and access to expert knowledge regarding the costs of projects to be undertaken, while officials do not. As to timing, business partners have pressures on them to "do the deal," do the project, then move on, whereas government officials must have a longer-term perspective on how the project serves citizens. Officials must thus envision long-term costs and liabilities, as well as benefits, which are of no concern to the for-profit partner. While government officials rarely have a personal financial incentive for undertaking a project, for-profit partners always do, which leads the latter to engage in hard bargaining with their public partner—at times when the for-profit partner already has leverage over its public partner due to its privileged access to the capital needed to invest in the partnership's projects. Ethical values surrounding contractual commitments differ between government officials and private partners: "tough, position-based negotiating tactics, including intimidation and deception" are elements in business ethics,[68] but this is far less often the case for administrators who feel bound by civil service regulations, and for elected officials who feel constrained by the need for scarce capital for projects, or, in another register, for their campaign financing. Given these incommensurable endowments and expectations that public officials bring to partnerships in contrast to for-profit enterprises, how is the public good to be assured?

Presumably, citizens are to benefit from public-private partnerships, but how can it be ensured that some citizen populations will not be victims of the externalities (unintended side consequences) of public-private partnership arrangements? How will the residents of an inner-city area who are projected for relocation due to an urban revitalization project involving for-profit builders be provided for, or compensated, when this is not a condition built into the contract of the public-private partnership? How will a partnership ensure that farmers who draw water off a river for their crops be protected from waste toxins dumped upstream by a factory that has been given public subsidies to locate in the county as part of a broader development initiative?

The Rise of the Nonprofit Sector: Privatized Social Services and Community-Oriented Public-Private Partnerships

The rise of neoliberalism with its disdain for government has meant that the nonprofit sector of American society has also come to play a much larger and more prominent role in governance. In the area of social services in particular, the nonprofit sector has in effect become an arm of the state and profoundly dependent on state funding in the form of contracts to it.[69] In 1980, more than 40 percent of government social services funding at all levels went to contract work with nonprofits, and the amount paid for these services to nonprofits tripled in absolute terms (in 1996 dollars) from $13 billion in 1977 to $40 billion in 1996.[70] Ironically, over the same period from 1977 to 1996, for all services provided, an increase in the proportion of the American population employed in the nonprofit sector has almost exactly offset the decrease in government employment, leading one study to conclude that "many of our government officials like to proclaim their success at reducing the size of government and point in particular to the decline in the direct employment of individuals. In truth, what has occurred in large part is that the government has increasingly paid others to perform the work it finances."[71]

In the "reinventing government" movement, nonprofit organizations, like for-profit firms, are portrayed as possessing virtues of flexibility that government agencies with their rigid "command and control" structures do not, yet nonprofits are seen as driven by altruism rather than the profit motive. As a result, according to Crenson and Ginsberg, they are said to "embody a self-conscious awareness of ends along with a flexible experimentalism in the choice of means—more accountability than the market, more responsiveness than public bureaucracy. Nonprofits are private groups dedicated to public interests."[72] Beyond neoliberalism as such, nonprofits embody a stronger social-services orientation that draws on the perspective of communitarianism, which relies on such mechanisms as redistribution of wealth, public funding, and official government oversight of services.[73] In this connection, we would add two points.

First, we note that in providing services community-oriented public-private partnerships involving nonprofit partners are less common than contract arrangements.[74] Here the rhetoric of relationship—how "partnership" is spoken of in specific circumstances—may be crucial. Whereas public-private partnerships with *for-profit* partners have more often than not been defined by capital-intensive projects for economic development where local governments have eagerly sought out businesses with capital on a putatively "equal" basis, that is, as a "partner," local governments are in a far more powerful position vis-à-vis most *nonprofit* organizations. This arises from the fact that nonprofits are competitors with one another in seeking to gain access to scarce government contracts and grants. Thus the connotations of equality and mutuality vis-à-vis government of the term "partner" are generally less applicable to the nonprofit, as much as it would like to assume them. Nonprofit organizations are thus far more often viewed as contractors than as partners.

Nonetheless, the literature reveals that community-oriented public-private partnerships exist as such but—at least in the United States—under distinctive circumstances.[75] These partnerships between local governments and nonprofits tend to exist and be recognized as such where (a) they serve locales that have come to be neglected or discriminated against by higher-level governments, thus leaving local and municipal governments starved for resources, such as in distressed large inner-city neighborhoods and in rural areas with historically underserved poor or minority populations; and (b) the nonprofit partner is able, for whatever reason, to bring a large amount of nongovernment resources to the table, for instance, large numbers of skilled volunteer staff ("human capital"), or autonomous funding such as a private foundation grant. In extreme situations of deprivation, governing nonprofits or mediating institutions emerge.[76]

Second, the phrase "nonprofit organization" has many meanings in the literature; scholars have typically assumed that such an organization is incorporated, that is, has legal tax-exempt status under sections 501(c)(3) or 501(c)(4) of the Internal Revenue Code, which is what confers eligibility on it to receive contracts from governments in privatization exercises or to serve as a partner in public-private partnerships. As Smith points out in his book *Grassroots Associations*, the dimension of legal incorporation excludes the vast majority of grassroots associations, which to him are small, locally based organizations made up primarily of volunteers and defined by their "voluntary altruism." He derives a "5-to-1 to 10-to-1 ratio of the estimated number of . . . [voluntary groups] not listed with the Internal Revenue Service (IRS) to the number of . . . [voluntary groups] so registered." Thus, in contrast to the National Red Cross or a private university, a group of city residents who are concerned about crime in their neighborhood and come together to lobby the police for more patrols, but have not registered their group with the IRS for tax-exempt status, do not belong to a nonprofit organization, although the group would be a grassroots association.[77]

And appropriately so, for we argue that a legal "nonprofit organization" is one that is becoming progressively incorporated into the mechanisms of state governance in two senses—first, in that it is legally required to comply with the terms of its tax-exempt charter, especially with respect to refraining from electoral politics, and second, in that only after it has registered as such is it eligible to receive a government contract. In contrast, unincorporated grassroots associations—whether they are composed specifically of activists and seek to make political change, or are dedicated to "nonpolitical" forms of altruism—remain outside the ring of incorporation into the state. When a group becomes registered as a tax-exempt organization, it crosses a special line.

In this chapter, we are most concerned with legal nonprofit organizations that receive contracts from state and local governments or serve as partners in community-oriented partnerships and provide public services to people as residents of places, not to individuals as such, for the focus of our research is on political participation by people in their communities.[78] Nonprofit organizations have taken on the responsibility through contracts or informal arrangements with government to provide housing, job training, child care, and elder care, to distribute food to the hungry via soup kitchens,[79] and to offer new public services such as rape-crisis and AIDS hotlines and battered women's shelters.

One example of social service privatization is New York City's Community-Based Organizations (CBOs), which, unlike most other nonprofits, are classified as such because they are organized around a particular geographic place, are expected to provide for the needs of their "disadvantaged" community members, and are characterized by the significant participation of community members in the organizations' own governance.[80] CBOs in New York City and elsewhere receive grants directly from local government agencies, which have been devolved from federal and state governments to the local level. Marwell's study reveals that CBO leaders engaged in competition with other CBOs throughout New York City to secure grants and other funding from local government agencies to finance their projects—in a beggar-thy-neighbor struggle over scarce public resources. The outcomes of competition were significant: "Which specific NPOs [nonprofit organizations] win contracts determine *where* services are available, *how* individuals access them, and ultimately *who* benefits from public spending for the poor."[81] The way contracts are awarded and on what criteria then become critical. Securing government contracts demands that leaders have scarce skills—being able to translate community needs in the discourse required by grant proposal guidelines, reporting their expenditures accurately, etc. At the same time, the leaders of nonprofits compete with each other for funding from foundations and private philanthropists.

The foregoing points to several strains that characterize the privatization of governance functions by nonprofit organizations, and leads us to ask the following concluding questions:

Does potential access to resources that comes with incorporated nonprofit status such as government contracts pose intolerable dilemmas for activists working in grassroots associations who seek to build their organizational capacities in order to accomplish their political goals? How can activists reconcile their need to gain control of resources with the risks that come with incorporated nonprofit status—having to curtail their political activities and, if they gain resources through government contracts, facing cooptation by the very governance structures they as citizen-activists hope to transform?

As is the case for for-profit contractors, we must ask of nonprofit organizations, How can citizens and local governments be sure that a contracted-out or partnership function has been adequately performed? Although clearly the asymmetries in information, market power, time orientation, and capacity for hard bargaining between a government and a nonprofit organization are fewer than they would be with a for-profit contractor, they still exist, particularly with respect to information. That is, "policymakers . . . know less about a program than those implementing it" due to difficulties in monitoring the performance of the nonprofit contractor such as determining whether "shortfalls of productivity" are due to a lack of effort or to extenuating factors.[82] These uncertainties about the performance of the nonprofit contractor may allow the contractor to misrepresent whether it has performed a service, the problems it faces, or even its costs of operation. Even without the moral hazard of misrepresentation, there are risks of accountability in dealing with nonprofit organizations as contractors, for their non–contract-based sources of funding are corporations, foundations, and private philanthropists who may make demands on them contrary to the conditions imposed by their contracts. If the leaders of a nonprofit organization have divided loyalties, will they follow the wishes of wealthy private donors or of government officials? How then is their performance to be monitored?

In the case of social services performed by nonprofit organizations (like CBOs) engaged in community building, they should be accountable to their members as well. How are the leaders of such nonprofits going to reconcile their accountability to members with their accountability to local governments in fulfilling their contracts or meeting partnership obligations? Are members citizen-constituents first—to whom leaders must be responsive democratically (i.e., involve members in deliberation and decision making)—or are they clients first to whom services are being rendered as determined by technical criteria? Crenson and Ginsberg pose the problem thus: "the most politically significant consequence of the new contractual relationship between government and nonprofits is the redirection of organizational energy from the mobilization of public constituencies to the 'treatment' of clients one by one. In the process, attention shifts to personal rather than political problems."[83] Can this—should this—shift be avoided?

How can the public good be served and democracy furthered given the all-too-common invidious competitions between different nonprofit organizations over reduced and limited government contracts and grants (and partnership arrangements)? When many entrants in this competition are deserving, yet those who succeed in obtaining contracts and grants are few, and when contract application procedures require leaders to use scarce organizational, writing, and lobbying skills, how can public resources be equitably distributed through democratic processes?[84]

7 Imagining Local Futures

Who Sets Priorities for the Present?

Visions of Creative Destruction

"In Durham, we are blessed with all this old industry that has left some great buildings behind," Jimmie Jordan, a real estate developer, said as he shifted his luxury sedan into second gear and turned the corner onto Duke Street. The car passed some renovated tobacco warehouse condominiums on the right, and left the downtown historic Brightleaf district on the way to check on a property in an upscale suburban development several miles away. The middle-aged white man turned again to Thad Guldbrandsen, the ethnographer riding shotgun: "That's the thing about adaptive reuse; it relies on changing economies and the decline of old industries. Downtown is surrounded by nice architecture. If we were not able to redevelop these buildings, downtown would be an island." There was a pause in the conversation as the two men considered the implications of these comments. The sedan left the historic downtown area and came to a stoplight at an intersection where an expanse of pavement and commercial development dominated the field of vision: a labyrinth of interstate highway ramps, fast-food restaurants, shopping mall parking lots, pawn shops, banks, and gas stations. Emphasizing the irony in his argument that declining industry was actually *good* for the local community, Jimmie explicated his point: "The decline of the Liggett [cigarette] factory is a blessing . . . otherwise Liggett would be a roadblock [for revitalizing downtown]."[1]

Ten years ago positive statements about the decline of Liggett and Myers's tobacco production in Durham would have been considered blasphemy in this

"City of Tobacco." Once home to the world's largest tobacco production empire and thousands of tobacco jobs, Durham was officially redesignated "The City of Medicine" in 1981. This was an attempt to reflect the new social and economic character of Durham's high-technology–, medical-, and pharmaceutical-dominated economy, closely linked with the region's world famous center for biotechnology and information technology, Research Triangle Park.

Harvey Catawba maintains a very different relationship from Jimmie to Durham's political economy by virtue of his position as an African-American man and former tobacco worker. Harvey and his cohort have not yet benefited from the demise of the local industrial economic base. He is a self-educated activist (and self-proclaimed socialist) who is most concerned with organizing labor in the face of the growing flexibility and strength of global capital. A divorced father of grown daughters nearing retirement from his current job with a local government agency, Harvey worked for American Tobacco until 1986, when he left his nearly $20-per-hour job just before the factory relocated operations. Now Harvey works tirelessly to help support and organize labor unions in the area and lobbies the local government to do its part in promoting livable wages in Durham. He mentors African-American teens, and generally devotes his spare time to concerns that promote a stronger community but will probably never yield him any personal profit. Harvey's vision of political action is not market oriented or profit driven, yet his vision of the future carries less weight than Jimmie's undeniably self-serving visions.

Harvey never granted a formal interview, but he and Thad traveled together on several occasions to friends' houses, picket lines (such as the UPS strike), secret labor meetings, public meetings on race and local politics, and local watering holes. The narrated view through Harvey's windshield stands in sharp contrast to Jimmie's.

On one occasion, as Harvey and Thad drove through the urban landscape, Harvey commented on the people they saw and periodically yelled out the window of his pickup truck to several of his acquaintances (neighbors, fellow activists, people who had recently relocated "back home South," and kids on the corner). Harvey pointed out his mother's house next to a convenience store where a number of young men and boys stood out front. He spoke of trouble with the police and the drug trade around the store. The police had not been able to do anything about the problems, he noted, but their presence "keeps life interesting" for his mother and her neighbors. Harvey and Thad looked at houses in various stages of disrepair, the presence of abundant trash, and seemingly abandoned automobiles. Harvey pointed out some notorious liquor houses, crack houses, gambling houses, and a house being renovated by Habitat for Humanity. When the two drove through more affluent neighborhoods with middle- to upper-middle-class houses, tree-lined streets, landscaped yards, new and working cars, and a pervasive sense of quiet, Harvey commented very little. As they drove on, Harvey pointed out people whose bodies were visibly ravaged by poverty and drug abuse. A man with the vacant look of a zombie staggered down the sidewalk, leaning forward slightly, arms hanging lifelessly by his sides, and a woman with encrusted hair sticking out in all directions scratched at what Harvey figured were needle tracks on her arms. Harvey shook his head out of empathy and frustration and, not knowing what else to say, said "Look at that."

Visions of the Future

Like Jimmie Johnson and Harvey Catawba, people in every community in America imagine the way they want their community to look in the future. According to their own personal experiences and interests, different people will have different visions for the future. Those visions may include more schools and day care centers, different shopping options, better streets and sidewalks, or perhaps different job opportunities. Some individuals may be involved in local government and have a great capacity to affect change in their community. Many people we spoke with in our research were activists trying to make their vision for the future a reality; others we spoke with never really considered where plans for the community had come from and did not imagine themselves as people who defined the future of their city. For a variety of reasons, the capacity to make one's vision of the future become a reality varies from person to person, and that fact has a significant effect on local democracy. In examining these five North Carolina communities to ask, Is this democracy? we must also ask, Whose vision for the future sets the course for how resources are allocated, what land is developed, what buildings get built, who benefits, and who defines the public good?

Throughout the 1990s, "Vision 2000" plans, "2020 Visions," and the creation of similarly named land-use planning documents (i.e., official planning visions) became a national pastime as cities all over the United States worked to "chart a new future" and present a positive public image. For example, Durham, North Carolina, Concord, New Hampshire, and Flagstaff, Arizona, each had their own "2020 Visions." Downtown Fayetteville, North Carolina, had the "Once and for All" plan (alternately called the "Marvin Plan," for the landscape architect hired to design it).[2] Communities administered their visions with different arrangements of governmental and nongovernmental actors. Some plans were administered by the municipal planning department; in other cities nongovernmental agencies took the lead. In most cases, much of the actual work was carried out by private businesses or nonprofit development agencies. Thus, much of the work of the public—the actual planning, design, and building of public space—was conducted outside the realm of government agencies and sometimes outside the realm of conventional public deliberation. These arrangements are the archetypal public-private partnerships introduced in the opening chapter of this book.

In Durham, downtown development partnerships were influential with their 2020 Plan, and in Fayetteville, the entire process of creating the downtown development plan was managed by a nonprofit organization for downtown redevelopment. In some instances, planning departments and/or nonprofit development partnerships invited input at public brainstorming sessions or question-and-answer meetings. Often, citizen groups had positive suggestions for making the plan better reflect their own interests, while at other times community protest caused planners to reconsider certain aspects of the plan. In other instances, plans operated without much participation or even awareness of the general populace. In Halifax County, few county residents even knew of the existence of economic development partnerships like Halifax Horizons, which among other things developed an extensive industrial park and shell building. By the time such plans were adopted by local elected officials, people had already formed important relationships to community leaders and organizations that connected them to their own neighborhood visions and real estate development plans. After Durham's countywide 2020 Plan and Fayetteville's downtown redevelopment plan had been adopted, they carried substantial political weight as real estate developers and community development organizations would stand before their city council declaring that a particular proposal should be approved because it fit into the plan. And that is precisely why the plans were developed: to orient thinking in a particular direction, to channel rhetoric, effort, and public resources in an attempt to make the vision a reality. Thus these vision plans took on a life of their own, becoming political actors in their own right.

These official planning visions had the dual purpose of articulating a plan for future city development *and* formalizing a public image of the way people wanted their city to be perceived. For some people, the goal of a given vision plan was not necessarily to produce the thing that was envisioned. For example, after all the political work performed to garner input and support for the Durham 2020 Plan, the plan was so broadly nonspecific that it was open to vastly different interpretations. On several occasions, the 2020 Plan was used rhetorically in public debate by opposing parties to support both sides of the argument. Such a plan could also (and often did) channel ideas and interests and thereby crowd out or cut down on the number of new initiatives. Insofar as vision plans are a way to articulate a community's self-identity, they help mediate the relationship among localities, state and federal governments, and outside investment, and they help to attract outside investment. A nongovernmental organization can articulate a vision for the future to win state funds, grants from federal agencies, grants from other NGOs, or capital investments from private corporations. Formalized vision plans communicated to residents and potential investors that a city was making strides toward improvement. Even if the 2020 Plan does not accomplish all that it set out to do, it still has operated as an important political and strategic device.

When communities competed with other locales for outside investment, vision plans operated as advertisements for each locale. Fayetteville's Once and For All Plan and Durham's 2020 Plan operated as catalysts of urban development and as public relations devices to show potential investors that these were enlightened cities with a vision for the livable, cosmopolitan future. Watauga County's tourism brochure articulated to the outsider ideas about how the community—or some members of the community—thought about itself as a bucolic mountain resort with an ethic of self-determination and hard work. In Halifax County, Halifax Horizons presented a vision to the world that the county was ready for industrial investment with the political will to help build infrastructure. Chatham County had a split identity, with half the county orienting itself toward industrial and agricultural development and their other half linking its fortunes to the Research Triangle, ripe for residential development. In the context of a competitive global economy, community vision plans in each of our five sites were an important part of local governance and of marketing to outside investment.

In this intense global competition between localities for coveted outside investment, local futures became more tenuous, and a cause for anxiety on the part of residents. Communities were often treated as commodities, measured for their exchange value in the global markets of businesses, tourists, retirees, and the like.

Sometimes places were evaluated in terms of their exchange value at the expense of their use value, a trend that ultimately challenges democratic inclusivity since visions produced for exchange value leave out the interests of a great proportion of the public. "Use value" refers to the "livability" of a place, whereby its value is considered in terms of people's ability to make a living and a comfortable home. "Exchange value" refers to the potential market value of real estate, and the purpose it serves in generating profits for owners, developers, and the businesses that gain from wealthier clientele.

As illustrated in the opening vignette of this chapter, Jimmie Jordon was interested in creating livable urban space for upscale shoppers and condo residents, but he was even more interested in exchanging that real estate for profits for himself and his associates. By comparison, Harvey Catawba was concerned with helping to create a more humane, livable environment for the great number of unemployed or underemployed residents who had not benefited from Durham's transition from a landscape of production to a landscape of consumption. The economistic logic of neoliberalism, which dominated public dialogue, privileged the Jimmie Jordans of our communities at the expense of the Harvey Catawbas. In this context, economic interests—business leaders, chambers of commerce, real estate developers—achieve supercitizen status, while others are demoted to the realm of special interests or even left out of the vision for the community's future.

The process of organizing and implementing vision plans was often exclusionary. We do not doubt that all residents of a place wish to improve the quality of life. Yet, different people have different interests in their community and its economy and often have conflicting notions of what an improvement in the quality of life would look like. Business interests have superseded other community interests in defining future directions for each of our five research sites. While contemporary trends in local governance and the increasing importance of volunteer organizations promised new kinds of political inclusion, their democratic potential was not fully realized for identifiable reasons.

The Traffic in Visions

Visions of the future can take many forms. They range in scale from one person's ideas about his or her immediate surroundings to grandiose plans for refashioning an entire city. They range from formal development strategies to taken-for-granted notions of what a community is and how people commonly identify it. Visions are manifested in numerous formats, such as in chamber of commerce web pages, city government statements of purpose, policies for policing crime, plans for economic development, and the assumptions people carry with them. Sometimes visions arise out of overt political debate when a community decides its future direction. At other times it is a mainline vision that has political force, even though it has, in many cases, never been subjected to a vote or *officially* decided. The amorphousness of visions makes them hard to name or study as distinct phenomena for the same reasons they challenge the abilities of everyday people to intervene on them in the public sphere. Visions are manifested at different times in different ways. They can be communicated, as when people talk about ideas for the future in official or unofficial capacities; built, as when a vision for the future comes to fruition and becomes manifest as a building or institution; or documented, as when the vision is written down, photographed, drawn, or calculated. Once documented in these forms, visions often take on a life of their own.

While web pages, agency reports, and planning documents are sites of political contestation, once they are written down, they take on characteristics of facticity and can better be deployed for strategic political ends. They can be public, as in reports or institutional web pages; quasi-public, as in reports, web pages, or memos of nongovernmental agencies, public-private partnerships, or private companies with substantial influence; or private, as in personal documents, personal web pages, to-do lists, or financial plans. Obviously, a personal or agency to-do list has limited impact on defining the public good. When such a to-do list is elaborated, institutionalized, presented in a report, and circulated through the media, it can have enormous weight. In that way, the media play an important role in defining the public good.

When the editorial staff of the local newspaper or a talk radio host adopts a vision for the city and propagates it through media channels, it can impact the way the community's self-identity and collective persona is presented to those outside the community. Local news media are part of the local growth coalitions discussed earlier, which have a strong interest in stimulating economic growth. Because local newspapers or television stations, for example, typically have a finite geographic area to serve, their own business is served by growing the local populations, stimulating internal markets, and bringing in outside investment. This ultimately brings more revenue to media outlets. Thus, there is an enormous bias toward economic growth and market-oriented democracy among the institutions that provide people the information they need to be informed citizens.

When a city or town is served by a media outlet located in other cities, representations of the city may have a different spin. For example, newspapers and television stations in Raleigh have contradictory relationships with Durham and Fayetteville. Raleigh news outlets have a stake in the economic well-being of Durham and Fayetteville that is buffered by their primary interest, which is Raleigh. As a result, economic development professionals in both Durham and Fayetteville find that the news from Raleigh is not always as flattering as that in their hometown newspapers, and they complain that the Raleigh *News and Observer* emphasizes their own cities' shortcomings to a much greater extent than the *Durham Herald* or the *Fayetteville Observer.* One of the key functions of the Durham Convention and Visitor's Bureau is to help the local media become aware of the good things happening in the city and help manage potentially negative stories. For a number of reasons, stories about struggles for social justice or economic equality in Durham or Fayetteville tended not to be a major ongoing focus of any of the local papers, while decisions about downtown real estate development were often front-page news.

A Shift in Vision

For a concrete example of the development of a vision, let us return to the City of Medicine. At a time when Durham residents thought of their city as "The City of Tobacco," and a place where the Dukes had built a multinational empire, and the well-being of the city was inextricably linked to the well-being of the tobacco production, visions of Research Triangle Park and Duke University Medical Center charted a new future, which would ultimately supersede the city's older industries. Even while the vision of the City of Tobacco was losing hegemony as the local economy diversified, tobacco production defined the city's identity well into the 1980s. Around 1980, when James Davis articulated his notion of "The City of Medicine," it was not simply a matter of naming a self-evident social order. The act of renaming the city was a political act, representing specific interests and requiring a significant amount of political work (spearheaded by James Davis and the chamber of commerce) to make the name fit. A chamber of commerce report argued, "No other city in America exceeded Durham's broad diversity of fine hospitals and allied medical facilities, prestigious teaching institutions, innovative research laboratories, and major healthcare corporations."[3] The idea caught hold as more people discussed and more public and quasi-public documents proclaimed it. The idea of the City of Medicine became a self-fulfilling prophecy. Today, one out of three Durham County residents is employed in medical-related fields, and the nickname becomes more taken for granted each time people pass the "Welcome to the City of Medicine" sign at the city limits. With every reading of the city's official stationery or web site, which states "Durham, North Carolina, The City of Medicine," the new name becomes more accurate, more taken for granted.

Nostalgia, Problems, Glorious Futures

Ironically, the visions of the future that we studied all relied heavily on images of the past. Nostalgic imagery played heavily in futuristic visions of each community. Romantic pasts were combined with future promise in a process of entrepreneurial and middle-class problem making (and solving). Redevelopment projects drew upon (largely invented) nostalgic sensibilities about community and combined them with new forms of architecture, transportation, community development, and policing to envision a more livable city. Even in Durham—the newly fashioned City of Medicine—visions of the future incorporated picturesque tobacco barns reminiscent of individual self-determination and quaint urban villages where neighborliness and civility reigned. In these visions, the Market House in Fayetteville invoked a bygone era when children walked downtown after school for a soda and there was no political conflict in its clearly prescribed social order, and the Market House now plays heavily in that city's plans for revitalization.[4] In Halifax County, Old Historic Halifax, with its white Jeffersonian yeoman farmers, also invoked memories of a self-sufficient economic prosperity and heroic self-government (for some). Chatham County, caught between a landscape of production and a landscape of consumption, flaunts its small-town pride and agricultural production while new subdivisions of half-million-dollar houses spread into its northern and eastern parts. Watauga's frontier past, where great American pioneers forged their own life in the rugged Appalachian wilderness, draws increasing numbers of history-loving tourists, who sometimes return as part-time residents to feed the second-home and retirement-home industries.

The entrepreneurial future makers who are most responsible for vision making also work to bring about public action to remake the city according to their vision. They use social problems as rhetorical devices to mobilize public commitment, often generating public debates, nonprofit organizations, the reallocation of public resources, and other political or institutional effects. In Durham, images of a crime-ridden and working-class downtown with many homeless people became a problem that inspired the allocation of significant public capital to clean up downtown. The sex industry's military-induced presence in downtown Fayetteville, in conjunction with a derelict downtown, was seized upon to incite a massive campaign to clean up the city's image. A lack of jobs and tax base in Halifax spawned a new publicly funded office park and debates about a new airport. And the concern for the degradation of Watauga's environment via tourism and retirement-home building has inspired multiple organizations to form and seek ways for the region to maintain its rural character and scenic beauty. It is important to pay attention to who defines these social problems, as labeling has serious ramifications for the way resources get channeled and which populations get served.

Another aspect of visions of the future in each of our five communities is that they promise a glorious future in which the problems associated with the present are eliminated. Thus we have official planning documents like Durham's 2020 Plan and Fayetteville's Marvin Plan that promise no racial problems, spreading economic prosperity, affluent consumers spending money downtown, and positive notions of rising property values. Watauga's plan heralds the preservation of the county's frontier past, its small, ostensibly safe communities, and its natural scenic beauty. A balance between growth and rural character shapes the vision plan in Chatham; a simultaneous industrialization and revival of its Revolutionary War past dominate Halifax's future plan. It is important to note that these visions entail the promise of economic dividends for those who, in the visionaries' judgment, appropriately invest in this future.

Public expenditure is called upon to realize these future visions. In Watauga County, a place where the tourism and service-oriented landscape of consumption has largely supplanted the previously agricultural landscape of production, the public good was often defined by economic growth and measured by increasing property values and the number of housing starts in a year. The vision for community development was dominated by nostalgic visions of Watauga's past repackaged as "the Watauga experience" to attract transplants and tourists. Meanwhile, the pressures of increasing cost of living and increasing property values make it difficult for farmers and other Watauga residents to maintain farms or even hold onto land in the county. The low-end service-sector jobs that Watauga's economy produces create a bipolar class structure that is similar to that of Durham and other landscapes of consumption.

As Watauga's historic reliance on agriculture (tobacco, cattle, dairy) is being turned to a new tourism/consumption-oriented economic base, local leadership has fashioned and publicized a new image for the county. Elected officials, government bureaucrats, chambers of commerce, and boards of tourism (in partnership with State of North Carolina agencies) are concerned to attract tourists, seasonal residents, and new full-time residents. To build a marketable reputation for the area, they emphasize the Blue Ridge Parkway, state parks, rivers and mountains, ski areas, and the pristine nature of a place that is fundamentally different and separate from the troubles of urban life. At the time of our study, local leadership had just started a secondary economic development strategy: attempts to attract small-scale businesses and to help, in their terms, incubate local businesses.

Additionally, another recent component of plans to attract new investment in real estate and the local economy highlighted telecommuting as a mode of economic development. The idea is that flexible markets, just-in-time production, and the increasing reliance on information technology and the shipping and transportation industries will deliver economic prosperity to places like Watauga County despite its relative isolation from urban centers of economic activity. If people can live wherever they want and telecommute, that is, work from home using the Internet and phone, they will be more likely to choose places like Watauga with natural beauty and a slow-paced, neighborly charm. The hope is that these people will expand the tax base by building nice new homes, paying property tax, paying sales tax, and supporting local business. Then one day, this small-scale economic activity might expand into larger businesses and develop local jobs. This is Watauga's business leaders' attempt to strategically use visions to attract outside interest and capital.

A Municipal Entrepreneur Empowered to Implement a Vision

As we describe in the previous chapter, among the many political changes that have occurred at the end of the twentieth century to alter the conditions of local politics in our five sites and in communities around the United States is the growth of the nonprofit sector and the increasing partnership among government, private entities, and other nongovernmental organizations. In connection with decreasing federal funds earmarked specifically for municipalities and increasing availability of federal moneys for nongovernmental entities, the nonprofit sector had become especially important to political relations in

American cities. At every level of government, agencies fundamentally altered the way they interacted with other agencies and the private sector. This resulted in a blurring of the boundary between public and private sectors. Under the free market rhetoric of neoliberalism, local governments were faced with more opportunities for autonomy and more responsibilities to meet the needs of their populace. At the same time, prevailing sentiments of fiscal conservatism made it difficult to fund them, so the city and county government in our research sites had, in effect, outsourced these new opportunities to the private and nonprofit sector.

Some of the most important political work in our research sites—in terms of governing the city, providing services, planning the future, allocating public resources, and defining public good—was not necessarily managed by public (government) institutions nor defined as political. Instead, when nonprofit organizations did the work of government, the work tended to be construed as voluntary or philanthropic activity. When government agencies outsourced work to private for-profit organizations, the action was construed as good business. In either case, such public work was not construed as political per se.

In this and subsequent chapters, we highlight the work of some key public-private partnerships to illustrate how political restructuring and nongovernmental organizations impact the extent to which various individuals and groups are included in efforts to shape the future of their communities. One organization, City Development Ventures (CDV), acted as a quasi-governmental organization and collaborated in numerous public-private partnerships oriented toward urban development in Durham, North Carolina. The case shows how government reorganization and new forms of activism offered a range of possibilities available to residents of Durham. However, capitalizing on these opportunities took significant time, resources, and knowledge. Ultimately, political restructuring privileged economic development interests, displaced social justice programs, and had clear anti-democratic tendencies.

Since the early 1990s, Frank Valek had been the chief executive officer (CEO) of CDV, a nonprofit organization that was devoted to urban development in central Durham and operated through a set of overlapping public-private partnerships. One of CDV's primary responsibilities was to help other people, particularly investors, implement their visions for particular properties or entire sections of the center city. We examine CDV and Valek here because CDV was successful, and it provides a model for understanding how public-private partnerships work. In fact, under Valek's tutelage other partnerships and nonprofit organizations prospered by emulating CDV's organizational strategies. While CDV was not representative of nonprofit organizations in Durham, other cities throughout the United States had similar urban development organizations. And, lastly, the work of CDV represents the possibilities for, and challenges to, local democracy posed by public-private partnership and non-governmental organizations. Valek was good at what he did, and CDV was relatively successful in achieving its goals, but we are concerned here with understanding the conditions that made CDV and its approach to shaping Durham's future possible and intelligible.

Thad first met with Frank early in 1997 in order to learn more about urban development in Durham and CDV's vision for how to develop the urban core. When he asked Frank to explain the details of CDV's vision for future urban development in Durham, Frank rose from his chair, stepped over a dozen or so manila folders of work-in-progress, and indicated some very general plans as he drew circles around sections of town depicted on a laminated four-foot Planimetrics map of Durham fastened to the wall.

> Well, there are basically five parts of downtown. [1] Within the loop is the office center where banks and institutions are located; I don't think we're likely to see any retail in there. [2] There's the Inner Village area that will probably be the biggest mixed-use area. [3] There is the Brightleaf area, which has retail, restaurants, and entertainment. Increasingly that is being considered [the center] of downtown. . . . Brightleaf is going to continue growing. [4] There's the Liggett and Myers [cigarette factory] area that will probably be mixed use, but you might see a major investor come in and do a lot with that property. We really don't know what is going to happen with that. . . . [5] Then there is the Ballpark area, which will probably have some retail right next to the ballpark. Then the rest, anything can happen. We've already planned some office space, but we don't know what will happen with the American Tobacco buildings. . . . This is all dependent on private interests and what they want to do with the properties. This is what we envision for the best-case scenario.[5]

One point to be made about this five-part vision pertains to the notable lack of industrial development or opportunities for blue-collar employment with livable wages and the predominance of service- or consumer-oriented development. In fact, later in the conversation Valek explained the need to be selective about the kind of development that does take place. He noted the undesirability of the potential development of new warehouses or adult entertainment venues. Mixed-use, articulated as the most desirable kind of development, in its ideal form, was imagined as a mix of upscale residential development (e.g., loft apartments) along with professional offices, boutiques, cafés, restaurants, and entertainment venues. (The Brightleaf Square tobacco warehouse district—on the western edge of downtown, not in the geographical center—was a good example of this.) So the urban development process was not, as Valek said, all dependent on private interests and what they want to do with the properties, but rather a process of steering certain kinds of investment while discouraging others.

The more significant issue to explore regarding this ethnographic encounter pertains to the basis of CDV's and Valek's authority and ability to influence urban development, particularly since CDV's plan for downtown coincided with, if not defined, the dominant vision for downtown revitalization in Durham in the 1990s. When Valek said, "*We* really don't know what is going to happen" or "*We've* already planned some office space, but *we* don't know what will happen," who was being invoked by the reference to "we"? How was that "we" connected to other institutions and the broader community? And what was the basis of their authority and influence?

The recent emphasis on market solutions through partnerships, entrepreneurialism, and greater commitment to private and nongovernment interests documented in chapter 6 has changed municipal government and the possibilities for democratic civic engagement. These conditions of political restructuring have made organizations like City Development Ventures, Halifax Horizons, and other groups described in this book both possible and influential. While one leader of an economic development agency often complained that his city government's inefficiency was one of his greatest obstacles for accomplishing his work, in fact his work was *predicated* on the relative weakness of local government.

Valek illustrated this in the following way:

It is hard to get things done in Durham because [city government] is not effective. If there is a dead tree downtown, you have to get four agencies to do anything about a tree box. So we just go and cut the tree down, and then the city agencies get pissed off at us. [Our agency] wants responsibility for downtown. City government is just too complicated. There is too much dead wood.[6]

Valek proposed that city government could be more streamlined if there were a "point person" or an agency that serves as a "one-stop shopping center" for business leaders who want to work with the city on economic development: "We want to make [the county economic development officer] in charge of city deals too. He takes care of deals with the county, and we would like to see that all consolidated."[7] In fact, the city did institute a new office for economic development in 1998. This had the effect of strengthening the position of nongovernmental interests by making city government more responsive to private interests and nongovernmental organizations.

The above dialogue drew attention to a municipal government that lacked resources to accomplish its ever-expanding demands, as well as the process in

which agents of public-private partnership circumvented government procedures. This did not, however, imply that such circumvention was unsanctioned
by city government. In fact, this organization was authorized to act as a quasi-
governmental institution, and largely defined the vision for future urban development.

In an interview, the city manager confirmed this. When asked about visions
for downtown redevelopment, he suggested that Thad talk with Valek and
explained that Valek had a clearer idea of what was happening in the urban
core. However, not everyone in city government—and certainly not all of the
city councilors—consented to the centrality of nongovernmental organizations
in acting as a catalyst of urban redevelopment, as was apparent on many occasions.

Valek himself described an ongoing conflict with one city councilor: "[The]
council makes it difficult for revitalization. They say they are for it, but . . .
[there is one city council member who] always asks, 'What does this do for
Northeast Central Durham' [a largely underserved, and relatively poor part of
the city]?"[8]

Thus there was a perception, and indeed a reality, that the market-oriented
tendencies of government and the strength of nongovernmental organizations
did not serve all residents of the community in the same way and neglected
entire neighborhoods. Northeast Central Durham, for example, was not considered to be in the domain of CDV, even though it was as close to the central
business district as Brightleaf Square. That neighborhood had its own community associations and nonprofit organizations, however ineffective and ill
equipped they may have been at promoting community improvement. In Halifax County, municipal boundaries sometimes excluded African-American
neighborhoods, thereby denying them access to public resources.

If the public-private partnerships in each of our research sites (e.g., CDV,
Halifax Horizons) were authorized to act on behalf of the public good, but not
entirely accountable to all residents of these sites, to whom were they accountable? The question of accountability can be answered in three parts. First, public-private partnerships like the downtown development partnerships in
Durham and Fayetteville and the regional economic development partnerships
in each of the counties had operating budgets that came partly from public
funds (city and/or county government) as well as from private donations, all of
which varied from year to year. The funding was contingent on the success and
agreeability of the organization's work. This is what is meant when political
leaders talk about a brand of government concerned with "empowering rather
than serving";[9] some oversight came from government and elected officials,
but CDV was inspired largely by its relationship to other nongovernmental
organizations and private interests (which also had strong influence in city and
county government).

Second, the organizational structures of the partnerships were in place, in part, to liaise with other community members. At the core of the partnerships were organizations, like many other nonprofit organizations, comprised of a board of directors, an executive board, and a chairperson, who oversaw any operating staff (such as Frank Valek). Although the boards were not exclusive, they were almost entirely comprised of business leaders and prominent members of related nonprofit organizations. The chairperson received input from the community and acted on behalf of the board to direct the actions of the operating staff.

Third, since these organizations typically had a 501(c)(3) tax-exempt status, their actions were monitored by the Internal Revenue Service (IRS). The IRS set limits on the way that nonprofit revenues could be used. For example, the IRS stipulated that nonprofit organizations should not operate for the financial benefit of individual stakeholders and that revenue may not be used for certain kinds of political lobbying.[10] Both of these stipulations, however, were too ambiguous to establish tangible criteria for oversight. In the matter of financial benefit, some of the board members were property owners in the areas they served, bankers, real estate agents, and business leaders who stood to benefit from the success of their respective organization. Although no member of any of these boards would stand to reap direct profits from the organization they served with, it was precisely the intent of CDV and Halifax Horizons, for example, to benefit the economic interests of real estate developers and others business leaders. And as far as lobbying was concerned, advocating for economic development was another stated goal of each economic development partnership. Yet, these actions were often seen as somehow being apolitical. For example, CDV was trying to be sensitive to what it portrayed as simple market demands, or to operate successfully within the market. Here, the market is construed as being outside the realm of politics.

This attitude highlights the way that, under neoliberal regimes, economic interests were often taken for granted as an integral part of the public good, an understanding that rendered opposing perspectives political as it elevated business interests to a supercitizen status. While Frank Valek benefited from a logic that defined economic development as an unquestioned good, his less influential counterparts in Northeast Central Durham, for example, were typically construed as special interest, political, and lacking the ability to partner with city government or other organizations. The same comparison could be made between the Halifax Horizons agenda and that of the Concerned Citizens of Thornton, introduced in chapter 3. Social-justice and human-service organizations had the same political status and, as such, were not able to operate as freely or raise funds as effectively as economic development organizations.

Furthermore, operating a successful nongovernmental organization required some expertise in addition to financial and symbolic resources. What little oversight was in place to monitor the actions of nongovernmental organizations was a disproportionately onerous burden for some small organizations. Maintaining an organization took time, some business acumen, and/or administrative resources. Neoliberalism and political restructuring also privileged people and organizations with clearly stated goals and measurable outcomes, which some social-service agencies struggled with. That put many social-justice and human-service organizations at a further disadvantage in relation to economic-development organizations.

"Selling out of an Empty Wagon": Visions and Omissions in Halifax Horizons

"Industry follows infrastructure." This was an argument commonly made by elected officials, chamber of commerce representatives, and economic development officers in Halifax County. Local leadership in Halifax and other counties used this slogan to justify all kinds of public outlays for such projects as the construction of airports, roads, sewer lines, and industrial parks. One Halifax County leader in economic development expressed this view as he explained the importance of building an industrial park and "shell building" (a hollow frame structure equipped with water, sewer, fiber-optics, and natural gas hookups), with the belief or hope that it would attract businesses to relocate to the area off I-95. He said,

> [Before we built the shell building] we didn't really have a product to sell. . . . We were trying to "sell out of an empty wagon." And that's very difficult to do. Now we have a product to sell. Economic development encompasses a lot of different areas. Product development is one of them. Not only does it involve going out and finding somebody to come in and establish a company and provide jobs and tax base for the county, but it also means that you've got to develop your product. And that's what we've been doing.

The "empty wagon" to which this man was referring is a sparsely populated county in northeastern North Carolina where once-large plantations gave way, after the Civil War, to smaller peanut, cotton, and tobacco farms and eventually to dispersed small factories and textile manufacturing. The current challenges of increased mechanization in local industrial and agricultural production and the departure of jobs from the county to other regions of the world are forcing local leadership to be creative. In this context, economic development schemes designed to bring outside investment to a locality like Halifax County and to retain existing companies have fostered important collaboration between government officials and local business leaders. Here again, this dual process of thinking about places in terms of their exchange value (rather than their livability or use value) and putting business interests at the center of decision making defines important aspects of the contemporary local political environments.

The people of Halifax County are well aware that jobs in the county are on the decline. It has become increasingly difficult to forge a livelihood out of the land in small-scale agricultural enterprises, and many of the remaining commercial and industrial jobs in the county offer very low wages. Halifax County continues to provide some of its residents with decent-paying professional jobs in local businesses and educational institutions; however, many residents are working more, getting paid less, and, often, having to commute long distances to work and shop. This sense of dire economic straits helped local Halifax County leadership to justify using public funds, infrastructure, and other resources to try to attract outside investment (such as feces plants) and/or jobs by trying to build a better airport, build better roads, expand telecommunications infrastructure, and steer other public services (such as sewer lines) to areas for potential business development, rather than to residences that still need them.

In 1997, a coalition of economic-development proponents from Halifax County government, the chamber of commerce, and other proponents of their vision of progress formed a public-private, nonprofit organization called "Halifax Horizons." Headed by representatives from the county's major businesses as well as current and past government leaders, this group of business- and market-oriented government leaders pulled together the funds and political will to build an industrial park and a shell building complete with municipal sewer collection system, natural gas, and enough water pressure and volume to douse an industrial fire.

Halifax Horizons was a public-private partnership comprised of some of Halifax County's key power brokers and economic leaders. While this group was a significant political force, it had not been subject to the processes of voting or public scrutiny. Furthermore, the group had highly exclusive membership. In 1997 its leaders came from a local affiliate of Nationwide Insurance, Heavenly Ham, *The Daily Herald*, Champion Paper, some smaller real estate agencies, Roanoke Valley Energy, and a pool of former elected officials. The county manager, a chamber of commerce representative, and the Halifax development commissioner were all ex-officio members.

Like other business-oriented public-private partnerships in our five communities, Halifax Horizons is an institution formed to redress the problems associated with economic restructuring and the complex issues associated with the increasing demands placed on restructured local governments. With tight budgets and with aspirations to attract wealth, public-private partnerships like the local Halifax Horizons economic development partnership and the regional "Northeast Partnership" (a quasi-governmental agency comprised of business and government leaders in North Carolina's sixteen northeastern counties) have attempted to pool the resources of local governments and businesses in order to court large-scale capitalist economic development projects. Based on the recommendations of the State Department of Commerce, Halifax Horizons established a four-point plan that the group thought would be most beneficial to the county's economic development: (1) create an industrial park with a shell building, (2) establish a grant program for relocating and expanding industrial prospects, (3) increase Halifax Development Commission's and the local chamber of commerce's marketing efforts, and (4) offer a revolving loan fund for new and expanding businesses. Their arguments were compelling enough for the local governing bodies to justify allocating tens of thousands of dollars of federal, state, county, municipal, and private monies to build the shell building and other similar projects for a (as yet unknown) company that *may* someday locate in Halifax. These incentives are in addition to all of the state-level benefits, such as good, low-tuition universities, community colleges, highways, low wages, absence of unions, industrial revenue bonds, association with Research Triangle Park, tax incentives/credits and abatements (especially in the state's neediest counties), tax-free bonds and loan guarantees, employment assistance and training in the state's community colleges, and, to the numerous public-private partnerships oriented toward developing new high technology, the area's natural beauty and inexpensive land.

As in many other places dominated by landscapes of production across the United States, this county has made great efforts to salvage its economy. This investment hadn't paid off by the end of our field work, as this Halifax County businesses/economic development leader suggested:

> When you look at our goals, [the] mission statement [of economic development agencies in the county] is "to increase the wealth of Halifax County and its citizens." And this is achieved by the creation of good-paying jobs and investment in the tax base. Well, we've done good on one, bad on the other. The good comes with the increased tax base, [which] comes with expansions. We've had new equipment installed. . . . Unfortunately in today's climate, every company is in a global economy—in a global market. They've got to compete with companies that have very low labor costs, so productivity becomes an issue that each employee has to be as productive as possible to compete with those low-wage countries like in the Caribbean Basin, Mexico, and areas like that. . . . The good news, I suppose, is that although there is some [company] downsizing going on, the commitment of the companies here to invest in the equipment to make the employees here more productive citizens speaks volumes to me.

The investments in economic development don't seem to be paying off as much as Halifax County residents would like. And other infrastructure needs have been neglected. Halifax County being one of the poorest counties in the state, more than 5 percent of its houses rely on outhouses or pipes that dump untreated sewage directly into the ground or a waterway.[11] Rather than building sewage systems and other infrastructure to provide for current county residents, business and government leaders spent resources to build infrastructure for possible businesses, believing that quality of life for residents is contingent on localities' ability to promote economic development.

Approximately five miles from the shell building down Highway 903, the Runnymede community has inadequate sewage treatment. The families of Runnymeade moved there in the middle of the twentieth century in part because the land and housing were accessible to African-Americans and affordable. People also have family ties to the area, some attend church, and they are enmeshed in the kinds of social networks that form the substance of people's lives. People have different relationships to place than do corporations. People are bound by a sense of home and a desire for livability. Conversely, businesses are governed by economic profit logic.[12] The high clay content of the earth in this part of northeastern North Carolina is well suited for the cotton, peanuts, and tobacco that have thrived here since colonial times, but it's not an ideal place to locate the kind of unimproved septic systems now used in many rural places. Put into service when the neighborhood was created, these septic tanks were failing. Yet few residents could afford to install newer systems that meet the new codes. The combination of standing water (from waste backup and flooding) and the outhouses that were used in the county pose health hazards and an inhospitable stench, especially in the long Carolina summers with temperatures regularly approaching a humid one hundred degrees.

Runnymeade was (and still is) a predominantly African-American unincorporated community that abuts the predominantly white township of Halifax to its east. For years Halifax Township resisted annexing Runnymeade partly because the cost of providing municipal services has been deemed financially imprudent for both the township and Runnymeade residents. Before Runnymeade was annexed, in 1998, widespread opposition to annexation was built around the argument that Halifax did not have the resources to incorporate this relatively low-income neighborhood into its borders and the less morally persuasive argument that residents of Runnymeade could not easily afford the increase in taxes that the annexation would precipitate.[13] Many people assume that it is an individual family's responsibility to provide for its own waste water disposal system, at least in rural areas. This has long been the case in Halifax County and throughout North Carolina.

The spatial exclusion of Runnymeade through unexamined assumptions is common. In this case, a predominantly African-American community had been systematically excluded from a municipality and thereby denied much-needed basic services until the summer of 1998, when it was finally granted some municipal service (but not annexed) after a long fight by a group of well-organized Runnymeade residents. Whether this spatial exclusion, with its consequences for Runnymeade, arose out of an overtly malicious plan, racist biases operating in conjunction with tight budgets have created a discriminatory environment in which this particular community has had few options but to deal with pools of raw sewage and the associated health hazards on its own. Meanwhile, the county and state continued to allocate money for sewage service (as well as high-pressure water service, electricity, natural gas, and fiber-optic telecommunications cables) to areas outside of municipalities where yet-unnamed industries may *someday* locate. And there is little evidence that if industries do locate in this area (and *if* they decide to stay), they will actually improve the quality of life for the majority of Halifax County residents. Comparing this investment in infrastructure to attract industry to the lack of investment in public schools and other public infrastructure highlights Halifax County as a striking example of the concept of "place over people," of putting the marketability of place over the well being of those who live in the place. The effects of this doctrine have brought some economic development to the county, but the poverty and lack of infrastructure that so many Halifax County residents face is evidence that perhaps it is time for a new approach.

Some Visions Do "Succeed": The Case of Research Triangle Park

Sometimes when a group of people has a clearly articulated vision for a community's future and the means to make that vision a reality, it can pay off in big ways. In the 1950s, a group of government and business leaders conjured up a vision of the Research Triangle Park (RTP) and "turned poor dirt into pay dirt." At the time, the state's dominant industries of furniture, tobacco, and textiles were starting to show signs of decline. In order to emulate the emerging successes of the university-business partnerships at Boston-Harvard-MIT (which would develop into the successful high-tech Route 128 region) and around Stanford (which laid the foundation for the growth of Silicon Valley), they bought hundreds of acres with public tax money and private donations from Wachovia Bank and other local business leaders, formed the Research Triangle Foundation (a nonprofit organization), and began courting high-tech research and development firms in the fields of computer technology, pharmaceuticals, government research labs, and so on. Operating outside the realm of public scrutiny, this partnership used public and private funds to fundamentally transform the region. Drawing from the resources at Duke University, UNC–Chapel Hill, and North Carolina State University, they formed formal and informal partnerships that would bridge the gap between scholarship and business. Among these partnerships was the North Carolina Biotechnology Center, a publicly funded research institution that offers services to businesses in RTP. Unlike Halifax Horizons, the vision of RTP *has* successfully transformed the region over the past four decades.

There are two important issues to remember when discussing the successes of RTP. First, focusing only on the successes obscures the fact that even North Carolina's RTP region has profound poverty. Durham County residents have one of the highest per capita incomes in the state, but also some of the worst poverty rates. With its extreme wealth gap, Durham's high-tech economic miracle needs to be coupled with the question, "miracle for whom?" Second, the RTP example also diverts attention from the fact that North Carolina, like many other states, has numerous office and industrial parks that lie virtually empty. They have the entire infrastructure in place, shell buildings ready for occupation, and subsidies ready to go. Despite significant public outlays, many publicly funded office parks, like the Halifax County shell building, have not produced all that their visions foresaw.

The idea that Durham has experienced an "economic miracle" has been firmly established in various fora. Durham has been dubbed "a best place to live and do business" by *Money Magazine,* "a great place for Gays" by *Out Magazine,* "one of the best places for women" by *Ladies Home Journal,* "a community of activists" by the *Utne Reader,* and so on. These designations may well be warranted, and they are a great compliment to the local community. However, such proclamations of community vitality paint a picture that hides the reality of ongoing profound poverty and the fact that not everyone in Durham is taking part in this economic miracle and democratic and pluralistic cornucopia.

Durham's current economy is simply not producing quality blue-collar jobs in the quantity that the city needs. And a large number of unemployed, underemployed, and underpaid people lack the qualifications to benefit from the new high-tech economy. So even though Durham is a great place to live for white-collar knowledge workers from far and wide, the decline of the older industrial (tobacco and textile) economic base has left many of Durham's residents with a much reduced source of income.

Some residents of Durham sorely miss the relatively high wages that tobacco factories gave high school–educated, unionized labor. In the late 1980s, tobacco and textile production left Durham for other areas of the American South and for developing countries with lower wages and lower real estate costs. The jobs that high school graduates can expect now in Durham are the low-wage retail or food-service jobs that are relatively abundant throughout the city or the temporary maintenance or janitorial jobs of the region's prosperous research and industrial parks. Even though Durham had an exceptionally low official unemployment rate (around 1.2 percent in 1997), the true figure was higher. Underemployment was a serious problem, and many fully employed people have trouble handling the costs of increasing property values and increasing costs of living. Despite this working-class reality, images of tobacco manufacturing and the city's blue-collar identity have become a per-ceived liability for certain sectors of a community that are trying to fashion the city's image as a high-tech Sunbelt success story.[14]

Much of RTP's success is attributed to a set of historical factors that are no longer present in Durham or the Research Triangle at large. RTP's leadership (past and present) conveyed to us that they do not think that anything like RTP could be created in our contemporary political landscape, largely because there would be too much political scrutiny. In the 1950s and 1960s, a private land development company was able to discreetly purchase thousands of acres with public and private funds and effectively redirect the region's future.[15] RTP's leadership (and retrospective accounts of the Park's history) notes that it was a sense of profound poverty and state of desperation that made the Park possible. Because North Carolina had the second-lowest per-capita income in the United States in 1955, and its three primary industries were waning, there was an intense political will to seek alternative economic possibilities. That desire for experimentation gave North Carolina's business and government leadership license to take liberties (e.g., to secretly purchase thousands of acres of private individuals' land and silently make arrangements for sewer, water, and roads on that land) that are unthinkable in the region's contemporary political climate. This kind of political work (at least on this scale) is widely considered a thing of the past in Durham.

To the city's business leadership's chagrin, much of the region's continuing poverty is concentrated in the eastern part of the city in an area stretching from Duke University through downtown and on toward RTP. The social costs of such poverty are myriad. For example, Durham is known as having one of the highest violent crime rates in the state.

Furthermore, for the last three decades development in Durham has taken place on the periphery of town in a pattern of growth, commonly known as "urban sprawl," that makes poor use of land, puts undue stress on water and natural resources, and causes traffic problems. Ironically, the successes of Research Triangle Park have helped to create the problems that contemporary urban planning and development seeks to redress.

As we have begun to outline earlier in this chapter, in an attempt to address these problems and ensure that other parts of Durham continue to prosper eco-nomically, urban planners and residents of Durham created the Durham 2020 Plan. This plan draws on ideas that have been successful in cities like Portland, Oreland, San Antonio, Texas, and Baltimore, Maryland. It aims to foster growth in high-density corridors and thereby reduce commuting distances and pro-mote public transit and other modes of transportation. The plan also calls for more mixed-use development where shopping, employment, and residential developments lie in close proximity. Furthermore, these high-density corridors are likely to change the character of the main gateways to the city so that people traveling from RTP will have attractive corridors for traveling to and from the city, if they choose to avoid the impoverished parts of town.

The Durham 2020 Plan emerges out of a different set of perceived problems and a different political climate than the vision for Research Triangle Park or Halifax Horizons. Whereas in Halifax people from Champion Paper and the local newspaper, along with other business and government leaders, formed a partnership to put together an industrial park and affect policy in Halifax, Durham's political arena has an entirely different policy. The Research Triangle Foundation and the corporations in RTP have an official policy of not weighing in on local political issues. As much as possible, they (officially) try not to affect local politics and to remain apolitical.[16] While companies officially remain politically neutral, they often encourage their employees to be active in their local communities, and indeed they are. Key leaders in local nonprofit organizations, citizen's boards, neighborhood associations, etc., all have strong RTP ties. Accordingly, they serve the interests (of class or otherwise) of RTP.

The 2020 Plan was an attempt to redress all of the problems of Durham. It aimed to decrease crime, build more livable/self-policing neighborhoods, improve auto traffic in South Durham (around the Research Triangle Park), increase public transit, and improve Durham's public face. The 2020 Plan turned out to be a plan that many different people with different interests could buy into. Diverse activists, business people, and others supported 2020 Plan.[17]

Visions and Omissions

During our research, one thing that soon became clear was that the people who benefit economically from shifting economies, movement of capital, movements of people, and speculation about the future have a unique perspective on the current condition. Such privileged perspectives in no way represent all people in their respective communities. In our interaction with contemporary developers, chamber of commerce leaders, architects, planners, and other visionaries of local communities, we noted that they often handily recast would-be problems as "opportunities." Where others we met were troubled with uncertainty and alienation, this class of affluent speculators at times seemed nearly giddy about the prospects that lay ahead for them. People who stood to prosper from contemporary economic change, like Jimmie Jordan, the Durham man introduced in the opening paragraph of this chapter, advocated for more change that reflects their notions of a better future. Meanwhile, people like labor organizer Harvey Catawba sought alternative ways to address a different set of public concerns. Others have tuned out official city politics altogether because such politics did not reflect their day-to-day experience or visions for what changes should be effected.

The political reorganization and economic restructuring described in earlier chapters made new kinds of local autonomy possible and relevant.[18] Ideally, these processes should have offered equal potential for all residents of a place to have a say in the development of their future. In this arena, business interests, above all other interests, came to define *the public good* and to dominate the allocation of *public goods*. Economic restructuring and government reorganization pose as many challenges to democracy as they inspire. Our research found that nonbusiness representatives (people who think primarily in terms of livability or use value) have had limited opportunities to allocate public resources in ways that they see fit. Individuals and community organizations were successful when they linked a community development project to more dominant projects that had the support of chambers of commerce and other business-oriented economic development coalitions. In short, alternative visions for the future and/or more community development projects have been successful only by virtue of their ability to form alliances with business-oriented projects. Part of this process had been the increasing dominance of public-private partnerships, nonprofit organizations, chambers of commerce, and even individual business leaders as centrally important players in the local decision-making game. Community development plans in our five research sites were part of a situation in which it is more likely for public resources to be devoted to creating the infrastructure for an office park than to ensuring that people only five minutes from that office park have the means to adequately dispose of human waste. City funds were more likely to be allocated to create downtowns as recreation areas and shopping centers for the wealthy while thousands of people who live within miles of such areas do not have easy access to public transportation, food shopping, or jobs. Vision plans like the Durham 2020 Plan, Fayetteville's Marvin Plan, and Halifax Horizons highlight a dynamic set of relationships and images of the future wherein partially public and private interests came together to redefine public policy measures.

In the opening pages of this chapter we introduced Jimmie Jordan and Harvey Catawba for two alternative perspectives on Durham's urban landscape. With Jimmie's vision for adaptive reuse of old tobacco buildings, we showed that his position as a real estate developer led him to see the world in such a way that he celebrated economic restructuring and the opportunities it engendered for the people in his field. We also looked to Harvey Catawba, another Durham resident, for an alternative perspective on the limitations of market-oriented visions that focus too heavily on the exchange value of a place at the expense of its use value. For Jimmie, economic and social change was an opportunity to accumulate capital. Durham was a landscape of financial opportunity. And those opportunities allowed him to look beyond the people who have not benefited from Durham's "new economy." For Harvey, economic restructuring has brought poverty and insecurity for people who struggle to find a foothold from which to assert their own interests. When he looked out across the same spaces in which Jimmie operates, he saw a landscape of destruction, marked by needle tracks and human bodies ravaged by the symbolic and physical violence endemic to abrupt shifts in the capitalist flows that moved an important category of jobs to another locality, marks that were largely invisible from Jimmie's privileged position. Thus, in reflecting on the new possibilities for direct civic engagement that were available to Frank Valek, Jimmie Johnson, the leaders of Halifax Horizons, and even Harvey Catawba, we can ask, Is this democracy?

Although Harvey was often frustrated by his inability to create the kinds of changes in Durham that would impact the lives of the urban poor, his narrated tours of the city were a reminder that he holds a relatively privileged position in local politics. He offers a strong voice in city council meetings, and other local leaders know him on a first-name basis. For other Durham citizens, working toward an alternative future for the city seems a distant possibility.

As Harvey and Thad drove out of one quiet, affluent neighborhood, they found themselves behind a large, beat-up sedan with four men inside.

"Reefer!" Harvey exclaimed. "You smell that? Take a whiff."
"Yeah, I smell it," Thad responded.
"Man that is strong!"

The driver of the car looked in his rearview mirror and saw Harvey's truck, which had previously been used by the police to transport evidence. Harvey had bought it at a city auction. The driver of the car seemed to throw something out the car window as he repeatedly and nervously glanced in his rearview mirror, swerving slightly, not watching where he was going, out of fear that he was under surveillance.

8 Public Business as Usual

Few Americans would really want government to act just like a business—making quick decisions behind closed doors for private profit. If it did, democracy would be the first casualty.

—David Osborne and Ted Gaebler, *Reinventing Government*

Introduction: Public Affairs in An Age of Market Rule

In this chapter we ask, Is public business now becoming a contradiction in terms? Is the public of citizens and residents becoming divorced from the institutions of local political life, and is public business instead becoming increasingly the province of business—of private enterprise? Are private entrepreneurs becoming supercitizens while other residents are increasingly treated as subcitizens in local public affairs? Unfortunately, when local elites act on the basis of these neoliberal preoccupations, they privilege the views and influence of business people and other elites and exclude many other citizens from full participation—and at times *any* participation—in the institutions of local democracy.

We will also examine the processes, mechanisms, and strategies by which a very large proportion of residents of North Carolina communities are either discouraged from participating in these institutions or, worse yet, excluded entirely from participation. We see these elite practices and processes of exclusion as a major impediment to the realization of a fuller and more democratic public life in our communities. The net effects are deeply corrosive of local democracy, and extend far beyond the empty polling places on election days and media stereotypes about apathetic or angry voters.

Central to the domination of neoliberal thinking in our communities has been the market logic by which economic development is now being judged—in short, as the shibboleth now goes, can the community "compete in the global economy"? Can it offer the attractions that will bring in roving global investors to revive the locale, which would otherwise surely undergo decline if left solely to its own devices or to the decreased largesse of national and local governments? In response to this challenge, the elites of communities in North Carolina and elsewhere in our country have with great inventiveness and at times cunning created new institutions and practices and maintained and reworked older ones that have quickly and often without much critical comment come to occupy a major role in public life. The new institutions are hybrids that bring together practices that were previously distinct to private enterprise, local government, or civic associations. As hybrids, they either incorporate market-oriented logics into collective policy goals by restructuring local governments in ways that move the latter away from the redistribution of resources toward the priority of market performance, or they incorporate the efforts of philanthropy to remediate the adverse consequences of policy decisions that incorporate such logics.

In what follows, we first examine two such hybrids—the market-oriented partnership most often called a "public-private partnership" (see chapter 6) and the task force. Market-oriented partnerships and task forces are principal mechanisms through which elites carry out the strategies that seek to attain their goals. Second, we consider informal, often unspoken practices of etiquette and elite networking that operate both within and beyond these institutions, which simultaneously include those who have mastered these practices and exclude those who have not. Third, having set out the elite *strategies* emerging within these institutional hybrids, we describe elite *tactics* for managing public life that exclude many from participation. Elites employ these tactics within the operation of market-oriented partnerships and task forces, but use them outside these institutions as well. These tactics are among the most effective yet insidious ways that class and white privilege operated in the five communities we studied. They include

controlling eligibility so that only certain groups and not others are defined as having "standing"—the recognized right to be represented in decision making;

controlling the degree of visibility and disclosure of affairs conducted "for" but not "by" the public in these partnerships and task forces;

setting and scheduling agendas such that certain issues never make it onto agendas and attendance at public meetings is impossible or difficult for groups whom elites see as bringing up "irrelevant" issues;

freezing out, by ignoring the presence and statements of those who dissent against majority opinions or decisions;

claiming the right to authoritatively represent the histories of minority or dissenting groups while erasing (or ignoring) their members' testimonies of the past.

These elite tactics represent the petty insults, the unkind little cuts, the small swipes at opportunity, that accumulate to make up a micropolitics of anti-democratic practice, and that reinforce class and white privilege.

Neoliberal Hybrids: A Market-Oriented Partnership for Fayetteville's "Revitalization"

Local political and economic elites have promoted market-oriented partnerships and the private nonprofit corporations associated with them over the last two decades as one variety of innovative response by "enterprising," "competitive," and "market-oriented" state and local governments to the crisis in government dating from the late 1970s. The crisis dates from the passage of Proposition 13, the prototypical "taxpayer's revolt" in California in 1978, in which local property taxes, traditionally the source of local government funding, were cut in half by law. Proposition 13 spawned a rash of similar laws and referenda in other states such as North Carolina in subsequent years. Faced with imminent declines in their fiscal bases and the national constraints on locales described in chapter 6, desperate municipal governments sought out the private sector and formed joint ventures with it. In addition to the urban "revitalization" projects like the one discussed in this chapter, local elites have formed market-oriented partnerships and private nonprofit corporations in other areas of municipal governance—the provision of utilities and waste management, and the operation of schools, prisons, parks, libraries, and homeless shelters.[1]

In each such arrangement, local governments expend public funds in ways that subsidize the private corporate operation of these facilities and programs on a for-profit basis benefit stakeholders—corporate shareholders, public agencies, private suppliers and contractors, and consumers or clients. Stakeholders who are market players (like investors, consumers, customers), who have the power to structure markets (like governments), or who have the resources to ameliorate their adverse effects (like nongovernment organizations) replace citizens and citizens' groups as constituents. The change is more than one of terminology. For instance, under the PRWORA law of 1996, TANF recipients administered to by for-profit corporations are treated as individual customers or clients—not as citizens who should have a collective voice in their own governance.[2] The claim goes that government has thereby reinvented itself.[3]

As recounted in chapter 6, market-oriented partnerships and associated private nonprofit corporations first came into existence as an entrepreneurial response to the 1970s fiscal crises of America's municipalities, and elites affected by neoliberal thinking promptly installed them as enduring institutions of local governance in North Carolina and elsewhere. These institutions now purport-edly provide local governments with the advantages of efficiency, low cost, accountability to civic stakeholders, and flexibility, and improve on the bad old years of rigid, inefficient, expensive, and unaccountable public service. For local elites, the very notion of urban revitalization, as we demonstrate below, is an extended metaphor based on the notion of the dying body of the city's center revived only by the vitality of the profit motive and private enterprise.

In urban revitalization, market-oriented partnerships consist of growth coalitions of local elected officials, public bureaucrats, financiers, and business people. They join together in projects that are in large part publicly funded to stimulate new investment in urban America's central business districts and downtowns, and to bring "bring back" the middle class.[4] In theory at least, they seek not only to create new profit-driven real estate and facilities that will attract businesses to relocate from outlying areas to the city's downtown core but also to ameliorate the living and working conditions of poorer downtown residents. However, as we shall see, there is much reason to doubt whether the latter goal is ever a serious priority. The private nonprofit corporation serves as the operational arm of the market-oriented partnership, and receives both pub-lic and private funds to execute the project envisioned by the partnership. (Such private nonprofit corporations, also known as "quasi-public redevelop-ment corporations," have special legal rights, such as being able to receive gov-ernment funds, condemn and consolidate land, issue tax-exempt bonds, and offer tax abatements—although they cannot engage in direct, for-profit activi-ties.)[5] In addition to local elected officials and bureaucrats from government agencies, the other partners of the partnership are private for-profit enterprises: land developers, bankers, and the proprietors and managers of finance compa-nies, real-estate construction businesses, architectural firms, and landscape design firms.

Let us turn to one such market-oriented partnership, the Marvin Plan pro-posed for downtown Fayetteville, and its associated private nonprofit corpora-tion, the Fayetteville Partnership. We discussed in the previous chapter the utopian visions of the future represented in market-oriented partnerships like Halifax Horizons—that is, their projective and imaginative dimensions. In this chapter, in contrast, we examine the tensions between the idealized vision of the Marvin Plan and its actual implementation in the operation of the Fayet-teville Partnership. These tensions revealed the Marvin Plan to be a rhetorical project, that is, an effort at persuasion directed toward citizens and citizens' groups who had yet "to get behind it." This demonstrates a more general point—that the rise of neoliberal thinking to dominance in our local democra-cies, exemplified in projects such as the Marvin Plan, is unfinished, uncertain, and still very much open to debate. These tensions also constructed the follow-ing "truth" of sorts: namely, that stakeholders and not citizens—particularly not citizens who are poor, undereducated, or African-American—*matter* in the formation and execution of public policy. Both the supporters of the Marvin Plan and its opponents, despite their disagreements, agreed to certain shared assumptions—one of which was the centrality of stakeholders and the irrelevance of some citizens to urban revitalization.

In 1994, a "grassroots committee of forty business and civic leaders" in Fayetteville was formed, and soon after that began working with the architectural firm of Robert Marvin and Associates of Columbia, South Carolina, to create the Marvin Plan, the revitalization plan for downtown Fayetteville. The Marvin Plan offered an idyllic image of the downtown's future as the center for North Carolina's fourth largest metropolitan area. Phase I of the Plan offered the following bird's-eye vision: "There's a 45-acre park in the middle of a thriving arts district, filled with theaters, museums, galleries, and restaurants. There's a performing arts center, an amphitheater, an open-air pavilion, and a series of lakes around which the people of this community play, live and work."[6] Among the amenities would be "a series of shallow lakes. . . . The displaced earth will be used to build an architecturally sculptured mound so unique that it will be as closely associated with Fayetteville as the battery is with Charleston, the arch is with St. Louis, and the River Walk is with San Antonio." Things were to improve further in Phase II: "Just over 100 acres . . . have been allocated for a public recreation area and the campus of a new magnet school. . . . The area will have a city-run fitness center, gymnasium, swimming complex, softball field, 11 tennis courts, a track, a senior center, picnic shelters, 30 acres of reforestation and 13 acres of open fields. A bicycle trail will wind along Cross Creek."[7]

This self-described "grassroots committee" sought to portray the vision of an urban consumers' paradise, rather than the nitty-gritty details of its making, for they argued that image as much as—perhaps even more than—substance was at stake in the revitalization of downtown Fayetteville: "As you study this plan on paper, imagine it in place. Some day soon, this could be the image everybody has of Fayetteville. All we have to do is focus."

The Marvin Plan was an envisioned solution to a problem, a prescription for an illness. The web site for the Marvin Plan presented the image of the modern city as a living body. Although Fayetteville "continues to grow along a myriad of arteries, it lacks something vital—a heart. The natural heart of any city is its downtown, and . . . much of it remains stagnant. Between pockets that have been neglected and areas that have become associated with high rates of crime, Fayetteville has developed a serious problem that threatens our very vitality."[8]

But for Marvin Plan supporters "far worse than the reality was the perception" of Fayetteville as "Fayette-Nam." Fayette-Nam was the nightmarish image of a mélange of a downtown of topless bars, street prostitutes, derelict buildings, addictive drugs, violent crime, rowdy young enlisted-rank male soldiers from Fort Bragg, and poor African-American residents. The image of Fayette-Nam, they said, above all prevented the attraction of badly needed businesses and consumers to downtown Fayetteville and the support of the North Carolina legislature. As one industrial recruiter put it, "when an industry is looking at a place, what they are looking at is if we are going to move fifty or sixty people [in], are they going to be happy?" Obviously they wouldn't be, in Fayette-Nam. Fayetteville's revitalization program thus sought above all else to redress the shortcomings of its downtown's image.

Its envisioners' strategy was two-pronged: first "cleaning up" downtown, then "revitalizing" it with the features of the consumer's paradise of the Plan. "Cleanup" had begun several years previously with the forced relocation of Rick's Lounge, Fayette-Nam's largest and most notorious topless bar, out of the downtown area to the city's outskirts. A new town hall and police station took its place. According to a staff member of the Fayetteville Partnership, much remained to be done: "Downtown is very poor. We will distribute Buena Vista Terrace . . . [hedging a moment], I can't say too much because that is really up in the air right now . . . but what is for sure we have to do something with the rundown housing and clean up crime. We are working very closely with the police department." By "distribution," he meant the relocation of the estimated five to eight hundred poor, predominantly African-American residents of the Buena Vista Terrace housing project downtown. By the "cleanup" of crime, he referred to the violent crimes committed in connection with the drug trade. Meanwhile, "rundown housing" was to be demolished or, in some cases, converted into historic landmark buildings. This in turn was quite controversial, as it turned out, because several prominent developers and land owners owned properties located in the area downtown to be revitalized by the Marvin Plan, and some of them sat on the committee heading up the market-oriented partnership behind the Marvin Plan.

The second phase of the Marvin Plan, "revitalization" as such, was to consist of the reconstruction of the infrastructure of downtown—the building of middle- and high-cost residential housing and a new school, to start with, to draw thousands of new affluent residents to the city center. Equally important, downtown was to be visually revitalized with the refurbishing of more historic buildings like the "Market House"—a restored structure from the antebellum period, which now served as an icon for a revitalizing downtown. In its heyday, however, it was Cumberland County's slave auction house, a historical fact bitterly preserved in the collective memories of local African-Americans.

The public backers of the Marvin Plan consisted of a relatively small coalition of economic and political elites of Fayetteville and Cumberland County. Many of them served as managers and executives of private (for-profit) corporations, public agencies, and community associations—with several individuals being associated with more than one such organization. They thus played on the ambiguities of their affiliations: it was unclear whether their presence as prominent sponsors of the Marvin Plan implied only their own individual support or represented endorsements by the corporations, public agencies, or voluntary organizations they headed. At the center of this elite coalition were three organizations: the "Once and For All (OAFA) Committee"—a self-described "grassroots committee of . . . business and civic leaders"—its associated thirteen-member "Management Team," and the Director and staff of the nonprofit, private Fayetteville Partnership. The Management Team included several appointed public officials (e.g., the city manager and county manager) and representatives from the local chamber of commerce, from the private, nonprofit Fayetteville Area Economic Development Corporation, and the Fayetteville Partnership itself.

The fifty-one-member OAFA Committee consisted of most members of the Management Team, and in addition boasted several former and current elected officials, the heads of public agencies such as the Public Works Commission (PWC), and numerous prominent property developers, realtors, bankers, attorneys, clergymen, and retired military officers. Forty-six out of the fifty-one members of the "grassroots" OAFA Committee were white, contrasted to a city population where approximately two of every five residents were African-American. It is not an exaggeration to describe the Management Team and the OAFA Committee as, by and large, the white male establishment of Fayetteville—its civilian economic and political elite. Outsiders referred to this establishment as "the downtown crowd" or "the revitalization crowd."

The operational arm of the Management Team and the OAFA Committee was the Fayetteville Partnership, in particular, its director and staff. The Partnership was the incorporated organization that, under the direction of the Management Team and the OAFA Committee, oversaw the progress of the Marvin Plan, received money for it, and paid its bills. It was thus the financial conduit for funds received from city and county governments and from private contributors. The vast majority of the funds it received or was promised came from public sources ($500,000 from city and county governments) in contrast to private sources ($80,000 from OAFA Committee members and the chamber of commerce). But as a *private* nonprofit organization, the Partnership was not legally required to make public its business transactions, minutes of its meetings, or other sensitive materials.

Despite the appearance of a formidable crowd of supporters, the Marvin Plan and Fayetteville Partnership had an ambiguous and uncertain status. They had not received the full endorsement by vote from either the city council or county commissioners: while both "support[ed] the concept" of revitalization and voted $500,000 seed money for the Partnership to pay for the design phase being undertaken by Marvin's architectural firm, they did not commit either city or county governments to the execution of the Plan under the Partnership. Moreover, by the end of 1997, the actual achievements of the Plan consisted only of the drafting of its "schematic design" by Marvin's firm and were otherwise hypothetical—as yet, no old building had been razed, no lakes dug, no performing arts center or amphitheater was under construction.

The Marvin Plan was therefore still very much an ongoing rhetorical project—an effort at persuasion. But persuasion of whom? We asked the staff member of the Fayetteville Partnership whom we quoted above to tell us how the initiators of the Marvin Plan gathered support. It is crucial to note the dissonance between the democratic language he used in invoking the phrases "grassroots" and "going to the people"—and the actual composition of the elite stakeholders supporting the Marvin Plan (the OAFA Committee et al.):

> [The Plan] needed to be grassroots and therefore we call the action "A Complete Fayetteville For Once and For All" . . . so we put fifty people together that were representative of all, trying to include everybody. So we went to [every group] and asked them about downtown. It was a very positive process. If they were opposed, we would explain to them the philosophy behind the plan. . . . Ninety percent of those opposed to revitalization were won over.

Expanding on this he stated,

> The process of going to the people has been central. . . . Revitalization has been discussed for many years, but never solidified into a solid project. When it was decided that it was to be big, it also had to be grassroots . . . it had to come from the citizens. They have ownership. To make the revitalization grassroots, we identified forty groups. We got churches involved.

Three years after the Marvin Plan's inception, organized opposition to it emerged. In 1997 a group called Fayetteville Taxpayers for Accountability (FTA) began making public statements in meetings of concerned citizens, radio talk show appearances, and letters to editors. A large proportion of FTA leaders were retired military professional officers and their spouses; they originally served at the nearby army base and later retired to the Fayetteville area. Moreover, like Marvin Plan backers, FTA leaders were mostly white and male. FTA representatives criticized not only the features of the Marvin Plan but also the Partnership's lack of accountability to the "taxpayers" of Fayetteville, its not being open to public scrutiny. FTA leaders claimed that because meetings of the Partnership were not open to the public, there was no timely way for taxpayers to know how public funds were being spent, or to have input into decisions about these expenditures. They argued that although FTA supported downtown revitalization, private investors and not taxpayers should pay for it. Moreover, "building a big expensive park" was not as important as other priorities for downtown—education, roads, and preventing crime. They also held that the profits of the city-owned utility, the PWC—whose managers were prominent supports of the Marvin Plan—should not be used to finance it but instead should be returned to PWC customers. Beyond their public pronouncements, FTA leaders avowed that the "revitalization crowd" or "downtown crowd" of developers, their clients, and friends behind the Plan acted as if the public (city and county) funds allotted to the Plan were theirs to dispose of as they, themselves alone, saw fit: "there is a certain perception that the downtown Revitalization Crowd is entitled to this money, is entitled to get paid." As one FTA leader put it, "people are not included. When I say "people," I mean the broader population in the community. Particularly, the people who have not been associated with what is termed the 'downtown crowd,' or the 'Old Fay group.'" FTA spokesmen demanded that the city hold a referendum on the use of city funds for the Marvin Plan.

Supporters of the Marvin Plan quickly counterattacked by stating that they always intended to bring the issue to the voters, but only after the design was completed and its costs known. The prominent backer of the Plan quoted above stated, "We have never tried to cram this down the people's throats as we've been accused of." Moreover, the executive director of the Fayetteville Partnership argued in support of city and PWC funding for the Plan, stating that the private sector could not be expected to invest in downtown if the public sector was not itself willing to ante up funds for revitalization.[9] However, the executive director of the Partnership had also gone on record previously for having argued that secrecy and confidentiality were crucial to the undertakings of the Marvin Plan, precisely because private capital was at stake and downtown property markets were speculative: "[T]he [OAFA] committee often discusses confidential issues that have to do with private developers interested in downtown. . . . [M]aking the information public could jeopardize development deals or push up land prices."[10] In her view—which presumably reflected that of the entire OAFA Committee—full disclosure of the proceedings of the Committee demanded by critics was incompatible with its business dealings with private investors, which she saw as making downtown revitalization feasible and cost-effective.

In fact, Marvin Plan backers encountered a formidable opponent in the FTA, its leaders and members, who came to have standing and gain voice as *the* opposition to the Marvin Plan, when, for instance, an FTA spokesperson was invited by a city council member to speak before it about the deficiencies in the Marvin Plan, or when FTA members were given radio air time or covered by the local newspaper. In public fora and individual interactions, FTA leaders and spokespeople alluded at times implicitly, at others explicitly, to their experience as military technocrats who got things done as their qualification to challenge the Marvin Plan: "while we do have a lot of give-and-take and we disagree, we are willing to make a decision, be decisive, and move on. We also know how systems work." One FTA leader, in an aside to us, described FTA members as forward looking and willing to take risks:

> We see the needs of the future, they see a need for a dirt mound which will have a private restaurant on top. There are very few people involved in the dialogue. . . . The military brings a perspective that challenges the status quo, we have experiences that have taught us how to adapt, so we understand that things can be different. "Old" Fayetteville opposes change; they want to keep things the same.

The conflict between Marvin Plan backers and the FTA was a public drama of contention: both sides achieved standing, that is, became recognized as having legitimate concerns, and both sides were given voice—their opinions and arguments, however opposed, *mattered* and were given extensive coverage in the media. From a more abstract perspective, it is perhaps unsurprising that the one ideologically sustainable challenge to this market-oriented partnership came from a group like the FTA that could draw on technocratic and modernizing authority arising from their professional qualifications within that truly global and globalizing force—the U.S. military.

Now we are in a position to ask, Who was left in, and who was left out, of the politics of Fayetteville's urban revitalization? Despite their many disagreements over the Marvin Plan and their contrasting social origins, Marvin Plan backers and FTA members had much in common. Taken collectively, both groups were predominantly white in racial composition, male, professional, and middle- or upper-class in their economic positions. Both groups in different ways distanced themselves socially from poor African-American residents of downtown and from those who in prior decades (albeit not so much recently) had been among downtown's principal patrons—young enlisted-rank soldiers. Persons on both sides of the conflict over the Marvin Plan saw downtown residents and enlisted soldiers as the *objects* of "revitalization"—people to whom and for whom "revitalization" had to be done—and not as the *subjects* of revitalization who should play a role in deciding about revitalization or other priorities. Marvin Plan backers spoke of the several hundred residents of the Buena Vista Terrace public housing project downtown as in need of "distribution," that is, relocation. FTA leaders, consistent with their technocratic and hierarchical approach, sought to manipulate African-Americans in the city rather than work with them as equals, as evident for instance in FTA's campaign against the set-aside of PWC profits for the Marvin Plan: "We got the blacks going; they hate PWC! To them, the

PWC represents 'the man.'" FTA leaders (as their group's name indicated) identified themselves publicly with "taxpayers"—that is, with those whom they saw as paying the property taxes that would finance downtown revitalization, *not* with a broader category of citizens or voters including poorer downtown residents—who also paid property taxes, albeit indirectly through their rents.

The groups targeted by revitalization (downtown residents, enlisted-ranks soldiers) were poor or working people, most often racial minorities, associated imaginatively in characterizations made of downtown by both Marvin Plan backers and the FTA with decay, crime, sex, dilapidated dwellings, and drug addiction. White privilege manifested itself in these statements of cultural stereotypes that constructed stigma and argued for exclusion. These statements incited those with power to exclude those who were poor and less powerful from participation in the decisions that directly affected their lives, and this had important social consequences. These stereotypes reinforced prevailing patterns of institutional racism, and did so irrespective of individual participants' opinions or feelings about members of one race or another. It is in this sense that we said above that the tensions between the ideals and actual under-taking of the Marvin Plan—manifested in the publicly recognized drama of contention between Marvin Plan backers and the FTA—created a certain truism: that only certain propertied, powerful, or otherwise qualified stakeholders should participate in such weighty decision making, and not the mere citizens it most directly affected. But truisms like this one are beliefs that shape people's lives.

Those directly affected by the Marvin Plan could and did speak for themselves and had their own representatives, but were marginalized in the public debate set by the terms of the controversy between the Partnership and FTA. For instance, the comments of one African-American city councilwoman who strongly opposed the Marvin Plan in any form, and whom poorer African-American residents of downtown saw as their representative, were rarely mentioned in media coverage. She was politely ignored in council debates and treated as an eccentric old woman. African-Americans in Fayetteville saw downtown and its revitalization as primarily white people's preoccupations that would require a large proportion of the city's financial resources and increase city taxes, and thus would leave fewer public funds to be dedicated to social needs such as education of African-American neighborhoods elsewhere in the city. For instance, one prominent African-American leader put it thus:

White folks are downtown. Why are we concentrating on downtown when we here, in the black community, really need just as much development, economically speaking and otherwise, as downtown does? . . . Another thing is, downtown is your vagrants, your homeless, your poor, or your down-trodden. Who are they? They are black folks! The middle-class income black folks are saying: The reason why you want to develop downtown is to chase the poor black folks out of downtown!

Poorer African-Americans living downtown and elsewhere in the city, especially in recently annexed districts, expressed widespread indignation about the donation by the city-owned PWC of $10 million of its profits toward the Marvin Plan, at a time when it had just introduced a new $7 cut-off charge that most frequently affected them. Many African-Americans also felt deep antagonism toward the Market House, which was refurbished at the city's expense ($800,000) and made into the centerpiece and icon of the Marvin Plan. As one African-American put it, "to us, when I say us I mean blacks, it symbolizes the history of slavery. . . . [We call it] the Slave House."

Managing Public Business: Task Forces in Durham and Siler City

A task force is a one-time-only group of persons mobilized by a formal organization to perform a specific task. The task force appears originally to have been a military form of organization, which has been brought into broader usage through its use and reworking within large private corporations. In both military and corporate contexts, task forces are organized hierarchically under a leader or team of leaders, extremely goal oriented (rather than process oriented), internally disciplined, single-task, and temporary, and bound more by instrumentalism (staying on task) and goal (completing the task) than by internal codes of rules or regulations. From the military and corporations, the task force has more recently become installed in American public life, supplementing citizen's commissions and boards of inquiry as a more flexible mechanism for drawing on citizen participation in investigating a situation or problem, reporting on it to those in charge, and recommending—not requiring—policy changes on the basis of its findings. In its latest transformation, the task force shows no vestige of the idea that a task force should be composed of complementary specialists whose authority derives from their certified qualifications. What does this mean for the processes of local democracy, particularly in a period where public agendas are increasingly being set by the market-oriented goals of neoliberal thinking? In what follows, we present two examples of such public task forces in North Carolina, and evaluate their operation, to ask, Does the operation of task forces lead to broadened democratic participation as was their ostensible purpose—since previously public administrators or officials may have consulted little with the public—or does it narrow or impede participation? In the first example, in Durham, we focus on the implications for democracy of the *processes* by which task forces operate, while in the second example, in Siler City, we examine the significance of the *end product* of the task force for democratic participation.

In 1995, the Durham Public School (DPS) system established a new "alternative school" for students labeled "disruptive." (For more on this controversial event, see chapters 4 and 5.) This came largely at the behest of the county chamber of commerce, whose leaders argued that such students threatened the attainment of high academic standards in local public schools—and by unspoken implication also threatened the attractiveness of the Durham area to outside capital investment. They desired the segregation of disruptive students in a separate facility. As one officer of the chamber put it,

> we at the chamber said, there needs to be an alternative classroom setting for these kids who disrupt so these kids who want to learn can learn. And the disruptive kids need to be in these settings until they are ready to play by the rules. So that is how we got involved with it. [This involvement] actually led to the establishment of the alternative programs for high school students and middle school students.

Despite the extreme sensitivity of this issue given the preponderance of African-American students among those deemed disruptive and the polarized racial politics of the Durham public school system, the alternative school was duly set up, but moved twice after that. In 1997, it was once more relocated by DPS to the George Street area, a poor, largely African-American neighborhood in central Durham. Residents were upset about being "dumped on," despite their own sympathies for the students, and they protested to the DPS against the school being located there. A Durham County judge, frustrated by having tried several students from the George Street Alternative School in her court, visited its grounds and was appalled by the poor conditions there. She thereupon enjoined the new Durham school superintendent and DPS to improve the deplorable conditions of the school. In response, DPS hastily convened a task force of more than fifty people by inviting community educators, business people, residents of the George Street neighborhood, and African-American community activists to meet with DPS administrators over the next six weeks to debate what to do about the alternative school program in general and the George Street Alternative School in particular.

Although the public at large was invited to join the task force, the newspaper notice was obscurely placed, leaving few beyond those already invited with any knowledge about the existence or goals of the task force, much less with a sense of welcome. But DPS officials could claim that the process of participation was open to all. Still, some who did join complained about the inconvenient meeting time (3:00 P.M.), while others said they were made to feel that they had "invaded" the meetings. At the first meeting, attended by the new school superintendent, the county judge, two DPS officials who were to chair the task force, and more than fifty interested citizens, the superintendent and her two subordinates spoke glowingly of the great potential of the task force for achieving results on behalf of "at-risk" children and "alternative education" and of the open-ended nature of its charter. The exhortation was to be imaginative, free-thinking, and innovative. One DPS official put it thus: "our goal is not to focus on what already exists because it will impede our ability to make our own vision of what could possibly be. I encourage you to assume that we already don't have a program [in place]." When asked by one of those invited to better define the goals of the task force—What kind of school should at-risk kids be expected to attend?—she replied, "let's not narrow the focus. This is the type of decision the task force is established for."

Over the next several weeks, however, the task force chairs' instructions to members changed radically from their early open charter to expansively reimagine the future education of at-risk children in Durham County. During the first two meetings, broken down into four working subgroups, members engaged in spirited debates: Was the at-risk student label a valid one, or was it an unfair stigma inflicted on a child due to racial stereotyping and the logistics of large class size and an impersonal bureaucracy? What should be the criteria for admitting a student to the alternative school—and who should apply them, principals from the sending schools, social service professionals, community leaders, or some committee composed of all of them? Was an alternative school really needed, or would it be better if disruptive students remained in their home schools for counseling or discipline? And above all, in response to the concerns of George Street neighborhood residents on the task force, should the alternative school remain at its present location in an impoverished minority neighborhood, or should it—as most residents wanted—be moved elsewhere?

By the fourth meeting, however, the tone of the proceedings had changed. The two DPS officials chairing the task force began to take a harder line, instructing members to have more "manageable" expectations, to be "more realistic," to "stay on task," to "not get bogged down." Members of the task force speculated with one another whether the officials already knew what they wanted the final report of the task force to say when it was presented to the school board for action. Members worried to one another about being on task when it was not even clear what the task really was. The four subgroups drew up their initial reports of broad recommendations to present to the task force as a whole. By the fifth meeting, attendance began to fall off. One of the DPS officials chairing the sessions complained to members, "We have a hodge-podge of ideas or program components, but do not have a program."

In the seventh and final session of the task force, the two school officials first outlined to the small number of remaining members—dictated, really—

what would happen next to their recommendations. The recommendations that people in this session came up with—not the written preliminary reports of subgroups—was to form the basis for the final report of the task force. The staff of the DPS central office, in particular the two officials themselves, was to draft the report. A copy of the final report was to be mailed out to all task force members, who would then have only a week to respond with further suggestions. The final report was to be revised by DPS staff with these suggestions in mind. The report was to then be sent to the superintendent, who would then comment on it, whereupon the report would be presented to the school board for review and action.

During this final session, as recommendations were presented orally by task force subgroups, the two school officials informed the members that the session's task was to be a much more narrow one than that defined over the previous six sessions. "We want to focus on what is going to happen next year" at the alternative school. Not only that, but in discussion, "if you get off target, we will cut you off." Among other revelations, members were told by one of the officials that the alternative school would remain in its present location—that this had already been decided by the DPS administration and was not subject to being changed by the task force. (The school was eventually moved, but not due to the efforts of the task force.) At one point, a white task force member asserted that the George Street neighborhood was "a criminally involved area," and therefore it was imperative to move the alternative school "to an area with less crime and more alternatives." Another task force member, an African-American, then objected, saying he took umbrage at this as a racist slur on the area. Members of the task force began to take sides along racial lines. But this exchange was really a last-minute diversion. By the end of the last session of the task force, it appeared the report would hardly be considered "the task force recommendations," as it had gone through so much steering, revision, and manipulation that it belonged more to DPS staff than the community members on the task force.

Subsequently, the DPS staff wrote up the recommendations of the task force, using educational jargon and stripping the report of the more complex issues arising from discussion by the citizens on the task force, and then presented it to the Durham school board. The final report and the response to it by the school board did at least achieve what appeared to have been the real if implicit goal of the task force—"cooling out" the county judge during DPS's delicate transition to a new white superintendent. When interviewed later, the judge showed her satisfaction, at least in one respect: "In the end, everyone came together and did a good job. In retrospect, it was a good idea. I don't think it could have been done a better way. The people that were pulled together were diverse. . . . It was an educational experience for everybody." The task force, the judge noted, worked in the sense that "the problem kids from George Street are no longer on my court docket." Whatever else it accomplished, the operation of the task force also succeeded in domesticating opposition.

Reflecting on the task force, one DPS administrator noted as much, in remarkably economistic language about stakeholders, etc., that suggests just how far the neoliberal logic of the market has encroached on educational policy making:

> If it's a big issue and you need a really large representative group to deal with it, you form a task force. . . . When you need a lot of people involved for one reason or another, to help take some responsibility for pieces of it, to help sell it, and then you want a more varied group than just educators. . . . It goes back to the buyer. . . . There are a lot of stakeholders who have been involved and are either supportive of what's been going on or opposed to what's been going on, or have ideas for how it could be done differently or better, and the only way to really deal with it is to bring everybody to the table. . . . Once you come up with those recommendations, then there are people to help sell it to the community, there are people to help provide those resources. . . . And because others have to help us do this, then you get their buy-in.

That the task force was more a facade of democracy than the reality of democracy was reflected in the fact that despite the diverse issues about which task force members had been initially charged with making recommendations, months later only one of its recommendations had been implemented: the relocation of the school. Although the location of the alternative school in their neighborhood was what first motivated George Street residents to participate, the outcome of the process of task force deliberations, and the procedures of the process itself, could hardly be said to encourage their participation; even the eventual relocation of the school does not appear to have occurred because of the efforts of task force members. The alternative school is now located in a DPS-owned office building in the middle of Durham's downtown district, ironically relocated there as part of Durham's revitalization effort, called City Development Initiatives (CDI), that seeks to bring more diverse activity to its declining downtown area.

Let us now turn to another example of a task force—one in which we focus not so much on the process of task-force operation but on its end product, and, again, see close connections to local reworkings of neoliberal thinking. This involves the white population of the town of Siler City and its relationship to Latino immigrant residents, which we encountered in chapter 4. In 1994, the mayor of Siler City appointed a six-member Hispanic Task Force to study issues concerning the influx of a large number of Latino immigrants to the area—the difficulties they faced, and the tensions arising from their interaction with a rural community largely consisting of white and African-American small farmers and industrial workers. Only one of the members appointed to this task force was a Latino.[11] After several months of deliberation, the task force came out with a printed brochure, translated into bad Spanish and entitled, "Available Services for You in Siler City," for distribution to Latino newcomers in the area. The task force brochure gives a clearer sense of who, in the task force's opinion, should be servicing whom:

> Please do not make excessive noise at any hour. You are not permitted to use radios or TV's after 10 P.M. If you do so, your neighbor will call the police and you will be investigated. Pets such as dogs and cats are permitted in Siler City. Keeping chickens or goats within city limits is illegal. It is illegal to have garbage in your yard or to work on your car in the street or in your driveway. . . . Drugs are illegal, and any person who sells or uses them will be arrested. Drugs are bad and very dangerous. In this country it is completely illegal for a husband to hit his wife or his children for any reason. A man who does this will be sent to jail and may lose his children. The thing that can help you most here is learning English. Anyone who wants to get a better job must learn English.

Why would a brochure supposedly about "available services" be written in this way? The pamphlet composed by Siler City's Hispanic Task Force framed Latinos in Siler City as a problem representing noise, dirtiness, illegality, violence, and disorderliness and thus, for the community of Siler City, essentially out of place. Because the task force put the full weight of its authority behind intimidating language that stigmatized Latino immigrants as racial and national others who were in no position to challenge its assertions, much more was at stake than the very infrequent incidents mentioned in the brochure. One could infer that the brochure was in effect aimed as much at local white residents as at the immigrants. What was at stake was whether the brochure's imaginative construction of negative features of immigrant identity would be allowed to justify whites treating immigrants as essentially different and dangerous others not entitled to public services, or to being treated with dignity.

As our analysis in chapter 4 of Latino migration to North Carolina makes clear, what we found in Siler City was a large, vulnerable population of several thousand transnational migrants—men, women, and children, many of whom were so-called undocumented workers illegally residing in the United States, available as a contingent labor force to work for the poultry plants and other local industries of the town and surrounding county.

This population of foreign workers presented a serious anomaly for reigning neoliberal thinking, because it was not supposed to exist in American communities. According to the neoliberal story of progress, Americans should continually upgrade themselves through education and training for high-technology jobs in order to remain globally competitive, and their access to high technology should constitute their comparative advantage in global labor markets. In the neoliberal story, Americans have no houses that they themselves clean, no elderly people or children requiring their care, no gardens or lawns they themselves maintain, no field crops they themselves pick, no poultry or hogs they themselves butcher—for each of these labor-intensive tasks is part of the old spit-and-sweat manual industrial economy that is no longer competitive, and thus rightfully disappearing.[12] But, of course, all these kinds of labor actually do have to be performed in America, and cannot be outsourced to the cheaper labor of foreign countries. The *necessary* existence of homegrown American demand for such labor is an open secret and a major embarrassment for neoliberal ideology—as was the physical presence of grossly underpaid and overworked American women, African-Americans and other minorities, and—most recently—Latino transnational migrants, who do the work. At most, neoliberal theorists speak glowingly if vaguely about the rise of a service economy, but spare the listener uncomfortable details about who's serving whom, and how.

The racial and national animosities evinced in the brochure of the task force must be seen in this light. For instance, Latinos working in the poultry plants of Siler City, like the African-American women who preceded them there, were dehumanized by those using what one of this book's authors calls "homegrown, socially conservative neoliberal" rhetoric: in this racist discourse, they were imaginatively decomposed into only the "arms" and "backs" needed by the poultry industry.[13] The labor they did in the poultry plant was tedious, filthy, dangerous, and perhaps in the view of many whites, polluting in its contact with killing and death.

Moreover, most Latino laborers were poor and badly paid—although this was in line with neoliberal thinking, since they deserved low wages because of the low level of skills required in their work. As chapter 4 makes clear, most Latinos could only afford to live in dilapidated, crowded houses and trailers, where they suffered from rent gouging and badly maintained rental properties. Thus the work and living conditions for most Latinos, when refracted through the racialist lenses of some white residents, provided fodder for the denigrating stereotypes that cast Latinos as a problem appearing as a many-headed hydra— here as drug addicts, litterbugs, and wife beaters, there as public parasites, country hicks letting chickens and pigs run wild, and menacing out-of-town gang members. If we view the perspective of many long-time residents in Chatham County sympathetically, the additional schooling, health care, and other community services required by the influx of Spanish-speaking immigrants posed a serious increased burden on a local government already stressed by threats of factory closings and reduced federal and state funding. Whatever the reasons, messages from employers, from elected town and county officials, from local news commentators—and not surprisingly from the Siler City Hispanic Task Force as well—all came down to saying to Latinos, "You are disposable, you are/you generate trash, you are a burden on us, you diminish our community."

Civic problems, however, had to be managed, and the brochure as a product of the Hispanic Task Force represented a publicly sanctioned effort to discipline these transnational immigrants who were "out of place." The outlandish restrictions placed on Latinos in the brochure ("You are not permitted to use radios or TV's after 10 P.M.," etc.) showed quite clearly that this disciplining cut along the divide between citizen and noncitizen, and between white and African-American citizens and Latino foreigners at that, for such demands could never, would never, be made upon American citizens. And—at least so goes the story—*real* American citizens did not use drugs, hit their wives or children, or litter their front yards. In this sense, the work of the task force sought to define who had standing—who was legitimately *in* and who was *out* of the national community—and why.

Viewed in this way, the Hispanic Task Force and others like it manifest the fact that the social responsibilities for dealing with the tensions and burdens generated by labor market–based decisions made by businesses have been offloaded, or in the current lingo, "outsourced" to local communities, and that resentful and overwhelmed citizens of these communities often stigmatize the new and relatively powerless immigrants as social problems as a result. The racial and national profiling found in the task force brochure, like the denigrating news commentaries and other manifestations of local animosity toward Latino residents we described in chapter 4, imaginatively constructed them as permanent subcitizens placed beyond the civic pale. In such a situation of intimidation and scapegoating, local democracy, which values equality and seeks to build an inclusive community, was bound to suffer. Or are we wrong to expect that our neighbors, whether they are legal citizens or not, should have not only responsibilities but also rights when engaged in the important work of creating North Carolina's new industrial economy?

Elite Networking and Political Style: Setting Agendas for Economic Development in Halifax and Watauga Counties

One informal mechanism by which market rule becomes incorporated into the public's business is the networking among elected officials, government bureaucrats, and local business leaders. Indeed, the existence of many such networking interactions—informal exchanges of information and favors between two individuals—can quite clearly be inferred from the new linkages we discovered above between public officials and private entrepreneurs in market-oriented partnerships and nonprofit private corporations, and in the formation and operation of task forces. We could infer the operation of such one-on-one deal making in the case of market-oriented partnerships when our informants told us of the way, for instance, a real estate developer in Fayetteville had "put together a package" by working with HUD officials to subsidize the cost of housing he sold, as we describe in another chapter. The secrecy surrounding such networking was frustrating not only to us as ethnographers but even more to citizens and residents, whose futures were being decided, in part, on the sly. We refer to this networking between political and economic elites as "elite networking."

Even where the formal institutions of market-oriented public-private partnerships and task forces are not present, however, elite individuals still engage in networking in ways that simultaneously reinforce neoliberal doctrine while they have negative consequences for the working of local democracies. Admittedly, networking for whatever purpose has long taken place because confidential exchanges between individuals provide each with things of value they each would not otherwise have—valuable information, or promises or commitments of resources. As a result, networking is not a new feature of local politics but long predates the rise of neoliberal thought. Still, elite networking within and across public institutions in North Carolina simultaneously excludes some from democratic participation *and* promotes neoliberal approaches to our social ills. Moreover, the two are closely linked in practice. Neoliberal thinking has become dominant in part because those who promote it exclude other voices and perspectives from our public life, and one of the principal means by which this occurs is networking. A brief example will have to suffice.

Steve O'Donnel, a local government official in Halifax County and a booster for economic development in the county, spoke in an interview with ethnographer Marla Frederick-McGlathery about officials at the State Department of Commerce in Raleigh as "[my] 'good friends.' After all, that's what business is all about. You get to know people, you like each other and so you do business together. The bottom line is people." The Department of Commerce serves as the state-wide agency that seeks to attract outside industry to invest in North Carolina communities by promoting the state's welcoming business climate, its low labor costs, and its hostility to labor unions. Its officials thus promote a world view based on neoliberal premises—the need for global competitiveness, a friendly local business climate, and disciplined local labor vis-à-vis the global economy.

O'Donnel saw the officials of the Department of Commerce in the capital, Raleigh, as his "good friends" because they made contacts with outside investors and referred them to his office in Halifax County. Speaking to Marla about a newly completed "shell building" and industrial park in the county, he said,

Now, we have something to go and sell. Now we have something that we can take to clients, to Commerce. The Department of Commerce, which is the lead economic development agency in the state, gets a thousand inquiries a year. Of those one thousand inquiries, 80 percent want to look at an existing facility. I talked to a client yesterday that is in the process . . . as it is they are very excited about our location, along [Interstate] 95, our equal distance between north, I mean, New York and Florida.

It is not surprising that O'Donnel's views reflect those of his "good friends," for instance, with respect to the issue of the need for an educated workforce in the global economy:

Employers . . . want to know "are the students educated to a level that they can come work for me? Are they going to make me [a] competitive player in the market?" Over the last two years Halifax County has lost over one thousand jobs. The national cry is downsizing. What that means is each employee is going to have to do more. [The focus of industry employers is] on the idea that our worker is going to have to outproduce. [Let's take] a sewing factory in Scotland Neck, the workers there are going to have to outproduce people in countries such as the Dominican Republic or Haiti. Otherwise, the businesses will simply relocate there in order to gain cheap labor. Industry leaders want workers who can come in, understand, think, and work to problem solve.

Despite this stark depiction of the challenges facing local workers, in particular the African-American workers to which he is implicitly alluding,[14] O'Donnel is enthusiastically expansive in describing the important potential role for local schools, the local community college, and the school-to-work programs in the county in training these Halifax County workers in the new skills required to outproduce in the global economy:

I see optimism in all the school systems really. A lot of activity is going on to try to educate teachers and students about what the workforce, what the world of work needs today and what it will need tomorrow. The chamber has several good initiatives. They sponsor youth leadership and also they sponsor school-to-work programs. . . . No, I think all the educational systems are making tremendous efforts to improve their product and their product of course is their educated students. The community college, of course my office is here, makes a big, big impact on training, on students in the county.

But even if such elite networking invariably includes some persons, it just as surely excludes others. This reality is particularly invidious where racial difference and the workings of market-oriented partnerships intersect, as in the case of elected African-American officials left outside the loop of functioning networks that plug into a white-controlled private sector. Let us contrast the views of O'Donnel, a white man who boasts of his networking with state officials in Raleigh, local educators, and chamber of commerce officials, with the perspective of James Bright, a prominent retired African-American educator and political leader, who served for several years as an elected official in Halifax County. He also referred to networking—by whites—to explain why in his view blacks in Halifax County have not succeeded economically:

> Decisions about personnel and representation are made at the Kiwanis Club. That's how we are excluded and they never think about that. [When I] served as the sole representative of [Company X] on the Chamber of Commerce, [I] was invited to a luncheon at the Holiday Inn where the president of BB & T was supposed to speak. I was only one of two blacks invited to this huge event. And this is where names are passed. Company executives get to meet young professionals. And there were only two blacks and five women present at the entire event. These are the kinds of setting where you get your exposure. How do you ever expect blacks to move up economically or socially if they're not exposed?

He noted that networking among whites also took place when it came to placing people for jobs in the county school system, which "is predominantly black, [but] whites want those jobs for themselves," and occurred face to face when "they [whites] get together at night in the Lions Club, Kiwanis Club, and they talk about those things." Moreover, he told Marla about the racially specific networking he encountered while serving as a public official:

> A woman called me up one day because her electricity was about to be turned off. I called the head of N.C. Power and told him about the situation, the executive told me to call someone and added, "if he doesn't satisfy you, then call me back." In other words, this man will surely handle your concern because I will call him before you and tell him to do this favor for you. I called and surely the woman's electricity remained on . . . it is these types of influential networks that African-Americans are by and large excluded from.

He went on to say that people would "be surprised at the number of whites who called him to help their daughter/son get a job, get out of prison. . . ." From his point of view, whites in the community actively utilized their networks in order to resolve issues in their lives.

Unlike O'Donnel's effusive account of job training, Bright describes the ways in which networking among whites in Halifax County and beyond operates to exclude African-Americans from all but the most menial jobs, and in fact *reserves* for them one such kind of job—but very few other jobs—as part of what he sees as part of a perverse economic development strategy of the county devised by local officials.

> What they're trying to do is reserve their jobs for their folks. All the good jobs, if you go to Frontier [a large corporate employer in the area] and the Ajax Company is probably the biggest employer in the county, all of your administrative jobs are being held by whites, and all of your office jobs are being held by whites. And this is true at North Carolina Power, this is true in Frontier, all of these banks, you go to the banks and see who have the administrative jobs, the loan officers, people of that nature. And they want to reserve jobs for us, you know where? You know where they want to reserve jobs for us? . . . It's [the] fast food industry. You know? Fast food industry. And these guys, they get together at night and at Kiwanis Club meetings and Lions Club meetings, and they talk about these kind of issues, reserving the good-paying jobs, high-profile jobs for whites, at the hospital.

Bright had an altogether more jaundiced view than O'Donnel of the relationship among educational institutions, training, and jobs—a relationship he sees as sustained by networking among members of the local elite—officials like O'Donnel, and local educators—and one central to the operation of the economic development programs of the county. He argued,

> This county here might get five million dollars a year for job training. Job training now, five million dollars a year for job training. . . . They'll spend four million dollars of that to subsidize salary [in] places like Hardee's and Burger King—all these fast food places. See what they do is . . . they would bring you in as a trainee, see, and through the community college, job training supervisor or whatever you want to call it, would have your name listed and Company B makes their report to him. And if they've got five trainees, then he starts sending them checks for the pay of about two-thirds of your salary, so Burger King's got to come up with a third of your salary. And they do that for fifty-two weeks, and then after fifty-two weeks, you know what they do? Let you go and get another one, and that cycle goes right over again.

Being cycled into entry-level jobs in the fast food industry was at best an ambiguous opportunity for young African-Americans. Whether or not Bright was correct in claiming that they were forced out of such jobs, local African-

Americans felt they deserved more say in the purportedly democratic arrangements that determined the economic prospects of their teenage daughters and sons, since public monies were being spent to subsidize these practices. Elite networking is never race free, and it perpetuates an institutional racism, which is all the more invidious given that such exclusion of African-Americans from market-oriented partnerships in which public resources are committed *is* exclusion from participation in the decisions made by local government officials over their economic futures. Race-favoring elite networking is part of the unspoken underside of what passes for neoliberal governance, particularly in a county and a state that have not thoroughly separated from their troubled racial pasts.

However, exclusion may take even subtler forms than networking, which at least is conscious and intentional, if not always acknowledged or recognized for its effects. One such form is political style, exemplified in a controversy over roads. Their construction, costs, and location have long been objects of contention in the mountainous western counties of North Carolina. This is particularly so for Watauga County, where self-described natives have come to clash over roads with large numbers of people they call transplants, people who have lived most of their lives outside of the mountains and have moved to Watauga. Most transplants retired from careers elsewhere, and many sought to spend the hotter summer months away from their winter bases in Florida in their seasonal vacation homes in the cool Blue Ridge Mountains. In contrast, natives of Watauga and other mountain counties felt that they had long been left behind in road construction by successive Democratic state governments and the state Department of Transportation.

More immediately, natives in Watauga County favored the building of new roads and expansion of older ones because they believed that more and better roads would attract industries into the county and allow less well-educated residents access to the industrial jobs found in distant lowland counties. They saw this employment as very badly needed because of the decline in family farming in the county and the rising price of land due to the influx of transplants. And natives owning small businesses or working in the tourist industry saw more and better roads as essential to drawing in more tourists. In contrast, affluent transplants residing in their vacation homes saw road construction as disturbing their recent but hard-earned tranquility, destroying the aesthetics of nature, polluting the environment, and thus, not incidentally, lowering the property values of their second homes. There was in part what local parlance called the "drawbridge" mentality—keep the drawbridge down until I pass through, then up it should go.

In 1996 a Tennessee corporation, the Marsdon Corporation, leased land for a plant that would produce asphalt for a nearby road then under construction. Neighboring property owners, the majority of whom were transplants, rose up to protest the plant opening on health, environmental, and aesthetic grounds. They formed an organization, Citizens Unite (CU). Its leaders were approached by and called on the advice of two veteran environmentalists. CU members made phone calls to state and federal agencies (e.g., the state's Department of Environment, Health, and Natural Resources, and the Federal Emergency Management Agency, FEMA) to lobby against the plant on various grounds, and put out press releases announcing their opposition. The leaders of CU then gathered signatures to petition the Watauga County commissioners to prohibit erection of the plant, and CU members and supporters appeared before two meetings of the commission. To express their indignation, several CU members donned painting masks at one of the meetings to signify the health dangers of asphalt fumes, aggressively addressed the commissioners (the majority of whom were natives of the county), and railed against the siting of the plant in their neighborhood or indeed elsewhere in the county or nearby. However, commissioners appeared hostile to these tactics and refused to act, noting at last that the lack of zoning laws prevented them from becoming involved in the conflict between CU and Marsdon. The commission did, however, support CU in its request for a Department of Air Quality hearing on emissions from the proposed plant. The failure of CU to make headway with the commissioners in these encounters precipitated countywide debate, both among individuals and in the media, about the causes of the stalemate: How was this failure, and the clear hostility between native commissioners and CU leaders, to be explained?

The transplanted CU leaders and members were educated professionals or business people from out of state, several experienced in confrontational municipal politics from elsewhere, proud of their ability to effectively network with state agencies, and in command of research and public speaking skills. CU encounters with the commissioners were almost always impersonal and distant, taking place in the constrained formal setting of the commission's public meetings or through formal letters and petitions sent to the commission. While a few CU members sought to act amicably and respectfully toward commissioners, the interactive style of most alternated between invoking scientific expertise and giving technical facts (such as about the pathologies attributable to asphalt fumes) and a grating and aggressive public oratory combined with elements of domesticated street theater (e.g., the wearing of painting masks).

Although it was clear that native commissioners favored the building of this and other roads, and certainly did not oppose the asphalt plant on philosophical grounds, what most affronted them and other Watauga natives was the political style displayed by CU leaders and members. Commissioners felt threatened by CU's confrontational group behavior and use of public fora such as meetings and the media. Commissioners preferred that CU leaders visit them personally, use a consensual tone, provide them with CU materials to preview before meetings, and make requests of them instead of demands. In the end, elite natives still controlled what should be said and how. Natives, who in number still predominated and elected the county's commissioners, thought appropriate political style between people of unequal status should be highly personalized. Persons seeking assistance and those they sought help from ideally interacted face to face, one on one, and informally ("on the front porch"). Moreover, they ideally interacted in private, that is, outside the public view of spectators and the media. Encounters were to be polite so as to avoid personal embarrassment—for instance, persons seeking support should inform individual commissioners beforehand what they intended to do in a public meeting so as to avoid unpleasant surprises. Furthermore, the persons interacting were to be mutually respectful, particularly avoiding what commissioners saw as condescending behavior associated with outsiders' assumptions that natives were provincial, ignorant, uneducated, and backward. According to informants, CU leaders had repeatedly violated these expectations for a political style suited to dealing with native powerholders.

It is likely that even *if* CU representatives had shown appropriate political style toward native county commissioners, they still would have been thwarted in their efforts to halt the building of the Marsdon asphalt plant. On the other hand, natives of the mountain counties of North Carolina have long had to suffer at the hands of exploitative outsiders endowed with superior material resources and bearing attitudes of superiority toward "hillbillies," "hicks," or "mountain yokels." Insofar as the behavior of several (but not all) CU representatives appeared to display these attitudes, the natives, both commissioners and other residents, viewed them as unneighborly and pretentious in a setting where neighborliness and a strong sense of individual equality are highly valued traits. One could understand why commissioners and natives saw the concerns of CU members about air quality and traffic congestion as less pressing than the needs for roads on the part of younger native men and women who couldn't make a living on the family farm or find work in the county but needed to commute to faraway factories, or of local businesses dependent on the autumn tourist traffic to pay their bills for the rest of the year. At the same time, there is no doubt that differences in political style, and in the way political style was interpreted, served as one mechanism through which CU and its transplant supporters were excluded from effective participation in local politics.

The anxieties of both natives and transplants in this controversy should be seen within the framework set by neoliberal thinking. On one side, natives' support for roads, and their arguments for the necessity of roads for local economic growth—that is, to attract outside industry and to allow local residents to bring income back from outside the county—are surely consistent with neoliberal premises about the need to market the industrial infrastructure and business climate of a locale to global investors. On the other side, however, the marketing of a locale to the outside world has a virtual as much as a real component. The outsiders to whom the image of Watauga County was being marketed as an attraction for its natural high-altitude beauty, its clean and pure mountain air, and its supposed preservation of an older and more peaceful, bucolic way of life were outsiders like the transplants of CU, seasonal tourists, and others drawn from afar to enjoy the amenities of the mountains. For transplants, more roads interfered with the appropriate consumption of natural beauty and a healthy environment and the preservation of high property values: roads merely represented more problems—if only roads were sufficient, but only just sufficient—to lead them there from Florida, New Jersey, or elsewhere, during late spring, and out again in autumn. In short, many transplants appeared either to be unaware of or to have forgotten the virtual furbishing of Watauga County as a landscape of consumption within the nationwide competition among aspiring retirement communities and vacation destinations for the investments of retirees, which brought them there to begin with. Moreover, they saw their residence and local property rights—however recently acquired—as conferring standing on them in the county, a claim disputed by natives.

Compared to most natives, transplants were members of the entrepreneurial, propertied, and technocratic elites whom the neoliberal account of the world casts as its heroes. We expect that political power in Watauga and similar mountain counties will soon pass from natives to transplants and other outsiders, where this has not already occurred. If so, native political style will no longer "work" as a set of excluding practices, but instead the new majorities will be able to view it nostalgically as an artifact of a bygone way of life, preserved if at all only in museums of vicarious experience, such as plays about the good old days performed in annual cultural festivals for the benefit of well-heeled newcomers.

The Petty Tactics of Exclusion

In distinction to the strategies of exclusion we describe above, we would like to conclude with a brief enumeration of the *tactics* of exclusion, which are exercised within or through these strategies.

Let us begin with the tactic of controlling eligibility, or standing. In the case of the Marvin Plan in Fayetteville, local elites deemed certain persons and groups to have standing in debates over the goals of the Marvin Plan. The director of the Fayetteville Partnership and a few others invited members of the OAFA Committee to join as part of the nominally grassroots effort, to demonstrate that they were representative of all. However, the lopsided race and class composition as well as the gender composition of the OAFA Committee speak volumes about the actual selection criteria for inviting persons to join, as it does in a negative sense, about those left out—residents of the Buena Vista Terrace housing project and members of nearby neighborhood community associations.

The leaders of the Fayetteville Taxpayers for Accountability achieved their standing as the legitimate and recognized opposition to the Marvin Plan on a different basis, by using public media adroitly while appealing to the authority of their military credentials and experience, and trumpeting their own status as representative taxpayers. It did not hurt them that most were white, relatively well-off, retired men.

Similarly, many of the original members of the Durham Alternative School Task Force were preselected through invitation, although it appeared that a broader solicitation to the public had been made, even if in such a way that it would not draw a lot of attention. It is worth recalling that residents of the George Street neighborhood also turned out at the first meeting, but were made to feel that they had invaded. They felt they were regarded by DPS officials as interlopers without standing—even though they would be affected as much as other groups that were represented on the task force by the continued operation of the center if it remained on George Street.

A second tactic of exclusion employed by leaders of market-oriented partnerships and task forces is controlling the degree of visibility and disclosure of affairs conducted *for* but not *by* members of the public. The informal practices associated with elite networking and distinctive political styles connected to access to officials reinforce this tactic. As one FTA leader observed about the lack of public scrutiny of important decisions made about Fayetteville's future by the Fayetteville Partnership:

> An issue that also concerns me is secrecy, and how Mr. Marvin suggested to this group that they form a separate group [the Fayetteville Partnership], so they can avoid the sunshine laws and hold meetings in secret and supposedly not take notes in these meetings, so they cannot be held publicly accountable for what they are doing. I'm concerned about the drift of public money into these private organizations, the money is then not accountable for, so we have no way of knowing how the money is used.

In a different way, the creation of the final report of the Durham Alternative School Task Force showed a similar lack of respect for public scrutiny. This final draft came not from the written or verbal recommendation of task force members but from the concluding analysis written by the two DPS administrators chairing the task force. Although in theory DPS officials gave members of the task force the opportunity to review and comment on this final report, they were given less than a week to do so, hardly enough time for citizens with busy lives and complex schedules to respond thoughtfully, if at all. By thus placing pressure on members to review the final draft so quickly, DPS officials sought to create conditions in which complete disclosure and consideration of their report were impossible.

Elite networking, as in the instance of the Halifax official in contact with Commerce Department officials in Raleigh, insofar as it involves the confidential exchange of information or favors between two persons only, clearly operates as a mechanism that limits public visibility and disclosure—and is most excluding of those who, like poorer African-Americans in Halifax, are most "out of the loop" in other ways.

Finally, native political style in Watauga County, however personally empathetic it may be, also clearly operates to exclude those who cannot or do not "sit on the front porch" with a county commissioner from a fuller knowledge of the public's business, and certainly CU's political style, even if it was self-defeating in dealing with the commissioners, is rightly grounded in the correct apprehension that "backroom wheeling-dealing" is not the most democratic way to conduct public affairs.

A third petty tactic of exclusion is the setting and scheduling of agendas for public meetings. Public meetings can be scheduled at inconvenient times, or even formidably difficult times for working residents, particularly parents, to attend: consider the 3:00 P.M. meeting times scheduled for the Alternative School Task Force, or the Monday morning regularly scheduled meetings of the Durham County Commission. Either public meetings may be scheduled in relatively remote sites, which are most accessible by car or time-consuming to travel to on the public transport that poorer residents have to rely on, or they can be located in places such as upscale hotels, imposing downtown office skyscrapers, or convention centers where entry by poor people, or by people of color but without property, is inhibited by the presence of armed security guards.

Getting a time to speak on the agendas of public meetings becomes a major obstacle placed on people whom authority does not want to acknowledge or listen to. When that hurdle is overcome and a group is given time on the agenda to address an issue during the public discussion period, it is often provided an absurdly short amount of time to do so, or its speaking time is scheduled late in the evening after all other business is conducted, when members of the town council, county commission, or school board are tired and impatient to go home, and most of the audience in the meeting hall has long since left to put children to bed or go to bed themselves to rise early for work the next day. In theory, such constraints on participation operate equally against all groups who seek to participate, but one of the main thrusts of this chapter is that they tend in fact to operate to the disadvantage of those least privileged in terms of their race and class by the practices associated with neoliberal doctrine and market rule.

A fourth tactic of exclusion we call "freezing out"—ignoring the presence of people who try to speak out, and the content of what they say, when they speak as representatives of groups dissenting against majority opinions or decisions. For instance, consider the situation of an African-American town councilwoman, one of the few city council members who voted against extending Fayetteville's contract with Robert Marvin. She was variously seen by other council members and Marvin Plan backers as cranky, old, and out of touch. In a classically stigmatizing move, she appeared to be treated by the white majority on the council as a mad "old maid" who was to be courteously but silently listened to when she spoke, but never acknowledged or responded to. In another setting, ethnographer Don Nonini observed a public meeting of the Durham school board where majority members studiously ignored African-American community leaders who, during the free comment period on the agenda, spoke out in favor of the pressing needs of poor minority students for instruction in African-American culture and history: while one leader spoke thus, white members of the school board carried on side conversations with each other, conspicuously not listening to what he was saying.

Freezing out is actually the penultimate recourse in face-to-face situations, when prior controlling of eligibility and setting and scheduling of agendas is ineffective in excluding those whose participation is an inconvenience or challenge to those in authority—penultimate, because there is even one more extreme option: removing dissenters via physical force by police or military from a public venue, or preventing them from entering it to exercise rights of assembly or free speech to begin with, when they are deemed potentially disruptive—an option most recently exercised with abandon by police in Seattle and Washington, DC, in controlling demonstrations against the WTO, IMF, and World Bank. This should be seen rightly for what it is (in addition to whatever else it might be): a tactic for excluding someone from democratic participation.

One more, less overtly violent tactic of exclusion is to claim the right to represent authoritatively the histories of minorities or dissenting groups, while ignoring their members' memories or testimonies of the past. Here we recall the role of the Market House, the refurbished centerpiece of Old Fayetteville and an icon of the Marvin Plan, in spite of its being widely despised by African-Americans in Fayetteville as the old antebellum slave auction house of the area, where the ancestors of many were bought and sold.

PART III

Struggling for Democracy

9 Against American Plutocracy

Democratizing Our Communities, One by One

Is America Democratic?

The preceding chapters have found much evidence of the adverse effects of inequalities in wealth and power and of racial and nationalist discrimination in the communities in North Carolina we studied. We discovered that these effects can be traced to institutional arrangements of class and race privilege. These arrangements constrained the way individuals viewed the possibilities for political participation and change (chapter 3). They dictated that the views of members of one race about development, progress, and the good life prevailed over those of other racial and national groups (chapter 4). They channeled the way schools were oriented and education defined (chapter 5). They determined which visions of a common future became dominant and in what ways (chapter 7). They profoundly shaped the way public business was conducted and who was included in or excluded from it (chapter 8).

Our findings press us to ask more encompassing and basic questions whose answers are vital if local democracy is to flourish and play a transformative role in American society. First, is the U.S. political system itself fundamentally democratic? Second, if it is not democratic but, as we argue, plutocratic, could the new grassroots activist groups that have emerged from the matrix of market rule during the last two decades provide the crucial necessary if not sufficient first step towards democratizing the American political system?

A Broader View of American Politics

The question of whether American politics is in actuality democratic is a question not only about the facts of American history and society but also about the theoretical and ethical implications of the facts. If the system is fundamentally democratic, then a variety of reform strategies for dealing with the challenges posed by market rule outlined in chapter 1 can be envisioned. However, if the American political system is fundamentally undemocratic, then a more profound set of theoretical and ethical questions must be asked about the nature of the system. These questions not only lead to a much more piercing examination of this system and of its relationship to market rule but also imply that the system as it now stands must be radically transformed. Much is at stake.

The overwhelming evidence demonstrates that the American political system has long been and is at present fundamentally undemocratic. It is a plutocracy, a form of rule by a power elite or an oligarchy formed from an upper class consisting of people with wealth and power, and not a democracy, or a form of rule by the people.[1] Moreover, the U.S. political system has been a plutocracy since its inception in the late eighteenth century, although the upper-class elites who have ruled and selected those who govern have shifted in composition many times from the wealthy merchants, planters, and soldiers of the late eighteenth century to an upper class defined today by its membership in the industrial and financial "corporate community."[2] This corporate community consists of business directors and owners who are socially interconnected with a social upper class distinguished by its largely inherited accumulation of wealth (in stocks, bonds, real estate, currency, art works, etc.).

This power elite dominates the American political system, including its electoral process. Members of the power elite select electoral candidates through campaign financing, lobby elected officials to follow a corporate agenda, make sure that members of the power elite are themselves appointed by these officials to high government positions, influence policy-formation networks by funding and serving as directors and trustees of foundations, universities, conservative think tanks, and policy discussion groups (e.g., Business Roundtable, Council on Foreign Relations), and work to popularize their pro-corporate policies through their private control of the electronic and written media.[3] As a result, for example, a majority of American presidents over the last century have come out of the corporate community or been selected by it.[4]

Domhoff shows that corporate control of labor markets has long been central to the conservative corporate agenda.[5] Corporate influence on politics and law has weakened labor union power and reduced claims by the working population on public wealth for subsistence, such as Social Security, Medicare, and unemployment insurance. Weakening the economic security of the working population reduces the capacity of most of the population to participate in politics, and thus has effects that are anti-democratic. The major transformations of the last thirty years show the effects of successfully promoting or even imposing that corporate agenda on the American people. Neoliberalism is, in effect, the philosophical and political rationale of rule by the corporate community and its power elite, and it confers prestige, standing, and even the presumption of expertise on the wealthy by dint of their wealth. The corporate assault that has weakened labor unions and demobilized their members more than those of other groups[6] has promoted the processes in which locales and local activists have become delinked from state- and national-level politics. Transnational corporate restructuring of the labor force through plant closings, outsourcing, offshorings, flexibilization, and retrenchments, which has defined a "race to the bottom" over the last two decades of globalization, has weakened the bargaining leverage of working people. Corporate lobbying of Congress now jeopardizes long-accepted understandings about citizens' rights to Social Security and other government redistributive programs that have been in place since the New Deal in the 1930s. Corporate plutocratic power is, without a doubt, historically at an apex in the American political system.[7]

Rule by a corporate power elite at the national level is most trenchantly supported by certain local elites—"local growth coalitions."[8] These growth machines are led by place entrepreneurs who seek to maximize property values and rents from buildings and land in a locale, and they include real estate owners, bankers and financiers, building developers, construction firms, and real estate brokers and attorneys.[9] Within growth coalitions, place entrepreneurs are supported by local elected and appointed officials (e.g., mayors, county commissioners), the local media, and some (but not all) small-business proprietors and professionals.[10] In our own research, we have found growth coalitions to also include North Carolina State Commerce Department officials and representatives from local chambers of commerce. Local growth coalitions seek to create what they believe (sometimes erroneously) to be a favorable business climate (e.g., low business taxes, physical infrastructure, right-to-work laws, and lax or absent environmental regulation). Members of growth coalitions believe that these conditions will lead to corporate investment from outside, stimulate local economic growth, and bring in jobs and people, which will in turn increase demand for real estate, and thus increase rents.[11] The practices of local growth coalitions formed by financiers, developers, and realtors are also central to the processes of structural racism that make white and class privilege possible. These processes create racial segregation in housing and schooling through such practices as banks' "redlining" African American neighborhoods and realtors' "steering" whites away from African-American neighborhoods.[12] Local growth coalitions support low-wage regimes that attract corporate investors but offer few opportunities for advancement to poor whites, African-Americans, or Latino migrants.

Under these circumstances, the rights of corporate elites to invest corporate resources wherever they wish, at lowest cost to them, or to disinvest from communities in accordance with self-interested market logics, all in the name of growth, go entirely unquestioned. Even where there are internal disputes within growth coalitions, these rarely challenge the rights of roving corporate investors, or the doctrine of growth.[13] Local growth elites are usually crucial to the electoral campaigns of local politicians, who thereby have (or soon acquire) pro-growth, pro-corporate policy orientations.[14]

At the local level, as at national and state levels, plutocratic rule has its own fault lines, however. The hold on local elites of the neoliberal doctrine of growth through competition in the so-called global market remains tenuous. Local growth elites are profoundly dependent upon and therefore ambivalent toward growth through competition with the global market's roving corporations, which can move out of communities and thereby devalue local real estate and reduce rents. Moreover, in accordance with neoliberal logics, one growth coalition has to compete with others in rival areas. In terms of local issues of concern to citizens, growth coalitions also have tense relations with groups formed by neighborhood residents to improve their own conditions of living.[15]

The claim that plutocracy, not democracy, best describes the American political system at all levels represents a painful but undeniable conclusion, not what one would expect in a book on local democracy, and certainly not one that we as the authors of this book celebrate. The weight of plutocratic rule on lives of ordinary citizens is extraordinarily heavy. It goes far toward explaining the peculiar stance of many Americans who appear to show reflexive pride in American democracy, celebrating it as a model for the rest of the world even as they themselves show a deep everyday cynicism about political life and have turned away from voting and participation in large numbers.

This would be a miserable conclusion if it were the whole story, but it is far from being so. Although the national political system is undemocratic because of rule by a power elite, this is not the same as saying that democracy does not exist in America, or that the potential for extensive democratic change does not exist. What this does mean is that the fight for democracy under the prevailing conditions of "the rule of the dollar" is an uphill struggle. American democracy at each level and in every locale can never be taken for granted, and must always be fought for. This is all the more reason for taking seriously the finding of the next chapter that there are widespread, effective efforts of democratic activism in local politics.

In fact, there have been notable democratic successes in the modern history of the United States, ones achieved through struggle and organizing of vast numbers of marginalized people. The most recent such successes have been those of the Civil Rights and the anti–Vietnam War movements in the 1960s.[16] The Civil Rights movement secured legal rights of equal access to the voting booth and equal pay and equal schooling for African-Americans and women at all levels of the political system. The protests against the Vietnam War helped bring an unjust war to an end, and prevented the use of nuclear weapons by the United States against the North Vietnamese and a probable catastrophic nuclear exchange between the United States and the U.S.S.R.[17] Viewed retrospectively, neither of these movements nor their successes were predictable given the anti-democratic structures of rule in America, yet both were hardwon victories that involved the creation of coalitions that brought together communities of people of color, intellectuals, religious groups, labor unionists, pro–Civil Rights and anti-war Democrats, and sympathizers within the upper class and the power elite itself.

Moreover, both movements led to longer-lasting institutional reforms in the American political system, which have been sources of popular empowerment and to which the power elite has had to respond. Skocpol describes the "advocacy explosion" coming out of these two movements, in which there was an "extraordinary proliferation of new and different civic organizations" managed by professional advocates working to improve the environment and to make more just the living and working conditions of women, minorities, immigrants, the disabled, and many other similarly disadvantaged groups.[18] Similarly, reform movements such as the consumer rights movement have since the 1960s led to an increasing prominence of expertise—legal, medical, scientific— in setting public policies, which can be seen as an improvement over issues being "decided by a few old bulls in the back room."[19]

Rule by a plutocratic power elite has therefore been by no means unproblematic in American history. Plutocratic rule is not simply a reflex of some set of enduring and unchanging structural arrangements, but is the outcome of sustained efforts by the power elite, which are limited by unforeseen popular mobilizations, and thus sometimes fail. Neither plutocratic rule nor democratic rule by ordinary citizens has foreordained outcomes. Instead, there is *the American conundrum of rule: plutocratic rule prevails most of the time because the structural rules of power are stacked in its favor and it is often unchallenged, yet it is also contingent, unstable, and even now and then unsuccessful when large numbers of people mobilize themselves democratically in spite of it, or even against it.* Similarly, there is a local corollary to this conundrum: although local growth elites prevail in local governance more often than not because of the rules set in their favor, their power is also uncertain and contingent because it can be challenged by mobilized citizens. Not only can their power be challenged but it has been—as examples in the next chapter demonstrate.

Moving toward Participatory Democracy in America's Communities, One by One: Citizens Organizing in Associations

Local participatory democracy is crucial if the American political system as a whole is to be transformed into a true democracy. Whether local politics provides citizens with the opportunities to cultivate the skills and habits of democratic participation or, conversely, discourages citizens from participating will have crucial implications for the resources that they can bring to their similar encounters with representative state and local political systems. Competencies such as becoming a good and close listener, a willingness to broaden one's own perspective to envision how one might share a common fate with other citizens, the capacity to act as either leader or follower, the ability to negotiate and to articulate not only one's own needs but also that of a group one represents are, after all, needed at all levels of politics.[20] If, as we maintain below, local politics that cultivates maximal inclusiveness of citizens in participation can serve as a school for democracy, then local politics can serve as a source for empowering citizens to work toward democratizing what is now plutocratic national politics. Most crucially, local politics can provide the imaginative optimism, based on actual democratic achievements, which could inspire citizens to engage in the efforts needed to democratize plutocratic rule. In this we are supported by the strong positive value placed on local democracy as the model for democratic politics in classical theory.[21]

If citizen participation is the sine qua non of democracy, citizens do not solely or even primarily participate as individuals, but come together in groups or associations to affect local politics. In fact, Americans form a great diversity of different civic groups—neighborhood groups working to improve the environment, church groups engaged in charity, parent-teacher associations, and many more. They are also increasingly joining groups that are part of more encompassing social movements independent of, but seeking to influence, government. Although we agree with observers who have argued that there has been an increasing tendency within American politics from the 1970s onward toward a "personal democracy" based on citizens' voting combined with (some) citizens' strategic access to remote advocacy groups,[22] there has also been widespread participation by citizens in associations engaged in the political process over the same period.

By "associations" we mean the part of society that is set apart from the state and consists of "the nexus of nongovernmental or 'secondary' associations that are neither economic nor administrative."[23] There is a growing and important social science literature that argues that associations, their internal organization, and their roles in broader governance are all crucial issues in democratic politics.

Associations Resisting Illegitimate Authority

How are associations a crucial feature of local democracy? How can they be organized in directions that further the democratization of American politics? From the perspective of participatory democracy, there are two crucial kinds of activities that associations in local politics could engage in to further democracy, and we focus on these here. First, associations may provide the imaginative and logistical resources needed to resist and check the illegitimate exercise of state power.[24]

There is a history of the associations of civil society coming together to exert a counter force to illegitimate state power. Scholars favoring this function of associations point to Solidarity during the last years of Communist rule in Poland, or the student groups in the case of the Tienanmen demonstrations in China, as paradigmatic examples. Generally, as these examples suggest, those who propose this function most frequently assume that it applies to "democratizing" societies, not fully "democratized" ones as the United States, supposedly, is.

However, given the actuality of rule by wealthy elites in the United States, this assumption should be revisited. Although the authority of, say, elected representatives who legislate in accordance not with the expressed needs of the voters of their electoral districts but with the wishes of their most generous campaign contributors among the corporate elite may be legitimate in a nominal sense, many would question just how real such legitimacy is. Instead of the mainstream legalistic definition of legitimacy, there are other ways of thinking about what is legitimate that could sanction (and have long sanctioned) fundamental changes in governance brought about by associations of citizens who have joined together in broader social movements at times of crisis: notions of legitimacy based on ideals of human and planetary sustainability, justice, and equality. We believe that America is now in such a period of crisis—where the indefinitely expanding economic system, unbridled corporate power, and militarization of American society have come increasingly into contradiction with human needs for survival, economic and ecological sustainability, and dignity.[25] The current widely discussed "crisis of legitimacy" is one in which these ideals increasingly challenge anti-democratic authority with new definitions of legitimacy, in this period in which "the old world is dying, and a new one has yet to be born." A participatory democratic perspective necessarily supports the idea that citizens organized into associations directed toward the broader societal goals of democratization and social justice have a vital role to play—first in opposing plutocratic power, and then in forming a crucial element within a transformed democratic society.

Toward a New Form of Democratic Power

Second, associations can play a direct role in self-governance, by being incorporated into the processes of governance (e.g., deliberation and decision making), in state functions of regulation, in the provision of services, and in policy formulation.[26] We are most excited by the possibility for local politics that associations can become self-governing, the venue for much if not all governance in a participatory democracy. There are three such theoretical-normative approaches to the relationship between associations and democracy.

One approach—"associative democracy"—proposes a devolution of the state to voluntary associations. Paul Hirst and his associates have proposed that associations consisting of voluntary members should assume most of the economic and governance functions of a new decentralized social order, in which a lean state would play only minimal roles of enhancing communication among associations, conducting foreign affairs, and ensuring "public peace and the rule of law."[27] Associations would compete among one another for citizen-members, and participation in one association rather than another would be voluntary.[28] While hypothetically such a minimal society might be attractive to many people, both its long-term viability and the process by which it might come into existence are in great doubt. What in such a society, for example, would limit competition among associations over resources to the legal sphere, instead of there being a transformation of voluntary associations into Mafia-like units intent on the violent dispossession of other associations? If the state were then to enter into a violent confrontation between groups, use armed force, and choose sides, where then does that leave the loser—and the state itself? If citizens could voluntarily join and exit such associations, what would prevent those with concentrated resources from exiting when the economic or social going got tough, and those who stayed had to pay a heavy price?[29] And, even more troubling, as Fung implies, how could we possibly envision a transition from the current institutionally complex American nation-state with its concentrated ownership of productive wealth in the hands of a wealthy minority into the lean libertarian state envisioned by Hirst and others, in which decentralized voluntary associations and their members owned and controlled the society's productive property?[30] Hirst's vision of transition is entirely schematic—an unjustified leap of political faith.

Another approach to the role of associations in participatory governance is that of Cohen and Rogers. This approach sees associations incorporated into a state much like the one that currently exists, but with associations gradually taking on more governance functions vis-à-vis the legislature and state bureaucracies.[31] The principal objective of Cohen and Rogers's proposals appears to be on the economic and environmental fronts—to demonstrate how the involvement of associations in governance could enhance economic efficiency and prevent environmental damage and abuses of the labor force. These governance functions would include helping formulate policy, coordinating economic activity within the framework of law, and enforcing and administering policy. Since these functions are organized around federal arrangements, associations performing these functions in cooperation with the other agencies of the state would exist on national, regional, and local levels. Associations would include all relevant groups and individuals ("be relatively encompassing"), would be accountable to their members, but would also possess powers of sanction over their members.[32] Associations would provide improved information to those who form policy and would assist in coordinating labor markets, production cycles, and locational decisions surrounding production. They would thus act in dialogue with employers' organizations and labor unions to ensure that workers were adequately represented, trained adequately for new jobs, and protected by adequate occupational safety and health standards.[33]

As with Hirst's imagined libertarian associational society, there are serious unresolved issues associated with Cohen and Rogers's vision of state associationalism. It is completely unclear, for example, whether such associations would in effect be merely advisory and facilitative vis-à-vis other agencies of the state, or instead would have real powers reserved to them. Even more problematic, as in Hirst's ideal society, it is difficult to imagine the processes of transition by which the current institutions of American politics controlled by the power elite, the corporate community, and allied local growth coalitions would surrender their powers to the citizens' associations envisioned by Cohen and Rogers. Why would the power elite allow the disturbance of "business as usual" by providing associations of citizens with resources and recognition to improve the representation of workers, facilitate their training, and ensure the health and safety of their work conditions—given the current ascent of neoliberal ideologies favoring market solutions, the processes of globalization, and the decline of organized labor, promoted by the power elite and its corporate supporters over the last two decades?

Empowered Participatory Governance

The approach we find most attractive is that of empowered participatory governance. Empowered participatory governance (EPG), as proposed by Fung and Wright, compared to the foregoing other two approaches, has two major advantages.[34] First, it seeks to maximize the participation of citizens rather than finding for them new forms of indirect representation, and second, it begins with the local political setting in ways that point to a path toward political transformation. According to Fung and Wright, there are three principles to EPG—a "practical orientation," "bottom-up participation," and "deliberative solution generation."[35] A practical orientation is one in which participants "focus on practical problems such as providing public safety, training workers, caring for habitats, or constructing sensible municipal budgets."[36] In most respects, the practical orientation to these problems, which is part of EPG, would not conflict, at least at first, with the agendas of local growth coalitions or their corporate supporters—and indeed, in some instances, such as providing public safety, may actually enhance the property values so beloved by these coalitions.

In addition to an orientation toward solving practical problems, EPG also adds two other features. One feature is bottom-up participation, in which there are "new channels for those most directly affected by targeted problems—typically ordinary citizens and officials in the field—to apply their knowledge, intelligence and interest to the formulation of solutions."[37] Within the new associations, the local knowledge of citizens would be more valued than that of experts, because the citizens and lower-level officials impacted by such problems provide a diversity of knowledge bases and perspectives that experts lack, and the increased participation by citizens makes them more accountable to the outcome of collective problem solution, as well as allowing them to put more direct pressure on political parties. The other feature is deliberative solution generation, in which participants in association deliberations "listen to each other's positions and generate group choices after due consideration"— that is, they focus self-consciously on the process of deliberation as one of their desired outcomes.[38] Thus incorporating as many views as possible, listening respectfully to the views of others, etc., becomes not only a means but also a by-the-way end of the reasoning and decision-making process, in addition to the performance objective itself. All three principles of empowered participatory governance are consistent with, and indeed advance, a participatory democratic program.

Unlike the other two approaches referred to above, one very promising feature of EPG is that it has actually been tried, more often than not with success—in a variety of settings ranging from "participatory budgeting" in the city of Porto Alegre, Brazil, to neighborhood councils governing schools and policing in Chicago, to empowered *panchayat* (village council) governance in Kerala, southwestern India, and to habitat conservation planning in the rural United States.[39] It is interesting that three of the four such examples of EPG used by Fung and Wright to illustrate how it works clearly involved *local* reforms— Porto Alegre, Chicago, and Kerala villages.

This is not to say that EPG can come into existence without its own critical preconditions set by the larger political order. Fung and Wright refer to three "design properties" of EPG—devolution of administration and politics from higher to lower levels of the system, "coordinated decentralization" between political levels for purposes of accountability and for dealing with scale-specific problems (e.g., the use of water within a multijurisdictional watershed), and the presence of a system that is "state-centered, not voluntaristic."[40] These design properties clearly involve changes at higher levels of the political system—control of government by state or municipal political parties in two cases (Kerala, Porto Alegre), passage of a law by a state legislature in one (Chicago), and a favorable federal government administration able to use executive regulations in the fourth (habitat conservation). In each case, such changes made possible a devolution combined with coordinated decentralization to locales, and a formal governance role for new local associations. Because of the dependence of local reform and decentralization on changes made at higher levels, it remains to be seen whether EPG could be instituted at the local level in the United States.

Nonetheless, there are promising signs. First, in many respects, EPG's practical orientation is already compatible with the changes associated with the rise of market rule in American local politics-the giving over by the present neoliberal state of many of its responsibilities to assist in solving the problems of local communities to the for-profit sector in the case of certain commodified services, and to the nonprofit sector that assists groups who cannot afford to pay for services. This provides an opportunity for new local associations of citizens to place pressure for democratization on those administering such privatized governance functions, and to seek changes along the lines of the EPG paradigm. Second, on the grounds of reducing "big government," both the federal government and state governments have already devolved certain powers to state and local governments; Community Development Block Grants are one example, but there are many others.[41] Seeking to restructure these institutions along the lines of EPG instead of allowing them to become the domain of local growth coalitions could be the first objective of local activist organizing efforts. Third, two examples cited by Fung and Wright— Chicago and Porto Alegre—show devolution occurring *within* or *below* the level of local government, a reform that many local governments have the capacity to implement, as in the case of neighborhood councils on schools and policing in Chicago, and participatory budgeting in Porto Alegre, which depends on dividing the city into sixteen administrative regions, with each region having its own residents' assemblies. Residents of communities are already in a position to place pressure on local governments to make these changes. Fourth, and central to the intrinsic appeal of local politics, the principles of empowered participatory governance *already* appear to make sense in the situations of the local activist groups we studied. Local activists' commitment to their own communities grounded in the sensory realities of local life, and their members' awareness that by working together they have the power to improve certain vital aspects of their own lives, are completely consistent with the practical, participatory, "bottom-up," and deliberative nature of local politics in the locales we studied. For these reasons, we are very encouraged by the role of associations within the empowered participatory governance approach.

We end with one important caveat. Although there is much reason for optimism that activist groups like those we studied and describe in the next chapter can advance empowered participatory governance and play a vital role in making American communities more democratic one by one, this is insufficient. What will also be needed is a widespread, popular scaling up of local associations through their translocal mobilization across communities to transform the American political system as a whole. We point to possible paths toward scaling up in the next chapter and conclusion to this book.

10 Counter Experiments for Democracy

Activism on New Political Terrain

Learning about Activist Organizing in a Neoliberal Age

Ethnographic research relies on the comparatively open-ended strategy of analytic induction and so is useful for, among other things, identifying new and emerging social practices and cultural forms.[1] Through ethnographic study of two dramas of contention in each field site, we encountered a number of activist groups or, in the terms of democracy theory, voluntary or secondary associations.[2] The organizations that turned up in our ethnographic research differed, not surprisingly, from the older, hierarchically organized federations of associations such as the PTA and the Elks Club, identified in Putnam's and Skocpol's accounts of the decline of the post–World War II civic life. The new organizations that we found had developed on a very different political terrain. Most had originated as small, grassroots groups, not local chapters of classic hierarchical federations. Some clearly participated in a form of translocal organization that differed from the hierarchical federations, and all, despite their struggles against market rule, were oriented to a government reorganized according to neoliberal precepts.

Three of the five groups reviewed here had become connected to one or two of the great variety of social movement networks that presently exist.[3] Movement networks are a form of translocal organization that Skocpol, for one, finds functionally similar to the older forms, "with a similar blend of national and local, political and social undertakings."[4] At the same time, she acknowledges the differences: contemporary movement networks are composed of

loosely coupled, partially competing components, from advocacy associations to chapter-based membership federations to small, grassroots groups oriented to particular places.[5] Correspondingly, analysts have increased attention to the significance of networks relative to formal organizations.[6]

Most the groups we met showed particular signs of having developed in response to recent economic and political circumstances, particularly market rule. They had originally started as grassroots groups, that is, "locally based and basically autonomous, volunteer-run nonprofit groups."[7] The longer-lasting ones had obtained 501(c)(3) nonprofit status with the Internal Revenue Service and, in some cases, had partnered with the government to provide public services.[8] They had been drawn into a relationship with government agencies reorganized according to the neoliberal projects described in earlier chapters. Nonetheless, despite this partnering with the government, several provided conceptual and physical spaces for counter publics oriented to addressing needs and interests and cultivating visions of society not being served by market rule.

The groups we describe did not necessarily oppose the state. In fact, they worked with the government at least to the extent that they maintained 501(c)(3) status by not engaging in political activities specified as off-limits by the tax code. But they were contentious in that they had visions alternative to neoliberalism and they acted on them. All promoted one or more democratic values (such as equality) and projected visions of the good society dominated by a focus not on pursuing profit but on being treated with respect, having a community with dense social ties, nurturing connections to history and place, or protecting the environment.[9]

What the Limits of Dramas of Contention Revealed

While the study of dramas of contention helped immensely in tracing the dynamics of local politics and identifying important types of activist groups, two limitations of the method were quick to surface. Enacting a reflexive stance on our research as it progressed,[10] we considered how too narrow a focus on dramas of contention might be obscuring important aspects of the new political terrain. From our general ethnographic study of downtown redevelopment in Durham and Fayetteville, for example, we noted that important participants and activities were not always visible in public meetings or in the media, even though they were addressing potentially explosive issues. This led to our increasing awareness and subsequent focus on public-private partnerships, how they functioned, and their centrality to market rule.

Another informative initial shortcoming of the dramas-of-contention approach concerned the role of faith-based groups in the new activism. Such groups did not come to the surface in the dramas at the time of the study but,

as described more fully below, have become more publicly present since. Fortunately, we had other sources of information on the importance of religion in activism.

The five groups we studied most intensively have varied disagreements with market rule, relations to the state, stances toward the history and social life of the communities they served, and reactions to the social movement networks that courted them. They also differed in resources and influence. Our research on these groups raises further issues about the problems with voluntary associations that would need to be addressed if these groups were to become more depended upon, as some democracy theorists advocate, for meeting shortfalls in the provision of public services and for ameliorating disappointments with representative democracy as practiced in the United States today.

Case Studies of Associations

Citizens Unite

Mountainous Watauga County contains beautiful valleys. Citizens Unite (CU) started as a neighborhood group opposing what members considered inappropriate uses of the bottomland in their local valley. A number of residents had been upset when a fairground and, later, a racetrack had been planned for the area; they formally organized in the spring of 1997 when they learned that Marsdon, a company with headquarters in Tennessee, planned to put an asphalt plant in the valley.

Some fifty persons showed up at Citizens Unite's first meeting. Perhaps showing their middle- and upper-middle-class backgrounds and their experiences in other parts of the country (almost all were newcomers to the area), they decided to hire a lawyer to make a presentation at the county commissioners' meeting. They assumed that once alerted to the unwanted land use, the government would take care of the problem. When the response turned out to be tepid—the commissioners agreed only to write a letter supporting a request for a public hearing—the group adopted other means. Under the tutelage of a seasoned environmental alliance, the Appalachian Defense Alliance, they organized a steering committee, a research committee, a fund-raising committee, and a committee to handle press contacts.

CU members, drawing upon this organization, presented their cause to the state Division of Air Quality via phone calls and letters and persuaded the state to grant a public hearing on the air quality permit for the plant. They held a press conference, wrote letters to the editors of the local papers, garnered support from regional environmental organizations, circulated petitions, raised funds to place ads in local papers, used protest tactics in another county commissioners' meeting,[11] and through these various means managed to mobilize a landmark turnout at the state-sponsored public hearing in Raleigh. Although it eventually granted the permit to Marsdon, the Division of Air Quality, for reasons partially related to CU's efforts, put a year's moratorium on the start-up of the plant.[12]

In their first weeks of activism, CU's members expressed anger and dismay. They saw themselves as citizens who, faced with unexpected disinterest on the part of the government, had to take up the burden of protecting the environment from an irresponsible corporation. As they continued, a sense of righteous indignation fueled their work.

CU may have begun from the threat of the asphalt plant in its members' own neighborhood, but they rapidly found tutors not only in effective organizing techniques but also in the discourses and rhetoric of the environmental movement. The Appalachian Defense Alliance primarily, but also other locally represented groups such as the Appalachian State University (ASU) chapter of Students Actively Volunteering for the Environment (SAVE) and ASU's Sustainable Development Program, all gave the group direction.[13] "We were one big emotional sore; [we] didn't know how to channel those feelings," one leader said.

Eventually, CU developed a vision that went beyond the valley. They were even important in galvanizing the takeover of the local Democratic Party by a younger set who had espoused environmentalism as one of their issues. In the election that followed CU's activities against Marsdon, two Democratic county commissioners were elected—the first Democrats in many years.

CU used the local issue to challenge larger processes. Members were important in convincing the Division of Air Quality's decision to declare a moratorium on the construction of asphalt plants across the entire state until measurements of fugitive emissions could be incorporated into the permitting process. CU continued to monitor state air policy, going in caravan to the state capitol, for example, to protest a proposed weakening of the state's Air Toxics Program. The group was eventually incorporated into regional environmental alliances, for which they served as a watchdog on environmental issues and mobilized the membership of affiliated groups on appropriate occasions.

EXPANDING THE DEFINITION OF THE PUBLIC GOOD

CU activists effected change not only through electoral politics and recognized channels for approaching government officials but also through contentious behavior in the public sphere. They engaged in cultural as well as conventional politics. Alvarez and her colleagues have interpreted "cultural politics" as the process enacted when sets of social actors shaped by, and embodying, different cultural meanings and practices come into conflict with each other. This definition . . . assumes that meanings and practices—particularly those theorized as marginal, oppositional, minority, residual, emergent, alternative, dissident, and the like, all of them conceived in relation to a given dominant cultural order—can be the source of processes that must be accepted as political. . . . [W]hen movements deploy alternative conceptions of woman, nature, race, economy, democracy, or citizenship that unsettle dominant cultural meanings, they enact a cultural politics.[14]

At stake in cultural politics are the very categories that frame political action. Activists make an issue out of unexamined, everyday notions about who deserves respect, for example, who has social value, and who does not. They challenge the boundaries of "citizen," "work," and other socially important categories. The effort to redefine the activities of housewives and mothers as work is an example of engagement in cultural politics; so, too, is urging people to recognize government buyouts of failing industries as "corporate welfare." CU's cultural politics worked to expand the definition of the public good to include environmental quality.

In interviews with the local newspaper and letters to the editor, the president of the Marsdon Corporation and Marsdon sympathizers fought back against CU's charges by promoting a negative interpretation of CU and redefining the issue at stake. They portrayed Marsdon as a reasonable capitalist company. They painted CU, on the other hand, as disingenuous and deceitful. As often happens in dramas of contention over environmental issues, they insinuated that CU was nothing but a NIMBY (not in my back yard) group with only its members' selfish interests in mind.

In Marsdon's account, both CU and the company were pursuing capitalist goals. The difference was that Marsdon was playing the game aboveboard while CU was not. CU members were pretending to be environmentalists, champions of the public good, and holders of the moral high ground when in fact they wanted to make a profit from selling their houses in coming years, just as Marsdon wanted to make a profit selling asphalt. If CU members wanted to play the capitalist game, if they wanted to participate appropriately in the world of capitalism, they should, it was claimed, use a legitimate route to block Marsdon, which was to call for zoning laws in the area.[15]

CU ignored this charge and instead continued to paint Marsdon as a company threatening the common good because it irresponsibly affected air quality. In keeping with the environmental perspective of its tutors, CU pursued a cultural politics aimed at claiming environmental qualities as a public good no matter whether the claims went beyond the limited legal liability theretofore granted to corporations. To the extent that the environmental movement, with CU as one particular manifestation of it, manages to redefine environmental qualities as public entitlements, the movement will have served to redefine, at least for the public, the limits of corporate power. Environmentalism is one area (in contrast to education, for example) where the definition of the public good is being expanded instead of reduced.

THE FIGHT AGAINST THE ASPHALT PLANT
AS A SPACE FOR AUTHORING PERSONAL IDENTITIES

CU members provide insight into the transformation of consciousness that can occur in the course of participation in a local associations of this type. At the time of the research reported in this chapter, CU was also one of twenty-one local environmental groups in western North Carolina and on the Delmarva Peninsula that comprised a separate research sample studied through participant observation and in-depth identity trajectory interviews with members; the researchers also interviewed respondents who had never belonged to any such group.[16] Comparison of those interviews shows that participation in local environmental groups tended to engender more discipline than was available to individuals whose environmentalism had formed primarily in the public sphere. The histories and practices of the individual members became enmeshed with the histories and practices of the groups. In practice, especially in the contentious practice of activism,[17] their identities (senses of self) as environmental actors had developed and solidified, becoming a basis for a range of actions.

In CU, as in many of the other 21 grassroots groups studied, a good number of the participants began to think of themselves as environmentalists for the first time. Before his work in organizing CU, for example, Ray had a few pro-environmental concerns, but they were not well orchestrated into a narrative, and he considered them unimportant. Other than that, he described himself as not having been "really concerned about the environment."

> This campaign [for air quality] has led me into being a fairly strong environmentalist. I see things now that I wouldn't have ordinarily seen in the past. When I see things happening, big exhaust coming out of trucks, the first thing I think of now is how much sulfur dioxide is going into the atmosphere, whereas before it was just smoke coming out of an exhaust. . . . I just was not environmentally minded up until six months ago [when the asphalt plant issue emerged]. Now, I am very environmentally minded.

Even more remarkably, perhaps, Ray switched political parties: the Democratic Party was responsive to CU's efforts to clean up the air of the county; the Republicans were not.

Along with these changes in consciousness and behavior, Ray shifted his understanding of himself—his identity—in relationship to the environmental movement. Before his abrupt immersion in the world of environmental action, he felt little responsibility for environmental degradation, seeing it as a reasonable exchange of material progress for environmental damage.

Then the asphalt plant came along. Ray and CU developed a narrative that blamed Marsdon for being an irresponsible company that violated environmental regulations and so threatened the health and welfare of the community. Especially when they discovered that local government officials would not intervene, they began to talk about themselves as environmental "watchdogs," as concerned citizens who had taken up the job of monitoring business and government. As he worked with CU to stop Marsdon, and as he talked and worked with experienced environmentalists, Ray's thinking went beyond the asphalt plant. He began to think of other industrial installations and waste dumps and to think of environmentalists as public-minded watchdogs monitoring the excesses of the hog industry, of the timbering industry, of landfills, of nuclear waste disposals. At some point he began to take these broader narratives personally and to see himself as a citizen concerned about air quality in the county as a whole.

Broughton Road Improvement Association

The Broughton Road Improvement Association (BRIA) was founded in 1988. Over the decade before we met them, BRIA members had made an outstanding effort to bring both material and symbolic resources into an African-American neighborhood near downtown Fayetteville. When Paul McCloskey, a retired Department of Defense employee, and Corrine Singleton, a community activist, began the group, the neighborhood was a place of dilapidated housing, drug dealing, prostitution, and nightclubs. In an earlier era of urban renewal, some of the houses in the area had been razed and their occupants dislocated. New construction had begun, but was abandoned when a change in government priorities redirected the funds. The area had a bad image. Even though residents were considered to be at risk from dangerous elements, police stayed away. The residents believed that because the people who populated the Broughton Road area were black and poor, the government had abandoned it. They also emphasized the need for "responsibility" and "respect" within the community.

The newly formed Broughton Road Improvement Association focused first on the nightclubs. By hiring a lawyer to represent them before the planning board, they succeeded in having the city rezone the area from commercial to residential. They insisted that the police check in the clubs for underage drinkers, and urged state Alcoholic Beverage Control officials to revoke the licenses of clubs caught selling alcoholic beverages to underage consumers. This crippled the businesses financially. BRIA members also petitioned for streetlights and police protection. Next they worked on drug dealers, notifying police that dealers were using sophisticated technology to overhear police plans to approach the area. They persuaded the city housing authority to put wrought iron fences in front of each residential project, to deter loitering and littering. They also got the housing authority to close off a dead-end street to all but pedestrian traffic and so made street dealing and getaways more difficult. To eliminate drug houses, they canvassed the neighborhood for abandoned or derelict buildings and for lots that were vacant and overgrown and conveyed the information to the city, requesting action.

Concerned about the general state of housing in the Broughton Road area, BRIA teamed up with a local chapter of Habitat for Humanity to build Habitat homes in the community. BRIA was also invited to partner with the city and a private developer in proposing projects to HUD for subsidized housing. To qualify for federal and other sources of funding, BRIA became a nonprofit organization. Because of these achievements, BRIA was put forward by the city as a model community development corporation for other community groups to emulate. In sum, BRIA engaged, with remarkable success given the barriers its community faced, in a do-it-yourself neighborhood revitalization program and in the process emerged as an effective political voice for the community in municipal venues such as the city council and the Fayetteville Revitalization Commission.

The Broughton Road area was not a locale that was inevitably, as posited by the ideology, prospering under market rule. Rather, it was experiencing profound government neglect. Area residents frequently had trouble procuring government services such as police and public health protection. The stories we heard from BRIA activists, to whom residents had brought their complaints, indicated the kind of prolonged and continuous effort it had taken and continued to take to overcome the image of the area and bring needed public services to the neighborhood. BRIA's agenda had to focus as much on the cultural politics of rebuilding the identity of the area and its people as on the pursuit of the area's interests through conventional politics.

When they did happen, government projects in the Broughton Road area had sometimes been left unfinished. One such case was the abandoned urban renewal project. Another, a year or so before the time of our research, involved ditches that the city had dug behind several houses in the neighborhood. Those affected argued that the city should at least cover the open, unfinished ditches, which were not only unsightly but also posed dangers to young children, who might fall into them.

When BRIA and the local chapter of Habitat for Humanity brought the issue before the city council, the votes against it caused anger. One councilor was remembered as having said that he was a hard-working American citizen and that the city's money could be better used in some other area. Residents thought the problem would have been quickly addressed had their neighborhood been white and wealthy. Further, instead of simply being discussed as a city project that needed to be completed, the issue escalated into a debate about whether a charge of racism was intended, or justified. Residents did feel that racism was involved; but what they wanted was not some sort of recognition of the racism but relief from the dangerous condition of the ditches.

Residents' apprehensions also conveyed to us their uneasiness with the treatment they were accustomed to receiving in public forums. Praising Corrine Singleton, one of the leaders of BRIA, a member said, "I have to give the credit to Corrine. She is one woman that stands up and speaks her mind to those people downtown. I will be down at those meetings and I would be drawing up. She doesn't draw up for nobody."

A former president of the Habitat for Humanity homeowners group, which was sponsored by BRIA, explained why Habitat members were reticent in voicing their concerns. In stark contrast to members of the dissident Fayetteville Taxpayers for Accountability (discussed in chapter 8), they did not feel entitled to speak in either BRIA or city council forums. They worried that their Habitat houses were "gimme" (largesse) deals that could be taken away if they "made noise." Those who did speak up felt they were treated poorly—a frequent theme in political autobiography interviews we conducted in Fayetteville and elsewhere. One BRIA leader's description of efforts to get the area rezoned was met with politics of exclusion (as described in an earlier chapter):

> There were any number of times that the zoning case would come up before the planning board, they would call us, and you go down there and sit throughout the whole meeting, and the case didn't come up. . . . When that happens two or three times? What are you doing? . . . Is this the way the system works? . . . Then I realized this is the way, when the system doesn't want to do something for you, this is the way they wear your patience.

People usually gave class and race as explanations for why the Broughton Road area was treated so poorly. One respondent used the concept of "environmental racism" to label his understanding of what had happened to the area:

> It has been happening for a while in particular black areas. . . . The area—they clean up every once in a while—but the area is basically dirty. You see trash everywhere, fields that need to be cut down. I mean I've called the city on several occasions about the area next to my house where the grass is growing up. They say: We don't know who owns the land. But when the situation

[arose] with the ditch, they knew who owned the land [and didn't do any-thing].

When asked what concerned him, he replied that the city treated the neighborhood poorly: "The first thing they ask you is where you live. As soon as you say 'Broughton Road,' the conversation kind of backs off."

A number of BRIA members saw the City of Fayetteville itself as the main obstacle to the improvement of the Broughton Road area. Nonetheless, BRIA did accept the city's invitation to become partners in a proposal for HUD revitalization funds. The city felt BRIA's participation would improve its chances; BRIA was attracted to the arrangement by the prospect of becoming even more of a resource center for the community and of being able to offer job training and job information.

Pondering this potential reversal of fortune, one BRIA member took a less optimistic perspective. A developer had bought up some of the land, he said, and wanted to put low- and middle-income houses on it; but because of the area's bad reputation, the developer could not attract buyers. So, for the sake of converting the bad area (with all manner of crime "going on down in those old raggedy houses," as he put it) into an area for profitable development, the city had teamed up with BRIA, the better to apply for federal money and to access Habitat for Humanity resources. He had doubted that this partnership would play out well for local residents, and found that in fact it didn't. White businesses going up in the surrounding areas were expanding into the Broughton Road area. Now, he concluded, "they are going to profit on it [the successful revitalization], but our taxes are going to go up."

Had BRIA, which has its heart in the community, been taken advantage of by the city and by the developer allied with the city? This was a recurrent theme of conversation about partnerships with the city. An African-American man associated with another community development corporation in Fayetteville gave us a similar assessment of the currently planned revitalization:

They come here and remove the blight, development comes in, dollars come in, and we don't get the benefit of development dollars. We don't have the businesses that are established there. Right? [They come in] to make it beautified, cultural, or whatever. So then they will change streets to go around or over our communities. So we are really like pawns in the game that can be shuffled. I'm not going to say it's racism, it's economics that does that! So we just have to be better at playing this economic game.

Ultimately Broughton Road residents remained suspicious of the city government. Theirs was a history of extensive efforts to procure public services that other areas received as a matter of course. Yet BRIA somehow managed to turn the tide and work in partnership with the city. Comments from outsiders and from some of the BRIA members themselves indicated a distrust of the public-private partnerships in which they engaged. The partners were perceived as not pursuing the same goals as BRIA, or even as playing the same game.

WHAT IS MISSED WHEN SERVING THE PUBLIC GOOD IS DEPENDENT ON MAKING A PROFIT?

Previously we have seen subtle but deep differences in citizens' views of economic development and other community issues depending on their social position—their race and class—and the circumstances of their lives. So it may not be surprising that we found divergent responses to public-private partnerships—that some black activists in Fayetteville thought it ironic at best that federal funds for those in need should end up benefiting private real estate developers, whereas city officials, in contrast, felt great about such an arrangement.

One municipal contact explained that instead of starting from scratch, "now we are working, leveraging our money with [the developer]. . . . He comes in and puts together a package. He goes to NC Housing Finance and makes a proposal. This project [part of the HUD proposal], we couldn't finance it to save our lives. We don't have that kind of money."

> This is an economically distressed area. It's an equation: how do I get housing [for the poor] at $80,000 a whack? You don't! So, you try to get someone to do it below market rate. It's a public-private partnership. Usually, you do whatever the market will bear. With affordable housing, we defray the costs. It's attractive, [to] get government involved in lowering the soft costs, which lowers the rent to make it function.

No doubt such "leveraging" of government resources with private resources makes good sense when neoliberal policies and programs are in place. But notice that an emphasis on leveraging can potentially turn the provision of services into nothing but an economic game where profit is expected. In neoliberal ideology, the economic game of pursuing profit in an allegedly free market is supposed to be miraculous in that it provides for all human needs. But it is important to ask whether a neoliberal vision sees only those needs that can be provided for in the pursuit of profit. Does the vision have a place for issues like respect? Are there profits to be made in providing respect? And, what about city services for poor neighborhoods in times when there are no federal programs to be leveraged?

Durham Inner Village

The core members of Durham Inner Village (DIV) were white male profession-als, a well-heeled group who between them had considerable acumen and pres-ence. As with the Broughton Road Improvement Association in Fayetteville, DIV's goal was to improve an area in a city. In this case, though, it was not an area where DIV members lived. Instead, they had been working together since the early 1990s to make over a commercial section of downtown Durham that contained infrastructure and buildings left over from the days when the city was a landscape of production, predominantly factories and warehouses for storing tobacco products. They wanted to convert the area, commonly consid-ered unsafe, useless, and unsightly, a hangout for alcoholics, into an inner vil-lage, a park ringed by new homes and shops busy with consumers and filled with walkways where resident families could enjoy a stroll—a place crowded and active enough to deter muggers and other undesirable visitors.

Whereas BRIA's emotional tenor was laced with anger and distrust, DIV members communicated excitement and enthusiasm accompanied by a sense of agency and creative capacity. Members described themselves as catalysts, not developers. True, they were likely to profit economically through an increase in their property values—or, at least those who lived nearby were. But the main profits would go to the developers who constructed or restored the buildings, along with the financiers, the real estate agents, and the insurance brokers.

An important motivation for the core group was the "revitalization" of Durham. They were excited to be movers in the resurrection of a part of the city from what they saw as a moribund state. They were enthusiastic about the New Urbanism movement and its gurus, including Andres Duany. (The DIV associates we met in the Durham City Hall complex at the opening of the book were planning for a visit from Duany himself.) They shared New Urbanism's concerns for promoting social engagement and thereby overcoming contempo-rary patterns of isolation. They responded to its architectural designs and the nostalgia these evoked for the early decades of the twentieth century when, to their way of thinking, healthier patterns of sociability prevailed. Sections of Baltimore and San Antonio had been redesigned to fit the principles of New Urbanism: Why not Durham?

While their vision was clearly formed from a middle- or upper-class vantage point, DIV members could not be accused of a disregard for diversity. Their vision included both racial and class diversity, and they made efforts to achieve that diversity. At the beginning of DIV's activities, members staged an event to gain input from at least a wider range of what they called "power centers" than they themselves represented. They raised money for a *charette,* an intensive process for exchanging views on a topic, which brought together a range of Durham's diverse institutions and activist groups.

Moreover, although they were not core members, the continuing members of DIV included a couple of white women and an African-American man and woman. Even so, despite the intention of diversity, the ways of talking and acting at the meetings created discomfort and a feeling of marginality for some of the members who were not male and white.[18] The future inner village seemed to some instead to exclude diversity and to be designed only for what one critic called "the beautiful people."

DIV's actions revolved around turning its vision into a built space. "Putting together the package" of funding and support necessary for their project required that members gain the respect of a number of different "players." They had to be accepted as legitimate and credible by a range of authorities and collaborators, including city officials, the experts from City Development Ventures (the public-private partnership, established and funded by the city council and others) who advised them, the pundits of New Urbanism who lent their plans an extra aura of excitement, the developers they expected to build the envisioned houses and shops, and the leaders of other nonprofit organizations whose cooperation they needed. They had to enlist others into their program to further broad community interests and build collective resources and, at the same time, to make their way through regulatory and bureaucratic thickets.

With government reorganization and the federal government's increasing disinclination to fund major urban rebuilding, large projects such as DIV were dependent on money being raised from other government sources and from private grants. At the time of our research, DIV had received expert advice from City Development Ventures but no direct funding from the city or the county. It hoped to fund the inner park primarily through a city bond referendum. The park would then supposedly draw private developers and other nonprofit groups, such as Habitat for Humanity, to take on the tasks of building the housing and shops that would constitute the desired village effect.

To nudge development toward this New Urbanist ideal, DIV members worked to ensure that the zoning of the area excluded businesses such as warehouses, which were not part of their plan. But beyond the practical tasks of securing proper zoning and the bond referendum, the most important part of their job was the alchemy of turning the concept of an "inner village" into an accepted goal and enlisting the public's interest and self-perception to the cause. Those who would eventually be approving the bond referendum, voting for the referendum, granting the zoning ordinances, and putting up the private capital to build the housing and shops needed to embrace DIV's conception of the future of this part of the city. To stir up public excitement, DIV sent books by Andres Duany to city council members, exercised its media savvy in the press releases it sent out, and launched its own web site.

Officials and citizens alike regarded this kind of public-private collaboration as relatively new to North Carolina, and many found it to have advantages.[19]

According to one Durham municipal official, "The city doesn't want to take on development projects on its own. . . . We use these leverages [building a parking garage] to attract development. . . . This is what we do now, we offer incentives." He explained that the federal government no longer participated in revitalization in the way it had done thirty years before.

Securing local support for the inner village plan probably would have been a quite different task in the past, as well. As a legacy of the city's racial and class struggles, Durham's black community has a long-standing, well-organized political network. Although one DIV member characterized the city as having a "super racial agenda," he felt that its public decision-making bodies, such as the city council, were sometimes difficult to galvanize into action because of the divisiveness of racial interests: developing a major project such as DIV's on an entirely public basis, as in the past, would be very difficult on such contentious political terrain. Under current conditions, with public-private collaborations and their relative seclusion from the public eye, the terrain was much easier to negotiate.

Government business was being accomplished by public-private partnerships and by nonprofits such as DIV in offices and meetings that were considered to be private and nongovernmental and therefore not obliged to be open to the public. While government contributed expertise, the funding for one or two of the components, and its legitimization of projects that it deemed to be of public benefit, it did not necessarily fund the projects fully. Other funding came from private individuals, businesses, and foundations. Nor did the government carry out the projects.[20] This reorganization of the government role made it possible for New Urbanists and other activists to take a major, relatively unsupervised, proactive role in the shaping of what was likely to be a significant public urban space.

COUNTER VISIONS TO MARKET RULE?

Although DIV's projects were motivated by visions and cultural imaginings that lay outside neoliberal schemes, their efforts dovetailed with the city's short-term goals for entrepreneurial development. Moreover, their vision of a revitalized Durham reflected their class background in terms of both taste and goals, such as reviving lost community ties. It is hard to imagine how New Urbanism and its vision could have similarly excited residents in poor, black neighborhoods of Durham, many of whom had different concerns on their minds and had tended to stay relatively close to home for college and jobs, never losing their networks of friends and kin. Despite DIV's efforts to achieve diversity, the group was mostly unsuccessful in this respect and their vision remained constrained by their own backgrounds. Critics of New Urbanism have argued even further that the rhetoric of New Urbanism presupposes the desirability of gentrification, a process with negative effects on established residents who are displaced and whose preferences and needs are undervalued in the process.[21]

Yet because of its members' visions of community and efforts to realize them, DIV was indeed going in a direction that neoliberal projects had neglected. This vision was not one of profit for individual shareholders, but rather of a community in which people had meaningful ties. Social movements such as New Urbanism, environmentalism, human rights, and gay rights have many middle-class adherents. While the activism of these movements is not necessarily directed to redistributing wealth by class or to eliminating the remaining structures that preserve white privilege, they do challenge other central dimensions of the status quo, such as the power of corporations to destroy the environment at will and with impunity. Or, like DIV, they may wish to develop and nurture qualities of urban community life that current styles of housing and consumption have undermined.

DIV's candidacy for consideration as an opponent to market rule comes from its New Urbanist participation in the cultural politics of community, where emphasis shifts from the business community to the neighborhoods where people live. Whether DIV and other New Urbanist projects will ultimately help to install an alternative discourse for describing and shaping the future of Durham and other cities is unclear. Perhaps DIV's ideals and discourse will simply be accommodated to neoliberal emphases on image and used to make Durham sell well to outsiders who have capital to invest. Nonetheless, at the point where we left off the study, DIV did have an alternative vision.

Concerned Citizens of Thornton

Our fourth example of citizen activism comes from the northeastern part of the state, Halifax County, and highlights some of the more powerful systemic arguments we heard. Concerned Citizens of Thornton (CCT) addressed a broader range of concerns than Citizens Unite, with its single-issue focus on air quality in Watauga County, and Durham Inner Village, which concentrated on transforming a specific urban area in Durham. Because it served a population (rather than a landscape) that had been neglected by the government, CCT's activist perspective derived from a set of race and class positions more like those of the Broughton Road Improvement Association in Fayetteville. But CCT took a different political stance than BRIA and managed to develop an array of public services comparable to what might be expected from a government.

Founded in 1978, CCT grew out of a twenty-five-year civil rights struggle to achieve equal education in Halifax County. At the time CCT was founded, citizens were opposing the potential loss of an important center and symbol of their community, the Thornton Chapel Elementary School.[22] According to its literature, CCT also had roots in mutual aid associations established by New

Deal resettlement projects decades before, and in even earlier African-American organizations such as burial associations.

One of the founders emphasized that his middle name means "Protector." Over the two decades that CCT had been in existence, this man had worked hard, along with others in the community, to protect the African-Americans of the area and to develop the community's resources. A shift from small farms to agro-industry, along with systematic discrimination within U.S. Department of Agriculture programs designed to support small farmers, had made it difficult for black farmers to hold onto their sources of livelihood.[23] According to its mission statement, CCT sought to protect the people of southeastern Halifax County and other nearby counties from the loss of their farmland and from the environmental degradation brought on by the large, intensive livestock operations trying to locate in the area.

CCT was a defensive activist organization, but it was also celebratory and generative. It commemorated the history of the region as a New Deal resettlement area; it celebrated the achievements of present-day citizens and groups; and it prepared for the future by training its children and young people for leadership roles. Where there was anger, it came not from a recent rupture in expectations of a helpful government and benign corporations, as with Citizens Unite, but from a long-standing history of racism, abuse, and neglect. Where there was excitement, it was not from a major visionary project soon to be realized, as was the case for Durham Inner Village, but from a feeling of agency in the existing community.

By the late 1990s, when we studied it, CCT was an accretion of groups and projects that had been formed over its history in efforts to secure health care and other basic needs. CCT's logo featured two hands holding a sphere that encompassed several buildings—a symbol of community—with the initials CCT rising above. On the two hands are listed seven different organizations, ranging from members' associations sorted by age group (the Nubian Youth, the Grown Folks Group, and the Open Minded Seniors) to associations focused on particular issues: the Area Health Committee, H.E.L.P. (Halifax Environmental Loss Prevention), the Land Loss Fund, and the Economic Development Committee.[24]

CCT had broadened to the point that it was practically a full-service community organization. It both supplied social, political, economic, and educational services and developed the abilities and skills of its clients and members to act on their own behalf.

HOW DID A SMALL CIVIC ORGANIZATION MANAGE TO ADDRESS ISSUES OF NEGLECT AND CONTRIBUTE TO ACTIVISM BEYOND THE COMMUNITY?

The scope of CCT's issues and projects is likely to challenge the imagination even of those who have had extensive experience with similar community organizations. CCT has worked for social transformation, first, through building community institutions that could directly provide important services; second, through challenging government agencies that withheld their services and failed to protect basic human rights; third, through developing critical perspectives and leadership skills among its members; and, fourth, through its efforts to develop the environmental justice movement in the area and region. Not only was CCT engaged in meeting the health and educational needs of African-Americans in Thornton, through such efforts as pushing for county health restrictions to slow the spread of the hog industry into the area, but it also took a leadership role in movement and activist networks that extended through and beyond the local community. Yet the organization lacked a guaranteed source of funding and made do with relatively meager amounts of money. CCT carried out its multitudinous activities through a bricolage, a mosaic formed opportunistically of funding, partnerships, and an integration of the efforts of its constituent units.

Whereas other groups we had studied formed committees responsible for different components of their current activist tasks, CCT, over its long existence, had built an organization that reflected its deep historical roots in the community and its simultaneous involvement in broader movement webs. At their frequent meetings, the Open Minded Seniors provided social and supportive activities, celebrating members' birthdays, offering sympathy to bereaved members, organizing religious and historical programs, celebrating Kwanzaa and Mother's Day, and contributing money to families in medical emergencies. Sometimes their meetings were dedicated to educational programs (for example, on diet, or lead poisoning), but these could expand to training about environmental racism and other pressing topics and frequently led to conversations about political issues. Members conferred on problems from unusually high family water bills to instances of environmental racism affecting their entire community. They discussed national and regional issues such as the Civil Rights Report from the U.S. Department of Agriculture on USDA discrimination against black farmers, or the legacies of slavery, and the fate of black youth in the criminal justice system. There was no lack of sociological imagination in this group!

In addition to field trips for fun and leisure, the Open Minded Seniors had participated in political protests and lobbying efforts in Raleigh and in Washington, DC. CCT chaired the Hog Roundtable (a coalition of groups concerned about the hog industry); when the group staged a rally in Raleigh in 1997, CCT seniors were among those present. Others went to Raleigh to help the Clean Water Fund lobby for tougher enforcement of state environmental laws; still others went to Washington to participate in a Congressional Black Caucus hearing on black land loss.

More locally, Open Minded Seniors and other CCT members attended a program on environmental justice organized by the Runnymeade neighborhood association; supported a young black scholar, athlete, and author in his fight against criminal charges for shoplifting; and participated in dedication ceremonies of the Thornton Volunteer Fire Department building. During the time of our study, CCT organized two national conferences on black land loss; Open Minded Seniors helped with the planning and other organizational work of the conferences. Two of CCT's members regularly monitored the Halifax County commissioners' meetings and reported back to the seniors. Larger contingents of Open Minded Seniors sometimes attended the meetings, and county commissioners and candidates for commissioner—and even Eva Clayton, the area's U.S. congressional representative—sometimes visited CCT and dropped in on Open Minded Senior meetings, to be grilled by CCT members.

Meeting monthly, the youth group engaged in some of the same political rallies in Raleigh and Washington as the Open Minded Seniors. And, like the seniors, they engaged in discussions that encouraged a critical perspective. Their programs also included informational sessions with speakers who could tell them about relevant concerns—college expectations, for example. Meanwhile, they engaged in fund-raising activities dedicated to realizing a project called Hoop Dreams, for building a community basketball court in Thornton. Several members volunteered time to the People's Health Clinic run by CCT, serving as Pre–Health Career Interns. They also traveled widely to participate in cultural programs in other communities and to support community residents who had achieved local and regional scholarships and other honors.

As with its funding, CCT oversaw a bricolage of activist projects. These had resulted from perceived need, discourses adapted from national movements, and possibilities for funding and services through partnerships (described below) and through the development and recycling of its own historical resources—such as the Resettlement Café, a business run by CCT on land that the organization had purchased. Labor for these projects, including the Resettlement Café, came in part from the members of the age-specific groups. The seniors and the youth were also sources of support for the community services that CCT offered to all residents of Thornton (regardless of membership in CCT) and for the various political struggles in which CCT engaged. In addition, the youth group helped with major social events, sponsoring, for example, a Sunday brunch for the entire community at the Resettlement Café.

CCT's mission was distinctly critical of the status quo. It grappled with issues of inequality and worked for social, economic, and environmental justice. In its oral and written presentations, CCT articulated an inclusive vision of the public good. Important to that vision were basic human rights in a just society, including access to health care and to a healthy environment. These were viewed as rights that should not depend on whether one was of a certain race or income level. Three examples drawn from its newsletters and historical documents communicate this vision:

- "Making the big medical/industrial complex the standard for health care delivery is a vital part of the changing face of politics in the U.S. and has created high-cost, unaffordable, medical care for African-Americans, for the poor and average citizen, and has led to the present health care crisis."[25]
- "When we speak of environmental justice, we often speak of hog factories and landfills and toxic waste sites. However, the denial of equal environmental health standards in the Runnymeade Association community is a perfect example of environmental racism."[26]
- "Access to good health care is a basic human right, and the denial of this right is unjust."[27]

CCT's mission did not mesh well with a neoliberal agenda. If CCT's issues of universal health care, environmental justice, and social dignity did occur on any neoliberal agendas, they did not loom large.

THE CULTURAL POLITICS OF HISTORY, IDENTITY, AND PARTNERING

During the period of our research, an article about Thornton appeared in the Sunday Journal section of the Raleigh *News and Observer,* a major state newspaper. The article, entitled "Still Here," portrayed Thornton as a town that time had left behind. Focusing on a woman who coincidentally turned out to be a member of CCT, the story used her as a symbol of Thornton's tenacity. The people had persevered through slavery, an unusually long history of tenant farming, then a respite in the form of a New Deal settlement program that helped them buy land. Now, because of lack of business savvy and the USDA's discriminatory loan programs, the farmers were losing their New Deal farms.

   Even though she was portrayed as an icon of tenacity in an outmoded place, the woman's story allowed other themes to emerge. She was described as a "woman who walks with a cane now and speaks with a rasp but is fiercely committed to community activism and public education." She expressly cited CCT's tradition of building activist skills:

> A lot of them [CCT members] came here, they didn't know anything about standing up, telling how they felt about something. Now most everybody here can stand up and talk. And then by them telling about their situations, that's helped make it. Because if anything comes up, everybody can know it and we can work on that particular thing. Instead of trying to do it yourself, everybody can turn out and try to help with that situation.

CCT and its Open Minded Seniors had created an organization that nurtured knowledgeable, active members who were ready to discuss problems facing the community and to act collectively to ameliorate them.

One reason CCT succeeded in this endeavor was that it forcefully engaged in cultural as well as conventional politics. It favored names with historical resonance for its buildings (for example, Currin House, where the clinic was located), for its business (the Resettlement Café), and in the focus of some of its celebrations: for its tenth-year anniversary, CCT celebrated Thornton's history as a New Deal resettlement area. It recycled and recreated the area's social and cultural resources, working to make its history a powerful source of identity and agency, instead of touting the charming but quaint and outmoded backwater image conveyed by the article in the Sunday Journal. CCT did not accept a definition of the area as having hopelessly lost in the competition for global attention. Instead, it focused on the rich and special heritage of its people, emphasizing the wealth of resources the community in fact possessed.

CCT carried this identity into the partnerships it formed and the movement webs in which it participated. CCT worked with regional and national social movements, even taking a leadership role in them. In supplying services to people in Thornton and the surrounding area, it relied upon forming partnerships with institutions and offices supported by public funds. Particularly striking was its insistence on treatment as an equal in its relations with its partners. It engaged in the cultural politics of self-definition and demand for respectful treatment.

CCT teamed up freely with members of the university communities in the state and with local government agencies. In one project avidly sought by CCT and funded by the National Institute of Environmental Health Sciences, it collaborated with the Halifax County Health Department and a faculty member from the School of Public Health at the University of North Carolina at Chapel Hill. The federal grant enabled the hiring of a health educator, housed in the county health office, whose charge was to educate people about environmental justice. This partnering furthered CCT's projects and relied upon a discourse of environmental racism—a concept drawn from the environmental justice movement—to fight the further encroachment of the hog industry into Halifax County and to argue against municipal and county neglect of failing sewer systems in African-American neighborhoods such as Runnymeade.

CCT, in 1998,[28] was instrumental in bringing about the first statewide summit of environmental justice organizations and, not long thereafter, in organizing the North Carolina Environmental Justice Network with others around the state, sharing its 501(c)(3) nonprofit status with affiliates.

Besides its teamwork in hiring the health educator, some of CCT's other projects—notably its health services and basketball court—came from partnering arrangements as well. CCT engaged in important cultural politics on this front. It insisted that these relationships be symmetrical, such that CCT was not expected to be the passive recipient of a magnanimous donor's largesse. When medical personnel from East Carolina University and Duke University served in its clinic, for example, CCT described them as participating in "CCT's Intern Learning Program." As stated in the booklet celebrating the clinic's tenth year (1997), the Intern Learning Program was shaped by the following precepts:

- Many of our interns are by chance Caucasian or from other European descent. They have had little or no experience in the real world of poverty, racism, the bureaucratic maze, and the political nature of health care distribution in the United States.
- We find that their intense training and education in their chosen fields of study tends to isolate them even more. Ours is a social change movement. . . . What we try to do is move our interns out of the nest of privilege and the isolation of university towers. Interns are required to live in local homes in the community. They must feel and experience, if only for a short time, what it is like to live without enough food, heat, and without indoor bathroom facilities, and to experience other difficulties and personal struggles of the people they will be working with.
- We do not want our interns to confuse their experience with the Thornton's People's Health Clinic with that of a health fair or a community rotation program. We want them to understand better the meaning of real social organization dealing with health distribution and consumer leadership.

Researchers came in for the same treatment: "We want everyone involved to be aware that community-based research must have community members as equal partners."[29] Our own research team was expected to abide by this stricture. Marla Frederick-McGlathery, our researcher in Halifax County, donated labor to CCT throughout much of the period that she resided in the county.

CCT went to great lengths to insure compliance with its protocols for partnerships, including refusing a physician said to have violated the clinic's guidelines. Unlike our experience with the Broughton Road Improvement Association, we heard no comments from members who feared that CCT might be being exploited by its partners.

GENERATIONS OF ACTIVISM: LESS STRIDENT PROTESTS,
MORE BUREAUCRATIC ACTIVITIES

The activist careers of some of the founders and early members of CCT spanned the end of the 1960s-era Civil Rights movement and the activism of the current era. Founded in the 1970s, CCT in the 1990s still objected to government mistreatment; but while its constituent groups sent members to protests, those events were calm and law abiding. Arrest records for civil disobedience were no longer common, and profiles of leadership no longer strongly featured heroic defiance.

In the early 1980s George Givens, then director of CCT, and some of the other members went up against the white-controlled school board. Even though school desegregation had been mightily resisted by whites, to the point that public schools in the area were mostly all black, whites still controlled the Halifax County school board and predominated among the county commissioners, some of whose rulings affected the schools. Givens won a seat on the school board and was part of a protest at a school board meeting that resulted in his arrest and that of five colleagues when the white-majority school board refused to hire a black superintendent. The group became known as the "Halifax Five plus One." In an interview with us, the "One," a middle-aged woman, pointed out how shocking the arrests had been for the younger people involved. By the time she and her peers were in their thirties, they had all had jail records from civil rights struggles. More recent generations had no such records.

In seizing the opportunities opened by government reorganization, activists at the time of our study had become, or made themselves ready to become, partners of the government. Instead of sponsoring civil disobedience to gain more control of governing institutions such as the school board, CCT had shifted its efforts toward opportunities and funding available through partnering efforts.

This shift was not total. CCT's form of activism included protests, but it put even more energy into piecing together funding and partnerships to provide services and build the social movement organizations to which it contributed. Becoming part of a government/civic-activist hybrid required procuring non-profit (501(c)(3)) status from the Internal Revenue Service, which made the organization eligible to receive government and other funding without incurring tax obligation. Maintaining the status required filing frequent financial reports and refraining from functioning like a political party or engaging in direct electoral activity.

Involvement with the government (including publicly supported institutions such as state universities) or with foundations and other sources of funding usually meant further entailments, such as writing grant proposals, having to shape proposals to meet funders' objectives, and reporting on funded activities. While it was possible to maintain objectives different from those of the government and avoid being overwhelmed by the required bureaucratic work, these tasks necessitated considerable effort. And such efforts also necessitated skills and styles of a different sort than those requisite to effective confrontational politics.

Laurel Valley Preservation and Development, Inc.

At the outset, one might suppose that Laurel Valley Preservation and Development, Incorporated (LVPD) and the associated Laurel Valley Community Council (LVCC) would be engaged by problems similar to those addressed by

Concerned Citizens of Thornton. One of the oldest communities in Watauga County, Laurel Valley lies in the mountainous part of North Carolina. Like the eastern, predominantly black counties of North Carolina, the western, Appalachian region of North Carolina has been subjected to pejorative stereotypes. Media and other sources, including earlier scholarship, had long portrayed impoverished white residents of the hollows and coves of the mountainous counties as inbred and either passive and fatalistic or prone to unprovoked violence. Thus, like CCT, the Laurel Valley group might have been much occupied with a cultural politics addressed to displacing negative stereotypes. But perhaps because members of LVPD were middle-class and either newcomers or natives who had returned to Laurel Valley after working outside the area for many years, they were less vulnerable to such negative attributions.

The commonality between the CCT and LVPD was rather more a matter of material and symbolic dislocation. In Halifax County, economic restructuring and government reorganization had introduced new burdens to the black, largely agricultural community as the land and economy became converted to hog factories and other forms of agro-industry. Laurel Valley and other places in Watauga County had similarly undergone massive disruptions of the cultural and economic landscape as agricultural production and rural community life gave way to ski resorts and other recreational land use, leisure centers, and activities organized around consumption.

Earlier in the twentieth century, residents of Laurel Valley had farmed, done agricultural labor, worked at light manufacturing jobs in the area, or commuted to work in furniture factories off the mountain.[30] By the late 1990s the manufacturing and agricultural jobs in the area had declined significantly, and the available jobs were low-paying service and retail work in the stores and restaurants of Boone, which lies ten miles to the east of Laurel Valley. Long-term residents were being bought out and pushed off their beautiful upland properties, and more "big box" enterprises—Wal-Mart, Lowe's, etc.—were being constructed in the fertile bottomland where, in previous generations, farms had flourished.

Laurel Valley gave less evidence of these changes than nearby towns, which are filled with tourism-based businesses, gated resort communities, and cars from other counties and states. In response to these broad-scale changes brought by corporate globalization and by the continuing consequences of specific local decisions that displaced Laurel Valley from its earlier preeminence in the county, citizens generated two organizations to steer the changes sweeping their community. These organizations had roots in the valley's earlier experience of resistance to the relocation of its important public buildings.

At the turn of the nineteenth century, Laurel Valley was the most developed community in the area. Its economic future looked brighter than that of any other place in the county. Then state officials decided to locate most of the county government and services in Boone. A state training school (which eventually became Appalachian State University) was also established in Boone. Laurel Valley's commercial and urban potential was undercut. A new highway built in the 1950s bypassed the center of the community, and more of the local businesses failed. In the mid-1960s, when Watauga County consolidated its schools, Laurel Valley lost its high school and associated athletic teams. In the mid-1990s the county school board relocated the elementary school, from the old stone building that had once housed the high school to a site several miles east. The old school, a beautiful stone building made by the Works Progress Administration (WPA) in the early 1940s, sat empty at the center of the community, a visible reminder of all these losses. The Laurel Valley community had been essentially gutted. As one of its leaders put it,

> This got to be a bedroom community [for Boone] after consolidation [of the high schools]. People just lived here and then went to work; there was very little interaction except if you went to church. But the thing at church is not to get involved with political, nonreligious matters. So [we did not address community political issues and] it didn't seem like a vital community anymore.

But beginning in the 1990s Laurel Valley residents began to make their reaction to these losses more public. In 1993 the federal government announced its plans to close the Laurel Valley Post Office, one of the last remaining public spaces where neighbors regularly saw and chatted with each other. With the leadership of a man whose great-grandfather had been the first postmaster, Friends of Laurel Valley Post Office formed and encouraged the citizens of the area to petition the government to leave the post office open. Most of the originators of the group were native residents and had extensive kin and friendship networks throughout the area. Their efforts were successful, and the post office was allowed to remain open. In the wake of these experiences, some of the organizers decided they wanted more control over what was happening to the area. They continued to meet, eventually becoming Laurel Valley Preservation and Development, Inc., and the Laurel Valley Community Council.

One of the continuing group's first efforts was meeting with county planners to discuss new, decentralized institutions called community councils, inspired by those newly formed in neighboring communities. The intent of the councils was to allow citizens more say in local affairs by giving them power to engage in land-use planning and natural-resource protection. In 1997, LVCC was officially recognized, with fifteen members. The council began to develop a proactive community plan that aimed both to protect farmland and waterways from encroaching suburban development and to encourage community-based economic development that would "preserve rural character." As groundwork for the plan, the council gathered community opinion by holding meetings and conducting a survey.

In another early project, the organizers worked to save the old school building, an effort guaranteed to garner wide community support.[31] By 1996 they had established LVPD as a separate group, secured its 501(c)(3) nonprofit status, and acquired control of the majority of the building. They leased the property from the county government, organized work parties to clean it up, and began raising funds for essential renovations.[32]

Leaders from these two organizations teamed up with Appalachian State University's Sustainable Development Program and successfully applied for a grant from a state foundation to hire a sustainable communities coordinator, to be based in Laurel Valley. The new coordinator, a native of a nearby area just across the state line in Tennessee, showed the same remarkable ability to develop public domain projects that we found in leaders and members of other activist groups. He used his considerable talents to organize two events: Farm Heritage Days, to celebrate the historic legacies of the area; and a Doc Watson concert, featuring the nationally famous local musician as its central performer. Wildly successful, those two occasions became annual events, bringing in funds for the organization and carrying out the groups' missions for preserving the area's character. Both events marked the distinctiveness of Laurel Valley. Heritage Days, for example, celebrates an agricultural history of self-reliance and preservation of rural ways and values: "The positive display of local identity functions to legitimate the continued preservation of the community lifestyle."[33]

In addition, the Laurel Valley organizations envisioned using their historic school building to house community services, such as a health clinic and a day care center. Several years later, and thanks in part to the considerable skills of its activist coordinator, the old school building had become a demonstration site for state-of-the-art geothermal heating, host to a health clinic and medical training center, and the location of a Doc Watson museum. It had also gained Internet connections via a rental agreement with an e-commerce tenant; at the time of our research, that business was scheduled to supply twenty-five new jobs for the area, helping to realize LVPD's goals for economic development. The grounds in front of the building had been cleared, and every evening people of the community gathered there to walk, talk, and play sports.

MAKING THE FUTURE AROUND YESTERDAY'S BUILDINGS
AND CULTURAL PRACTICES

When asked why the old school building was so important, an LVPD leader explained that it was "a picture of what we're trying to do." It provided a "vision" and a "history." It allowed the organization to "preserve the history but build the future at the same time." It helped to locate and define the community. It gave the group direction, purpose, and vision. Much like CCT's use of the buildings and other symbols of Thornton's past as a New Deal resettlement community, LVPD found a means of anchoring its vision of the future to a tangible sense of its past.

LVPD's successes show that such symbols have more potential to unite people from disparate backgrounds than might be expected. The school and the celebratory events of Farm Heritage Days and the Doc Watson concert were effective, meaningful symbols not only for native residents but also for people who had moved into the community from other parts of the state and the country. The newcomers had arrived long after the building had served as a high school, but they too found ways to understand and value the school and its place in the history of the community. Oldtimers and newcomers alike saw in the center a basis from which to resist the wholesale reorientation of Laurel Valley to a landscape of consumption.[34]

Place-Oriented or Movement-Oriented?

A thread of similarity and a sign of difference among the groups surveyed in this chapter can be surmised from the discussion of the importance of historic buildings. The commonality is the degree to which the groups oriented their efforts to a particular place and its history or to a region or beyond. This question is important to those who wonder whether local activism's small-scale efforts can ever hope to affect globalization or the other large-scale changes to which they are, in part, a reaction.

Citizens Unite, the group initially concerned about the asphalt plant, and Laurel Valley Preservation and Development both began in reaction to the ongoing transformation of Watauga County into a landscape of consumption. But CU's trajectory led to involvement in the regional and statewide environmental movement, whereas Laurel Valley's led to a focus inward on place and a wide array of community issues.

In its beginning phases CU was tutored by more experienced environmentalists. It eventually became connected to environmental groups that were active in the western region of the state, forming a chapter of the Western North Carolina Alliance, and began to work informally with at least one other organization that also participated in environmental issues statewide. CU took on tasks involved with monitoring state regulations and enforcement of regulations pertaining to air quality. On the other hand, CU's contributions to the immediate local community were much more limited in scope than those of LVPD.

In the process of establishing the community council, LVPD organizers accepted some tutoring from the county, but they were less open than CU to involvement in wider movement networks. At one point, the director of LVPD's public-sector partner, the Sustainable Development Program at Appalachian State University, tried to enlist LVPD into the sustainable development movement. He invited the group to officially join the sustainable communities effort and incorporate an organizing document—the Local Agenda 21 strategies from the 1992 United Nations Earth Summit in Rio de Janeiro—into the materials they planned to circulate in the community. They declined, on the grounds that LVPD needed to be seen by the community as a completely local effort.[35]

Concerned Citizens of Thornton, in contrast, had a history of both addressing a broad range of community problems and, at the same time, engaging in, even taking leadership roles in, regional, state, and national movements to stop black land loss and to promote environmental justice. CCT has been important in disseminating the notion of environmental racism not only to the citizens of its own area but also to a more extensive environmental justice network.

The activist projects of two of the five groups described in this chapter were primarily place based. They and the groups that carried them out could best be characterized as locally focused. The others were more engaged with regional, national, and even international movements. Complicating the picture, CCT and (to a lesser extent) Durham Inner Village could be characterized as both locally focused *and* movement focused. In assessing the significance of these groups and their effectiveness, it is important to realize that they are not simply isolated islands of effort to reshape the public good. The groups were active contributors to social movements connecting their members to broader imagined communities—in the case of CU, for example, of "people who care about the earth"—and to networks of people and institutions beyond the local.

Religion and Faith-Based Organizations in the Public Sphere

Missing so far from this discussion of activism and community groups is the role that churches and religious organizations played in the configurations of civil society and in the counter experiments in democracy we studied.

Religion is certainly important in the lives of a majority of North Carolinians. A study completed in 2000 reported numerous religious faiths and denominations in the state, mostly Christian, and total membership of over 3.5 million, nearly half of the state's population.[36] This was an underestimation, as the study had no method for including unaffiliated or regional denominations and congregations (many of them historically black) that do not keep national records. One reviewer supplied more data: "If the 1990 numbers for . . . two historically black churches (AME Zion and the Black Baptist) are added, the NC proportion of adherents would rise to 55 percent of the population, well above the national mean."[37]

More or less nondenominational religious and social movements organized via the Internet and televangelism—such as the "New Christian Right"—also have a strong following in North Carolina.[38] The growing popularity of large-arena conferences like Bill McCartney's Promise Keepers, which have been hosted in at least three North Carolina cities, Charlotte, Greensboro, and Raleigh, and T. D. Jakes's ManPower and God's Leading Ladies[39] is further evidence of widespread religious involvement. These para-church movements are aimed at shaping individual lives with the goal of transforming society. Through a type of neoconservative emphasis upon personal responsibility and transformation and taking strict biblical cues from their evangelical and Pentecostal backgrounds, these conferences have focused on issues such as abuse, self-esteem, personal finances, marriage, and sexuality.

Nonetheless, there were several reasons why, despite the religious involvement of many North Carolinians, faith-based organizations were not so visible in dramas of contention and thus no religious organization became a focus of our research on local politics. One reason has already been mentioned. For many adherents, religion was better practiced at a distance from politics—a traditional position staunchly upheld by such venerable figures as the internationally respected North Carolina evangelist Billy Graham.[40]

A second factor was that churches phrased contentious issues and conflicts in spiritual terms and addressed them in the context of church doctrine, policies, and programs, rather than through the mechanisms of secular politics.[41]

Third, our study took place before such organizations were promoted, in G. W. Bush's first term, as legitimate partners for government. Since the study, religious groups as such have become more prevalent in dramas of contention and a segment of the religious population in the United States has become more visible in mixing religion and politics in the public sphere. Both the 2000 and 2004 presidential elections amply demonstrated that point.[42]

Even though churches and other faith-based organizations were seldom direct participants in dramas of contention, spirituality and religious outlook did constitute an important mediator for some in the reformation of their personal lives and, in cases of involvement in local activism, in the framing of their participation. As described in the chapter on political autobiographies, religious convictions were often cited by those we interviewed as the wellspring for civic action, and fellow church members were often named as key sources of information about local issues and politics, broadly defined.

In Halifax County, this blend of religiously informed personal activism with more direct engagement in the public sphere could be seen in members of

Concerned Citizens of Thornton. Some actively listened to and participated in the ministries of popular evangelists like T. D. Jakes, but their work in CCT drew on an integrated spiritual and political understanding of the complexity of the challenges facing residents of their own county.[43]

Moreover, as might be expected, despite the low level of direct involvement of religious groups in dramas of contention at the time, prayer and other religious practices, as well as references to religious themes such as stewardship of the land, were not uncommon in the civic activist groups we studied. Moreover, and certainly not surprisingly, some of the groups (CCT, for example) contacted local churches in order to notify people of their civic actions and to recruit community support. Nonetheless, faith-based groups qua religious organizations were not central players in the dramas of contention that we followed.

Discussion: Changed Conditions for Activism and Its Possibilities

Looking across the places where we did research, we see that market rule has altered the terrain of activism and community organizing. The targets of action, along with the conditions to which community-oriented activists are responding, are clearly linked to the prevalence of neoliberal arrangements and rhetoric.[44] Yet, as we and several democratic theorists have noted, there is an opening in market rule for extending democracy.[45] There are unforeseen possibilities in market rule's support of potential partners for government, even partners with alternative, not-for-profit visions of the common good. Acting to resolve community problems shaped by corporate globalization and seizing upon possibilities created by this government reorganization, the associations described in this chapter developed projects and programs, sometimes in close partnership with government.

Because of the increasing significance of public-private partnerships, including market-oriented public-private partnerships and outsourcing, the role of the government in structuring and providing services is more diffuse than in the past. The boundary between government and business has become less distinct, as has the line between government and civil society. As the government has entered into partnerships with more and more businesses or with civic activists, its role as a target for dissent has become less clear. Who should be blamed for the shortfalls and mishaps in social services: the government, its partners, or even, in neoliberal logic, the consumers of the services?[46]

While the image of heroic activism from the Civil Rights and student movements of the 1960s may still linger in popular imagination, and indeed some activist groups do stage protests either occasionally or (as with the Global Justice Movement) as their signature activity, members of today's organizations are less likely to be imagined as sign-carrying protestors; instead, they are neighborhood people rushing around to myriad meetings and staying up late to write yet one more proposal. With relatively little funding, they serve the community and region and sometimes the country in various ways. One or more of the organizations we reviewed

- conducted cultural politics by attracting media attention that circulated alternative definitions of the public good and not-for-profit visions of the good society (all groups), creating positive valuations of what poor people have to teach others (CCT), and redefining the environment as a common good (CU, CCT);
- served as a sustained source for expressing citizen concern and provided a space for formulating alternative ideas about economic and community development (CCT, CU), environmental safeguards and health protection (CU, CCT), urban design (DIV), and racism (CCT);
- supported or took leadership roles in translocal social movements (CU, DIV, CCT);
- helped to transform sentiment and consciousness regarding the environment (CU, CCT);
- communicated local input to state politicians and officials (CU, CCT);
- helped to prevent unwanted land use and economic development in their area (CCT, LVPD);
- reduced crime in their neighborhood (BRIA, CCT);
- created a more positive community identity (BRIA);
- fought government neglect of neighborhoods and populations (BRIA, CCT);
- planned, promoted, and were on track to redesign an urban area (DIV);
- provided health services to neglected populations (CCT);
- recycled local history not as a tourist commodity, but as a resource vital to public life (CCT, LVPD, DIV);
- created a space for and attracted small businesses (LVPD).

These efforts constituted counter experiments for democracy and assisted communities with the challenges brought about by neoliberal governance and economics. As discussed in the previous chapter, advocates of associational democracy see a great potential in such associations.[47] They promote designs that would channel more government resources to associations and would pass on to them more responsibilities for governance.[48] Cohen and Rogers, for example, see associations as potentially

> providing a distinctive form of social governance, alternative to markets or public hierarchies. . . . In providing a form of governance, associations figure more as problem solvers than simply as representatives of their members to

authoritative political decision makers, pressuring those decision makers on behalf of member interests. They help to formulate and execute public policies and take on quasi-public functions that supplement or supplant the state's more directly regulatory actions.[49]

Fung and Wright, for their part, as we have seen, forward a more modest, and perhaps more feasible, proposal that encourages empowered participatory governance. They call for devolution of administration and politics from higher to lower levels of the political system, for coordinated decentralization, and for a state-governed system. They want to expand citizens' deliberation and decision making in the provision of services and other state processes, through mechanisms such as participatory budgeting and resident assemblies and through direct involvement of citizen associations such as those we have featured here. These increased opportunities for participatory projects extend democracy beyond infrequent elections that typically offer only a weak choice among fairly similar candidates, usually wealthy, and always backed by wealth. They whet citizens' tastes for challenging the strongly plutocratic features of the present system.

Whether associations like the Broughton Area Improvement Association or Citizens Unite can play a larger role of the sort that these democracy theorists think they can is another question. Can they ultimately be a force for opposing the tendencies of U.S. democracy toward plutocracy? Or, are they prone to debilitating developments such as Marwell's account that intimates such organizations are too easily caught up in exchange relationships with politicians, and too easily tamed?[50] Our research indicates areas where such associations show promise, others that signal major problems and difficulties to be overcome.

Democratic theory, building on de Tocqueville, has long looked to voluntary associations for their role in sustaining democratic governance—or, in opponents' views, they have been eyed suspiciously as narrow interest groups potentially challenging democratic governance. For those who see them as crucial to democracy, such associations are viewed as engaging their members in participatory democracy and providing them with opportunities to develop their skills, sentiments, and sensitivities for democratic governance. This is clearly the case for Concerned Citizens of Thornton and others of the associations reviewed.

Also important is their role, as we have seen, in focusing and shaping public opinion, thus fulfilling a responsibility of civil society to democratic governance. The associations provided conceptual and physical spaces for the development of counter public spheres, and they attracted media attention that often distorted, but nonetheless aired, dissent from those who occupy less favored social positions and who offer nondominant visions of the good society. As we also observed, such organizations were sometimes linked to translocal social movements seeking to halt wanton environmental degradation, for example, or to eliminate racism and poverty, or to transform the socially negative aspects of contemporary urban life.

Judged from the perspective of empowered participatory governance, Concerned Citizens of Thornton, Laurel Valley Preservation and Development, Inc., Citizens Unite, and the other local associations considered here are outstanding arenas for participatory projects that address immediate, community problems. Participants' commitments to their communities, their knowledge of local interests, needs, and conditions, and—especially as seen with Durham Inner Village, Concerned Citizens of Thornton, and Laurel Valley Preservation and Development, Inc.—their efforts to build on local history engage bottom-up participation. And in each project there is the opportunity for members to deliberate about organizational goals and strategies and to tie discussion to action.

But, as we note, the voluntary associations were not spontaneously responding to all needs. There are no guarantees. In undertaking the job of revitalizing its neighborhood, BRIA, for example, did a great service to the area. Yet the formation of the group and its voluntary embrace of the task occurred, in some sense, by happenstance. Had BRIA not existed, the task would probably not have been carried out. The same was true of the work undertaken by the other groups described in this chapter. There were no mechanisms in place to ensure the encompassment of all the populations who need services.[51]

The high level of skills and knowledge necessary to prevail in the stiff competition for funds and resources both from the government and from philanthropic sources was evident in our research. Moreover, it was clear that community-oriented activist groups' social and political expertise had to be considerable to achieve any measure of success in delivering public services.

There are further problems to be solved if such associations are expected to take on a greater burden of governing. In effect, activist groups elect themselves to the roles they undertake as public-project activists and as suppliers of public services, and there are no controls. Standards for internal democratic practices are not necessarily pursued. Even when the groups themselves work hard to bring in a diverse membership, as in one of the cases discussed (Durham Inner Village), they do so of their own accord and may lack either sufficient will or the know-how to achieve it.

Our study strongly suggests that if voluntary associations are to take on more of the burdens of distributing public goods and public services, as some theorists urge, or, even additional tasks urged by the vision of empowered participatory governance, there will have to be some mechanisms for encouraging the development of more associations. Those who espouse further dependence on community associations for government services need to specify a mechanism to make sure that every segment of the population has a group carrying out public-project activism on its behalf. There must be some way to assure that all segments of the population have associations that can form community-oriented public-private partnerships that work effectively to serve their needs, and to fund them.[52]

It is reasonable to imagine that groups of associations might form broad alliances to press for these changes and undertake some themselves. Because these groups do fill in for government to some extent, and so in a sense make neoliberal cuts in services more palatable, they might even have some success.

Hirst calls for associational organizations to "rebuild from below," to assume greater collaboration and self-conscious coordination in providing services and in creating conditions for their own expansion.[53] As we've argued elsewhere, Hirst's overall proposal needs to be reformulated, but, conceivably, "rebuilding from below" and taking other steps toward extending empowered participatory governance, especially if they were to develop into a broader democracy movement, could significantly erode arenas of plutocratic control and bring the nation closer to democracy.

11 It's Up to Us

From Local Politics to a Democratic America?

Our Findings

American politics has never stood still. Viewed historically, the United States has cycled between long periods of anti-democratic consolidation of plutocratic power interspersed with widespread, successful campaigns by active, organized citizens that have fundamentally transformed the political system in more democratic directions. In dynamic process since the nation was established on the contradictory foundations of slavery and liberty, American politics is now passing through a phase of radical reformation—but its direction is uncertain. Are we moving into another period of firming up the structures of plutocratic rule, or are we entering an era of popular mobilization and democratization? The postwar political system in place up to the 1970s is being profoundly reshaped by challenges arising from globalization, economic restructuring, and government reorganization. Because people's everyday lives are deeply affected by these changes, communities across the country have responded to them. Citizens now emphasize local politics in a new way as a source of redress and satisfaction. There people find familiar barriers to participation, but, at the same time, new democratic possibilities. The consequences are as yet unclear. We are at a pivotal moment.

In the course of our ethnography, we discovered a major shift in political terrain that we had not fully imagined. By listening carefully to people and observing their daily democratic practices and the context for them, we found that only an extraordinarily broad definition of politics could describe this shift, one beyond more common notions of politics. We learned the value of ethnography for teaching us about the new demands placed on and the possibilities for local politics, particularly when we listened to the views of those ordinary citizens who are usually absent from public deliberations and media imagery. We discovered that the political pundits' claims about the angry or apathetic voter missed much of what we heard and observed. It has always been clear to any observer of American life that some people are excluded when political decisions are made, while others play a preponderant role. To the extent that journalists cover the machinations and corruption in Washington and in state legislatures, people can read about the influence of money and powerful corporate interests on political deliberations. However, until we began our study, we had only a thin idea about what exactly is now necessary for effective political participation on the local ground where politics occurs across American communities.

Local politics is never transparent. It is instead an enormously complex and changing process that few have the time or wherewithal to investigate and understand. Doing so requires going beyond the myths that tell us how politics works, whether those myths come from classic conservative, liberal, or libertarian paradigms. One of the most striking features of the new political terrain of market rule we observed is the expanded importance of public-private partnerships, which create what could be called outsourced government. These partnerships include both market-oriented, for-profit and community-oriented, not-for-profit partnerships. Whereas commentators, newspapers, television shows, and college textbooks define politics in relation to representative democracy with its emphasis on voting, elections, and political candidates, government's for-profit and nonprofit partners are now extremely influential in governance and the provision of public services. Even more recently, we have seen the rise of the idea that government should partner with faith-based organizations to design and implement public programs.

The idea of politics needs to be expanded beyond the familiar electoral processes to include the availability and workings of these partnerships. A whole new layer of complexity, with both dangers and opportunities for democratic participation, is now in play. To have a say, local residents must deal with powerful people and processes that have no mandate to include, and in fact often exclude, them from participation and, less well recognized, many must either participate or have advocates who participate in partnerships with government.

So important is this newly expanded political arena that we are simultaneously apprehensive and excited about its present openness. It allows, and to some extent supports, the development of alternative visions of the good society, as imagined by groups such as those we studied. On the other hand, government-private partnerships frequently become not much more than for-profit development schemes that allow few avenues for public oversight of decisions of governance and the expenditure of public funds.

Of the many examples we found, one of the most striking was the public-private partnership called the Marvin Plan in Fayetteville, which pursued the revitalization of the downtown area without getting input from all who stood to be affected, thereby excluding, for example, one of the largest and most long-suffering groups of residents in the downtown area, poor African-Americans. Amelioration of their poverty and underemployment was not in the plan except, as some might argue, as a trickle-down effect of enhancing the profit-making capacity of downtown landowners. Supposedly, the greater profits would be reinvested in the area to create jobs and bring more people (though not necessarily or even probably the poor), and so, in the developers' terms, increase safety and security in the downtown area.

In any event, whether we look to the bright or to the dark side, outsourced government with its heavy reliance on public-private partnerships is frighteningly devoid of guarantees that all segments of the public will be served. If a particular segment of the population is for some reason unable to organize itself into associations that can effectively partner with the government, then it most probably will experience neglect, and even real social harm.

At the same time that the federal government, in agreement with politicians' neoliberal commitments, has scaled back government by cutting the social services it provides, state and local governments are encountering new challenges brought about by globalization, associated flows of labor, goods, and capital, and suburban sprawl. For example, in a relatively brief period Siler City in Chatham County has seen its population expand and shift dramatically as it incorporates a large influx of Latino workers and their families. City schools must adjust to much higher numbers of children who need ESL classes, housing stock is strained, and older inhabitants' tolerance of diversity is called into question. Moreover, the conditions of labor in the poultry plants where the new laborers are offered jobs are grim. The geographer David Harvey has compared them to factory conditions prevalent in England over 150 years ago.[1] When we began our research, we thought that race stereotypes and notions of who is a real "American" would probably make political input from the new immigrants from Central and South America unwelcome. But we found that the tests put to democratic incorporation were even more severe than we had imagined. We learned how much the dehumanizing work and living conditions of immigrants is part and parcel of their political disenfranchisement. As Bob Hall of Democracy North Carolina tells us, those who process pork and chicken for our tables are being physically mangled and discarded so that when they are disabled, they lose their jobs as well as health, and are forced to return to their places of origin in Latin America.[2] While in the United States, they are worked so hard, so long, and under such difficult conditions that they have little time for politics, and many, particularly those who are undocumented, are excluded by intimidation, while vulnerable to harassment from anti-immigrant citizens and police.

Economic restructuring challenges local communities in yet other ways. The shift from small farms to agribusiness and the impact of agribusiness operations on the environment provide another example. In the name of keeping capital investment from moving elsewhere, government is often hesitant to regulate the massive environmental impacts of such operations. People who live with the stench and water pollution produced by tens of thousands of hogs or chickens are told that their greater interest and that of the community require their cooperation and silence: the market has decided, community elites say, jobs are at stake, and so political life should not concern itself with effects on the environment.

Another case is found in the rise of the landscapes of consumption we examined in chapter 2. The economic successes of some of these places of tourism, retirement, and educational and other services appear to a minority of their residents as one of the great payoffs of neoliberal reform. But here, two distinctive populations have been created: market forces largely unimpeded by public regulation favor upscale consumers while others—people who are in effect subconsumers—get poorly paid service and retail work, higher costs for housing, food, and health care. These costs, as well as the layoffs and casual work arising from economic restructuring, mean that in some areas old timers experience the disappearance of their former occupations, are funneled into service work, and lose their previous ways of life. Meanwhile, the hopes for and perspectives on local politics of those in service jobs are different, as we have seen, from those of the people who are served. And, the voices of the latter are often more dominant in local political venues than those of the former.

These challenges and schemes of government reorganization are putting heavy burdens on local political institutions. At the same time, responses to these challenges are being shaped mostly by a select few. As we have documented in this book, older means of exclusion from regular politics are still prevalent and also characterize the new political terrain with its privatization and public-private partnerships. Perhaps the exclusionary mechanisms we observed have come as a surprise to some readers, especially those who have not yet tried to have input on local issues. We observed how racial discrimination sidelined even city and county legislators in several of our communities. And we heard people, no matter what their race or ethnic group, speak of their experiences with marginalization and subtle public shaming that dissuaded them from trying to present their views in public discussions. We saw how powerful individuals started task forces in communities and only recruited "diverse" others from less powerful segments of the community in order to get their "buy-in" and input. But a variety of forces—including the initial interests that created the task forces in the first place—limited their input and caused them to drift away.

Moreover, we noted a subtle but powerful means of unequal influence on political decisions. Since the 1970s, neoliberal thinking has come to dominate local government, and is now a dominant language spoken by local elites—elected and appointed officials and the members of growth coalitions that influence them. It is this language that has the most influence over local resource allocation and priority setting. This for-profit mentality assumes that market rule *naturally* makes for a good society. However, market rule privileges citizens with disposable income, and it focuses on the values of consumption, assuming that people are not first citizens with rights as well as responsibilities with respect to society and government but instead are individual consumers responsible for satisfying their own individual needs by making smart, economical choices in the market place. This orientation produces a highly individualistic vision of the good society, one that is blind to issues of social justice and equity. In such a society, which one person we spoke with likened to "crabs in a basket," politics is no longer a place for conversation and contest over conflicting ideas about goals for the community. Market-oriented, neoliberal, for-profit thinking puts forward instead the idea of society as a technocratic arrangement for individuals pursuing wealth and economic growth, even as it is clear that some, the so-called good market performers, will benefit significantly more than others. It has the goal of profit making, with social benefits supposedly emerging as a byproduct of the unfettered pursuit of individual wealth.

This neoliberal blueprint sets the stage for a select minority being players while the rest exist off (or exit from) the map of the new political landscape. When community development and local political discourse are organized on such grounds, business people are cast as supercitizens while those without the means to contribute—that is, without business know-how or capital to invest—emerge as de facto subcitizens. This blueprint also leaves serious social problems unrecognized and so unsolved, especially the material, social, and spiritual costs that unregulated markets visit on people. People we talked with recounted these costs to us. They include the stresses that economic restructuring produces locally: high rates of individual mobility and the attendant transient, impersonal, and fragile social relationships among members of any community, whose political life is thus undermined; labor influxes of the sort experienced in Siler City with the unaccounted and publicly unaddressed costs in new housing, schooling, transportation, health, and security needs; as well as retraining of those downsized. Local infrastructure suffers whiplash from the new fiscal demands placed on it and an incapacity to plan for the future, as corporations' hypermobility is valorized as good for the whole. Meanwhile, local pro-growth policies connected to land speculation for space-extensive development encourage suburban sprawl that disinvests in older communities, increases people's commute times and energy use, pollutes the air and water, and devastates outlying farming and natural ecosystems.

Neoliberalism's privileging in these ways of powerful individual market players, if unchecked, threatens the permanent destruction of the three-legged stool of democracy posited in chapter 1. One of the crucial assumptions of any democratic polity is that there is a "public good" or "public interest" that is greater than the (imaginatively) summed up individual interests within a diverse population. Those committed to the public good, for example, value preserving environmental quality for future generations over protecting the monetary interests of those who stand to gain in this generation by ignoring the accumulating injuries due to global warming. However, neoliberalism asserts by fiat that the common welfare is no more than the sum of the interests of self-interested individuals, and argues moreover that since this is the case, the market—not government—is the prime and generally only appropriate means for ensuring the interests of the individuals who compose it. Democracy's counter claim is that the common welfare—the group interest in question, whether of a community or a nation—is greater than the sum of the material interests of the individuals who form that collective and that this common good can only be achieved through the "rule of the people," that is, the collective effort of citizens working together, not through the competition between individuals that market rule requires.

Turning for a moment to consider the unintended positive possibilities of the experiment with market rule, we found striking and evocative alternative visions and counter experiments of what community development could consist of. Several of these visions—those of the Concerned Citizens of Thornton, for example—drew powerfully on local history and place not primarily, or even secondarily, to make money, but to create and nurture a sense of community belonging, identity, and interdependence.[3] Just as importantly, the activist groups we studied provided experiences of participatory democracy with an emphasis on conversation and debate, surely a core feature of any political process that claims to value equality and openness. Even though the Durham Inner Village group had difficulties reaching the level of diversity it wanted, the group provided a good example of the way politics could be remade in a manner that valorizes the exchange and discussion of ideas. Through such conversation, residents become citizens once again and not just consumers. We have only to remember the words of the older member of the Concerned Citizens of Thornton quoted earlier: "A lot of them [CCT members] came here [to CCT], they didn't know anything about standing up, telling how they felt about something. Now most everybody here can stand up and talk."

While the new political terrain does allow these alternatives to be developed on a small scale, we note sadly that these views—for example those of the Concerned Citizens of Thornton or of the Broughton Road Improvement Association—falling as they do outside the neoliberal orthodoxy, are largely ignored in public and official discourse.

One crucial reason for the exclusion of alternative visions, despite their intense popularity, is racial and class privilege. In our sites wealthy whites still set the terms of debate, although with strong contenders in Durham. In combination with overt prejudice, African-Americans and Latinos face more subtle forms of race and class privilege. There is still ongoing race-specific networking of power brokers. Also of great significance is the even more nuanced race privileging afforded by the dominant market logic, which marginalizes alternative African-American and other racially and ethnically inflected views of development. For-profit emphases exclude or crowd out efforts toward social justice, equity, and noncommodified community ties. These exclusions compromise democracy.

We have already raised another concern with the new hybrid forms of government: the partnerships of the several sorts we have described do not by themselves insure that all interests will be served. First, the kind of private organizations that communities now depend on to supply public services often do not serve the general interest. While members of excluded groups organize some of them, it is more favored groups and individuals who run them more often than not. Second, social problems around which people have not yet organized will not be spoken to, and their needs will go unmet. Further, there is no guarantee that a community-oriented partnership or group will step forward with the necessary material, cultural, capital, and organizational resources to meet the pressing social needs previously addressed by local, state, and national governments. For example, when requirements for federal food stamps have tightened, nonprofit organizations that provide food distribution and community kitchens have not always risen to meet the need, and some people, including children, have gone hungry.

There are now fewer guarantees than before that the governing process is meant to serve and be visible and accountable to everyone. The leaders of nonprofit groups, operating under 501(c)(3) status, can direct their efforts when and where they want in contrast to a public social service agency, whose services must be defined by elected or employed agents of the public as a whole. Especially when the public good comes to be defined by the market, as it is in the case of for-profit partners with government, there is no necessary assurance that all or even most will be served. Leading actors in the new political economy redefine *political* debates as irrelevant at best, anathema at worst. This follows from both the notion that efficiency is a paramount value and the idea that there is nothing to debate: there is just economic science and its wisdom about the magic of the market to put to work.

On the other hand, these new conditions of local governance can foster the growth of groups of all political stripes, as people recognize that they can and need to take initiative if things are going to improve for themselves or others. The burdens of time and effort have increased on citizens and on those groups, especially those most in need of public or collective assistance, who do not agree with market rule and the reigning neoliberal logic and its less than vigilant attention to social justice, environmental protection, and other such concerns. Where once ordinary citizens could, again at least in theory, call on government, political parties, and political interest groups to work on their behalf to allocate public resources to their specific needs on an ongoing basis, they now must think of forming associations that address such issues by seeking out whatever public and private funds they can find. They must rely on leaders with the crucial social and communications skills needed to secure such funds. The possession of these skills is often itself a form of privilege separating leaders from other members, and those who are organized in groups from those who are not. Moreover, these groups now compete with each other as they troll for more resources. This reshaping of volunteering and activism may be celebrated by some as the flowering of an American spirit of social entrepreneurial initiative and generosity, but it makes the attainment of the public good far more uncertain than it would be via a more guaranteed collective and cooperative means.

For Citizen Activists

The foregoing account brings insights from our ethnographic study of people engaged in politics in the places where they live together with debates on large-scale economic transformation and government reorganization. Here we summarize related points for those seeking to participate in local politics.

From the vantage point of our study, market rule has some things to offer citizens, but much for citizens to fear. Neoliberal reorganization of government has produced a mixed outcome promising several potential futures. Which future it holds depends in good part on how people use the opportunities now and in the next ten to twenty years. If most accept the position proffered them by neoliberal thinking and identify themselves as *consumers* of education, health, and other services, then the United States will continue to develop as a consumerist society primarily serving those with money to spend or a willingness to carry extensive consumer debt. More and more those in charge of educational, medical, pension or retirement, and social service programs will claim to be compelled to purge their rolls of those whose needs cut into profits. Equally important, the services will be aimed not at building community or encouraging social justice and equity or even individual well-being, but at ensuring profits for shareholders.

On the other hand, some citizens have opted instead to participate in the widened opportunities for a variety of nonprofit groups to design and implement local projects and services. Right now, market rule is inadvertently open to groups whose members are committed to alternative visions of the good society—ones that call for such activities as building community, serving as stewards of the environment, striving for social justice, and overcoming racism. At present, it is possible for such groups to enter into partnership with the government in order to provide public services. This option, in counter distinction to a consumerist society with a merely formal democracy and thus infrequent input at election time, offers a more hands-on, participatory democracy. In our research, we have seen how groups provide prototypes for empowered participatory governance that would make local politics far more democratic than at present. Whether such associations and mechanisms develop to the point of creating a truly democratic politics is very much an open question. Nonetheless, groups of local citizens can and are devising counter experiments *for* democracy.

For those who are unhappy with the current movement of American politics toward entrenched plutocracy, fearful that they or their children might one day need a government-provided safety net, irritated that their neighborhood is neglected, unhappy with the current lack of environmental protection, or worried that their area will be stranded by the government in the midst of a disaster, we make the following points from our study.

The first point recognizes that American politics is undergoing a significant makeover. *Contemporary politics involves not just politicians and government agencies but also nonprofit and for-profit partners of government. Now, more than ever, there is more to politics than voting and contacting institutions of government.* Market rule and its associated government-by-outsourcing have changed the way the government serves or doesn't serve the people. Public-private partnerships therefore deserve to be a major topic of political conversation and media coverage. The issue of whether the government should directly partner with faith-based organizations is properly a hot news item, but there are many other issues that should be aired. While there are some exciting possibilities associated with the new governmental arrangements, there are no guarantees that all will be served. It is a new system that needs to be critically examined *as a system.*

A related point constitutes the second message of the book for citizens and activist groups: *The day-to-day participation of people in voluntary associations is just as important as whether they vote.* Most of the people involved in Citizens Unite, in the Concerned Citizens of Thornton, and in the other groups described in the book had little if any experience serving as politicians or government officials. Many had not even participated in prior activist groups. Yet, when we met them, they were engaged in activities that provided important public projects and services such as supplying health care to poorer people in the area, making decisions on the part of the community about local development, and informing the state government about local air quality. As the government hands over services that its agencies used to provide to non-governmental partners and for-profit business, the development and flourishing of non-governmental groups is key to the political health of particular locales.

The issue of who gets elected to office is still important. Voting is still a significant act that deserves to be a defining feature of citizenship. Nonetheless, citizen participation in nongovernmental groups that partner with the government is now important in a way that goes beyond membership in the Shriners Club or the Kiwanis Club or some other voluntary associations that helped with public works in the past. Assistance from such organizations has been important in many places, but the public projects of those segments of civil society were supplemental, and not expected to carry the heavier burden that nongovernmental groups bear today. Through these latter groups, everyday people, not just politicians and paid officials, take on the work of furthering the public good. Since members of these groups are active in shaping public services and visions of the public good, they must also be recognized as engaged in politics—not electoral politics, but politics broadly defined.

This book is also clear on a third point: *In order for local democracy to become strong, communities have to become more economically and environmentally sustainable, which makes it possible for individual citizens to have the high degree of individual economic and social security they need to participate actively in democracy. Measures citizens take toward sustainability are also steps toward more democratic communities.*

After all, we are referring to the survival of communities. We are referring to inextricably linked economic and environmental sustainabilities to the protection of the human rights of individual citizens to their livelihoods, to a quality of life marked by material dignity, and to their capacity to pass down the economic, social, and environmental commons that is a collective inheritance to future generations.

The three processes of globalization, corporate disinvestment in communities, and the dynamics of suburban sprawl promoted by local growth coalitions generate economic insecurity among citizens and the lack of economic and environmental sustainability of communities. These outcomes force citizens to surrender their democratic rights and their human rights to dignity and enhanced survival.[4] Large-scale job loss and community economic devastation due to plant close-downs, and the creation of "throw-away cities" whose housing and public facilities are devalued through the development policies of suburban sprawl all increase economic inequalities among citizens and among the places they live, and impede democratic participation and cooperation.

The wastefulness inherent to these three processes jeopardizes the use of tax revenues in ways that make local democracy more feasible. For example, these processes lead to irreversible degradation of local and regional environments through the "destructive creation" of new settlements—leading over time to uncontrolled pollution of air and rivers, the destruction of forests and wetlands, and the deterioration of living standards. Adverse environmental changes place even greater burdens on local politics by exacerbating conflicts over land use between neighbors (and neighboring communities), and by forcing the expenditure of valuable public monies to redress environmental problems.

These processes also directly corrode and even destroy the local social institutions and political groups essential to local democracy.[5] Moreover, when processes of globalization, corporate relocation, and accelerated suburban sprawl lead to job loss and devaluation of community assets and places, citizens belonging to the majority begin to scapegoat immigrants, racial minorities, women, and other marginalized groups as the source of their misfortunes—for, for instance, "unfairly" taking jobs previously held by white men who "work hard and have families to support." The majority condemn affirmative action policies costing "more than the market can bear." Such scapegoating is a double injury. It is an injury to vulnerable racial and other stigmatized groups who far more often suffer from greater job loss and destruction of their assets than the majority when economic traumas do occur. It is also an injury to democracy itself, because members of these groups are driven away from participating in local politics.

The evidence provided in the rest of this book shows that where communities, such as those we studied in North Carolina, have little control over their local economies and environments, then local democracy appears to be impossible. Fortunately, in this respect another America is possible—in fact, in an increasing number of communities, due to the hard and at times amazing efforts of citizen activists on behalf of sustainability, it is already coming into existence.

The fourth major point is that alternative visions of the good society are important: *Even though most politicians support market rule and practices of outsourcing government, a significant number of local activist and social-movement groups advocate alternative visions oriented to community, social justice, or some other not-for-profit vision of society.* A proportion of the government's partners are those championed by neoliberal thinking. They are bottom-line groups, either for-profit businesses or nonprofit groups whose orientation is nonetheless to business concerns. Still, groups exist that are not dominated by profit-making goals or the idea that the free operation of the market constitutes the public good. Some place a premium on services designed to encourage sociability and build community; others think that respect for all groups is important;

others want to serve people even when or especially when doing so is not profitable; others revere the environment for itself rather than its market value; others care whether its members develop as informed citizens. Many such groups, moreover, are attentive to the means by which they seek to achieve these goals, and pay respect to the actual processes of democratic deliberation and decision making in their own operation.

What is the significance of and support for these alternative visions? It may well be that visions of community, social justice, environmental stewardship, humanitarian concern for those in need, equal rights, and democratic process have more appeal as life values for a large proportion of people in the United States than the for-profit dreams and drives of the business world.

A fifth and related point concerns the timeliness of pursuing empowered participatory governance now: *The cultivation of voluntary associations and other forms of empowered participatory governance is not only necessary but promising at this point in the country's history.* The reorganization of government, with its emphasis on outsourcing and public-private partnerships, makes local-level organizing to pursue the public good crucial. Moreover, such efforts are now more eligible for public resources than they were at many times in the past. These are opportunities to design and craft services to fit other than for-profit values and additionally to experiment with and expand participatory democracy. Local associations such as the ones we've described allow citizens much greater input than simply casting ballots every few years. Through being a reflexive practitioner in these groups or in related activities such as participatory budgeting, one develops a deeper understanding of local problems and the way to solve them and thereby develops further as a citizen and a contributor to the transformation of local politics and community.[6]

One source of hope and encouragement is that, despite the odds against it, citizens working together have already accomplished so much on behalf of a more just, sustainable, and democratic society. The examples of community organizations described in this book need to be considered along with other counter experiments for enhancing democracy and community that are occurring in other sites and locales. In addition to the groups discussed in the previous two chapters, there are many examples of functioning, successful local-level institutions that encourage participatory democracy as well as the economic and ecological sustainability of communities:

- locally based consumer cooperatives, community-owned corporations, and nonprofit corporations (some of which engage in for-profit business enterprise);[7]
- community-supported agriculture that not only supports local farming but also provides poor and middle-class residents with nutritious and low-cost fresh foods;

- employee stock ownership plans (ESOP) and workers' cooperatives that greatly enhance local economic sustainability, increase local economic equality, retain wealth generated within the community, and further workplace democracy;
- Community Development Corporations that provide jobs, low-cost housing, and other employment and business opportunities to community residents, and Community Development Financial Institutions that support the retention of local wealth, like credit unions, and micro-enterprise loan funds;
- living wage ordinances, local currencies, buy-local policies, and economically targeted investments by public pension funds that increase the incomes of residents, create local jobs, and generate multipliers that minimize the amount of wealth flowing out of communities;
- state- and municipal-owned enterprises that provide utilities such as electricity and water, operate facilities such as airports and hospitals, engage in real estate and other business enterprises—and by so doing add jobs that stay in communities, retain locally generated profits for in situ reinvestment, and meet the essential needs of residents.[8]

There are similar developments in North Carolina.[9] The promotion and encouragement of these institutions also provides citizens with a long-term agenda to achieve local economic prosperity, environmental sustainability, *and* local democracy.

A final point for participants in local democracy is more on the order of a postscript. *Ethnographic research is a means for democratic listening useful to those citizens and activists hoping to converse with others and work to better their communities.*

Since completing the study, we have begun to hear of activist groups adapting and developing ethnographic research as part of their activities. For example, Durham Congregations and Neighborhoods (CAN) seeks to answer questions about the communities it serves by using ethnographic tools such as participant observation to discover underlying problems and issues. Another example is the work of Parent U Turn, with UCLA's Institute for Democracy, Education, and Access (IDEA) as the academic partner.[10] Parents, after being trained in qualitative and quantitative methods, use survey methods, GIS mapping, and participant observation to argue with city and county leaders for more equitable schooling. Currently, a project in two rural North Carolina counties seeks not only to train parents as advocates for their children but also to use ethnographic methods as part of the curriculum so that they can begin to identify and "research" key questions that impact the structure of the children's schooling experiences.

At the core of ethnographic research is the premise that understanding human life in general and political behavior in particular demands observation of both the daily processes that make them up and the meanings that people, differentiated by resources and privilege, give to these events. We see the cultivation of ethnographic skills as another prerequisite for the development of informed citizens. There is no reason why citizens and activist groups should not ask how diverse groups in their communities interpret changing economic circumstances and act on their interpretations. In a place like Watauga County, for example, how is the intensification of place as a landscape of consumption being interpreted by different groups? Or, in a place like Chatham County, what problems has the expansion of agribusiness led to and how are different segments of the local population responding? As part of their participation in the politics of place, citizens could ask, What is the vision of the future being promoted in the community? Where are that vision's origins? Does it include everyone's interest in it? Who will benefit if the vision becomes a reality? Who will be left out?

These are the sorts of questions that ethnographic research both encourages and helps to answer. Of course, ethnographic research does not answer the question of how anyone *should* use his or her resources and energy, but it does provide a means for broadening one's perspective on how and why a community or neighborhood is changing and developing and who is trying to steer that change in what direction. Ethnography calls for noticing how these changes are interpreted and how different parties attempt to have their way through these interpretations. It encourages citizens who are trying to see the world and such things as desires for development from the different perspectives and life circumstances of those involved. In short, it develops the democratic art of listening in its broadest sense.[11]

Scaling Up: How Can Associations Be Mobilized toward a National Political Transformation?

While local democratic politics may provide the interpersonal and organizing abilities and imagination necessary for citizens to work effectively toward democratizing the national political system, it is clear that these capacities are insufficient in themselves for effective political action aimed to attain this goal. As we note above, the last two decades have been marked by the demobilization of locally based but nationally active citizens' organizations, notably, but not only, labor unions.[12] Over the same period, however, translocal networks and institutions such as those that compose the environmental and New Urbanism movements have been indicators respectively of shared, translocal, organized discontent.[13] Whether and how these various movements eventually coalesce will affect whether there is a long-term entrenchment of market rule and plutocratic governance, at all levels of government including the national.

It is imperative that citizens' associations now scale up into mobilized translocal coalitions acting regionally and nationally if the democratization of one, two, many locales is to lead to—that is, catalyze and even bring about—the democratization of national politics. We find most promising the models manifested in two social movements, one that draws on our own local ethnography, the other that, like the organization that inspires it, comes out of translocal research: the environmental movement in the United States, and the global justice movement.

First, like Skocpol, we have found that the environmental movement, whose activism we discovered in the locales we studied, not only provides values of vital importance to a real democracy (e.g., protecting the global environmental commons) but may also give us an actual example of the way active citizens in local groups can ally together in translocal federations to effectively seek and achieve democratic rather than corporate rule nationally by focusing on the environment and our common fate with it.[14]

Second, the global justice movement provides a singularly innovative organizational form, a hybrid that combines local groups affiliated with the movement with local activism and protest focused on specific sites like Seattle, Genoa, Davos, and Cancun where the rites of corporate globalization (e.g., meetings of the WTO, World Bank, IMF, World Economic Forum) are performed and with transnational and translocal organizing undertaken by activists on specific issues—and with this collective effort amplified by electronic technologies like the Internet and cell phones for intramovement communication and public dissemination of its positions.[15]

Both the environmental and global justice movements provide alternative promising models for scaling up via translocal mobilization in order to further democratization, and both, notably, target plutocratic rule in American politics and seek to transform it.

In this book we have relied upon ethnographic research methods and upon the simultaneously detached yet engaged perspective provided by ethnography to step back from the usual questions asked about the health of democracy in the United States. In their place, we have asked whether the shape of democracy has been altered by the intense social and economic changes of the last thirty years and, finding a new terrain, we have asked what the possibilities for this new politics are. Above all, we have sought to describe the circumstances that compel us to ask, Under current conditions, how can local politics be made more democratic? How can revitalized democratic local communities become part of, the source of empowerment for, and the grassroots bases for a mobilization of citizens in a broader movement to make the American political system more democratic?

The "puzzle of contemporary democracy" that opened chapter 1 juxtaposed contradictory images—one of the empowered associates of Durham Inner Village seeking to realize their vision of a transformed downtown; the other, a couple estranged from government to the point that they apparently lack the confidence to enter the City Hall Complex and pay their water bill. In answering how these contradictory images reflect the changing shape of democracy in the United States, we have described the openings inadvertently provided by market rule and government reorganization that some citizens are now using to build new pro-democracy projects. We have pointed out that some translocal organizations and networks have means for mobilizing those who dissent from politics as usual, on the national as well as local and regional levels. On the other hand, we have also described the myriad forms of exclusion faced by those seeking to have public input. Market rule and the outsourcing of government have risen to dominance over the last thirty to thirty-five years. If, going forward, this form of governance continues to set the context for democracy, then progressive visions must attend both to the activists of New Urbanism and to the couple who turned away. We have advocated ideas for advancing empowered participatory governance through both voluntary associations that provide public services and formal mechanisms of participatory democracy, such as participatory budgeting. At the same time, this call for refiguring democracy from the ground up must find ways to insure that all are served by, and, more ideally, themselves participate in shaping those services. Those like the couple on the sidewalk must derive benefit from an expanded participatory democracy as they, too, imagine the possibility of democracy at all levels of government.

Appendix: Democracy and Political Theory

Why Participatory Democracy?

Theorizing Participatory Democracy and Its Alternatives

Ethnographic projects display a strange interplay among data, analysis, and theorization. The associations forming the counter experiments in participatory local democracy we were taught about by our informants described in chapter 10 led us to subsequently theorize the importance of participatory democracy and empowered participatory governance in chapter 9. As we began to rigorously conceptualize what our ethnographic data revealed, we began to assess what theoretical purchase on them, if any, political theory and political science might have to offer. We discovered that opposed to the approach to participatory democracy that our ethnographic data validated and our personal values supported, there were conservative theoretical views within political theory that rejected this approach and favored elite representative democracy, while more critical approaches within political theory both opposed these views and buttressed our own. What follows is an exploration of the issues raised by our research within political theory as we see them.

If American Politics Is Undemocratic, So Much the Better! (Two Cynical Views)

One View: Public Choice Theory

Public choice theory basically adopts a free-market economics or market fundamentalist view of politics—the profoundly cynical view that the American political system is a deformed market, and that in vital areas of economic life it would be better to dispense altogether with government in order to allow self-correcting free markets to do their work unimpeded by politics and generate optimal solutions to social problems.[1] In this view, voters, elected representatives, and civil servants alike are rationally selfish, "utility-maximizing" individuals,[2] and politics is no more than bad economics, encompassing as it does a rigged market for public wealth displayed in the hypocritical drag of democracy.

Grounded in possessive individualism, public choice theory makes several related claims.[3] First, political parties and interest groups represent only the

249

aggregation of the economic self-interests of the people belonging to them, and aim primarily to gain access to public wealth.[4] Second, competition in politics, unlike in real free markets, is bogus "because of the power of incumbents, agenda setters, single-purpose groups, and the ignorance of voters."[5] Third, citizens rarely make informed choices because the costs of acquiring information far outweigh its value to them.[6] Fourth, there is a ubiquitous rent-seeking process where "politics creates profit opportunities or rents" by creating artificial scarcities, e.g., through regulatory licensing, allocating patronage projects, paying above-market salaries to officials, or providing public funds to welfare recipients.[7] Fifth, there are free riders in public life, since a rational individual will not expend her or his own effort on behalf of collective goals because the cost will exceed an uncertain return, and thus political actors will take advantage of gains others have secured. As a result, legislative politics will be dominated by smaller and more narrowly focused groups (where fewer share the spoils gained).[8]

In general, rarely have the five claims made by early public choice theorists been subjected to empirical test. Ironically, there are elements of truth in several of these claims. As to the second claim, the power elite described in chapter 9 injects the corporate agenda in the national political arena, ensuring that decision-making outcomes are usually fixed—in favor of corporations—much as in "real" markets.[9] As to the third claim, although citizens often work hard to learn more about public issues, since the 1960s most have indeed been *less* well-informed about issues, given the manipulation and use of technical, legal, and scientific expertise by corporations to further the corporate agenda.[10] As to the fourth claim, it is quite clear that when rent-seeking occurs, it best characterizes major outlays of public wealth—defense and weapons contracts, tax-code giveaways, pharmaceutical price protections, and much more—that are forms of corporate welfare.[11] Moreover, *more* accountability to citizens through procedures of public disclosure is what prevents corruption and abuses of public office from becoming systemic, but this is precisely what public choice theory rules out as impossible because it assumes uninformed citizens.

The other two claims—that political parties and interest groups are defined by economic self-interest and only seek public wealth, and that free riders are ubiquitous in political life—convert anecdotal observations into theoretical generalizations based on the cynical assumption that political actors are always possessive individualists. But human beings are far from always being possessive individualists; the doctrine that they are, as Macpherson demonstrated, draws on cultural assumptions about human beings specific to Western industrialized societies.[12] Moreover, both claims assume extraordinarily narrow and economistic definitions of self-interest, as if *all* citizens who engage in politics were no more than market actors.[13] These two assertions are thus false as empirical generalizations about political life. Many citizens, the movements they make up, and elected and appointed officials—as distinct from corporations and their lobbyists—engage in disinterested or civic-minded behavior in national politics; others of course do not.[14] Many citizens and their movements seek not to gain a free ride from public wealth but rather to add to it or even redefine it by new conceptions of the public interest, as in the environmental movement's proposing the environment as a commons and public good.[15] American civic life is rich beyond counting in such examples of selflessness and public-spiritedness.[16]

Much more consequential than its limited intellectual contributions is public choice theory's rhetorical message replicating a cynical "common sense" about "real life." On one side, popularized versions of public choice theory signal to ordinary citizens that their participation in politics is indeed futile. On the other side, it provides a prescriptive primer of cookbook abstractions and how-to maxims to the power elite: it proposes how economically self-interested actors—particularly corporate representatives and their supporters—*ought* to act when they get the chance. Public choice theory serves to further the aims of uncontested plutocratic rule. But then, as such, it is part of the problem, not part of the solution.

A Second View: "Realism," or the Theory of Procedural or Minimal Democracy

Allied to public choice theory is the theory of minimal or procedural democracy most closely associated with the views of Joseph Schumpeter.[17] Like public choice theory, this realist theory holds that the political system can only be undemocratic or minimally democratic, yet like public choice theory it fails to acknowledge that this is due to enduring structures of economic and political inequality. And like public choice theory, procedural democracy theory has contempt for the ordinary citizen and his or her capacities to participate actively in governance. But rather than claim that the market (i.e., corporate community) substitutes for citizens' pursuit of public interest, this theory proposes that the only democracy possible, given citizens' incapacities, is a formal procedural or minimal democracy—a set of institutional arrangements where governance is almost all the time in the hands of elites.

Schumpeter's view is basically that democracy should be all it can be but that when it comes right down to it that isn't much. Schumpeter argued that citizens should be limited in their participation in politics to the vote: democracy is not rule by the people as such, but rather rule by elites *approved* by the people.[18] Political parties are like firms competing in the market, votes, like profits to be competed over by politicians, and policies, the goods and services priced out through elections. In this scenario, voters are like consumers, voting with their votes rather than dollars for one party's candidates rather than the other.[19] However, the political "market" is "open" to citizens to "shop" (i.e., vote) once every two or four years, and the rest of time is accessible only to elites, the market makers. Other than their episodic convening as voters, Schumpeter assumed most citizens have no capacity, interest, or role to play in democratic politics.[20]

The theory of procedural or minimal democracy first proposed by Schumpeter in the 1940s has had at least two reincarnations since then. Some pluralist approaches have focused on the function of interest groups in insulating the national political system from citizens who could be irrational, extreme, and erratic in their demands on it. Citizens could become a threat to democracy and its institutions; and only through their being led and guided by political elites who controlled these interest groups might democratic stability be ensured.[21] As a result, political scientists by the 1960s "had converged on a 'low citizenship' model of democracy . . . that could be sustained, and even enhanced, by only modest levels of popular interest and participation."[22]

Since the 1940s, the notion of polyarchy, or the institutionalization of formally democratic institutions of governance, has become popular.[23] Dahl argues that whereas the democratization process in which democracies emerge from nondemocratic polities ("closed hegemonies") involves two different dimensions of change—public contestation by opposition parties and voting as the right to participate in government—increasing liberalization can change in one or both dimensions.[24] There are different degrees of polyarchy, rather than a single, fixed democracy. Still, for Dahl, a minimal criterion for a polyarchic (and thus potentially democratic) polity is that there be a periodic vote of citizens who elect the candidates put up by one or more political parties as their choice of rulers but who otherwise have little to do with processes of governance.

The notions of Schumpeterian, polyarchic, or low-intensity democracy are diminished, downsized versions of democracy, ones simply not good enough for the citizens of the United States—or of the rest of the world. Democracy is above all *rule* by the people, not just voting by the people for elites who do the actual work of rule. As we show below, Schumpeterian and other elite theories of rule do a disservice to citizens by casting them as necessarily ignorant, irrational, and incapable of forming a general *will*. Certainly, citizens today find it difficult to penetrate the mystifications of experts in Washington, DC—who, even among experts, does not? However, local activists are capable of and committed to informing themselves about complex political issues, and lead other citizens toward the greater understanding needed for critical democratic participation.

A Response: Rational Citizens, a Deliberative Public, and the Passions

Basically, realists' or minimalists' indictments of citizens' capacities come down to three claims—that citizens cannot form a rational public to decide on how to govern, that citizens are not individually reasonable, and that citizens are too emotional and intolerant to play the active roles in governing that participatory democrats call for. If these views were correct, then there would be little hope for participation as an essential design feature of local democracy, much less of democratization of the national political system. They bear close examination.

In new research, Marcus and Hanson and their associates suggest that all three characterizations of citizens by realists are theoretically flawed, inaccurate empirically, or simplistic.[25] In actuality citizens come together to form rational publics capable of debating and deciding on complex issues, they are individually reasonable, and political intolerance toward marginal groups is not so much a widely shared emotion as a selective outcome of public debate mobilized by elites. Much of this new research is based on sympathetic questioning of ordinary citizens—i.e., on ethnography—rather than on the superficial and "framing" methods of opinion surveys. We have found that the "truth" needed for the best democratic decision making always comes out of debates by citizens' publics. Where truth is not arrived at, it is not because individual citizens or the publics they form are irrational but because citizens are not sufficiently informed about their interests or not sufficiently involved as participants in governance to begin with, or because elites act demagogically.

Let us examine each of these claims. Realists claim that most people aren't interested in politics, aren't sufficiently knowledgeable, or have unchanging opinions; the result of their governing would be chaos, disunity, or rule by an ignorant majority. But new research demonstrates instead that the public as a whole deals with political issues carefully and intelligently by means of a process in which individual shortcomings are compensated for by the strengths of others brought out in collective debate; and that individual citizens often change their opinions as an issue is debated.[26] Through deliberation, citizens "discover and modify their preferences in light of other people's needs and interests"—common interests are defined and recognized, as are collective procedures for determining what their interests are.[27] Opinion leaders—whether arising within the public itself, from among its elected leaders, or from among experts—play a crucial role in the debate process, because they are in positions to educate or deceive the broader public. As John Dewey argued, it is the public airing of issues and opposed policies by their advocates that brings leaders to account—that allows democratic politics to progress toward discovering accurate information and achieving just and fair policy solutions.[28]

The second claim by realists is that individual citizens are impatient and impulsive when they try to understand complex issues, ignorant but not aware that they are ignorant, and prone to using emotion rather than reason. However, "new evidence points to previously undetected capacities for deliberation and moderation" among citizens.[29] Moreover, citizens' views of the range of personal freedom they have to express their opinions vary, and while some speak out, others self-censor. "Apathy" is most often better seen not as indifference or lack of interest but as self-censorship arising from fear of being abused by either government officials or other citizens. This is particularly true for people who are members of racial minorities or are poor, with personal experiences of being abused by authority or majorities.[30] We found in our own research (chapter 3) that people are often fearful of involvement in local politics because of unspoken intimidation that inhibits their participation. Moreover, most adults have sophisticated ideas about citizenship, realizing that it confers not only individual rights but also individual obligations.[31] It also turns out that contrary to realists' anxieties that citizens will be doctrinaire, citizens have a tolerance for the uncertainty and ambiguity that arises in political debates.[32] They display "ideological flexibility" or open-mindedness by showing—often through their silence—that they are uncertain about how specific political principles should apply to issues they are debating. People try to resolve these personally felt conflicts through investigation and further discussion.[33] But these actions are signs of reason at work, not of irrationality or doctrinarism. The critical social contexts for the formation of a rational citizenry are the civic associations in which people work together toward common goals, engage in dialogue and argue, and learn both specific civic virtues (e.g., a sense of generalized reciprocity and trust) and political skills (e.g., how to conduct a meeting or confront a representative). (See chapter 10.)

The third realists' claim is that citizens are too driven by passion and too intolerant to play a major role in governing. Early research using opinion survey methods seemed to confirm that elites were more tolerant than ordinary citizens of dissenting groups.[34] However, there is no evidence that people found to be intolerant through opinion survey research actually act upon their feelings in public life,[35] while the new subject-centered research suggests that a rational public may not necessarily be a tolerant one.[36] Citizens' tolerance for dissenting or marginal groups (e.g., U.S. Communist Party, Ku Klux Klan) depends on the extent to which they fear these groups.[37] What therefore appears to matter more than individuals' opinions about whether groups should or should not be tolerated is whether such opinions enter into public debate. And even more crucial is one implication of the way debates are structured around elites' roles in debate: whether elites *mobilize* resentments toward disliked groups by ordinary citizens, as occurred during the McCarthyist Red Scare of the 1950s,[38] and as has taken place in the post-9/11 period. In addition, the positive place of emotion or passion in processes of democratic rule should not be underestimated.[39]

The new evidence suggests strongly that citizen-publics are rational, that individual citizens are reasonable, and that the intolerant opinions held by citizens insofar as they exist toward certain unpopular groups only matter when they enter into public debate and are mobilized by elites who promote majority intolerance.

Is the American Political System Pluralist?
The "Upper-Class Accent" of "The Heavenly Chorus"

In staking out the position that the American political system is undemocratic, we reject the widespread pluralist account of the political system.[40] That account argues that class is irrelevant to politics in the United States because there is a plurality of interest groups, of which business groups are only one, vying for power and influence over the legislature and executive. Pluralists argue that the proliferation of these interest groups creates a more representative, more inclusive politics even as the two main political parties decline. Pluralism represents what Aronowitz calls "the common sense of contemporary American politics"—that "what you see is what you get," and what you see is a diverse number of interest groups, some allied with business, some with labor, some with minorities, some with environmentalists, etc., each contending to gain decisive control over the legislative process, and each occasionally winning what it wants.[41]

Pluralists have failed to pay attention to the American conundrum that plutocratic rule is effective most of the time on critical issues but is also unstable and occasionally fails due to democratic mobilization against it. That is, pluralists have taken the occasional, rare lack of success of the corporate agenda and legislative successes by groups not sponsored by the corporate community on peripheral issues to imply that there is no power elite, much less plutocratic rule. This is the classic nominalist fallacy of mistaking each legislative and executive decision-making outcome, however trivial, as equally significant for defining rule. However, when it comes to issues crucial to challenging upper-class interests and developing democratic potential, such as providing citizens with more power to make decisions in the workplace vis-à-vis corporations, spending public funds to empower an increasing number of citizens to participate in politics (e.g., funding income support, more leisure time, adequate health care), and placing curbs on corporate capacities to move capital or pollute the environment, the power elite's opposed corporate agenda virtually always wins out.

The power elite and its allies within local growth coalitions exercise power not only when it affects the outcome of a decision but also when it prevents issues that threaten their perceived interests from ever reaching the public domain of legislative deliberation.[42] The pundits and conservative think-tanks subsidized by the power elite and given airtime in the media it controls spend much of their time generating and disseminating definitions of reality acceptable to it—even if damaging to the needs and interests of ordinary citizens—and preventing dangerous views from entering the public domain. Citizens may not even be aware that they are affected by nondecisions, for their needs and sense of interests can be shaped in ways that prevent issues from ever coming up, through the use of spin and manipulation of data by the power elite and the intellectuals and experts beholden to it. Those who set agendas through these strategies may not even be aware that they are doing harm to specific groups of citizens.[43] In these ways, the power elite and its pundits engage in issue-definition control as much as issue-outcome control. It was in part for this reason, as we state in chapter 1, that we developed our ethnographic method of, on one hand, studying dramas of contention in which media have played a prominent role in constructing narratives about public issues and, on the other, interviewing citizens who were nonparticipators and concerned about public issues that had not congealed into mediatized political dramas.

When it comes to dealing with these critical forms and dimensions of power, pluralists' obsession with appearances, which leads them to count specific decision-making events, and who wins and who loses, is simply not up to the conceptual task.[44] The criticisms of pluralism advanced here apply to local politics as much to other levels of the political system. The structural domination of plutocratic rule through these arrangements and stratagems leads us to agree with Schattschneider that "the flaw in the pluralist heaven is that the heavenly chorus sings with an upper-class accent"—when, we would add, it bothers to sing at all about major issues of pressing concern to the majority of citizens.[45]

Notes

Preface

1. Goodman and Watts 1997; Harvey 1989; and Sassen 1988.
2. Some models do exist. We were inspired, for example, by Lamphere (1992).
3. Pathbreaking ethnographic work on democracy has been done by Paley (2001) and Gutmann (2002)
4. One consequence of our approach is that reoccurring actors, particularly the activist groups we followed, are presented and analyzed from a variety of angles, including in their own words, appearing in one chapter as successful at some endeavor, in a second, as less successful in another regard. We have endeavored not to present a seamless evaluative portrait of these groups but rather to present them in their complexity as actors in a variety of fields of action, including, for example, challenging local cultural codes, participating in social movements, resisting market rule, creating potential resources for increasing democracy, and being judged by other community members. It is also the case that we as individuals had different relations and reactions to these groups and thus our overall tone toward each group is not necessarily consistent. We see this complex picture as an advantage.
5. "Empowered participatory governance" is a term employed by Fung and Wright, (2003) who call for more opportunities for democratic input to government decision making through increased roles for voluntary associations and through governing procedures such as participatory budgets.

Chapter 1

1. Unless indicated otherwise, we substitute pseudonyms for the names of people and organizations who participated in our research.
2. Quotations are close to verbatim (taken from handwritten notes at the meeting).
3. See, for example, Couto with Guthrie 1999; Cohen and Rogers 1992; and Hirst 1994.
4. "Neoliberalism" sounds as though it might refer to political liberalism with its focus on government intervention for the public good. Instead, neoliberal ideas come from an earlier period in history. The liberalism in question highlights economic, not political, matters.
5. The sources of philosophical neoliberalism are many. A major source is the right-wing libertarianism that arose from the influential writings of Ludwig Von Mises and Friedrich Hayek in the 1950s and 1960s. More recently, libertarian thinkers include those working within the free-market–economics approach pioneered by Milton Friedman and the Chicago School, and the public choice theorists in economics and law who are influenced by this approach. Another strain comes from the public policy advocates associated with the Cato Institute. See Kuttner 1997 and Hardisty 1999.
6. In the name of getting rid of "big government," many elected political leaders, in order to "starve the beast [government]," have repeatedly mobilized the populace to call for reductions in the taxes that have funded these programs.
7. We have been helped inestimably in our thinking about what neoliberalism is (Is it "discourse," "ideology," "political rationality," "governmentality," "received wisdom," "ethos," or "world view"?) by the keen reflections of John Clarke, both in his recent book (Clarke 2004) and in personal communications.
8. We cannot discuss the many theoretical and factual shortcomings of neoliberalism here. For critiques, see Bilmes 1985; DeMartino 2000; Polanyi 1957; Sclar 2000; Stiglitz 2002: 21; and Yates 2003.
9. In 1998, the wealthiest 20 percent of the population owned over 80 percent of all such wealth in the country (Wolff 2002, 2003, 2004).
10. Reagan 2004.

11. Moyers 2004: 6.

12. Ibid.

13. The German philosopher Jurgen Habermas and his critics provided us a beginning set of ideas about what he calls "the public sphere" and its relation to government. Our concern with social diversity guided us to Habermas's challengers (e.g., Garnham 1992), who have questioned his disregard of the media's role in shaping public opinion or who have taken issue with his failure to address the way some are excluded from the public arena and that there are in fact multiple and contending publics (e.g., Fraser 1992).

14. McChesney 1997; Bagdikian 2004.

15. Economist Joseph Schumpeter (1950) coined the phrase "creative destruction."

16. Year by year voting statistics are available online at www.infoplease.com/ipa/A0781453.html. The percentages are based on voting-age population. Since the time of our study, some researchers have attributed the decline in voter turnout not to increasing apathy but to increasing numbers of ineligible voters. McDonald argues that voting percentages should be based on the voting-eligible, not the voting-age, population. The number of ineligible voters (primarily noncitizens and those who have been or are in the prison system) has been rising steadily since the early 1970s. Eighteen and a half million residents of the United States were not allowed to vote in the 2004 election (McDonald and Popkin 2001).

17. Voter turnout was up some points in both 2000 and 2004. (The trend in voter registration is less positive—see Jamieson et al. 2002: 11.) Nonetheless, the voting rates still translated into a relatively small proportion needed to win the presidential election. George Bush was credited with receiving the votes of roughly half (50.7 percent) of those who voted in 2004. Those who voted for Bush constituted only 28 percent of the voting-age population.

18. Putnam 1995, 2000.

19. Putnam's concept of social capital is relevant to a dimension of community or solidarity as we define it, but is only tangentially related to the questions we address. By social capital, Putnam means "features of social organization such as networks, norms, and social trust that facilitate coordination and cooperation for mutual benefit" (Putnam 1995: 67). For additional references to the debates, see Boggs 2001; Durlauf 2001; Foley and Edwards 1996; Montanye 2000; Muncy 2001; Newton 2001; Shapiro 1997; and especially Jackman and Miller 1998.

20. Kempton et al. 2001.

21. See Amin 1996; Couto with Guthrie 1999; Evans and Boyte 1986; Hirst 1994; Hirst and Bader 2001; and Putnam 1995, 2000.

22. Skocpol 2003; Evans and Boyte 1986.

23. Kempton et al. 2001.

24. Couto with Guthrie 1999.

25. See Fung and Wright 2003 for more on empowered participatory government.

26. Dagnino 2003.

27. For this method, we drew on Turner's (1974) social dramas in the anthropology of political process.

28. See Zukin, *Landscapes of Power* (1991). We chose our five sites to represent the range: Durham and Watauga County have transformed into landscapes of consumption; Chatham and Halifax Counties remain landscapes of production; Fayetteville and Cumberland County, affected as they are by a large military presence, constitute a landscape of the state. We also paid attention to racial divisions and sought out communities that varied according to the local power base for African-Americans. We located two cities (Durham and Fayetteville) where African-Americans lived in significantly large numbers and had developed institutions with a successful role in local politics; and three (Halifax, Chatham, and Watauga Counties) in which they had not.

29. Liebman and Wuthnow 1983; Smith 2002.

Chapter 2

1. A landscape of production is defined by an ethos that values productive labor, such as growing food or manufacturing textiles or chemicals. In landscapes of consumption, an ethos of consumption dominates everyday life—whether we are speaking of consuming the experience of a university education, summering in a vacation home, shopping for the latest fashions, or using the specialist medical services of a regional hospital. Los Angeles, despite its

aircraft industry and its large neighborhoods of sweatshops and unemployed people, is primarily a landscape of consumption, its culture and economy dominated by shopping, tourism, and movie making. Landscapes of the state are those places in which the effects of localized institutions of government are so great that they generate a dominant ethos in which residents orient their lives toward these institutions, their goals, and their resources.

2. Floren 1997.

3. North Carolina Rural Prosperity Task Force Web site.

4. Warrick and Stith 1995.

5. Williams 2001.

6. Wood 1986; Bluestone and Harrison 1982.

7. Price 1996.

8. Boyd and Watts 1997; Cecelski and Kerr 1992; Gouveia 1994; Hall 1989; Heffernan and Constance 1994.

9. Giardina and Bates 1991.

10. Boyer et al. 1993.

11. Lutz 2001.

12. Southern Exposure 1995.

Chapter 3

1. See Merelman's (1991) study of popular culture, which helps explain the types of democracy present in three English-speaking countries.

2. The very distinction between public and private lives is a culturally constructed one.

3. Cantrill and Roll 1971.

4. Bellah et al. 1985.

5. Dahl 1996; Voet 1998.

6. The realists include Lippmann (1925) and Sartori (1987). The participatory theorists include Pateman (1970), Dahl (1985), and Flacks (1988). See appendix.

7. Hanson and Marcus 1993: 5; see also Conover et al. 1993; and Hochschild 1981.

8. The questions posed were the same. We asked each person to characterize his or her "involvement in local public issues," and to describe a memorable moment during which they "got really concerned about a local issue." Each person was asked, "What draws you to the idea of getting involved?" "What would you say encouraged you to get involved?" and "What discouraged you from getting involved?" Each person described his or her thoughts and actions or inaction concerning nominated issues of concern. We also asked them to say where "you talk with others about these issues."

9. Schudson 1998.

10. Verba et al. 1995.

11. Parenti 1996: 46, 47.

12. Ibid.

13. Teske 1997.

14. Ibid.

15. Mitchell 2002.

16. Schor 1991.

17. Retirement as a concept is very important to democracy on this score. As more people retire at earlier ages and live longer, fresh blood for democratic life is produced. In those cadres, of course, class and racial and gender divisions do not disappear.

18. U.S. Census Bureau 2006.

19. These included mainly African-American and Latino individuals whom we interviewed, with approximately 5 percent of the people we interviewed mentioning that they had been harassed or threatened with harassment.

20. Mills 1959: 5, 6.

21. See Pfister and Schnog 1997.

Chapter 4

1. For more information on racist violence in North Carolina see reports by the NCARRV (1982–present).

2. The black belt region in North Carolina is characterized as the eastern region of the state, but especially the northeastern region, where the largest number of African-Americans live and also where the strongest impact of the slave trade was felt.

3. Black belt counties like Halifax often have the lowest literacy levels in the state. In 1997, in the five counties studied, 38 percent of Halifax residents—compared to 24 percent of both Durham and Cumberland residents, 22 percent of Chatham residents, and 12 percent of Watauga residents—scored at the lowest levels of literacy (National Institute for Literacy 1998).

4. Edwards and Ladd 1998; Olson and Lyson 1999.

5. UNC epidemiologists examined the location of approximately two thousand five hundred intensive hog-production facilities, or confined animal feeding operations (CAFOs), across North Carolina and found that "these facilities are located disproportionately in communities with higher levels of poverty, higher proportions of nonwhite persons and higher dependence on wells for household water supply." The health concerns that such placements raise are exacerbated because CAFOs are locating in areas that already have "the highest disease rates, the least access to medical care and the greatest need for positive economic development and better educational systems" (Wing et al. 2000: 229).

6. Stull et al. 1992: 51.

7. Chatham Community Health Improvement Project 1997.

8. Perea defines nativism as "the intense opposition to an internal minority on the grounds of its foreign (i.e., 'un-American') connections," resulting in immigration restrictions and discriminatory legislation (1997: 1).

9. Ungar cites statistics showing that illegal immigrants "may draw on such services as free medical care, unemployment insurance, and welfare less often than is generally supposed . . . [due to their] fear of being caught and deported. . . . [P]ractically no 'illegals' receive Social Security payments, but 77 percent of them put money in, and 73 percent have federal income tax withheld from their wages" (1995: 96).

10. Mahtesian (1997) discusses Enfield officers, as well as elected officials from various other parts of the country from Arkansas to Tennessee, who have boycotted government meetings in protest of the lack of attention given to minority concerns.

11. Churches in many regards served as the central meeting place not only for political activity but also for schools, camps, stores, weddings, and community events. For a further discussion of the church as a black public sphere see Higginbotham 1993 and Glaude, Jr. 2003. Also, for a discussion of the religious activism of African-American Protestants, see Wilmore 1972; Lincoln and Mamiya 1990; Paris 1985.

12. Lubiano 1997.

13. Moss 2003: 3.

14. Hinojosa and Park 2004: 229.

15. See Emerson and Smith 2000: 96.

16. Ibid.: 98. Emerson and Smith also consider the influence of religious conservatism on African-Americans, concluding that African-Americans in general place greater emphasis on discrimination and lack of educational opportunity as an explanation for racial inequality than whites, with African-American religious conservatives placing even greater emphasis upon structural problems. They conclude that religious conservatism has an opposite effect on blacks and whites.

17. Hartigan 1997: 496.

18. Luebke 1990; Key 1949.

19. Chafe 1998.

20. U.S. Department of Commerce 1997.

21. Winant 1994: 1.

22. Goldfield notes that the "Spirit of 1776" had already developed what W. E. B. DuBois named the "American Blindspot" (1997: 118).

Chapter 5

1. Labaree (1997) describes three overarching goals that have shaped public education in the United States: democratic equality, social efficiency, and social mobility.

2. For insightful accounts of contemporary corporate influence, see Borman et al. 1993; McGuire 1990; Molnar 1996; Rigdon 1995; Shipps 1997; and Useem 1986. For a helpful typology of business involvement, see Mickelson 1999. For general treatises on market approaches to education, see Apple 1995, 1996; and Wexler 1987.

3. For a lucid explanation of competing interests in public schools, see Labaree 1997. See also Ray and Mickelson 1990, 1993; and Sola 1989.

4. Boutwell 1997; Boyles 1998; Gelberg 1997; National Association of Partners in Education 1995.

5. McEwan 2000.

6. See Howell et al. 2001, 2002.

7. McEwan 2000.

8. On charter schools generally, see Bulkley and Wohlstetter 2004; Cookson 1994; Dougherty and Sostre 1992; Fiske and Ladd 2000; Fuller et al. 2003; Fuller and Elmore 1996; Gewirtz, et al. 1995; Rasell and Rothstein 1993; U.S. Department of Education, Institute of Education Sciences 2005; Wells et al. 2000; Wells 2002; Whitty 1996.

9. See Nelson et al. 2004; Wells 2002.

10. Wells 2002.

11. Ascher et al. 1999; Wells et al. 2000.

12. Frankenberg and Chungmei 2003; Wells 2002.

13. Bulkley and Fisler 2003; Fuller et al. 2003.

14. Quality Counts 2002.

15. Kohn 1999, 1992.

16. Crouse and Trusheim 1988; Firestone 1995; Frederiksen 1984; Heubert and Hauser 1999; Jencks and Phillips 1998; Kelly-Benjamin 1990; Kornhaber and Orfield 2001; McNeil 2000; Medina and Neill 1990; Montagu 1999, Odden and Dougherty 1982; Valdes and Figueroa 1994.

17. Beatty et al. 2001; Heubert and Hauser 1999; Shepard 1991.

18. Levin 2001.

19. See Luebke (1990), who distinguishes between *modernizer* and *traditionalist* fragments within the old southern Democratic Party. Modernizers characteristically urged education as a respectable route to social mobility (shielding themselves from more radical considerations of economic redistribution). See also Rothenberg 1984.

20. Bifulco and Ladd 2004: 10.

21. Ibid.: 1.

22. Ibid.: 9.

23. Clotfelter et al. 2002.

24. Common Sense Foundation and North Carolina Justice and Community Development Center n.d.: 8.

25. Horn 2003.

26. North Carolina Justice and Community Development Center and the North Carolina Education and Law Project 2002: 4.

27. Horn 2003.

28. Ibid.

29. Heubert and Hauser 1999; Shephard and Smith 1989; Shepard 1991.

30. See Common Sense Foundation and North Carolina Justice and Community Development Center n.d.; North Carolina Justice and Community Development Center n.d.; and North Carolina Justice and Community Development Center and the North Carolina Education and Law Project 2002.

31. For more on growth elites, see Logan and Molotch 1987.

32. Conway 1979: 116.

33. "Roanoke Rapids Herald 1996 Survey" 1996. For more on bias in standardized testing, see Hilliard 1991; Jencks and Phillips, eds. 1998; McNeil 2000; and Medina and Neill 1990.

34. Cecelski 1994.

35. See Cecelski (1994) for an account of how desegregation in one North Carolina community destroyed the black middle class's economic base.

36. Delpit 1995.

37. Fordham 1996.

38. For an account of how cities manage education conflict in order to protect their image in national business circles, see Ray and Mickelson 1990, 1993.

39. *Chatham News* Jan. 12, 1995.

40. Between 1984 and 1990, poultry companies earned an annual average of $1 billion in profits (Stull et al. 1995: 219).

41. Levin et al. 1995.

42. Rosenstein and Brooke 1997. See also Institute for Southern Studies n.d.

43. *Chatham News* July 3, 1997.

Chapter 6

1. Hackworth 2002: 712, fig. 1.

2. Conlan 1998: 219–20.

3. Peterson 1995: 80.

4. Ibid.: 74.

5. Kincaid 1999: 136.

6. Ibid.

7. Zepezauer 2004: 1.

8. Ibid.

9. Nathan 1996.

10. Kincaid 1999: 141; Conlan 1998: 235.

11. Quoted by Conlan 1998: 237.

12. We distinguish *administrative devolution*—greater flexibility and discretion provided to state and local officials in meeting the requirements set by federal funding—from *substantive devolution*—the turnover by the federal government to state and local governments of policy making as well as administration with respect to an area of governance (Kincaid 1999: 135–36). Complete devolution would also provide new direct sources of revenue to state and local governments to replace their fiscal dependency on the federal government, e.g., through revenue sharing.

13. Cho and Wright 2004.

14. Kelleher and Yackee 2004: 264, 267.

15. Ibid., 260.

16. See Morgen 2001.

17. Kincaid 1999: 145.

18. See Morgen 2001.

19. Conlan 1998: 204–10; Kincaid 1999: 157.

20. Bowman and Krause (2003: 310–11) also point out that centralization has not been a steady trend over this period but has been interrupted briefly by short episodes of decentralization and devolution. They note that these episodes occurred under Republican presidents in 1953, 1955, 1972, and 1981. See also Conlan 1998: 305–15; Kincaid 1999: 136–40, 153–58.

21. Schudson 1998.

22. Kincaid 1999: 158–59.

23. Ibid.

24. Sbragia 1996; Hackworth 2002.

25. Sokolow 1998.

26. Hackworth 2002: 716–19.

27. Ibid., 715.

28. Ibid.

29. Ibid., 713.

30. Chamber of Commerce of Durham 1997.

31. Mayer 1994: 326.

32. Harvey 1989: 141–72; Harrison 1994: 189–218; Henwood 1997: 263–94.

33. New York Times 1996.

34. Mishel et al. 2003: 97–112; Heintz et al. 2000: 34–35; Schor 1991.

35. Mishel et al. 2003: 288, 299.

36. Greider 1997.

37. Vita and Eilperin 2000; Brainard 2001; Dicken 1998; Mishel et al. 2003: 181–82.

38. MDC 2000; Mishel et al. 2003: 181–82. We thank Jefferson Boyer for being the first to point out the utility of this concept in the case of North Carolina and elsewhere in the U.S. South.

39. Smith-Nonini 2005. Against a new nativist chauvinism, evidence is accumulating that this massive immigration has been prompted by processes of rural economic decline in Mexico and Central America created by NAFTA and IMF-induced structural adjustment promoted by the U.S. government (Andreas 2000: 105; Bacon 2004: 42–59; Greider 1997: 265–76).

40. Williamson et al. 2003: 85–89.

41. Ibid., 91.

42. Schor also makes the following point: "Support for public goods, and for paying taxes, has eroded. Education, social services, public safety, recreation, and culture are being squeezed. The deterioration of public goods then adds even more pressure to spend privately" (1998: 21).

43. Williamson et al. 2003: 2–3.

44. Ibid., 80–81.

45. Skocpol 2003.

46. Greider 1992; Skocpol 2003; Crenson and Ginsberg 2002.

47. Osborne and Gaebler 1992.

48. Crenson and Ginsberg 2002: 203.

49. Ibid., 202.

50. Sclar 2000; Lynn 2002: 70–71; Kuttner 1997: 356–58.

51. Crenson and Ginsberg 2002: 220.

52. Savas 1977; Stevens 1985.

53. Sclar 2000: 68.

54. Ibid., 36–42.

55. Ibid., 45.

56. Kuttner (1997: 358–59). Kuttner gives an interesting example in the privatization of ambulance services in the Boston area:

> The actual cost of operating an ambulance is roughly comparable, whether the operator is a public agency or a private ambulance company. The main difference is that the private contractors are more aggressive at billing health insurance companies.
> The private companies, however, avoid the city of Boston, with its high concentrations of uninsured people. Suburban taxpayers save money, because their towns no longer have tax-supported ambulances. But there is no net gain to "efficiency" or to society.

57. Sclar 2000: 114–18.

58. Ibid., 13–15.

59. Crenson and Ginsberg 2002: 204.

60. Clarke 1998; Levine 1989; Walzer and York 1998.

61. Peters 1998: 12–13.

62. Linder (1999: 42–47) points to six distinct but related meanings of public-private partnerships circulating within the neoliberal discourses of participants, scholars, and media pundits.

63. See, e.g., Fosler and Berger (1982) for a discussion of successes, Rubin and Stankeiwicz (2001) for evidence of failures.

64. Stephenson 1991: 114–15.

65. Ibid., 117; see also Barnekov et al. 1981: 89–90; Davis et al. 1986.

66. Stephenson 1991: 125.

67. Ibid., 119–20.

68. Ibid.

69. Hall 1987; Lynn 2002.

70. Steuerle and Hodgkinson 1999: 90.

71. Ibid., 88.

72. Crenson and Ginsberg 2002: 220.

73. Etzioni 1995.

74. See Brinkerhoff 2002; Brinkerhoff and Brinkerhoff 2002.

75. Marwell 2004; Brinkerhoff 2002; Brinkerhoff and Brinkerhoff 2002.

76. See Hula et al. (1997) and Hula and Jackson-Elmoore (2001) on governing nonprofits; see Couto with Guthrie (1999) on mediating institutions.

77. D. H. Smith 2000: 9, 12. Smith includes incorporated "nonprofit organizations" within his definition of "grassroots associations," while we, on the basis of our research, find such organizations to have a fuzzy and ambiguous status—are they "grassroots," "the establishment," some of both, or sometimes one, sometimes the other?

78. We thus exclude universities, nonprofit hospitals, nonprofit managed care organizations, etc., that receive research grants, or Social Security, Medicare, and Medicaid and similar contracts for services from federal and state governments that administer to individuals.

79. The nonprofit organization America's Second Harvest now feeds more hungry people nationally than are fed by USDA food stamps.

80. Marwell 2004: 270.

81. Ibid., 267.

82. Gates and Hill 1995: 139.

83. Crenson and Ginsberg 2002: 223.

84. Ibid.; Lynn 2002: 69.

Chapter 7

1. This conversation is near verbatim. Unless otherwise noted, other quoted speech cites text or tape-recorded speech.

2. Each of these plans had a different focus. The Concord and Fayetteville plans, for example, focused primarily on downtown redevelopment, while the Durham plan was a county-wide land-use plan. Durham's downtown redevelopment plan was not initiated until the end of 1997. In 1998 the city brought in a planning firm from Indianapolis to create a plan, with the help of the local public-private partnerships and citizen input.

3. http://www.durhamchamber.org/living/cityofmed.html.

4. Local African-Americans have an entirely different view of the heritage represented by the Market House, as the next chapter discusses.

5. Quotation close to verbatim.

6. Quotation close to verbatim.

7. Quotation close to verbatim.

8. Quotation close to verbatim.

9. Osborne and Gaebler 1992.

10. United States Code 26 § 501(c)(3) 1996.

11. See "Houses to Do Without" 1999.

12. Businesses are not so bound to specific places (in many instances, exceptions are real estate and newspapers). Businesses are concerned with profit margins, not livability.

13. This bears comparison with arguments made about the different missions of the three Halifax County school systems. People say integrating the district would dilute the success of Roanoke Rapids schools. The reason for this, the argument goes, is that the county needs at least one strong school system for the children of the business leadership.

14. Exceptions exist when such imagery connotes the quaintness of a bygone era.

15. On behalf of government, business, and university leadership, Pinelands Development Corporation was backed by Wachovia Bank to discreetly secure land for the park. The current location of the park was determined by two factors: both its proximity to the three major universities and the Raleigh-Durham International Airport, and the availability of affordable land. Wachovia Bank donated the first plot, a sizeable piece of forested land. Subsequent purchases were in the vicinity of that original plot.

16. There are important exceptions to this, however. For example, in 1997, when the city of Durham considered a plot of land north of RTP for a landfill, RTP effectively snuffed out the discussion entirely. Furthermore, this does not prevent individual employees of RTP or RTP companies from being politically active.

17. Only two small groups of people were publicly critical of the plan (of course a lot of people didn't know about the plan): extreme free-market capitalists (who are opposed to public subsidy of public services, transit, zoning, etc.) and one predominantly African-American neighborhood adjacent to Duke University whose residents were concerned about gentrification.

18. See Conlan 1998; and Zukin 1991.

Chapter 8

1. Osborne and Gaebler 1992: 335–36.
2. Crenson and Ginsberg 2002: 223–25.
3. Osborne and Gaebler 1992.
4. Keating et al. 1996: 59.
5. Levine 1989: 23.
6. Robert Marvin and Associates 1997. See also http://www.ccbusinesscouncil.org/downtowndevelopment.
7. Robert Marvin and Associates 1997.
8. Ibid.
9. Kinsler 1997.
10. Childs 1996.
11. Levin et al. 1995.
12. Folbre 2001: 22–52.
13. Nonini 2003.
14. He mentioned Scotland Neck, for example, which is a small, predominantly African-American town in rural Halifax County.

Chapter 9

1. Mills 1956; Domhoff 2002; Aronowitz 2003. Domhoff summarizes a vast amount of social, economic, and political data, including his classic research on institutional connections ("interlocks") among (a) corporate directors and owners; (b) members of a social upper class belonging to exclusive prep schools, universities, and social clubs; (c) elected and appointed highest-level national government officials; (d) trustees and officers of the largest and financially best-endowed foundations and think tanks; and (e) owners of the corporate media. This data is drawn together for his book, *Who Rules America?*
2. Fraser and Gerstle 2005; Domhoff 2002.
3. Domhoff 2002.
4. Ibid., 141–42.
5. Ibid., 147–80.
6. Corporations sought to weaken the linkages between union locals and state and national labor federations as part of their overall assault on labor unions from the 1960s onward. This corporate campaign has been a sustained one up to the present, and includes refusing to open new unionized plants, closing and relocating unionized plants to nonunion areas, promoting conservative anti-labor think tanks like the American Enterprise Institute, using "advocacy advertising" against unions, funding electoral campaigns of anti-labor candidates, and engaging in an at-first-secret effort by a "blue ribbon commission" to delegitimize pro-labor decisions of the National Labor Relations Board in the 1970s (see Clawson 2003).
7. For histories of class rule in the United States, see Fraser and Gerstle 2005; and Phillips 2002.
8. Domhoff 2002: 39–40.
9. Logan and Molotch 1987: 32–34.
10. Ibid., 66–84.
11. Domhoff 2002: 40; Logan and Molotch 1987: 64–66.
12. Oliver and Shapiro 1997; Galster 1990.
13. "Cleavages within the growth machine can nevertheless develop, and internal disagreements sometimes break out into the open. But even then, because of the hegemony of the growth machine, *its* disagreements are allowable and do not challenge the belief in growth itself" (Logan and Molotch 1987: 64–65).
14. Ibid., 63.
15. Domhoff 2002: 40–41.
16. Other successes by popular movements vis-à-vis corporate power elites include the passage of the National Labor Relations Act in 1935 and the establishment of the Occupational Health and Safety Agency in 1970 (ibid., 169–75).

17. Ellsberg 1981.
18. Skocpol 2003: 138, 146–47, table 4.2. She notes an increase from approximately 5,843 organizations listed in the *Encyclopedia of Associations* in 1959 to 22,878 in 1999.
19. Greider 1992: 47.
20. See, for example, Bickford 1996.
21. Derthick 1999: 4.
22. Crenson and Ginsberg 2002; see also Skocpol 2003.
23. Fraser 1992: 133.
24. Fung 2003: 522–23.
25. We adopt the concept of dignity from the Zapatistas of Chiapas, Mexico. Holloway (1998: 169–70) writes that dignity is "the struggle for recognition, but for the recognition of a self currently negated. . . . Dignity is the cry of 'here we are!'" To recognize dignity in humans is to recognize their right to self-determination irrespective of class, race, or nationality.
26. Fung 2003: 526.
27. Hirst 1994; Hirst and Bader 2001; Bader 2001: 2.
28. Hirst 1994.
29. Streeck 1992.
30. Fung 2003: 527; Hirst 1994.
31. Cohen and Rogers 1995.
32. Ibid., 55.
33. Ibid., 79–90.
34. Fung and Wright 2003.
35. Ibid., 16–19.
36. Ibid., 16.
37. Ibid.
38. Ibid., 17.
39. Ibid., 5–14.
40. Ibid., 20–23.
41. Crenson and Ginsberg 2002: 226–33; Williamson et al. 2003: 105–64.

Chapter 10

1. Davies 1999; Denzin 1989.
2. Cohen and Rogers 1992: 393.
3. Social movements have multiplied over the last sixty years (Calhoun 1993). Following closely on the beginning of the Civil Rights movement in the 1950s and the student movements of the 1960s, a number of social movements emerged, including the women's movement, the peace movement, the environmental movement, the human rights movement, the gay movement, the animal rights movement, and a variety of quality-of-life efforts such as those addressed by "new urbanism." Analogous attempts to influence patterns of culture, social action, and social relations in a more conservative direction produced other movements, including those of the Christian Right, the Promise Keepers, and the anti-abortion movement.
4. Skocpol 2003: 268.
5. These characteristics are also reported for the contemporary feminist movement in Latin America (Alvarez forthcoming; see also Della Porta and Andretta 2002).
6. See, e.g., Melucci (1989) on "new social movements," and Alvarez et al. (1998) and Leyva Solano (1998) on Latin and Central American movements under conditions of neoliberalism. Note that Putnam's critics (e.g., Ladd 1999) fault him for not sufficiently considering whether less well structured and/or only loosely connected groups have replaced the older hierarchical organizations.
7. D. H. Smith 1997: 269.
8. Groups discussed in depth in the chapter formed alliances with some state-supported institutions, such as universities. With one exception, these particular groups did not take on any of the large-scale, government-originated services, such as a welfare-to-work training program.
9. Apropos of this complex relation between oppositional groups and the state, social movement theorists McAdam and his colleagues (2001) intentionally theorize across the dis-

ciplinary boundaries that have artificially segregated these topics since the 1960s. This is a timely move, especially in the face of the government reorganization discussed here. Still, we take a broader view. The vision of McAdam and his colleagues (2001) may well bring together previously clannish students of different forms of contentious politics, and thus benefit understanding; but for our purposes, it prematurely places the state in a central position (see 2001: 5). Instead, more reminiscent of European theorists of social movements such as Touraine (e.g., 1988), Melucci (e.g., 1989), and Habermas (1981), we are also interested in activism developing in response to entrenched cultural codes and to systemic conditions and transformations (e.g., postmaterial society, neoliberalism, market rule) that are not fully localizable to the state.

10. Reflexivity, an important criterion of rigorous ethnographic research, demands repeated scrutiny and reporting of the research encounter (broadly conceived) for its possible effects on the research outcome (Davies 1999).

11. They wore painters' masks as signs of protest. This unconventional approach to the commissioners was "too active, too demonstrative," and "too political" for some people, who dropped out of the group. It and some of CU's other confrontational tactics also upset nonmembers, particularly natives to the area. CU, as discussed in an earlier chapter, relied upon a political style that was counter and offensive to natives' sensibilities.

12. Bartlett and Boyer, forthcoming.

13. In the description of Citizens Unite, only "Citizens Unite" and the "Appalachian Defense Alliance" are pseudonyms.

14. Alvarez et al. 1998: 7.

15. Marsdon was trying to gain sympathy from those who subscribed to the local hostility to zoning. Company spokespeople may also have been suggesting that CU was akin to another group who opposed a road project favored by many natives. The members of that group, too, claimed to be environmentalists, but were suspected of simply trying to protect the value of their property.

16. See Kempton and Holland 2003; Allen et al., forthcoming; Holland 2003.

17. See also McAdam et al. (2001), which emphasizes the importance of contentious practice in the development and transformation of movement identities.

18. Guldbrandsen 2001.

19. Ibid.

20. This is not to say that the federal government has no presence in these politics. The federal government retains tremendous influence, but it does so with relatively small amounts of funding and agency involvement (see Guldbrandsen and Holland 2001).

21. See, e.g., N. Smith 1996.

22. North Carolina schools were desegregated in a painful manner. Black schools were often closed, and most of the decision-making power African-Americans had had over schools was taken away (Cecelski 1994; Givens 1997; Hill 1997; Gottovi 1997). All but five of the 298 black high schools statewide were closed. Even during our study in the late 1990s, when the events of school desegregation were seemingly a thing of the past, a black community in Chatham County rallied against the further alienation of a building that had been an all-black school before desegregation.

23. A major thrust of black land loss activism concerned claims against the USDA for withholding loans from black farmers and improperly foreclosing on existing loans to them. Cases began to build in the early part of Reagan's presidency, when the enforcement of civil rights claims was given low priority.

24. Interestingly, many of CCT's activities had a learning component, but the school system as a target of protest had been dropped. In fact, as an earlier chapter indicates, during the time of our study, we found no efforts in any of our sites to halt the massive redirection and undermining of public schools that had begun in the 1980s.

25. *Tenth Anniversary Brochure* 1988: 6.

26. CCT Newsletter, January/February 1998: 8.

27. *Tenth Anniversary Brochure* 1998: 11.

28. North Carolina has one of the deeper histories of activism on environmental justice in the country. Warren County is frequently cited as a birthplace of the movement, in the 1970s, when residents protested the state's placement of a PCB-laced landfill in a black section of the county.

29. CCT Newsletter, January/February 1998: 8.

30. Tourism has affected the area and jobs since the 1800s; the presence of a state school, since 1899. The completion of the Blue Ridge Parkway in 1939 brought more middle-class tourists (as opposed to the richer ones of earlier periods). Tourism boomed beginning in the mid-1960s, making the area one of the state's most popular destinations. By 1990 service and retail together accounted for nearly 65 percent of all employment in the county, and 50 percent of land parcels were owned by people living outside the county (Bartlett and Boyer, forthcoming: 560–64; Bartlett and Boyer 1997; Boyer et al. 1993).

31. The community council debated mechanisms that would enable the community to maintain control of development in the area. Concerned about possible backlash from those in the community who resisted government interference with property rights, the council decided to make the historic school the centerpiece of its plans.

32. Bartlett and Boyer, forthcoming.

33. Schumann 1997: 68.

34. For more detailed analyses see Bartlett and Boyer 1997; Bartlett and Boyer, forthcoming; Schumann 1997.

35. See also Bartlett and Boyer, forthcoming.

36. Jones et al. 2002.

37. Jones et al. 2002; see also Stuart 2004.

38. Liebman and Wuthnow 1983. In our survey in Chatham County, 7.9 percent of the respondents reported participating in local activist groups aligned with issues of the Christian Right.

39. Jakes has hosted conferences in both Charlotte and Greensboro. Although these conferences are all integrated (speakers and participants), McCartney's generally attract a larger, white, male Protestant following; Jakes's ManPower and Woman Thou Art Loosed/God's Leading Lady draw a largely African-American audience.

40. In 2005, Graham admitted on the *Today Show* that he is a registered Democrat, but he has generally kept his political affiliations and opinions silent. According to him, he has maintained his silence on political issues in order to stay focused on his main message, the gospel of Jesus Christ, a stance historically consistent with that of early-twentieth-century evangelicals who believed that involvement in politics corrupted the message of their faith.

41. Hassett's recent study (forthcoming) of the conservative movement within the worldwide Anglican Communion provides a good example of the way particular churches, such as the ones she studied on the North Carolina coast, participate in dramas of contention: whether on a local, national, or international scale, these take place within the church community.

42. For accounts of the recent rise in evangelicalism in American society, its implications for race relations and political involvement, and assessments of the president's emphasis on faith-based initiatives, see C. Smith 2002; Emerson and Smith 2000; O. P. Smith 1997; R. D. Smith 2003, 2004; Wuthnow 2004; Wuthnow and Evans 2002.

43. Frederick's book (2003) on her research in Halifax County treats this complex connection between religion and activism in depth.

44. Other conditions that have transformed activism are the Internet and the worldwide web, but these are not central to the issues of this chapter.

45. For example, Fung and Wright 2003; see also Fung 2003.

46. At the same time, mechanisms of racial dominance have shifted from overt, physical coercion and exclusion to less obvious practices that more subtly privilege white elite styles (as in schools) or protect white areas (as from toxic waste dumps and landfills). This shift in oppressive forms is probably another reason why opposing sides, even in their efforts to achieve social and economic justice, are (or were, before the environmental justice movement) less clearly demarcated than in the past.

47. See, e.g., Hirst 1994; Hirst and Bader 2001; Cohen and Rogers 1992, 1995.

48. See also Couto with Guthrie 1999; Amin 1996.

49. Cohen and Rogers 1992: 425.

50. Marwell 2004.

51. The survey we conducted in Chatham County suggests that the percentage of people actually involved in any one type of community-oriented association is relatively small.

Responses to a question about membership in six types of local organizations showed that the top two groups were those addressed to environmental issues (18.2 percent) and social justice issues (11.6 percent). Other surveys of membership in local environmental groups with more inclusive samples provide figures between 3 percent and 9 percent, the latter being the most recent (Dunlap 2000; Kempton et al. 2001). Considering that environmentalism is only one of many activist interests, it is likely that members of activist-based groups do constitute a significant minority of the population. Yet it is also likely that a very large number of people are neither participants in activist groups nor recipients of their benefits to nonmembers.

52. At the time of our study in the late 1990s, Latinos in our study areas had formed no activist groups to address the difficulties that confronted them. Since the time of our research, Latino activism has burgeoned.

53. Hirst 1994: 479.

Chapter 11

1. Harvey 1996.

2. Hall 2001.

3. The organization funded some of its operations through renting spaces to small businesses, and it valued the local jobs provided by these businesses.

4. Williamson et al. 2003.

5. Membership in civic organizations, social networks, local grassroots organizations, and simple personal relationships are all threatened when economic decline causes members of a community to lose their jobs, experience increased financial and familial stress, and perhaps move away. . . . When the economic underpinnings of a community erode, social networks and institutions—such as families, schools, churches, soccer leagues, and civic organizations—are also weakened, with predictably damaging results. Ibid., 3–5.

6. Strand et al. 2003: 29.

7. Community initiatives developed to meet needs not being satisfied by neoliberal governments and corporations frequently mix concepts and practices taken from the business community with the pursuit of goals beyond profit making. "Social entrepreneurism" is emerging as a term for these hybrid activities (e.g., Bornstein 2004).

8. Williamson et al. 2003.

9. For instance, the Self-Help Credit Union in Durham is a nationally renowned model for a Community Development Financial Institution—providing credit to hundreds of local businesses and poor residents, and generating two thousand jobs since it began in 1980 (ibid., 223–24).

10. See IDEA's web site at http://www.idea.gseis.ucla.edu.

11. See Bickford 1996.

12. Crenson and Ginsberg 2002; Skocpol 2003.

13. Religious movements are likewise setting visions for the country. They, too, are indicators of discontent, though politically conservative ones are currently content to form alliances with the advocates of market rule, if not to present themselves as fully compatible with its tenets.

14. Skocpol 2003: 268.

15. Notes from Nowhere 2003; Fisher and Ponniah 2003; Brecher et al. 2000.

Appendix

1. Public choice theory is allied ideologically and conceptually to the free market economics of Milton Friedman, Gary Becker, and the Chicago School of Economics; to the "law and economics" tradition most notably tied to the views of Justice Scalia, and to the anti-tax, anti-regulatory views of the judicial theorist Richard Posner (see Kuttner 1997).

2. Buchanan 1988: 10.

3. Macpherson 1964; Kuttner 1997: 328–62.

4. Buchanan and Tullock 1962; Downs 1957.

5. Kuttner 1997: 334; see Downs 1957.

6. Downs 1957.

7. Buchanan 1988: 8; see also Tullock 1967; Buchanan and Tullock 1962.

8. Olson 1965: 2.

9. Domhoff 2002: 123–80.

10. Greider 1992: 35–59.

11. Grassroots Policy Project et al. 1998; Nader 2000; Whitfield 2001; Zepezauer 2004.

12. Macpherson 1964.

13. Economic anthropology has found that self-maximizing behavior is often far from defined by narrow economic interest. Determination of costs and benefits and of how the two are to be balanced have often not been defined by material wealth but by individuals' needs to be accorded prestige or reputation for ensuring group welfare. Costs and benefits are always *culturally* and *historically* specific, and not—as neoclassical economists would have it—universal and transhistorical (Sahlins 1976).

14. Crenson and Ginsberg 2002: 20; Kelman 1987.

15. Barnes 2004.

16. For recent empirically informed work in public choice theory and allied "rational choice theory," see Mueller 1989; Schofield 2000; and Johnson 2002.

17. Schumpeter 1950.

18. Ibid.

19. Ibid.; Shapiro 2003: 57.

20. For a critique of the elitist and minimalist conceptions of Third World democracy held by neo-Schumpeterians like Samuel Huntington and Adam Przeworski see Shapiro 1996: 79–101.

21. Kornhauser 1959.

22. Crenson and Ginsberg 2002: xvii.

23. Dahl 1971, 1979, and 1989.

24. Dahl 1971.

25. Marcus and Hanson 1993.

26. Page and Shapiro 1993; Hanson and Marcus 1993.

27. Hanson and Marcus 1993: 9; Mansbridge 1993.

28. Kingdon 1993; Hanson and Marcus 1993.

29. Hanson and Marcus 1993: 11.

30. Gibson 1993; Hanson and Marcus 1993.

31. Conover et al. 1993; Dietz 1993; Hanson and Marcus 1993.

32. Hochschild 1993.

33. Ibid.; Hanson and Marcus 1993.

34. Stouffer 1955; Prothro and Grigg 1960; McCloskey 1964.

35. Hanson and Marcus 1993.

36. Kuklinski et al. 1993.

37. Theiss-Morse et al. 1993.

38. Hanson and Marcus 1993: 17; Hardisty 1999.

39. Hanson and Marcus 1993: 15; Moon 1993.

40. Dahl 1961; Truman 1951.

41. Aronowitz 2003: 96.

42. Bachrach and Botwinick 1992: 52–54.

43. McChesney 1997 and 1999; Lukes 1974; Bachrach and Botwinick 1992: 54.

44. For a fuller critique of the pluralist conception of rule, see Aronowitz 2003: 96–106; and Bachrach and Botwinick 1992: 49–74.

45. Schattschneider 1960: 35.

Bibliography

Allen, K., V. Daro, and D. Holland. "Becoming an Environmental Justice Activist." In *Environmental Justice and Environmentalism: Contrary or Complementary?*, ed. Phaedra C. Pezzullo and Ronald Sandler. Cambridge, MA: MIT Press, forthcoming.

Alvarez, S. *Contentious Feminisms: Cultural Politics, Policy Advocacy, and Transnational Organizing in Latin America*. Durham, NC: Duke University Press, forthcoming.

Alvarez, S., E. Dagnino, and A. Escobar. "Introduction: The Cultural and the Political in Latin American Social Movements." In *Cultures of Politics/Politics of Culture: Revisioning Latin American Social Movements*, ed. S. Alvarez, E. Dagnino, and A. Escobar, 1–32. Boulder, CO: Westview Press, 1998.

Amin, A. "Beyond Associative Democracy." *New Political Economy* 1, no. 3 (1996): 309–33.

Andreas, P. *Border Games: Policing the U.S.–Mexico Divide*. Ithaca, NY: Cornell University Press, 2000.

Apple, M. *Cultural Politics and Education*. New York: Teachers College Press, 1996.

———. *Education and Power*. 2nd ed. New York: Routledge, 1995.

Aronowitz, S. *How Class Works: Power and Social Movement*. New Haven, CT: Yale University Press, 2003.

Ascher, C., R. Jacobowitz, and Y. McBride. *Standards-based Reform and the Charter School Movement in 1998–99: An Analysis of Four States*. New York: New York University, Institute for Education and Social Policy, 1999.

Bachrach, P., and A. Botwinick. *Power and Empowerment: A Radical Theory of Participatory Democracy*. Philadelphia: Temple University Press, 1992.

Bacon, D. *The Children of NAFTA: Labor Wars on the U.S./Mexico Border*. Berkeley: University of California Press, 2004.

Bader, V. M. Introduction to *Associative Democracy: The Real Third Way*, ed. P. Q. Hirst and V. M. Bader, 1–14. London: Frank Cass, 2001.

Bagdikian, B. H. *The New Media Monopoly*. Boston: Beacon Press, 2004.

Barnekov, T., D. Rich, and R. Warren. "The New Privatism, Federalism, and the Future of Urban Governance." *Journal of Urban Affairs* 3 (1981): 1–14.

Barnes, P. "Sharing the Wealth of the Commons." *Dollars and Sense* 256 (2004): 22–26.

Bartlett, L., and J. Boyer. *Laurel Creek Resolves: A Community Assessment of Needs and Priorities*. Report prepared for the Laurel Creek Community Council and the Watauga County Department of Planning and Inspections. Boone, NC: Appalachian State University Sustainable Development Program, 1997.

———. "Participation versus Mobilization: Cultural Styles of Political Action in an Appalachian County." In *Social Capital in the Mountain South*, ed. Sue Keefe. Boone, NC: Appalachian State University, forthcoming.

Beatty, A., et al., eds. *Understanding Dropouts: Statistics, Strategies, and High-Stakes Testing*. Washington, DC: National Research Council Committee on Educational Excellence and Testing Equity, 2001.

Bellah, R., et al. *Habits of the Heart: Individualism and Commitment in American Life*. Berkeley: University of California Press, 1985.

Bickford, S. *The Dissonance of Democracy: Listening, Conflict, and Citizenship*. Ithaca, NY: Cornell University Press, 1996.

Bifulco, R., and H. Ladd. *The Impacts of Charter Schools on Student Achievement: Evidence from North Carolina*. Terry Sanford Institute of Public Policy Working Papers Series. Durham, NC: Duke University, 2004.

Bilmes, K. "Freedom and Regulation: An Anthropological Critique of Free Market Ideology." *Research in Law and Economics* 7 (1985): 123–47.

Bluestone, B., and B. Harrison. *The Deindustrialization of America: Plant Closings, Community Abandonment, and the Dismantling of Basic Industries.* New York: Basic Books, 1982.

Boggs, C. "Social Capital and Political Fantasy: Robert Putnam's Bowling Alone." *Theory and Society* 30 (2001): 281–97.

Borman, K., L. Castenell, and K. Gallagher. "Business Involvement in School Reform: The Rise of the Business Roundtable." In *The New Politics of Race and Gender: The 1992 Yearbook of the Politics of Education Association,* ed. C. Marshall, 69–83. Washington, DC: Falmer Press, 1993.

Bornstein, D. *How to Change the World: Social Entrepreneurs and the Poser of New Ideas.* Oxford: Oxford University Press, 2004.

Boutwell, C. *Shell Game: Corporate America's Agenda for Schools.* Bloomington, IN: Phi Delta Kappa Educational Foundation, 1997.

Bowman, A. O. M., and G. A. Krause. "Power Shift: Measuring Policy Centralization in U.S. Intergovernmental Relations, 1947–1998." *American Politics Research* 31, no. 3 (2003): 301–25.

Boyd, W., and M. Watts. "Agro-industrial Just-in-Time: The Chicken Industry and Postwar American Capitalism." In *Globalizing Food: Agrarian Questions and Global Restructuring,* ed. D. Goodman and M. J. Watts, 192–225. London: Routledge, 1997.

Boyer, J., J. Monast, and R. Moretz. *Steps toward a Sustainable Economy in Western North Carolina: Ashe and Watauga Counties.* Report for the Z. Smith Reynolds Foundation, Center for the Development of Social Responsibility and the Sustainable Development Program. Boone, NC: Appalachian State University, 1993.

Boyles, D. *American Education and Corporations: The Free Market Goes to School.* New York: Garland Publishing, 1998.

Brainard, L. "Textiles on the Front Lines," *The News and Observer* (Raleigh, NC), December 30, 2001.

Brecher, J., T. Costello, and B. Smith. *Globalization from Below: The Power of Solidarity.* Cambridge, MA: South End Press, 2000.

Brinkerhoff, J. "Government-Nonprofit Partnership: A Defining Framework." *Public Administration and Development* 22 (2002): 19–30.

Brinkerhoff, J., and D. Brinkerhoff. "Government-Nonprofit Relations in Comparative Perspective: Evolution, Themes, and New Directions." *Public Administration and Development* 22 (2002): 3–18.

Buchanan, J. M. "The Economic Theory of Politics Reborn." *Challenge* 31, no. 2 (1988): 4–10.

Buchanan, J. M., and G. Tullock. *The Calculus of Consent: Logical Foundations of Constitutional Democracy.* Ann Arbor: University of Michigan Press, 1962.

Bulkley, K., and J. Fisler. "A Decade of Charter Schools: From Theory to Practice." *Educational Policy* 17, no. 3 (2003): 317–42.

Bulkley, K., and P. Wohlstetter, eds. *Taking Account of Charter Schools: What's Happened and What's Next?* New York: Teachers College, 2004.

Calhoun, C. "'New Social Movements of the Early Nineteenth Century." *Social Science History* 17, no. 3 (1993): 385–427.

Cantrill, A., and C. Roll, Jr. *The Hopes and Fears of the American People.* New York: Universe Books, 1971.

Cecelski, D. S. *Along Freedom Road: Hyde County, North Carolina, and the Fate of Black Schools in the South.* Chapel Hill: University of North Carolina Press, 1994.

Cecelski, D., and M. L. Kerr. "Hog Wild." *Southern Exposure* 20, no. 3 (1992): 8–15.

Chafe, W. H. "Epilogue from Greensboro, N.C.: Race and the Possibilities of American Democracy." In *Democracy Betrayed,* ed. D. S. Cecelski and T. B. Tyson. Chapel Hill: University of North Carolina Press, 1998, pp. 281–82.

Chamber of Commerce of Durham, NC. "Ten Reasons to Locate Your Business in Durham." 1997. http://herald-sun.com/dcc/.

Chatham Community Health Improvement Project (CCHIP). *The Health of Chatham, 1996–1997.* Chapel Hill: Center for Public Health Practice, School of Public Health, University of North Carolina–Chapel Hill, 1997.

Childs, J. W. "Downtown Plan Updates Sought," *The Fayetteville Observer,* June 2, 1996.

Cho, C. L., and D. S. Wright. "The Devolution Revolution in Intergovernmental Relations in the 1990s: Changes in Cooperative and Coercive State-National Relations as Perceived by State Administrators." *Journal of Public Administration Research and Theory* 14, no. 4 (2004): 447–68.

Clarke, J. *Changing Welfare, Changing States: New Directions in Social Policy*. London: Sage Publications, 2004.

Clarke, S. "Economic Development Roles in American Cities: A Contextual Analysis of Shifting Partnership Arrangements." In *Public-Private Partnerships for Local Economic Development*, ed. N. Walzer and B. Jacobs, 19–46. Westport, CT: Praeger, 1998.

Clawson, D. *The Next Upsurge: Labor and the New Social Movements*. Ithaca, NY: ILR Press, 2003.

Clotfelter, C., H. Ladd, and J. Vigdor. "Segregation and Resegregation in North Carolina's Public School Classrooms." Terry Sanford Institute of Public Policy Working Papers Series, SAN02–03, August 2002.
http://www.pubpol.duke.edu/people/faculty/clotfelter/san02–03.pdf.

Cohen, J., and J. Rogers. "Secondary Associations and Democratic Governance." *Politics & Society* 20, no. 4 (December 1992): 393–472.

———, eds. *Associations and Democracy*. London and New York: Verso, 1995.

Common Sense Foundation and North Carolina Justice and Community Development Center. *A Closer Look: A Parent's Guide to Standardized Tests in NC Schools*. Raleigh, NC: Common Sense Foundation, n.d.

Conlan, T. J. *From New Federalism to Devolution: Twenty-Five Years of Intergovernmental Reform*. Washington, DC: Brookings Institution Press, 1998.

Conover, P. J., et al. "Duty Is a Four-Letter Word: Democratic Citizenship in the Liberal Polity." In *Reconsidering the Democratic Public Press*, ed. G. E. Marcus and R. L. Hanson, 147–72. University Park: Pennsylvania State University Press, 1993.

Conway, M. *Rise Gonna Rise: A Portrait of Southern Textile Workers*. Garden City, NY: Anchor Press/Doubleday, 1979.

Cookson, P. *School Choice: The Struggle for the Soul of American Education*. New Haven, CT: Yale University Press, 1994.

Couto, R. A., with C. S. Guthrie. *Making Democracy Work Better: Mediating Structures, Social Capital, and the Democratic Prospect*. Chapel Hill: University of North Carolina Press, 1999.

Crenson, M. A., and B. Ginsberg. *Downsizing Democracy: How America Sidelined Its Citizens and Privatized Its Public*. Baltimore, MD: Johns Hopkins University Press, 2002.

Crouse, J., and D. Trusheim. *The Case against the SAT*. Chicago: University of Chicago Press, 1988.

Dagnino, E. "On Confluences and Contradictions: The Troubled Encounters of Participatory and Neoliberal Political Projects." Paper presented at the 23rd Congress of the Latin American Studies Association (LASA), Dallas, TX, March 27–29, 2003.

Dahl, R. *Democracy and Its Critics*. New Haven, CT: Yale University Press, 1989.

———. "Is Civic Virtue a Relevant Ideal in a Pluralist Democracy?" In *Diversity and Citizenship: Rediscovered American Nationhood*, ed. G. Jacobsohn and S. Dunn, 1–16. Lanham, MD: Rowman and Littlefield, 1996.

Dahl, R. A. *Polyarchy: Participation and Opposition*. New Haven, CT: Yale University Press, 1971.

———. "Procedural Democracy." In *Philosophy, Politics and Society*, ed. P. Laslett and J. Fishkin, 97–133. New Haven, CT: Yale University Press, 1979.

———. *Who Governs? Democracy and Power in an American City*. New Haven, CT: Yale University Press, 1961.

———. *Preface to Economic Democracy*. Berkeley: University of California Press, 1985.

Davies, C. A. *Reflexive Ethnography: A Guide to Researching Selves and Others*. London and New York: Routledge, 1999.

Davis, P., Academy of Political Science (U.S.), and New York City Partnership. *Public-Private Partnerships: Improving Urban Life*. New York: Academy of Political Science, 1986.

Della Porta, D., and M. Andretta. "Changing Forms of Environmentalism in Italy: The Protest Campaign on the High Speed Railway System." *Mobilization* 7, no. 1 (2002): 59–77.

Delpit, L. *Other People's Children: Cultural Conflict in the Classroom*. New York: New Press, 1995.

DeMartino, G. F. *Global Economy, Global Justice: Theoretical Objections and Policy Alternatives to Neoliberalism.* London: Routledge, 2000.

Denzin, N. K. "An Interpretive Point of View." In *The Research Act: A Theoretical Introduction to Sociological Methods,* 3rd ed., 1–33. Englewood Cliffs, NJ: Prentice-Hall, 1989.

Derthick, M. *Dilemmas of Scale in America's Federal Democracy.* Cambridge and New York: Woodrow Wilson Center Press and Cambridge University Press, 1999.

Dicken, P. *Global Shift: Transforming the World Economy.* New York: Guilford Press, 1998.

Dietz, M. "In Search of a Citizen Ethic." In *Reconsidering the Democratic Public,* ed. G. E. Marcus and R. L. Hanson, 173–86. University Park: Pennsylvania State University Press, 1993.

Domhoff, G. W. *Who Rules America?* 4th ed. New York: McGraw-Hill, 2002.

Dougherty, K., and L. Sostre. "Minerva and the Market: The Sources of the Movement for School Choice." *Educational Policy* 6, no. 2 (1992): 160–79.

Downs, A. *An Economic Theory of Democracy.* New York: Harper, 1957.

Dunlap, R. E. "Americans Have Positive Image of the Environmental Movement." *Gallup Poll Monthly* 415 (April 2000): 19–25.

Durlauf, S. N. "Bowling Alone: A Review Essay." *Journal of Economic Behavior & Organization* 47 (2001): 259–73.

Edwards, B., and A. Ladd. "Environmental Justice, Swine Production, and Farm Loss in North Carolina." Paper presented at the 2nd Annual National Black Land Loss Summit Academic Conference, Tillery, NC, February 2, 1998.

Ellsberg, D. "Introduction: Call to Mutiny." In *Protest and Survive,* ed. E. P. Thompson and D. Smith, i–xxviii. New York: Monthly Review Press, 1981.

Emerson, M. O., and C. Smith. *Divided by Faith: Evangelical Religion and the Problem of Race in America.* New York: Oxford University Press, 2000.

Etzioni, A. *Rights and the Common Good: The Communitarian Perspective.* New York: St. Martin's Press, 1995.

Evans, S. M., and H. C. Boyte. *Free Spaces: The Sources of Democratic Change in America.* New York: Harper & Row, 1986.

Firestone, W. "The States and Educational Reform." In *Continuity and Contradiction: The Futures of the Sociology of Education,* ed. G. Noblit and W. Pink, 255–78. Cresskill, NJ: Hampton Press, 1995.

Fisher, W. F., and T. Ponniah. *Another World Is Possible: Popular Alternatives to Globalization at the World Social Forum.* London: Zed Books, 2003.

Fiske, E., and H. Ladd. *When Schools Compete: A Cautionary Tale.* Washington, DC: Brookings Institution Press, 2000.

Flacks, R. *Making History: The Radical Tradition in American Life.* New York: Columbia University Press, 1988.

Floren, G. "Agriculture Clash! Chatham County's Hog Farm Debate Smells Like Trouble," *Independent* (Durham, NC), 1997.

Folbre, N. *The Invisible Heart: Economics and Family Values.* New York: New Press, 2001.

Foley, M. W., and B. Edwards. "The Paradox of Civil Society." *Journal of Democracy* 7, no. 3 (1996): 38–52.

Fordham, S. *Blacked Out: Dilemmas of Race, Identity, and Success at Capital High.* Chicago: University of Chicago Press, 1996.

Fosler, R. S., and R. A. Berger. *Public-Private Partnership in American Cities.* Lexington, MA: Lexington Books, 1982.

Frankenberg, E., and L. Chungmei. "Charter Schools and Race: A Lost Opportunity for Integrated Education." In *The Civil Rights Project.* Cambridge, MA: Harvard University Press, 2003.

Fraser, N. "Rethinking the Public Sphere: A Contribution to the Critique of Actually Existing Democracy." In *Habermas and the Public Sphere,* ed. C. Calhoun, 109–42. Cambridge, MA: MIT Press, 1992.

Fraser, S., and G. Gerstle. *Ruling America: A History of Wealth and Power in a Democracy.* Cambridge, MA: Harvard University Press, 2005.

Frederick, M. *Between Sundays: Black Women and Everyday Struggles of Faith.* Berkeley: University of California Press, 2003.

Frederiksen, N. "The Real Test Bias: Influence of Testing on Teaching and Learning." *American Psychologist* 39 (1984): 193.

Fuller, B., et al. *Charter Schools and Inequality: National Disparities in Funding, Teacher Quality, and Student Support*. Berkeley, CA: PACE Working Paper Series, 2003.

Fuller, B., and R. Elmore, eds. *Who Chooses? Who Loses? Culture, Institutions, and the Unequal Effects of School Choice*. New York: Teachers College Press, 1996.

Fung, A. "Associations and Democracy: Between Theories, Hopes, and Realities." *Annual Review of Sociology* 29 (2003): 515–39.

Fung, A. and E. O. Wright. *Deepening Democracy: Institutional Innovations in Empowered Participatory Governance*. London, Verso, 2003.

Galster, G. "Racial Steering by Real Estate Agents: Mechanisms and Motives." *Review of Black Political Economy* 18 (1990): 39–63.

Garnham, N. "The Media and the Public Sphere." In *Habermas and the Public Sphere*, ed. C. Calhoun, 359–76. Cambridge, MA: MIT Press, 1992.

Gates, S., and J. Hill. "Democratic Accountability and Governmental Innovation in the Use of Nonprofit Organizations." *Policy Studies Review* 14, nos. 1–2 (1995): 137–48.

Gelberg, D. *The "Business" of Reforming American Schools*. Albany, NY: SUNY Press, 1997.

Gewirtz, S., S. J. Ball, and R. Bowe. *Markets, Choice, and Equity in Education*. Buckingham, UK: Open University Press, 1995.

Giardina, D., and E. Bates. "Fowling the Nest: The Poultry Industry Pollutes Fields and Streams with 14 Billion Pounds of Manure and 28 Billion Gallons of Waste Water Every Year." *Southern Exposure* 19, no. 1 (1991): 8–12.

Gibson, J. L. "Political Freedom: A Sociopsychological Analysis." In *Reconsidering the Democratic Public*, ed. G. E. Marcus and R. L. Hanson, 113–38. University Park: Pennsylvania State University Press, 1993.

Givens, G. "May the Circle Be Unbroken: An Intergenerational Discussion between African American Women." Ph.D. diss., University of North Carolina–Chapel Hill, 1997.

Glaude, Jr., E. S. "Of the Black Church and the Making of a Black Public." In *African-American Religious Thought: Anthology*, ed. C. West and E. S. Glaude, Jr., 338–65. Louisville, KY: Westminster John Knox Press, 2003.

Goldfield, M. *The Color of Politics: Race and the Mainsprings of American Politics*. New York: New Press, 1997.

Goodman, D., and M. J. Watts, eds. *Globalising Food: Agrarian Questions and Global Restructuring*. London: Routledge, 1997.

Gottovi, N. "The Serious Problem of Mundane Racism:A Case Study of the Marginalization of African-American Parents in U.S. Schools." Ph.D. Diss., University of North Carolina–Chapel Hill, 1997.

Gouveia, L. "Global Strategies and Local Linkages: The Case of the U.S. Meatpacking Industry." In *From Columbus to ConAgra: The Globalization of Agriculture and Food*, ed. A. Bonanno, et al., 125–48. Lawrence: University of Kansas Press, 1994.

Grassroots Policy Project, Sugar Law Center for Economic and Social Justice, and Sustainable America. *Public Subsidies, Public Accountability: Holding Corporations to Labor and Community Standards*. Washington, DC: Grassroots Policy Project, 1998.

Greider, W. *One World, Ready or Not: The Manic Logic of Global Capitalism*. New York: Simon & Schuster, 1997.

———. *Who Will Tell the People: The Betrayal of American Democracy*. New York: Simon & Schuster, 1992.

Guldbrandsen, T. "Bull City Futures: Transformations of Political Action, Inequality, and Public Space in Durham, North Carolina." Ph.D. diss., University of North Carolina–Chapel Hill, 2001.

———. "Sunbelt Dreams: Race, Class, Gender, and the Transformation of Public Space." Paper presented at the Mellon-Sawyer Seminar Series, "Reading Regions Globally: History, Place, and Power," University Center for International Studies, University of North Carolina–Chapel Hill, 2000.

Guldbrandsen, T., and D. Holland. "Encounters with the Supercitizen: Neoliberalism, Environmental Activism, and the American Heritage Rivers Initiative." Special issue, ed. K. Harper, *The Anthropological Quarterly* 74, no. 3 (2001): 124–34.

Gutmann, M. *The Romance of Democracy: Compliant Defiance in Contemporary Mexico*. Berkeley: University of California Press, 2002.

Habermas, J. "New Social Movements." *Telos* 49 (Fall 1981): 33–37.

Hackworth, J. "Local Autonomy, Bond-Rating Agencies, and Neoliberal Urbanism in the United States." *International Journal of Urban and Regional Research* 26, no. 4 (2002): 707–25.

Hall, B. "Chicken Empires." *Southern Exposure* 17, no. 2 (1989): 12–17.

Hall, P. D. "Abandoning the Rhetoric of Independence: Reflections on the Nonprofit Sector in the Post-Liberal Era." *Journal of Voluntary Action Research* 16, nos. 1–2 (1987): 11–28.

Hall, R. "Local Democracy? An Uncertain Future?" Workshop, University of North Carolina–Chapel Hill, March 2, 2001.

Hanson, M. "Educational Marketing and the Public Schools: Policies, Practices, and Problems." *Educational Policy* 6, no. 1 (1992): 19–34.

Hanson, R. L., and G. E. Marcus. "Introduction: The Practice of Democratic Theory." In *Reconsidering the Democratic Public*, ed. G. E. Marcus and R. L. Hanson, 1–32. University Park: Pennsylvania State University Press, 1993.

Hardisty, J. V. *Mobilizing Resentment: Conservative Resurgence from the John Birch Society to the Promise Keepers*. Boston: Beacon Press, 1999.

Harrison, B. *Lean and Mean: The Changing Landscape of Corporate Power in the Age of Flexibility*. New York: Basic Books, 1994.

Hartigan, J., Jr. "Establishing the Fact of Whiteness." *American Anthropologist* 99, no. 3 (1997): 495–505.

Harvey, D. *The Condition of Postmodernity*. Oxford and New York: Blackwell, 1989.

———. *Justice, Nature and the Geography of Difference*. Malden, MA: Blackwell, 1996.

Hassett, M. *Global Transgressions: Episcopal Dissidents, African Allies, and the Anglican Communion's Struggle with Homosexuality*. Princeton, NJ: Princeton University Press, forthcoming.

Heffernan, W., and D. H. Constance. "Transnational Corporations and the Globalization of the Food System." In *Columbus to ConAgra: The Globalization of Agriculture and Food*, ed. A. Bonanno, et al., 29–51. Lawrence: University of Kansas Press, 1994.

Heintz, J., N. Folbre, and the Center for Popular Economics, eds. *The Ultimate Field Guide to the U.S. Economy*. New York: New Press, 2000.

Henig, J. *Rethinking School Choice: The Limits of the Market Metaphor*. Princeton, NJ: Princeton University Press, 1994.

Henwood, D. *Wall Street: How It Works and for Whom*. London and New York: Verso, 1997.

Heubert, J., and R. Hauser, eds. *High Stakes: Testing for Tracking, Promotion, and Graduation*. Washington, DC: National Research Council, 1999.

Higginbotham, E. *Righteous Discontent: The Women's Movement in the Black Baptist Church, 1880–1920*. Cambridge, MA: Harvard University Press, 1993.

Hill, V. "Local Histories/Local Memories of Desegregation: Extending Critical Theory to Improve Understanding of Continuing Problems." Ph.D. diss., University of North Carolina–Chapel Hill, 1997.

Hilliard, A., ed. *Testing African-American Students*. Chicago: Third World Press, 1991.

Hinojosa, V., and J. Park. *Journal for the Scientific Study of Religion* 43, no. 2 (2004): 229–38.

Hirst, P. Q. *Associative Democracy: New Forms of Economic and Social Governance*. Amherst: University of Massachusetts Press, 1994.

Hirst, P. Q., and V. M. Bader. *Associative Democracy: The Real Third Way*. London and Portland, OR: Frank Cass, 2001.

Hochschild, J. L. "Disjunction and Ambivalence in Citizens' Political Outlooks." In *Reconsidering the Democratic Public*, ed. G. E. Marcus and R. L. Hanson, 187–210. University Park: Pennsylvania State University Press, 1993.

———. *What's Fair: American Beliefs about Distributive Justice*. Cambridge, MA: Harvard University Press, 1981.

Holland, D. "Multiple Identities in Practice: On the Dilemmas of Being a Hunter and an Environmentalist in the USA." In "Multiple Identifications and the Self," ed. Meijl T. and H. Driesson, special issue, *Focaal: European Journal of Anthropology* 42 (2003): 23–41.

Holloway, J. "Dignity's Revolt." In *Zapatista! Reinventing Revolution in Mexico*, ed. J. Holloway and E. Peláez, 159–98. London: Pluto Press, 1998.

Horn, C. "High-Stakes Testing and Students: Stopping or Perpetuating a Cycle of Failure?" *Theory into Practice* 42, no. 1 (2003): 30–41.

"Houses to Do Without." Editorial/Opinion Section. *The News and Observer* (Raleigh, NC), April 7, 1999.

Howell, W. G., P. J. Wolf, D. E. Campbell, and P. E. Peterson. "School Vouchers and Academic Performance: Results from Three Randomized Field Trials." *Journal of Policy Analysis and Management* 21, no. 2 (2002): 191–217.

Howell, W. G., P. J. Wolf, P. E. Peterson, D. E. Campbell, J. P. Greene, and D. Goldhaber. "Raising Black Achievement: Vouchers in New York, Dayton, and D.C." *Education Matters* 1, no. 2 (2001): 46–65.

Hula, R. C., and C. Jackson-Elmoore. "Governing Nonprofits and Local Political Processes." *Urban Affairs Review* 36, no. 3 (2001): 324–358.

Hula, R. C., C. Y. Jackson, and M. Orr. "Urban Politics, Governing Nonprofits, and Community Revitalization." *Urban Affairs Review* 32, no. 4 (1997): 459–89.

Institute for Southern Studies. "Ruling the Roost: Findings and Fact Sheet." Durham, NC: Institute for Southern Studies, n.d.

Jackman, R. W., and R. A. Miller. "Social Capital and Politics." *Annual Review of Political Science* 1 (1998): 47–73.

James, W. "Oration upon the Unveiling of the Monument to Robert Gould Shaw," Boston Music Hall, Boston, MA, May 31, 1897. http://www.holycross.edu/departments/english/sluria/wjspeech.htm.

Jamieson, A., H. B. Shin, and J. Day. *Voting and Registration in the Election of November 2000*.Washington, DC: U.S. Census Bureau, 2002.

Jencks, C., and M. Phillips, eds. *The Black-White Test Score Gap*. Washington, DC: Brookings Institution Press, 1998.

Johnson, J. "How Conceptual Problems Migrate: Rational Choice, Interpretation, and the Hazards of Pluralism." *Annual Review of Political Science* 5 (2002): 223–48.

Jones, D., S. Doty, C. Grammich, et al. *Religious Congregations and Membership in the United States, 2000: An Enumeration by Region, State, and County Based on Data Reported for 149 Religious Bodies*. Nashville, TN: Glenmary Research Center, 2002.

Keating, W. D., N. Krumholz, and P. D. Star, eds. *Revitalizing Urban Neighborhoods*. Lawrence: University Press of Kansas, 1996.

Kelleher, C., and S. W. Yackee. "An Empirical Assessment of Devolution's Policy Impact." *The Policies Studies Journal* 32, no. 3 (2004): 253–70.

Kelly-Benjamin, K. *The Young Woman's Guide to Better SAT Scores: Fighting the Gender Gap*. New York: Bantam, 1990.

Kelman, S. *Making Public Policy: A Hopeful View of American Government*. New York: Basic Books, 1987.

Kempton, W., and D. Holland. "Identity and Sustained Environmental Practice." In *Identity and the Natural Environment: The Psychological Significance of Nature*, ed. S. Clayton and S. Opotow, 317–41. Cambridge, MA: MIT Press, 2003.

Kempton, W., D. Holland, K. Bunting-Howarth, E. Hannan, and C. Payne. "Local Environmental Groups: A Systematic Enumeration in Two Geographical Areas." *Rural Sociology* 66, no. 4 (2001): 557–78.

Key, V. O. *Southern Politics in State and Nation*. New York: A. A. Knopf, 1949.

Kincaid, J. "De Facto Devolution and Urban Defunding: The Priority of Persons over Places." *Journal of Urban Affairs* 21, no. 2 (1999): 135–67.

Kingdon, J. W. "Politicians, Self-Interest, and Ideas." In *Reconsidering the Democratic Public*, ed. G. E. Marcus and R. L. Hanson, 73–90. University Park: Pennsylvania State University Press, 1993.

Kinsler, L. "Referendum Sought on Downtown Plan." *The Fayetteville Observer*, March 10, 1997.

Kohn, A. *No Contest: The Case against Competition*. Boston: Houghton Mifflin, 1992.

———. *The Schools Our Children Deserve: Moving beyond Traditional Classrooms and Tougher Standards*. Boston: Houghton Mifflin, 1999.

Kornhaber, M., and G. Orfield, eds. *Raising Standards or Raising Barriers: Inequality and High Stakes Testing in Public Education*. New York: Century Foundation, 2001.

Kornhauser, W. *The Politics of Mass Society.* Glencoe, IL: Free Press, 1959.
Kuklinski, J. H., et al. "Thinking about Political Tolerance, More or Less, with More or Less Information." In *Reconsidering the Democratic Public,* ed. G. E. Marcus and R. L. Hanson. University Park: Pennsylvania State University Press, 1993.
Kuttner, R. *Everything for Sale: The Virtues and Limits of Markets.* New York: Knopf, 1997.
Labaree, D. "No Exit: Public Education as an Inescapably Public Good." In *Reconstructing the Common Good in Education: Coping with Intractable American Dilemmas,* ed. L. Cuban and D. Shipps, 110–29. Stanford, CA: Stanford University Press, 2000.
———. "Private Goods, Public Goods: The American Struggle over Educational Goals." *American Educational Research Journal* 34, no. 1 (1997): 39–81.
Ladd, E. C. *The Ladd Report.* New York: Free Press, 1999.
Lamphere, L. *Structuring Diversity: Ethnographic Perspectives on the New Immigration.* Chicago: University of Chicago Press, 1992.
Levin, H. *Privatizing Education: Can the Marketplace Deliver Choice, Efficiency, Equity, and Social Cohesion?* New York: Ford Foundation; Philadelphia: Pew Charitable Trusts, 2001.
Levin, K., et al. *Latinos in Siler City: Community Perspectives.* Chapel Hill: UNC School of Public Health, 1995.
Levine, M. "The Politics of Partnership: Urban Redevelopment since 1945." In *Unequal Partnerships: The Political Economy of Urban Redevelopment in Postwar America,* ed. G. D. Squires, 12–34. New Brunswick, NJ: Rutgers University Press, 1989.
Leyva Solano, X. "The New Zapatista Movement: Political Levels, Actors, and Political Discourse in Contemporary Mexico." In *Encuentros Antropológicos: Power, Identity, and Mobility in Mexican Society,* ed. V. Napolitano and X. Leyva Solano, 35–55. London: Institute of Latin American Studies, 1998.
Liebman, R. C., and R. Wuthnow. *The New Christian Right: Mobilization and Legitimation.* New York: Aldine, 1983.
Lincoln, C. E., and L. Mamiya. *The Black Church and the African-American Experience.* Durham, NC: Duke University Press, 1990.
Linder, S. H. "Coming to Terms with the Public-Private Partnership." *American Behavioral Scientist* 43, no. 1 (1999): 35–51.
Lippmann, W. *The Phantom Public.* New York: Harcourt Brace, 1925.
Logan, J. R., and H. L. Molotch. *Urban Fortunes: The Political Economy of Place.* Berkeley, CA: University of California Press, 1987.
Lubiano, W. "Introduction." In *The House That Race Built.* New York: Pantheon Books, 1997.
Luebke, P. *Tar Heel Politics: Myths and Realities.* Chapel Hill: University of North Carolina Press, 1990.
Lukes, S. *Power: A Radical View.* London and New York: Macmillan, 1974.
Lutz, C. *Homefront: A Military City, and the American Twentieth Century.* Boston, MA: Beacon Press, 2001.
Lynn, L. E., Jr. "Social Services and the State: The Public Appropriation of Private Charity." *Social Service Review* 76, no. 1 (March 2002): 58–82.
Macpherson, C. B. *The Political Theory of Possessive Individualism: Hobbes to Locke.* London and New York: Oxford University Press, 1964.
Mahtesian, C. "Feature: Council Boycotts Quorum Busters." *Governing: The Magazine of States and Localities,* November 1997, 32–33. http://66.23.131.98/archive/1997/nov/boycotts.txt.
Mansbridge, J. "Self-Interest and Political Transformation." In *Reconsidering the Democratic Public,* ed. G. E. Marcus and R. L. Hanson, 91–112. University Park: Pennsylvania State University Press, 1993.
Marcus, G. E., and R. L. Hanson, eds. *Reconsidering the Democratic Public.* University Park: Pennsylvania State University Press, 1993.
Marwell, N. P. "Privatizing the Welfare State: Nonprofit Community-Based Organizations as Political Actors." *American Sociological Review* 69, no. 2 (2004): 265–91.
Mayer, M. "Post-Fordist City Politics." In *Post-Fordism: A Reader,* ed. A. Amin, 316–37. Cambridge, MA: Blackwell, 1994.
McAdam, D., S. Tarrow, and C. Tilly. *Dynamics of Contention.* New York: Cambridge University Press, 2001.

McChesney, R. W. *Corporate Media and the Threat to Democracy.* New York: Seven Stories Press, 1997.

———. *Rich Media, Poor Democracy: Communication Politics in Dubious Times.* Urbana: University of Illinois Press, 1999.

McCloskey, H. "Consensus and Ideology in American Politics." *American Political Science Review* 58 (1964): 361–82.

McDonald, M. P., and S. Popkin. "The Myth of the Vanishing Voter." *American Political Science Review* 95, no. 4 (2001): 963–74.

McEwan, P. "The Potential Impact of Large-Scale Voucher Programs." *Review of Educational Research* 70, no. 2 (2000): 103–49.

McGuire, K. "Business Involvement in the 1990s." In *Education Politics for the New Century: The 1989 Yearbook of the Politics of Education Association,* ed. D. Mitchell and M. Goertz, 107–17. London: Falmer Press, 1990.

McNeil, L. *Contradictions of School Reform: Educational Costs of Standardized Testing.* New York: Routledge, 2000.

MDC. *The State of the South, 2000: A Report to the Region and Its Leadership.* Chapel Hill, NC: MDC, Inc., 2000.

Medina, N., and M. Neill. *Fallout from the Testing Explosion: How 100 Million Standardized Exams Undermine Equity and Excellence in America's Public* Schools. 3rd ed. Cambridge, MA: National Center for Fair & Open Testing (FairTest), 1990.

Melucci, A. *Nomads of the Present: Social Movements and Individual Needs in Contemporary Society.* London: Hutchinson, 1989.

Merelman, R. M. *Partial Visions: Culture and Politics in Britain, Canada, and the United States.* Madison: University of Wisconsin Press, 1991.

Mickelson, R. "International Business Machinations: A Case Study of Corporate Involvement in Local Educational Reform." *Teachers College Record* 100, no. 3 (1999): 476–512.

Mills, C. W. *The Power Elite.* New York: Oxford University Press, 1956.

———. *The Sociological Imagination.* London: Oxford University Press, 1959.

Mishel, L., J. Bernstein, and H. Boushey. *The State of Working America, 2002/2003.* An Economic Policy Institute Book. Ithaca, NY: Cornell University Press, ILR Press, 2003.

Mitchell, T. *Rule of Experts: Egypt, Techno-Politics, Modernity.* Berkeley: University of California Press, 2002.

Molnar, A. *Giving Kids the Business: The Commercialization of America's Schools.* Boulder, CO: Westview Press, 1996.

Montagu, A., ed. *Race and IQ.* New York: Oxford University Press, 1999.

Montanye, J. A. Review of *Bowling Alone: The Collapse and Revival of American Community,* by R. D. Putnam. *The Independent Review* 5, no. 3 (2000): 541.

Moon, J. D. *Constructing Community: Moral Pluralism and Tragic Conflicts.* Princeton, NJ: Princeton University Press, 1993.

Morgen, S. "Agency of Welfare Workers: Negotiating Devolution, Privatization, and the Meaning of Self-Sufficiency." *American Anthropologist* 103, no. 3 (2001): 747–61.

Moss, K. *The Color of Class: Poor Whites and the Paradox of Privilege.* Philadelphia: University of Pennsylvania Press, 2003.

Moyers, B. "This Is the Fight of Our Lives." Keynote speech, "Inequality Matters Forum," New York University, June 3, 2004. http://www.commondreams.org/views04/0616-09.htm.

Mueller, D. C. *Public Choice II.* Cambridge and New York: Cambridge University Press, 1989.

Muncy, R. "Disconnecting: Social and Civic Life in America since 1965." *Reviews in American History* 29 (2001): 141–49.

Nader, R. *Cutting Corporate Welfare.* New York: Seven Stories Press, 2000.

Nathan, R. "The 'Devolution Revolution': An Overview." *Rockefeller Institute Bulletin* (1996): 5–13.

National Association of Partners in Education. *Handbook of Education Partners.* Alexandria, VA: National Association of Partners in Education, 1995.

National Institute for Literacy. "The State of Literacy in America: Estimates at the Local, State, and National Levels." Washington, DC: National Institute for Literacy, 1998.

Nelson, F. H., B. Rosenberg, and N. Van Meter. *Charter School Achievement on the 2003*

National Assessment of Educational Progress. Washington, DC: American Federation of Teachers, August 20, 2004.

New York Times. *The Downsizing of America.* New York: Times Books, 1996.

Newton, K. "Trust, Social Capital, Civil Society, and Democracy." *International Political Science Review* 22, no. 2 (2001): 201–14.

Nonini, D. M. "American Neoliberalism, 'Globalization,' and Violence: Reflections from the United States and Southeast Asia." In *Globalization, the State, and Violence,* ed. J. Friedman, 163–202. Walnut Creek, CA: AltaMira Press, 2003.

North Carolina Justice and Community Development Center. *Testing Our Children: Why North Carolina's High Stakes Testing Policy Goes Too Far.* Raleigh: North Carolina Justice and Community Development Center, n.d.

North Carolina Justice and Community Development Center, and the North Carolina Education and Law Project. *The Achievement Gap 2002: An Update.* Raleigh: North Carolina Justice and Community Development Center, 2002.

Notes from Nowhere, ed. *We Are Everywhere: The Irresistible Rise of Global Anticapitalism.* London: Verso, 2003.

Odden, A., and V. Dougherty. *State Programs of School Improvement: A 50-State Survey.* Denver, CO: Education Commission of the States, 1982.

Oliver, M. L., and T. M. Shapiro. *Black Wealth/White Wealth: A New Perspective on Racial Inequality.* New York: Routledge, 1997.

Olson, M. *The Logic of Collective Action: Public Goods and the Theory of Groups.* New York: Schocken Books, 1965.

Olson, R., and T. A. Lyson, eds. *Under the Blade: The Conversion of Agricultural Landscapes.* Boulder, CO: Westview Press, 1999.

Ong, A. *Flexible Citizenship: The Cultural Logics of Transnationality.* Durham, NC: Duke University Press, 1999.

Osborne, D., and T. Gaebler. *Reinventing Government: How the Entrepreneurial Spirit Is Transforming the Public Sector.* Reading, MA: Plume/Addison-Wesley, 1992.

Page, B. I., and R. Y. Shapiro. "The Rational Public and Democracy." In *Reconsidering the Democratic Public,* ed. G. E. Marcus and R. L. Hanson, 35–64. University Park: Pennsylvania State University Press, 1993.

Paley, J. *Marketing Democracy: Power and Social Movements in Post-Dictatorship Chile.* Berkeley: University of California Press, 2001.

Parenti, M. *Democracy for the Few.* New York: St. Martin's Press, 1996.

Paris, P. *The Social Teachings of the Black Churches.* Philadelphia: Fortress Press, 1985.

Pateman, C. *Participation and Democratic Theory.* Cambridge: Cambridge University Press, 1970.

Perea, J., ed. *Immigrants Out! The New Nativism and the Anti-Immigrant Impulse in the United States.* New York: New York University Press, 1997.

Peters, B. G. "With a Little Help from our Friends: Public-Private Partnerships as Institutions and Instruments." In *Partnerships in Urban Governance,* ed. J. Pierre, 11–33. New York: St. Martin's Press, 1998.

Peterson, P. E. *The Price of Federalism.* Washington, DC: Brookings Institution Press, 1995.

Pfister, J., and N. Schnog. *Inventing the Psychological.* New Haven, CT: Yale University Press, 1997.

Phillips, K. *Wealth and Democracy: A Political History of the American Rich.* New York: Broadway Books, 2002.

Polanyi, K. *The Great Transformation.* Boston: Beacon Press, 1957.

Price, J. "Perdue Has Buyer for Plant." *The News and Observer* (Raleigh, NC), June 14, 1996.

Prothro, J. W., and C. W. Grigg. "Fundamental Principles of Democracy: Bases of Agreement and Disagreement." *Journal of Politics* 22 (1960): 276–94.

Putnam, R. D. "Bowling Alone: America's Declining Social Capital." *Journal of Democracy* 6, no. 1 (1995): 65–78.

———. *Bowling Alone: The Collapse and Revival of American Community.* New York: Simon & Schuster, 2000.

Quality Counts. *Building Blocks for Success* (Special Report). Bethesda, MD: Education Week, 2002.

Rasell, E., and R. Rothstein. *School Choice: Examining the Evidence*. Washington, DC: Economic Policy Institute, 1993.

Ray, C. A., and R. A. Mickelson. "Corporate Leaders, Resistant Youth, and School Reform in a Sunbelt City: The Political Economy of Education." *Social Problems* 37, no. 2 (1990): 178–90.

———. "Restructuring Students for Restructured Work: The Economy, School Reform, and Non-College-Bound Youths." *Sociology of Education* 66 (1993): 1–20.

Reagan, R. "The Case against George W. Bush." *Esquire*, September 2004.

Rigdon, M. "The Business of Education Reform: An Analysis of Corporate Involvement in Education Reform Movements in Kentucky, Milwaukee, and Chicago." Ph.D. diss., University of Wisconsin, 1995.

"Roanoke Rapids Herald 1996 Survey." *Roanoke Rapids Herald*, November 7, 1996.

Robert Marvin and Associates, Inc. *A Complete Fayetteville Once and for All*. Master Plan prepared for the City of Fayetteville and the Once and for All Committee. Walterboro, SC: Robert Marvin and Associates, Inc., 1997.

Rosenstein, D., and C. Brooke. *The Impact of the Poultry Industry on Chatham and Lee Counties*. Siler City, NC: Helping Hands Center, 1997.

Rothenberg, R. *The Neoliberals: Creating the New American Politics*. New York: Simon & Schuster, 1984.

Rubin, J. S., and G. M. Stankeiwicz. "The Los Angeles Community Development Bank: The Possible Pitfalls of Public-Private Partnerships." *Journal of Urban Affairs* 23, no. 2 (2001): 133–53.

Sahlins, M. D. *Culture and Practical Reason*. Chicago: University of Chicago Press, 1976.

Sartori, G. *The Theory of Democracy Revisited*. Chatham, NJ: Chatham House, 1987.

Sassen, S. *The Mobility of Labour and Capital*. New York: Cambridge University Press, 1988.

Savas, E. S. *The Organization and Efficiency of Solid Waste Collection*. Lexington, MA: Lexington Books, 1977.

Sbragia, A. *Debt Wish: Entrepreneurial Cities, U.S. Federalism, and Economic Development*. Pittsburgh, PA: University of Pittsburgh Press, 1996.

Schattschneider, E. E. *The Semisovereign People: A Realist's View of Democracy in America*. New York: Holt, Rinehart, and Winston, 1960.

Schofield, N. "Constitutional Political Economy: On the Possibility of Combining Rational Choice Theory and Comparative Politics." *Annual Review of Political Science* 3 (2000): 277–303.

Schor, J. *The Overspent American: Why We Want What We Don't Need*. New York: Harper Perennial, 1998.

———. *The Overworked American: The Unexpected Decline of Leisure*. New York: Basic Books, 1991.

Schudson, M. *The Good Citizen: A History of American Civic Life*. New York: Martin Kessler Books, 1998.

Schumann, W. R., III. *Between Class and Subjectivity: A Case Study of Grassroots Resistance in Rural Southern Appalachia*. Boone, NC: Appalachian State University, 1997.

Schumpeter, J. *Capitalism, Socialism, and Democracy*. 2nd ed. New York: Harper & Row, 1950.

Sclar, E. *You Don't Always Get What You Pay For: The Economics of Privatization*. Ithaca, NY: Cornell University Press, 2000.

Shapiro, I. *Democracy's Place*. Ithaca, NY: Cornell University Press, 1996.

———. *The State of Democratic Theory*. Princeton, NJ: Princeton University Press, 2003.

Shapiro, M. J. "Bowling Blind: Post-Liberal Civil Society and the Worlds of Neo-Tocquevillian Social Theory." *Theory and Event* 1, no. 1 (1997): 1–31.

Shepard, L. "When Does Assessment and Diagnosis Turn into Sorting and Segregation?" In *Literacy for a Diverse Society: Perspectives, Practices, and Policies*, ed. E. Hierbert, 279–98. New York: Teachers College Press, 1991.

Shepard, L., and M. Smith, eds. *Flunking Grades: Research and Policies on Retention*. London: Falmer Press, 1989.

Shipps, D. "The Invisible Hand: Big Business and Chicago School Reform." *Teachers College Record* 99, no. 1 (1997): 73–116.

Skocpol, T. *Diminished Democracy: From Membership to Management in American Civic Life*. Norman: University of Oklahoma Press, 2003.

Smith, C. *Christian America? What Evangelicals Really Want.* Berkeley: University of California Press, 2002.

Smith, D. H. *Grassroots Associations.* Thousand Oaks, CA: Sage Publications, 2000.

———. "Grassroots Associations Are Important: Some Theory and a Review of the Impact Literature." *Nonprofit and Voluntary Sector Quarterly* 26, no. 3 (1997): 269–306.

Smith, N. *The New Urban Frontier: Gentrification and the Revanchist City.* London and New York: Routledge, 1996.

Smith, O. P. *The Rise of Baptist Republicanism,* New York: New York University Press, 1997.

Smith, R. D., ed. *Long March Ahead: African-American Churches and Public Policy in Post–Civil Rights America.* Vol. 2. Durham, NC: Duke University Press, 2004.

———, ed. *New Day Begun: African-American Churches and Civic Culture in Post–Civil Rights America.* Durham, NC: Duke University Press, 2003.

Smith-Nonini, S. "Federally Sponsored Mexican Migrants in the Transnational South." In *The American South in a Globalizing World,* ed. J. L. Peacock, et al., 59–79. Chapel Hill: University of North Carolina Press, 2005.

Sokolow, A. D. "The Changing Property Tax and State-Local Relations." *Publius: The Journal of Federalism* 28, no. 1 (1998): 165–87.

Sola, P. "The Corporate Community on the Ideal Business-School Alliance." In *The New Servants of Power: A Critique of the 1980s School Reform Movement,* ed. C. Shea, et al., 75–86. New York: Greenwood Press, 1989.

Southern Exposure. "Eminent Domain: Special Section." *Southern Exposure* 23, no. 2 (1995): 18–47.

Stephenson, M. O. J. "Whither the Public-Private Partnership: A Critical Review." *Urban Affairs Quarterly* 27, no. 1 (1991): 109–27.

Steuerle, C. E., and V. A. Hodgkinson. "Meeting Social Needs: Comparing the Resources of the Independent Sector and Government." In *Nonprofits and Government: Collaboration and Conflict,* ed. E. Boris and C. E. Steuerle, 71–98. Washington, DC: Urban Institute Press, 1999.

Stevens, B. J., ed. *Delivering Municipal Service Efficiently: A Comparison of Municipal and Private Service Delivery.* Technical report prepared by Ecodata Inc. for publisher. Washington, DC: U.S. Dept. of Housing and Urban Development, Office of Policy Development and Research, Community Development and Fair Housing Division, 1985.

Stiglitz, J. E. *Globalization and Its Discontents.* New York: Norton, 2002.

Stouffer, S. *Communism, Conformity, and Civil Liberties.* New York: Doubleday, 1955.

Strand, R., S. Marullo, N. Cutforth, R. Stoecker, and P. Donohue. *Community-based Research and Higher Education: Principles and Practices.* San Francisco: Jossey-Bass, 2003.

Streeck, W. "Inclusion and Secession: Questions on the Boundaries of Associative Democracy." *Politics and Society* 20, no. 4 (1992): 513–20.

Stuart, A. W. "Religion." The North Carolina Atlas Revisited. 2004. http://www.ncatlasrevisited.org/Religion/ rlgnTitle.html.

Stull, D., M. J. Broadway, and K. C. Erickson. "The Price of a Good Steak: Beef Packing and its Consequences for Garden City, Kansas." In *Structuring Diversity: Ethnographic Perspectives on the New Immigration,* ed. L. Lamphere, 35–64. Chicago: University of Chicago Press, 1992.

Stull, D., M. J. Broadway, and D. Griffith, eds. *Any Way You Cut It: Meat Processing and Small-Town America.* Lawrence: University Press of Kansas, 1995.

Tenth Anniversary Brochure. Tillery, NC: Concerned Citizens of Thornton, 1988.

Teske, N. *Political Activists in America: The Identity Construction Model of Political Participation.* Cambridge: Cambridge University Press, 1997.

Theiss-Morse, E., et al. "Passion and Reason in Political Life: The Organization of Affect and Cognition and Political Tolerance." In *Reconsidering the Democratic Public,* eds. G. E. Marcus and R. L. Hanson, 249–72. University Park: Pennsylvania State University Press, 1993.

Tocqueville, A. de. *Democracy in America.* Vol. II. Trans. H. Reeve, with introduction by J. Bigelow. Aldine ed. New York: D. Appleton and Company, 1899.

Touraine, A. *The Return of the Actor: Social Theory in Postindustrial Society,* trans. M. Godzich. Minneapolis: University of Minnesota Press, 1988.

Truman, D. B. *The Governmental Process: Political Interests and Public Opinion.* New York: Knopf, 1951.

Tullock, G. *Toward a Mathematics of Politics*. Ann Arbor: University of Michigan Press, 1967.

Turner, V. *Dramas, Fields, and Metaphors: Symbolic Action in Human Society*. Ithaca, NY: Cornell University Press, 1974.

Ungar, S. J. *Fresh Blood: The New American Immigrants*. New York: Simon & Schuster, 1995.

U.S. Census Bureau. "Table 293. Crimes and Crime Rates by Type of Offense: 1980 to 2003. Statistical Abstract of the United States: 2006." Washington, DC: U.S. Census Bureau, 2006, http://www.census.gov/prod/2005pubs/06statab/law.pdf.

U.S. Department of Commerce, Economics and Statistics Administration. "Statistical Abstract of the U.S.: Table #744." Washington, DC: U.S. Department of Commerce, 1997.

U.S. Department of Education, Institute of Education Sciences. *America's Charter Schools: Results from the NAEP 2003 Pilot Study*. The Nation's Report Card. Washington, DC: U.S. Department of Education, Institute of Education Sciences, 2005.

Useem, E. *Low Tech Education in a High Tech World: Corporations and Classrooms in the New Information Society*. New York: Free Press, 1986.

Valdes, G., and R. Figueroa. *Bilingualism and Testing: A Special Case of Bias*. Norwood, NJ: Ablex, 1994.

Verba, S., K. L. Schlozman, and H. E. Brady. *Voice and Equality: Civic Voluntarism in American Politics*. Cambridge, MA: Harvard University Press, 1995.

Vita, M., and J. Eilperin. "House OKs Historic China Trade Bill." *News and Observer* (Raleigh, NC), 2000.

Voet, R. *Feminism and Citizenship*. London: Sage, 1998.

Walzer, N., and L. York. "Public-Private Partnerships in U.S. Cities." In *Public-Private Partnerships for Economic Development*, ed. N. Walzer and B. D. Jacobs, 47–68. Westport, CT: Praeger, 1998.

Warrick, J., and P. Stith. "Boss Hog 2: Corporate Takeovers." *The News and Observer* (Raleigh, NC), February 21, 1995.

Wells, A. S., ed. *Where Charter School Policy Fails: The Problems of Accountability and Equity*. New York: Teachers College Press, 2002.

Wells, A. S., J. J. Holme, A. Lopez, and C. W. Cooper. "Charter Schools and Racial and Social Class Segregation: Yet Another Sorting Machine?" In *A Notion at Risk: Preserving Education as an Engine for Social Mobility*, ed. R. Kahlenberg, 169–222. New York: Century Foundation Press, 2000.

Wexler, P. *Social Analysis of Education*. Boston: Routledge, 1987.

Whitfield, D. *Public Services or Corporate Welfare: Rethinking the Nation State in the Global Economy*. Sterling, VA: Pluto Press, 2001.

Whitty, G. "Creating Quasi-Markets in Education: A Review of Recent Research on Parental Choice and School Autonomy in Three Countries." *Review of Research in Education* 22 (1996): 3–47.

Williams, B. "Black Farmers' Plight Not Over." *News and Observer* (Raleigh, NC), June 24, 2001.

Williamson, T., D. L. Imbroscio, and G. Alperovitz. *Making a Place for Community: Local Democracy in a Global Era*. New York: Routledge, 2003.

Wilmore, G. *Black Religion and Black Radicalism*. New York: Doubleday, 1972.

Winant, H. *Racial Conditions: Politics, Theory, Comparison*. Minneapolis: University of Minnesota Press, 1994.

Wing, S., D. Cole, and G. Grant. "Environmental Injustice in North Carolina's Hog Industry." *Environmental Health Perspectives* 108, no. 3 (March 2000): 225–31. http://ehp.niehs.nih.gov/docs/2000/108p225–231wing/abstract.html.

Wolff, E. N. "Changes in Household Wealth in the 1980s and 1990s in the U.S." Working Paper no. 407. Annandale-on-Hudson, NY: The Levy Economics Institute of Bard College, 2004. http://www.levy.org/default.asp?view=publications_view&pubID=fca3a440ee.

———. *Top Heavy: The Increasing Inequality of Wealth in America and What Can Be Done about It*. 2nd ed. New York: New Press, 2002.

———. "The Wealth Divide: The Growing Gap in the United States between the Rich and the Rest. An Interview with Edward Wolff." *Multinational Monitor* 24, no. 5 (May 2003): 11–15.

Wood, P. J. *Southern Capitalism: The Political Economy of North Carolina, 1880–1980.* Durham, NC: Duke University Press, 1986.

Wuthnow, R. *Saving America? Faith-Based Services and the Future of Civil Society.* Princeton, NJ: Princeton University Press, 2004.

Wuthnow, R., and J. H. Evans, eds. *The Quiet Hand of God: Faith-Based Activism and the Public Role of Mainline Protestantism.* Berkeley: University of California Press, 2002.

Yates, M. *Naming the System: Inequality and Work in the Global Economy.* New York: Monthly Review Press, 2003.

Zepezauer, M. *Take the Rich off Welfare.* Cambridge, MA: South End Press, 2004.

Zukin, S. *Landscapes of Power: From Detroit to Disney World.* Berkeley: University of California Press, 1991.

Index

Page references in italics refer to illustrations.

Activism: African American, 74–75, 167, 260n11; antiwar, 8, 46, 191; because of corruption, 46; changed conditions for, 227–31; citizen, 213, 214, 217, 239–45; civil rights, 8, 16, 39, 50, 191, 227, 266n3; common sense in, 44, 46; for crime reduction, 228; cultural politics in, 202–3, 206, 217–19, 228; cultures of, 38–47; delegitimation of, 51–52; educational, 244; effect of Internet on, 268n42; effect of migration on, 40; effect on market rule, 227–31; emotions in, 46; ethnographic research on, 244–45; fear concerning, 50–51; heritage, 228; heroic, 227; for historic buildings, 224; Latino, 269n52; motives for, 43–45; participatory theorists' model of, 37–38; realist model of, 37; reasons for, 36–38, 45, 259n8; religious, 200-201, 225-27, 233, 260n11, 268nn38–43; in response to cultural codes, 267n9; retaliation against, 51; revitalization of democracy, xii; role of family in, 38–40; role of media in, 41–42; role of schools in, 42–43; social aspects of, 44–45; social conditions enabling, 56; sources of, 38–43; textbooks ideals of, 43–45; time barrier to, 49–50; for urban development, 228

Activists, professional, 117–18

African Americans: as community representatives, 76; educational vouchers for, 87; exclusion of, 82; farmers, 21, 214, 215, 218; in fast food industry, 177; fear of harassment, 259n19; influence of religious conservatism on, 260n16; loss of land, 216, 267n23; redlining of, 189; religious activism of, 260n11; in workforce, 63–64, 175

African Americans (Durham, N.C.): activism of, 74–75, 167; in local economy, 27; middle-class, 77, 98; political exclusion of, 76–77; political networks of, 212; power base of, 258n28; in school system, 77, 167–70; violence against, 59

African Americans (Fayetteville, N.C.), 160; in Broughton Road Improvement Association, 205–9; on OAFA Committee, 161; poor, 164–66, 234; power base of, 258n28

African Americans (Halifax County), 59, 60–65, 143; basic services for, 148–49; effect of economic restructuring on, 221; exclusion of, 176–78; farmers, 214; on poverty roles, 60–61

Agribusiness: in Chatham County, 245; effect on small farmers, 19; new forms of, xii; in North Carolina, 22, 24

Agriculture, community-supported, 243

Aid to Dependent Families and Children (AFDC), 110

Alperovitz, G., 117

Alternative School Task Force (Durham, N.C.), 166–70; elite management of, 168; exclusionary tactics of, 182–83; public meetings of, 183

American Enterprise Institute, 265n6

America's Second Harvest (nonprofit), 264n79

Anglican Communion, conservative movement within, 268n41

Animal rights movement, 266n3

Anthropologists: economic, 270n13; educational, 100

Anti-war movement, 8, 46, 191

Appalachian Defense Alliance (pseudonymous group), 201, 202

Appalachian region, stereotypes of, 221

About the Authors

Lesley Bartlett is Assistant Professor of Comparative and International Education at Teachers College, Columbia University. She has published widely in the fields of anthropology of education, comparative and international education, and literacy, language, and schooling.

Marla Frederick-McGlathery is Assistant Professor of African and African American Studies and the Study of Religion at Harvard University. She is the author of *Between Sundays: Black Women and Everyday Struggles of Faith* (California, 2003).

Thaddeus C. Guldbrandsen is Director of the Center for Rural Partnerships and Research and Assistant Professor of Anthropology at Plymouth State University in New Hampshire.

Dorothy Holland is Cary C. Boshamer Professor of Anthropology at the University of North Carolina at Chapel Hill. She is coauthor of *Educated in Romance* (Chicago, 1990). She is coeditor of *Positioning and Subjectivity: Narcotraffikers, Taiwanese Brides, Angry Loggers, School Troublemakers* (Ethos Special Issue 32[2]), *History in Person: Enduring Struggles, Contentious Practice, Intimate Identities* (School of American Research, 2001), and *The Cultural Production of the Educated Person* (SUNY, 1996).

Catherine Lutz is Professor of Anthropology at Brown University and author of *Homefront: A Military City and the American 20th Century* (Beacon, 2001), *Reading National Geographic* (with Jane Collins) (Chicago, 1993), and *Unnatural Emotions* (Chicago, 1988).

Enrique G. Murillo, Jr., is founding editor of the *Journal of Latinos and Education* and the *Handbook of Latinos and Education: Theory, Research, and Practice,* as well as Associate Professor of Language, Literacy, and Culture in the College of Education, California State University, San Bernardino. He serves as a Professional Expert for the Los Angeles County Office of Education and is coeditor/author of *Postcritical Ethnography in Education* (Hampton Press, 2004) and *Education in the New Latino Diaspora: Policy and the Politics of Identity* (Ablex, 2001).

Donald M. Nonini is Professor of Anthropology at the University of North Carolina at Chapel Hill, author of *British Colonial Rule and the Resistance of the Malay Peasantry, 1900–1957* (Yale Southeast Asian Studies, 1993), and coeditor of *Ungrounded Empires: The Cultural Politics of Modern Chinese Transnationalism* (Routledge, 1997).